Frontispiece is an original pen and ink sketch
by David F. Driesbach, DeKalb, Illinois.

To Phil,
I hope you
enjoy it!
Love and Best
Wishes,
Joan
Metzger
5-10-05

THE GRIFFITH LETTERS

The Story of
Frank Griffith
and the
116th New York Volunteer Infantry
in the Civil War

Edited by
Joan Metzger

HERITAGE BOOKS
2004

HERITAGE BOOKS

AN IMPRINT OF HERITAGE BOOKS, INC.

Books, CDs, and more—Worldwide

For our listing of thousands of titles see our website
at
www.HeritageBooks.com

Published 2004 by
HERITAGE BOOKS, INC.
Publishing Division
65 East Main Street
Westminster, Maryland 21157-5026

International Standard Book Number: 0-7884-2557-9

"What a cruel thing is war: to separate and destroy families and friends, and mar the purest joys and happiness God has granted us in this world; to fill our hears with hatred instead of love for our neighbors, and to devastate the fair face of this beautiful world."

General Robert E. Lee: letter to his wife, 25 December 1862

to
Allan H.
because nothing means
more to me than your love

TABLE OF CONTENTS

ILLUSTRATIONS

MAPS

vii

ACKNOWLEDGMENTS

The book you hold in your hands would not have been possible without the assistance and support of many people. Without the encouragement of Dr. Glen Gildemeister, Director and University Archivist of the Regional History Center at Northern Illinois University, I might never have started this project. Glen and Cindy Ditzler, Curator of Collections at the Regional History Center, have covered for me when I was absent researching the Griffith letters, given needed advice, and provided editing assistance. In addition Glen produced the scanned images of the Griffith letters which appear in this volume. I have been fortunate to work with two such understanding and helpful people.

Dorothy Jones, former Reference Librarian at NIU's Founders Memorial Library, graciously read over the manuscript and provided helpful comments, and also searched out obscure information for me. The Information Delivery Services staff of Founders Library, especially Ron Barshinger, did an outstanding job in obtaining many old and scarce volumes that provided information to help fill out the story of Frank Griffith and the 116th New York Volunteer Infantry.

Northern Illinois University is fortunate to have an excellent cartography program, enabling me to enlist the services of Andrew Serek, a cartography student. Andy went above the call of duty to produce the maps in this volume, and I wish him well pursuing his dreams in the real world.

Phyllis Kelley of the Joiner History Room in Sycamore Illinois, provided background information in the initial stage of my research. Lauree Zielezinski, librarian at the Sandwich Public Library, aided my search for obituary information on members of the Griffith family. Joan Hardekopf, of the Sandwich Historical Society, opened the doors of the museum to me and helped me search the old bound volumes of newspapers. She has a great memory and an eye for detail and not only provided information on the career of Frank Griffith, but also located the only two identified photographs of Frank Griffith.

I was fortunate to come into contact with Esther Williams, whose great-grandfather was also a member of the 116th New York Volunteer Infantry. She generously provided me with copies of material she had gathered on this unit, and the names of others interested in the history of the 116th. One of these contacts, Gordon G. Ryther graciously sent me copies of letters written by his grandfather, James F. Ryther. Esther also sent a copy of a beautiful, full-color Military Register of Company K of the 116th which appears on the cover of this volume. Well known artist David F. Driesbach, my friend and neighbor, produced the original pen and ink sketch for the frontispiece.

Dr. Bruce Kenamore of Wilmette, Illinois is an internist who formerly specialized in infectious diseases. He took the time to review the symptoms Griffith mentioned in his letters and provide a diagnosis of his condition.

Sally Stassi of the Williams Research Center, in New Orleans, Louisiana helped me not only identify the site of the Marine Hospital in New Orleans, but also provided me with views of this Hospital where Griffith recuperated during the summer of 1864.

My New York research was aided by a number of people. My niece Susan Fairhead took time out from her busy schedule to do research for me at the New York State Library in Albany. She not only located some very interesting information on the members of the 116th NYVI, but also was persistent in making sure that the needed materials were photocopied in a timely manner. Coriann Bolt, Town Clerk in Springville, New York responded to my inquiry for additional information on the Griffith family. My research time in Buffalo, New York was aided by Mr. Robert M. Gurn, Head of Special Collections, and his staff at the Buffalo and Erie County Public Library, and by Mary F. Bell and Linda M. Kennedy of the Buffalo and Erie County Historical Society. Both institutions have preserved material on the New York units that fought in the Civil War as well on the citizens of Erie County who lived through those uncertain times.

My friend Bruce Dinges, Editor of the *Journal of Arizona History*, gave me editing advice and reassurance.

Last, but not least, I must thank my husband, Allan H. Metzger, and our best friend, Ed Fischer. They not only provided encouragement throughout the past four years, but also chauffeured me to and around Buffalo, New York to do research. They photocopied materials for me so that I could continue my search for additional information, and even double checked to see that all the pages were there. Without their loving support, gentle prodding, and laughter when I began to take myself too seriously, this volume might never have been completed.

INTRODUCTION

"Well, we have had a pretty rough time of it the last six days. We have marched 102 miles and fought two big battles in that time, lived on half rations, and if we get two hours sleep in 24 we done well. .... Darling, I don't want you to ask me to describe a battle to you nor the field after the battle is over, it is too horrible to think of. I can hear the groans of the poor fellows when there could nothing be done for them, and I cant get it out of my mind."[1]

Even after 140 years, letters by Civil War soldiers such as Frank E. Griffith of the 116th New York Volunteer Infantry, continue to be discovered and made public. The letters of the Griffith family contained in this volume show how one Erie County, New York family was affected by the war. While not unique, what is interesting is that in addition to the 106 letters (which have survived) written by Frank Griffith to his wife Thankful, the collection also contains seventeen additional letters from various family members. They include seven letters from Thankful to Frank, and four to Thankful from her brother Albert E. Myers, of the 78th and later the 102nd New York State Infantries. All contribute to form a more complete picture of one family's struggles and concerns during the Civil War, as well as providing insight into a soldier's life.

From his enlistment on September 2, 1862 until he was injured in the Battle of Pleasant Hill, Louisiana on April 9, 1864 Frank Griffith served as a private in Company K of the 116th. As E.B. Long states, "the regiment became a second home; usually the men were from the same area, and they often had known each other in civilian life."[2] Frank and Thankful both knew many of the men serving in the 116th, they were neighbors, friends, and one, Ashley Stanbro, was a favorite nephew. Following the Battle of Pleasant Hill Frank was sent to the Marine Hospital in New Orleans to recuperate from his wounds. Although his wounds healed other health problems prevented him from returning to the 116th and he was transferred to the Veteran Reserve Corps on June

---

[1] Letter of Frank Griffith to his wife Thankful, written 13 April 1864 from Grand Ecore on the Red River, Louisiana following the Battle of Pleasant Hill.

[2] E.B. Long with Barbara Long, *The Civil War Day by Day: An Almanac 1861-1865* (Garden City, NY: Doubleday & Company, 1971), 716.

30, 1864. He served as a hospital steward in New Orleans until September of that year when he was sent to Washington, D.C. where he served in Company I, 9th Regiment of the Veteran Reserve Corps. While in Washington Griffith performed duty as a hospital aid, a barber, and a cook until mustering out on June 6, 1865.

Frank Elnathan Griffith was just an average Union soldier. From his military record we learn that he was 5 feet 8 inches tall, had blue eyes, dark hair, a dark complexion, and was employed as a "mechanic" at the time of his enlistment. There is little information about his early life, but we do know a bit about his family. His father John Griffith was born in Stephentown, Rensselear County, New York in 1796. John married Harriet Sanford in 1827 and in 1833 they followed his brother Hezekiah Griffith to Erie County, New York. John and his family settled in an area of Concord township known to the locals as "Waterville," located north of the village of East Concord. Frank Griffith was the middle of nine children. His four older sisters were Catharine, Cynthia Eudora (called Dora), Nancy Eveline, and Martha Esther. He was followed by Sarah Ellen, Caroline E. (Carrie), William Henry, and Marcus Eugene. Frank Elnathan was born April 26, 1835. Prior to his marriage all existing documents list him as Elnathan, the name of his paternal great-grandfather.

John Griffith was a farmer, but he also served as a Justice of the Peace in Concord for a time. Frank grew up a farm boy, but "thanks to that dear Mother and Father I believe that I have a liberal Education at least so that what I fail to accomplish with my hands I may make up with my head."[3] The Griffith family apparently valued education as Frank's sisters Dora, Sarah, and Carrie all became teachers. By the time Frank was twenty the 1855 New York State Census shows him employed as a carpenter, still residing with his parents.

On April 6, 1859 Frank married Thankful Myers at Ashford, just across the county line in Cattaraugus County, not far from the home of Thankful's parents Jacob and Mary Peirce Myers in Yorkshire. For the first few years of their marriage they lived with Frank's parents, where Frank helped on the farm. Frank and Thankful's first child, Carrie Annette "Nettie" was born there on June 5, 1860. Just six months after the Civil War began, on Christmas Eve of 1861, Frank, Thankful and

---

[3] Letter from Frank Griffith to his wife Thankful Griffith, 16 January 1865, from Washington, D.C.

little Nettie moved to their own home in Evans township. Here, on April 7, 1862 their daughter Gertrude Mary "Gertie" was born.

One wonders what Frank and Thankful talked about as the war continued. Frank mentions in a letter dated December 19, 1863 that "I came from home an abolitionist." He must have been torn between the love of his young family and his duty to his country, especially since Thankful's 18 year old brother Albert, who had lived with them for a time, had enlisted in the 78th New York State Volunteer Infantry on November 27, 1861.

Governor Edwin D. Morgan, on July 7, 1862, issued an order for new regiments to be formed in each of New York's 32 senate districts. One can imagine Frank's inter turmoil as the 116th New York Volunteer Infantry is being formed in Erie County and he sees many of his friends and neighbors enlisting. Finally, on September 2, he too steps forward to enlist and is assigned to Company K, the last company in the regiment to be formed. As the 116th was set to leave Buffalo on September 3, 1862 the members of Company K were given a brief furlough to enable them to settle affairs at home, and they joined the regiment later in Baltimore.

Thankful Griffith was left with two young daughters; Nettie was just past two years of age, and Gertie only five months. Although they had been living in Evans when Frank enlisted, Thankful and the girls moved back with Frank's parents. It was not an easy life. People who owed money to Frank refused to pay Thankful, while those Frank borrowed from demanded payment. Thankful's brother-in-law, Horatio Hurd, who had been in partnership with Frank in Evans before the war, also took advantage during Frank's absence. In addition to financial problems, Frank's father developed cancer on his lip and was unable to work, and Frank's younger brothers were barely able to keep the farm going. By the time the war ends John Griffith is near death. Thankful not only worked to help the family, she also contributed to the war effort by joining the Waterville Aid Society, and was named President of the group.

Frank Griffith was a man whose love of family was only matched by his love of country. He missed his family desperately, yet was willing to die for his country. As one would expect his letters tell of his training and travels, guard duty and battles, hospital life, and the temptations a soldier faced in cities such as New Orleans and Washington, D.C. He commented favorably about the beauty he saw in Louisiana. Frank had strong views on issues such as slavery, religion, temperance, and the Union cause. Both Frank's wife and Mother spoke eloquently of their faith in God and His divine plan. When Frank was transferred to Washington he joined a temperance society and regularly attended their meetings.

From almost the beginning of his enlistment Frank experienced problems with his health. Health problems aside, Frank would speculate about leaving New York once the war ended whenever he got fed up with the way he and his family were treated concerning financial dealings at home. If unable to do physical work, Frank planned to use his mind to earn a living, perhaps even to study law. Despite his desire to leave the state, he vowed that as long as his parents needed him he would be there for them.

When the war ended Frank was honorably discharged June 6, 1865 at Camp Fry, Washington, D.C. and he returned to the family farm in East Concord. According to the 1865 New York Census, John Griffith died between June 1 and July 4, 1865. Perhaps Frank returned in time to see his father before his death. A letter from "Cousin Nettie" Sanford, written April 1, 1866, offered condolences on the recent death of Frank's mother. Nettie also expressed the hope that Frank would get over his disease of "Missouri on the brain," his desire to leave New York for greener pastures.

Following his Mother's death, Frank, Thankful and the girls moved to a home in Angola, Evans township. They were living there December 18, 1867 when the "great railroad disaster" took place. As an express train crossed over the bridge at Big Sister Creek the last two coaches full of passengers detached from the train, plunged into the frozen water below, and immediately caught fire. A large number of passengers died, and many of the injured were taken to Frank Griffith's home located near the scene of the tragedy.[4] 1870 finds the family living in Evans where Frank was employed as a carpenter, and on April 17, 1871 Frank purchased property in the township from Elbridge and Mary Ann Bundy.

In his May 20, 1912 declaration for a pension Frank stated he came to Sandwich, Illinois in 1875. His family apparently remained in Angola at least through the first three months of 1876 according to

---

[4] H. Perry Smith, ed., *History of the City of Buffalo and Erie County*, Vol. 1, (Syracuse, NY: D. Mason & Co., 1884), 576-577; and "The Angola Train disaster of 1867" http://www.bufnet/~macdowel/cross/train.htm, on 10/23/00.

Carrie Griffith's grade report from the Angola Union Free School for the term ending March 7, 1876. Sandwich, Illinois in 1875 was a small village of approximately 2000 residents, located on the southern edge of DeKalb County, about 60 miles west of Chicago. Perhaps Frank's move from Erie County was the fulfillment of his long expressed desire to get away from those who had treated his family poorly during the war years. Perhaps he moved to be near his friend and messmate from Company K, A.E. "Eb" Ames who had come to the Sandwich area in 1868. Perhaps it was the result of the panic of 1873 and the "despondency of 1875" which had hit Erie County.[5] The Griffith family now included two more daughters, Cora Elsie, born in 1868, and Harriet M. "Hattie" born in 1871, however daughter Gertie had died at the age of eight sometime in the second half of 1870. Frank and Thankful's only son, Edwin Clare was born in Sandwich, December 29, 1877.

The Voters and Tax-Payers of DeKalb County, Illinois published in 1876 listed F.E. Griffith as a Republican, employed as a millwright, an occupation he held at least until 1880.[6] He later worked as a carpenter and building contractor, able to build anything from cabinets to homes to factory additions, with a reputation of "thorough honest workmanship of a master builder."[7] A civic-minded man, Griffith helped found the Excelsior Lodge No. 67 of the Ancient Order of United Workmen on March 23, 1877, and served as the first "M.W." (the second highest office) and later represented his lodge in the Grand Lodge.[8] He was a loyal member of the Grand Army of the Republic, Sandwich Post, No. 510, and was elected Commander in December 1900.

---

[5] "Early Erie County History" http://www.hopefarm.com/erieny.htm, on 7/30/99.

[6] Henry F. Kett, *The Voters and Tax-Payers of DeKalb County, Illinois* (Chicago: H.K. Kett & Co., 1876), 203; 1880 Federal Census.

[7] Frank Griffith's obituary, <u>The Sandwich Free Press</u>, 24 November 1921.

[8] *Portrait and Biographical Album of DeKalb County, Illinois* (Chicago: Chapman Brothers, 1885), 878. The Ancient Order of United Workman was one of the first fraternal insurance organizations, established in Meadville, PA in October 1868 to provide financial protection, and a collective voice to its members. "The History of Neighbors of Woodcraft" http://www.nowfbs.com/history.htm, on 9/14/99.

Frank's beloved wife Thankful died January 7, 1900. A faithful member of the Baptist Church, Thankful had also been a charter member of the Woman's Relief Corps No.182 which was organized May 28, 1891 in Sandwich. It was a civic organization dedicated to relieve suffering and perform charitable work, and Thankful served as chaplain of the WRC for the last seven years of her life.[9]

Although Frank continued to be employed as a carpenter and building contractor at least into mid-1910, his health had been deteriorating for a number of years. In June 1892 he applied for a pension stating that he was largely unable to earn a support due to the wound he had received in his right thigh at Pleasant Hill, as well as "dyspepsia" (digestive difficulties) and "piles" (hemorrhoids). His friend A. E. Ames submitted an affidavit on his behalf stating he was at Griffith's side when he was wounded. This request was denied, but in May 1904 Frank again applied for an Invalid Pension, stating that he was partially unable to work due to "general debility from age and deafness." Frank spent most of the remaining years of his life living with his daughter Hattie Bernard and her two young children, first on Somonauk Street, later on West Center Street, in Sandwich. Meanwhile, his only son Edwin died April 1, 1906 in Lincoln, Illinois. On September 9, 1918 Frank suffered a cerebral hemorrhage leaving him paralyzed and bedridden. Hattie cared for him at home until his death at the age of 86 at 9 p.m. on November 17, 1921. Frank Griffith's obituary stated that although "at times, suffering greatly, he was cheerful and uncomplaining to the last."[10] He was buried in Oak Ridge Cemetery, Somonauk, Illinois.

It has been a most interesting experience to become involved in the lives of Frank Griffith and his family, as well as to see the Civil War and the South through their eyes. With his vivid descriptions, and earnest and honest revelations of his thoughts to his wife, it was easy for me to become fond of Frank as I transcribed many of his letters, and to wonder what happened to him after the war. With his many physical complaints I feared his life might be a short one. I also wondered about the many people mentioned in his letters. Who were these people he called brother, sister, and friend? I have attempted to learn the answers

---

[9] The Sandwich Free Press, 11 January 1900, 2 June 1898.

[10] The Sandwich Free Press, 24 November 1921.

to my questions, and hope that my efforts may enlighten others who are interested in the men who served in the 116th New York Volunteer Infantry, the Griffith family, or who are just eager to learn more about the Civil War. The "Rebellion" affected ordinary people all over the North and South, not just those in uniform, and Frank Griffith's plain spoken letters may also help shed light on their lives.

The letters which appear in this volume are part of the F.E. Griffith Family Collection (RC 89) which is deposited in the Regional History Center at Northern Illinois University, DeKalb, Illinois. The collection came to the Center in March of 1980 from Mr. William C. Burrows following the death of his wife, Elizabeth Ann Baird, great-granddaughter of Frank and Thankful Griffith.

These letters provide a view of the Civil War and its effect on a family that is rarely seen. Not only do we hear Frank's view of the war, and see how much he misses his family back in East Concord, New York, but we also see how the family he leaves behind struggles to get along without him. In order to convey how this family was changed and challenged by the Civil War I have chosen to include all of the letters in their entirety, misspellings and all. The loving concern of all the family members shines through despite the differences in writing skills. Frank's letters make up the bulk of this collection, and he in particular seemed to write nonstop, not taking the time for such niceties as punctuation. For the convenience of the reader I have added minimal punctuation and paragraphing to clarify meaning and improve readability. For the sake of uniformity the dates on the letters have been moved to the upper left corner. The use of capital letters has not been changed. Double words have been eliminated. If the sender left out a word, or a letter from a word, that makes the meaning of a sentence unclear, then the missing or misspelled word is inserted between brackets [ ]. Correct spellings of personal and proper names are also inserted into brackets [ ]. A word that could not be recognized is noted as [*illegible*]. The notes preceding the chapters will attempt to put the letters in context.

For the convenience of the reader the footnotes immediately follow the letters. The footnotes identify family, friends and members of the 116th New York Volunteer Infantry, as well as place names, and other textural clarifications. In addition, there are three appendices which provide additional information on those mentioned. Appendix A lists the family members and gives a brief biographical sketch of each.

Appendix B is a listing of all the members of Company K of the 116th with as much biographical information as is known about the individuals' service records and life after the war. Appendix C lists all the officers and other members of the 116th mentioned in Griffith's letters. Appendix D gives a chronology of the 116th from the time the regiment was formed in August 1862 until it was disbanded in June 1865, as well as Frank Griffith's location.

Although I acknowledge the help of many people with this volume, any mistakes that may be found are my responsibility.

Chapter 1

"I came here to serve my country"
Baltimore, MD - Fall 1862

On July 7, 1862 Governor Morgan issued orders to raise new regiments in each of New York's thirty-two senatorial districts. Between August 11 and September 3 the 116th New York State Volunteer Infantry was raised in Erie County, New York. Companies A through I muster in at Fort Porter in Buffalo on September 3, but Company K, the last formed, musters in the next day and is granted a short furlough in order to settle affairs at home. The 116th, minus Co. K, leaves on September 5 for Baltimore, where they arrive on the 7th, and are attached to Emory's Brigade of the 8th Army Corps. Near Druid Hill in Baltimore, the 116th establishes "Camp Belger," receiving instruction and drill under Col. Edward P. Chapin. Company K leaves Buffalo on September 10 and arrives at Camp Belger the following day.

The 116th N.Y.S.V. Infantry is among those units who head to Gettysburg, Pennsylvania on an expedition against Stuart on October 12. It was a futile trip, and they arrive back at Camp Belger on the 16th. Two days later the camp is renamed "Camp Chapin" in honor of Colonel Chapin. On November 5 the 116th leaves Baltimore to join General Nathaniel P. Banks expedition to Louisiana, where Banks is now in charge of the Department of the Gulf, 19th Army Corps. They arrive at Fortress Monroe, Virginia on November 13, and remain there until December 4 when they board the steamship *Atlantic*. After a rough sea voyage the 116th arrives at Ship Island, Mississippi on December 13, where they spend two weeks at "Camp Canaan" drilling in the sand.

Frank E. Griffith enlisted in Company K of the 116th on September 2, 1862. His brief note of September 9 informs his wife Thankful that he (and the men of Co. K) will be leaving Buffalo the next day. In the next six letters written from camp in Baltimore, Maryland, Frank expresses his loneliness, and explains what life is like in camp. As he put it "this Soldier life makes [us] tough if we do not die seasoning." He describes the trip to Gettysburg by train, and regrets that they missed seeing the "Rebels." Frank mentions the friends that are with him in the 116th, and asks about family at home.

On October 20 Albert E. Myers writes his sister Thankful from his hospital bed in Frederick, Maryland, not realizing that his brother-in-law Frank is also in Maryland, training to be a soldier. Albert Myers was eighteen years old, and had enlisted in the 78th New York Volunteer Infantry November 27, 1861 and had mustered in December 11, 1861. Presuming that Albert had written other letters, Frank would have had some knowledge of what "soldiering" entailed before his own enlistment.

On November 6 the 116th leaves Baltimore by ship. Frank recounts his good fortune to have had a "lame back" when they board the steamship *Atlantic*, thus getting the Captain's sympathy and a good night's rest in the officer's quarters while the rest of the men suffered on the open deck during a storm. During a brief stop at Fort Monroe, Virginia at the entrance to the James River) Frank wonders how many of those at home miss him. We learn that Frank, like most of the men has been seasick. The men also suffer from other illnesses. Frank's nephew, Lanson "Ashley" Stanbro, contracts typhoid fever.

The 116th spends about two weeks on Ship Island, a sandy island located at the mouth of Mobile Bay, Mississippi. Their final destination is still unknown, "but the talk is New orleans,"and Frank expresses the opinion that he will be home in the spring.

Buffalo
Sept 9th 1862

Dear wife,
    I shall leave here tomorrow morning at Eight for washington.
I have got a very bad cold but I hope nothing serious. please accept
the within present from your own,
        Frank

P.S. I shall send some pictures by John[1]. Please give them to my
sisters[2] in haste.
        Good bye,
                Frank

———————

Camp Belger
Sept 12th 1862

Dear Wife,
    I improve the present opportunity of writing a few lines to you
to let you know that the sceshers have not got me yet. we arrived in
Baltimore on Thursday morning [11th] about 6 Oclock tired and
hungry, marched two miles to Camp with[out] breakfast. I tell you I
thought if this is soldiering I for one don't like it. well after a while
we got dinner and felt better. went and laid down in Birnys[3] tent and
took a short nap before I went to sleep and felt gooder, began to like it

———————————————

[1] Most likely Frank Griffith's brother-in-law, John F. Morse.

[2] Frank had six sisters: Catharine (Mrs. Henry Stanbro), Cynthia Eudora
"Dora" (Mrs. Charles Cornell), Nancy Evaline "Eva" (Mrs. John F. Morse), Martha
(Mrs. Fayette Treat), Sarah Ellen (Mrs. Charles Spencer) and Caroline "Carrie."
See Appendix A, The Family.

[3] James B. Weber, like Griffith, was from Concord, New York. He was 19
when he enlisted and was was a sergeant in Co. F of 116th. New York Adjutant
General's Office, *Annual Report of the Adjutant-General of the State of New York
for the Year 1903, Registers of the New York Regiments in the War of the Rebellion*,
Vol. 35, (Albany: Oliver A. Quayle, 1904), 492. Hereafter referred to as *Registers*.
See also reference in Appendix C.

better. got my supper, helped pitch tent, went to bed, slept first rate. waked up this morning and liked it first rate which I sincerely hope I shall continue to do. we had a hard rain last night and some of the boys got swearing wet, but they will have to get used to it.

I have got in to a first rate mess[4] in our tent. they all belong to the church (but me). we read in the Bible and have prayers night and morning which makes it more home like.

We expect to move our camp down onto the river in a day, or live where we shall be on one side of the river and the rebels on the other, where I hope I shall have the supreme satisfaction of trying my rifle on the enemy pickts. we are Electing our officers this morning. I do not know whether I shall get any thing or not but I will let you know in my next. we can get plenty of fruit here, but I do not dare to eat it for some of our boys have been poisoned. there is 7 or 8 men sick in the hospital now some of which will probaly die. I suppose you have heard that we were all killed by this time. I will send you some postage stamps. they will pass in dixie.

Pl[e]ase write as soon as you get this and tell me all the news, how you and the little ones[5] get along.

Direct your letter to Baltimore M.D. 116 Regt N.Y.V. in care of Col Chapin.

Please accept this from your ever loving husband,
　　　F.E. Griffith
P.S. kiss the Ba[6] for pa

_____

Camp Belger
Sept. 25 [1862]

Dear wife,

_____

[4] A mess was a group of men who cooked and ate together.

[5] Frank and Thankful had two daughters at this time, Carrie Annette "Nettie," born June 5, 1860, and Gertrude Mary "Gertie," born April 7, 1862. See also Appendix A.

[6] The baby, Gertie.

I find myself seated under a tree this morning to write a few lines to you. I am on guard this to day so I have a few hours to my self. I received your very welcome letter yesterday and was very glad to hear from you. Nick[7] sits by my elbow talking in his old granny way as usual so you can gues how well I can write. I have got the tooth ache this morning and it does not feel good much. the talk is now that we shall go to Fortress Monroe in a few days but we can not tell any thing about it here in Camp. the weather is very pleasant here. it has not rained here but twice since we have been in camp. it is as hilly here as it is in Cattaraugus[8] only more so. you want to know wheather I have got any office or not. I answer no and do not want any thing but a high private in the rear rank.

Camp Belger
sept 26 1862

Well, dear wife,
I thought I would finish this poor scrawl in time for the mail in the morning. I stood guard all night last night, that is two hours on and four hours of[f], and I had to lay on the ground to sleep out doors with my musket for a pillow, the consequence of which is I have got a cold some. the days are very warm, but the nights are cold enough to freeze a dog. I have been out of camp tonight down to the railroad and saw two teams of paroled soldiers going home to Ohio and Pensylvania, and another of soldi[e]rs going to Washington. there is lively times her[e] in military matters. Please send me a paper once in a while so that I can see what is going on there.

Saturday 27.
Dear,
we have sad news this morning in camp. a man tried to run the guard, the natural consequence of which is that he got a bayonet

---

[7] Probably Nicholas Fedick, who served in Co. K with Griffith. He was 26, and from Evans, New York. *Registers*, 404. See also Appendix B.

[8] Cattaraugus is the county directly south of Erie County.

Front cover of booklet used by members of the 116th New York Volunteer Infantry. Courtesy of the Buffalo and Erie County Historical Society.

run through him and he lays in the guard house dead[9]. I think I will not try the expirament. Provisions are rather steep here. Butter is 30 cts, milk 4 cts a pint, cheese 40 cts a pound, and other things in proportion (in camp). Please write often wont you for it is so lonesome here. do not wait for me to write for I have so many to write to. tell Nettie to wait till pa comes, and kiss the dear little ones for me wont you? tell mother I will write to her in a day or two. Please do take good care of your self for my sake. give my love to all. tell sister Carrie I have not received a letter from her yet. tell George & Libbie[10] I should like to see them very much.

Please excuse all mistakes, and accept this with my love.
Frank

Camp Belger
Oct 17 [1862]

Dearest wife,

I take the present time to write you a little note to let you know that I am back in Camp Belger again safe and sound. I hope you did not worry much about me. we had a most splendid trip up in Pensylvania of about 60 miles to a town called gettysburgh. but when we got there the Rebels had (skedadled) back across the river, so like all the rest of the army movements it all came to naught. the Rebels took about 1500 horses and all the provisions they wanted and then went back and left us to sneak back to camp. I believe that we might have taken them if it had not been for so much (Red tapeism). but here we cannot move till we have (orders) so we were two days and nights in going sixty miles by Railroad so when we got where the

---

[9] William J. Story, age 42, from Buffalo, was a member of Company E. He had successfully gotten out of camp and was caught attempting to re-enter. "Killed, September 27, 1862, by bayonet wound received while attempting to run the guard at Baltimore." *Registers*, 479. Orton S. Clark, *The One Hundred and Sixteenth Regiment of New York State Volunteers*, (Buffalo: Matthews & Warren, 1868), 31. Hereafter referred to as Clark.

[10] Thankful Myers Griffith's brother and sister, George and Libbie L. Myers.

rebels were they were not there. I tell you traveling on the railroad is not the funyest thing in the world. I stayed three days and two [nights] in a freight car loaded with Commissary stores, and all the way ther[e] was to sleep was to roll myself up in my blanket and lay down on the boxes and barels with my Knapsak for a pillow. perhaps you think I did not sleep much, but I have not slept any better since I left home. this Soldier life makes [us] tough if we do not die seasoning. I can lie down on the ground and go to sleep in five minutes any time.

you want to know what I do here in Camp. I will give you a Program of one day. the first thing in the morning is Reville and roll call at six Oclock, then every man has to answer to his name or go on guard. next wash ten minutes, then go out and drill one hour, then Breakfast, then at nine Oclock go out and drill till noon (dinner), two Oclock Battalion drill till five, dress parade till six, supper, at nine Tatoo and roll call, go to bed on the ground in your tents[11]. we have roll call every time we go out. do you wonder that we can sleep. (grub) for breakfast we have potatos and mush coffee, for dinner we have bean soup and coffee, for supper we have rice and molasses and coffee good enough for soldiers (eh!). I am getting pretty tough again. I think I shall stand it first rate after a while.

Battalion drill and supper, and now I will try to finish this poor scrawl. I have just got your box tonight. you cannot tell how glad I am to get it, it seems so like home. I told my mess that I wish I could sit down to the table with yourself and the children to eat some of the good things you were kind enough to send me, and they all said (amen). do not think that I am getting uneasy for I never was more at home in my life. I have made up my mind to take the world as it comes. Lon[12] wants John to send him some money and I think he had

---

[11] Concerning all the drilling James F. Ryther of Company H wrote to Carmi Ryther from Camp Belger, October 9,1862: "Our Col. is determined to make this a good regiment and we have to drill very hard, but I am getting used to it & it don't tire me as much as it did in the first places. We have company drill in the morning & forenoon and Battalion drill in the afternoon & the boys are learning fast." Original letter held by Gordon G. Ryther, West Oneonta, NY.

[12] Probably Alonzo F. Killom, age 26, and like Griffith from Concord and a member of Company K. *Registers*, 433. See also Appendix B.

better send him right off for it is uncertain when we shall get our pay, and it is hard to be here with out any money especialy when we are sick. we can not get any thing to eat but what we buy.[13] but it is time to go to bed so I shall have to go to bed. Nick sends his best respects and says he is very much obliged to you for remembering him so kindly. so good night for the present.

Saturday morning, Oct 18
       I shall have to hurry and finish this before the mail goes. we have just had a pole raising this morning and named our camp. you will please direct your letter to Camp Chapin hereafter[14]. be careful to put the Company on the directions for our letters get mixed if you do not. if we go into winter quarters here I want you to send me some butter for we cannot get it here without paying 80 cts a pound for it. Tell Carrie I will answer her letter next, but she must not wait for me. I shall have to stop writing for our breakfast is ready. please write often and do not wait for me. I do not think you can read half of this for I have to write in a hurry.
       Kiss the children for me and accept this from yours.
       Frank

PS have you sent me any money yet? if not, do so if conveniant please.
       Frank

Frederick City, MD
Oct 20th 1862
Bethel Hospital

Dear Sister,
       I have made rather awkward work heading this letter but I

---

[13] It was common practice for sutlers to follow troops and sell the soldiers food, drink and supplies. Mark Mayo Boatner III, *The Civil War Dictionary*, (New York: David McKay Company, 1973), 822. Hereafter referred to as *Dictionary*.

[14] Camp Belger was renamed Camp Chapin in honor of Col. Edward P. Chapin of the 116th. See Appendix C.

Frederick - CITY. (Oct# 20th

Bethel Hospital. M. D. /1862.

Dear. Sister

I have made rather awkard work heading this letter but I thought I would make it plain so if you could see the directions and then you would have no excuse for not weighting to me I think I have wrote to you once before since I have been here but I will not be sure I can hardly remember whether I ever wrote a letter or not I am a sitting up in bed to weight this to you I am a little better than I have been for a good while I was not able to sit up in bed now I am able I am going to weight a few lines my hand trembles so I can hardly weight now how long since you heard from our folks the boys are all through work I suppose have they began drafting yet when they do begin it will bring some poor fools from behind the counter went it

Letter written by Albert E. Myers to his sister, Thankful Griffith, on October 20, 1862 from Bethel Hospital, Frederick, Maryland. Griffith Papers, Regional History Center, Northern Illinois University.

thought I would make it plain so if you could see the directions and then you would have no excuse for not wrighting to me. I think I have wrote to you once before since I have been here but I will not be sure. I can hardly remember whether I ever wrote a letter or not. I am a sitting up in bed to wright this to you. I am a little better than I have been for a good while. I was not able to sit up in bed now I am able. I am going to wright a long letter. my hand trembles so I can hardly wright now.

how long since you heard from our folks? the boys are all through work I suppose. have they began drafting yet? when they do begin it will bring some fine boots from behind the counter wont it. Are you afraid they will draft F. [Frank] or H.[Horatio][15] or are they not liable to a draft? I suppose the boys are all enlisting around those parts. I see in a paper that mother sent me that they are just got waked up in Collins Center. I hope they will send all of new york here before they will see the Union Army retreat for the Rebels as far as they did before. it was worse for us than it would have been to lose twenty five thousand men in a battle.

Has there been any snow out in evans yet this fall? it is growing very cool here but not cold yet. have the boys got there job done yet? do you calculate to stay there all winter? Netty must be a large girl by this time. does your other girl look any thing like her, and is she as rogueish as Netty is?

Well, I would like very well to be at home this winter, but as I find out I cant I will have to stand it the best I can. my Regt[16] has been badly cut up since I came to this hospital it now is at or on Lowden Hights[17] in camp, resting.

---

[15] Horatio Hurd, married to Thankful and Albert's sister Sarah.

[16] Albert was a member of Company G, 78th New York Volunteer Infantry. The 78th had been fighting at Antietam, Maryland, Sept. 16-17. Frederick H. Dyer, *A Compendium of the War of the Rebellion*, Vol. III, (New York: Thomas Yoseloff, 1959), 1435. Hereafter referred to as Dyer.

[17] Louden Heights is located near Harpers Ferry, West Virginia. Sullivan F. McArthur, Co. E, 78th NYV wrote in a letter dated September 30, 1862 that "we are now camped on Louden Heights a high mountain on the S. East side of Harper's F[erry], we are up considerably in the world. we can see for 30 miles around us."

I hope you will not get out of patience reading my letter for I have nothing to do, only wright and sit and hear Catholic Priest lecture to me. there is a large Catholic Church and Hospital near hear for soldiers of that denomination. well, it is nearly night and I will stop till another time, perhaps tomorrow.

Oct 21st 1862

It is quite cool this morning. I am getting better every day. I think I shall be able to join my command in a couple of weeks if I keep on gaining, but don't know how it will be for they are in a cold place.

well, how do you like to live in Evans as well as you do in Waterville?[18] Birney Weber & Marion Johnston and Henry Shoemaker has enlisted, so has Dr. Lynd enlysted to[o].[19] who has enlisted out there? is Emmans Smith[20] at home yet? of course he is as much of a man as ever. Well, I cant think much more to wright as I have no news to tell, only ask sarah[21] if she knew Urettie Hammond at East Ashford. she is married to an old Batcherlor, forty years old, a pretty nice match I think. Please wright and answer this. wright often and l—o—n—g.

Buffalo and Erie County Historical Society, A64-38 McArthur Family, Folder 2.

[18] Before Frank and Thankful moved to Evans they lived with Frank's parents John and Harriet Griffith in Concord township. The specific area where the Griffith home was located was known to the locals as "Waterville," so called because two branches of the Buffalo Creek met there. Albert was unaware that Frank had enlisted and that Thankful and the children were back living in Waterville. Erasmus Briggs, *History of the Original Town of Concord*, (Rochester: Union and Advertiser Company, 1883), 241. Hereafter referred to as *Concord*.

[19] Weber mentioned in letter of 12 September 1862; Marion Johnston, age 18, from Ashford, in Co. F of 116th. *Registers*, 430, see also Appendix C; Henry Shoemaker, age 18, from Concord, in Co. F of 116th. *Registers*, 472, see also Appendix C; Dr. Uri C. Lynde, age 28, originally from Concord, mustered in as assistant Surgeon for 116th. *Registers*, 441, see also Appendix C.

[20] Emmons F. Smith died July 24, 1863, age 19 years, 8 months and 26 days, and is buried in the Brant (NY) Cemetery.

[21] Sarah Myers Hurd. See also Appendix A.

respectifully yours obediant servant
Mr. A. E. Myers, Esq

Direct to Frederick City
Bethel Hospital
East Third Street
Mayerland

1862
Perhaps you cant read the directions. if you cant I will get it printed
and send it to you. tell frank to wright often as he can.

*(upside down on top of last page in different handwriting, probably
Sarah's)* I am better so that I am going to try & do my work next
week. all well, sarah

Camp Chapin
Oct 23 [1862]

Dearest wife
          perhaps you will be looking for a letter, so I will not
disappoint you If you can read this poor scrawl. I am well and tough
at present, though I have been sick about half of the time since I have
been here. I went up to the Quartermasters[22] today and weight myself.
I weighed 140. I think I shall weigh 160 in three months if I am well.
you want to know if I have got any office yet. I answer no, and do not
want one yet. I think the time will come when I can do better.
          I think the prospects of the war is that it will close before the
first of January. they are enlisting men from the regiments about here
for the regular service. some of the boys talk of going if they will take
them for three years. perhaps there will enough enlist to break up the
regiment, and if this is we shall be sent home as minute men. I think
some of enlisting. do you want I should, dear, or had you rather I

---

[22] Willet H. Fargo served as quartermaster for only two months. He was 25
when he mustered in September 30, 1862 at Baltimore as first lieutenant and
quartermaster of the 116th. He resigned November 25, 1862. *Registers*, 403.

would come home? I do not get disheartened for I came here to serve my country, but when I see the way that things are managed here I sometimes get discouraged. I thought we came here to put down the rebelion, but I have found we came to fill the pockets of our officer. I think if I was at home I should see my duty in quite a different lite.

do you think that I could ever forget home? I know you do not for in the noise and tumult of camp, or when I lay down to sleep or wake, and in my dreams your dear face is ever present with me. Oh, if it was not for this you might say I was lonesome. I have not been homesick since I came here for I made up my mind to stay three years when I came. If we are sick here we are taken good care of as we can be, so do not worry about that.

Friday morning [October 24]

well, dear, I slept cold last night so I am not in the best humor posible this morning as you will remember. I think I shall draw another blanket this morning and see if that will do any good. the boys are all crazy about going into the regular service this morning. I shall not enlist till I hear from you again. it looks as though we should be sent home as minute men what there is left. how do you like that? if we are sent home we shall not be call on, I do not think, in this war. Lewis Ludlow[23] and I are coming home on foot when we are discharged, so you may look for us about new years some[time]. but I shall have to go and (drill) so I shall have to stop writing, and I want this to get in the mail this morning. please write to me often, do not wait for me to write. have you heard from Albert[24] lately? I want to know where he is so that I can write to him. Give my love to all the folks, and kiss the children for me, and tell nettie to wait till pa comes.

Good bye for the present,
Frank

———————

Camp Chapin

———————————

[23] Lewis Ludlow was 25 when he enlisted at Evans in Co. K, 116th. *Registers*, 441. See also Appendix B.

[24] See previous letter from Albert Myers.

116th New York Volunteer Infantry at Camp Chapin, Baltimore, Maryland, in the fall of 1862. Courtesy Buffalo and Erie County Historical Society.

Nov 3 1862

Dear wife,

I have received your letter and I find myself trying to answer it. I do not know where I shall write the next one for we have got marching orders and we shall not stay here long. I think that we shall go to either New Orleans or Texas. we have not got our pay yet, but as soon as we get that we shall go somewhere, but then it is uncertain. we do not know one day what we shall do the next. if we go to New Orleans we shall go to Washington and then to Fortress Monroe, and I will try to write again. we may go in a day or two, and then we may not go in six months.

I went down town yesterday to guard the Hospital and there is where we see some of the horrors of war. some of the boys have their legs sahd of[f], some with their arms, and others with their bodys mangled to pieces most horribly. it makes me shuder to think of it. I saw one poor fellow with his under jaw shot entirely off. but I must not write so to you, dear, for you will not sleep any for a month. yet all the boys feel well. they will talk and laugh and joke with you. they all say they want to go back again. you must not think that it scares me to see them for I have though[t] it all over before I came here, when you thought that I was asleep. I came here knowing that hardships were before me, that I should have to endure hardships such as I never dreamed of at home.

Oh dear Thank, I think if I am spared to come home to you again I shall know better how to appreciate your loving kindness. and I hope I shall know better how to govern my own high temper so that I may never cause you to weep at my unkindnes. and for all the hours of pain and suffering I have caused you dear wife, I hope you will forgive me, and pray that if never permitted to meet again on earth we may meet in heaven where partings shall be no more.

Tell Mother I was very glad to hear from her and I hope she will write to me often. I will try to answer her letter soon. tell Lydia[25] that I have got her letter which was thankfuly receive[d], and I want her to write to often and not wait for me to answer for I can hardly get time to write to you. I shall write to Albert as soon as I get time. I

---

[25] Lydia E. Myers, sister of Thankful and Albert. See also Appendix A.

would like to go and see him, but that is out of the question now. give my love to Father and tell him I think of him often if I do not write to him. how long are you going to stay there?[26] I suppose it is not so lonesome there as it is at home, though I do not see how mother gets along without Nettie. how I want to see her, though if I am gone three years she will not know me, will she? but I shall have to stop writing for it is drill time. take good care of yourself, dear, for my sake. you want to know what I do here. I will tell you as near as I can next time I write. Direct your letters as usual and it will follow [the] Regt.

     from your own,
       Frank

Camp Chapin
Nov 4th 186[2]

Dearest,

     you will perhaps be surprised to get this so soon after my other note, but as this is probaly the last night that we shall stay in Baltimore I thought I would improve it in writing to you. we have orders to cook three days rations to be served out to us in the morning, so we shall go somewhere proba[b]ly, though for all that we may not go in a month. I am well at present and enjoying myself as well as I can when away from (you). you will be anxious to know where we are going. all I have to say is I don't know. Charleston, Florida, New orleans, Texas are all talked of in camp, but a soldier is not supposed to know any thing about it or what he is going to do. but when we get there I will write you. in the meantime do not worry for me for I feel that I shall come to you again, though when no one can tell. but I want you to take all the comfort you can till I get there.

     how long do you intend to stay with your folks? I presume you do not find it so lonesome there as you do at home. I sent you a book today to read. have you sent me any more papers? I was very glad to get the[m] and I want you to send them often for it is like getting a letter from home. if we get to Texas we shall not have the

---

[26] Thankful is visiting her parents, Jacob and Mary Myers, in Yorkshire, Cattaragus County, New York. See Appendix A.

mail only once a month and I shall look for lots of letters from you every time. you will not disappoint me will you?

There was a man shot here to day, but it did not kill him.[27] he is in the hospital, but I do not think he will live, it was done fooling with a revolver.

Oh dear Thank, I wish I could see you tonight. I could tell you more in an hour than I can write in a week, but as I can not there is no use wishing, so I shall have to stop writing. I will write again before we embark if I can get a chance. it is very cold here to night and I think I shall sleep cold on the ground, but we *[next page missing]*

On board the steamship Atlantic
of[f] Fortress Monroe[28]
Nov 13th 1862

Dear wife,

I think I will try to write a few lines to you just to let you know that I am in the land of the living and well, though I expect to be seasick pretty soon. we left camp Chapin last Thursday [Nov. 6] morning and came on board of this ship on Friday morning after laying on the deck of the Robert Morris all night in the snowstorm. it rained and snowed great guns all night. you ought to have heard the

---

[27] "While waiting the final order to move, private Henry W. Weeks, of Company "B," was accidentally wounded by the discharge of a pistol in the hands of a member of Company "G." It was not considered a dangerous wound, but it rendered it impossible for him to accompany the regiment." He was sent to Stewart Mansion Hospital in Baltimore. He was discharged for disability on June 4, 1863. Clark, 38; *Registers*, 493. See also Appendix C.

[28] Fortress Monroe, or Fort Monroe, was located on the tip of the peninsula between the James and York Rivers, 75 miles southeast of Richmond, Virginia. Occupying a strategic position on Chesapeake Bay, it was one of only a few southern forts that did not fall to the Confederates, and as such it served as an excellent staging area for many land and sea expeditions. Robert B. Roberts, *Encyclopedia of Historic Forts: The Military, Pioneer, and Trading Posts of the United States*, (New York: Macmillian Publishing Co., 1988, 815 & 817; David S. and Jeanne T. Heidler, eds., *Encyclopedia of the American Civil War: A Political, Social, and Military History*, Vol 2 (Santa Barbara, CA: ABC-Clio Press, 2000), 741-743, hereafter referred to as *Encyclopedia*.

boys sware, but it was of no use as they all lay down on the deck. well, about that time your humble servant had a most terrible lame back and the captain came along and took me to the officers quarters where they were making themselves comfortable so I just lay down on the sofa and went to sleep till morning. I tell you I am learning to for[a]ger pretty fast, don't you think so? well, the next morning [Nov. 8] we went on board the big ship and got our breakfast and supper of the night before and started for the Atlantic Ocean. we went about half a mile and run aground where we stayed four days, when we got off and started for here.

I suppose you will want to know where we are going. well, I cant tell, but I will tell you what we have got on board. there is three hundred tons of powder and two large siege guns in the hold, 1,000,000 rounds of rifle cartridges, and six months rations for one thousand men. there is about 1300[29] men on board, so you see we are in a first rate plase for a fire on board. and you will have to guess where we are going. but I will write when we get to our destination.

I have had a letter from Albert. he said he had received a letter from you. he said he was getting better. but the mail boat is coming and I shall have to close this in haste which after I will write again as soon as I have a chance.

from your dear husband,
Frank

Fort Monroe
Dec 2 1862

Dear wife,

I take the present opportunity to write a few lines to you for I do not know but you have put your threat in execution not to write till I answered all your letters. I have written once a week and sometimes more since I left home and I have not had a letter from you in almost two weeks. I am well at present though I have been complaining some. the boys are half of them in the Hospital with the Fever and the measles and one thing and another till we can not muster only about

---

[29] Twelve hundred men were on the ocean steamer *Atlantic*. Clark, 39.

five hundred men fit for duty. Loren[29] and May Johnson and Birney have been in the Hospital for a week though I do not think they are very sick. we went on shore last night and pitched our tents and this morning we took them down again and came on board the ship. so I think that there is a right smart chance of our leaving here, and we may go to day. so I thought I would write to you for this may be the last time I shall have to send a letter to you in a great while. the orders are for us to be ready to start at four Oclock to night, but we may not go in a week for all that.

The weather is very pleasant here. the days are warm as they are in September, but the nights are cold. we have not had any snow here yet and the trees look green. I suppose you have had good sleighing there by this time. would not you like to take a sleigh ride with me on Christmas? did you have any Thanksgiving dinner? we did here, Hard Tack[30] and coffee. well, if I ever live to get home I think I can appreciate good living. I don't think I shall be quite so dainty as I used to be. wont you be glad of it?

I have had one letter from Mother and one from Carrie since we left Baltimore, and that is all I have heard from home since you went away. I guess they do not miss me at home much or they would write to me oftener. and I do not know but that is the case with you, or perhaps they are waiting for me to write. but if they could see how I am writing this they would not wait any longer. The boys were singing the other night and they sung 'do they miss me at home' and home sweet home. and after they were all asleep I lay and thought of my own dear home, and I wondered if they missed me, that amid all comforts of home and pleasures of everyday life they thought of the absent one. do they ever think of the sacrifices that the soldier makes

---

[29] Lorenzo Johnston is the brother of Marion "May" Johnston mentioned in Albert Myers letter of October 20/21, 1862. Lorenzo was 25 when he enlisted at Concord. He was a member of Company F in 116th. *Registers*, 430. See also Appendix C.

[30] Hardtack was a hard flour and water cracker, approximately 3 inches square and ½ inch thick. The Commissary authorities considered ten or twelve crackers a full bread ration. Bell Irvin Wiley, *The Life of Billy Yank: The Common Soldier of the Union*, (Baton Rouge: Louisiana State University Press, 1998), 237, hereafter referred to as Wiley; *Encyclopedia*, Vol. 2, 927.

when he takes his life in his hand and goes to the service of his Country? But I know that there [is] One dearer to me than my own life who misses me and prays that I may be again restored to her, and the thought cheers me through many lonely hours. and when this dreadful war is over I know there will be one that will wealcome me back though I may be a poor cripple for life. and trusting in your own dear faith I go forth cheerfuly to my duty hoping and praying that I may be soon restored to you.

     Please write to me often, and accept this with much love from your own,

     Frank

Direct your letters as before

On board the steam ship Atlantic at Sea
Dec 7[th] 1862

Ever rememberd and beloved wife,

     it will perhaps be a long time before you will get this letter but you will perha[p]s be glad to get this poor scrawl. I am well at present with exception of a slight seasickness. I think I will keep you like me to keep a Journal of what I see and hear on the voyage. We left Fort Monroe on the 4th of Dec. we had a very pleasant trip altho it rained all day, but at night it blowed great guns and most all of the boys cast up their accts with Jonah. I went on deck and tried, but I guess I don't owe him anything for I could not pay. the weather is cold and overcoats are comfortable.

8th

     it rains today and the sea is rough. it makes the ship roll and the boys continue to be sick. we are going slow waiting for the rest of the fleet.

Ship Island [Mississippi] Dec 13

Dear wife,

     you see I have broke of[f] my journal rather short, but I have been some seasick, and you do not know how good one feels. but as there may be a chance to get this of[f] before we leave I thought I would write a few lines. they have got me on the sick list for the first time since I left home. I don't know what the matter is, but I guess some kind of fever. I guess now you must not worry about me for I shall be around in a day or two. Ashley[31] layes here by me sick with the Typhoyd fever. he has been verry sick, but he is better now and with good care he will get around in a few weeks. There is about fifty sick in the Hospital now and if we stay on board the ship two weeks longer we shall all be sick. Leroy Oatman[32] has been verry sick but is better now. Alonso is tough an[d] well.

If you want to know where we are you can look on the map at the mouth of Mobile Bay and there you will [see] ship island. and if you want to know where we are going you will have to guess for I do not know, but the talk is New Orleans. it does not matter to me where we go if we can only get through wit[h] the war and get home again for I am getting homesick doing nothing, and living pened up like hogs, and living on food that a Dutchman would not feed to his hogs. our hard Tacks are mouldy, and it is no uncommon thing to find grubs in them an inch long. I thought I would send you one but I have thought better since. but you remember those Albert sent in that box, well they were pretty good ones. and our meat stinks so you can smell it all over the ship. but I live in hopes that the war will not last forever and then I can get something to eat.

I got three letters from you the day we left Fort Monroe, but I did not get them till I had mailed mine. you do not know how glad I was to hear from you and the children, and how I long to hold you in my arms again. Oh Dear Thank, I never knew how dear you were to me when I was at home with you and had all the comforts of life about me. now you must not think that I am getting homesick and discontented because I write so much about home.

Monday, Dec 15th
Well Dear,

---

[31] Lanson Ashley Stanbro was Frank's nephew. Stanbro was born in Concord in 1842, the son of Catharine Griffith and Henry C. Stanbro. He married Thyrsa Bryant in April 1862 and four months later he enlisted in the 116th, serving in Company C. *Registers*, 478.; and *Concord*, 475. See also Appendices A and C.

[32] Leroy S. Oatman was 18 when he enlisted at Evans, serving in Company A of the 116th. *Registers*, 454. See also Appendix C.

here we are encampt on the sand on ship Island. we came on shore yesterday and pitched our tents (you see we do not have any sundays here) and today we have been looking around. the Island is about five miles long and half a mile wide and is covered with sand and fleas from one end to the other so that we walk, talk, eat, drink and sleep in the sand, and have sand in our coffee, sand on our bread, sand in our meat[34]. and when we get up in the morning we have sand in our hair, sand in our mouths, sand in our ears, and all over generally, and on the whole we have a sandy time generally. but we do not expect to stay here more than a week or so an then we shall go to New Orleans or to Vicksburgh. The government is building a fort on the island an I have been looking around it today. it is built of brick and will cost the government about one million of dollars and will take about two years to finish it. there is a lot of rebels prisoners at work on it. they have got some of them fixed with a ball and chain around their leg, and they will have to pound stone for the next three years.

17th

as the mail is going out this afternoon I finish this and send it. we heard that Richmond was taken last night and such a shout as the boys sent up would make the infernal rebels quake for the next months. but I shall have to close this in haste. please write often and direct your letters to Washington, 116 Rgt NYV. Ashley is getting better all the time, but I guess I have got the Ague[35] for I had a shake this morning. I think we shall go to N Orleans in a few days. kiss the

---

[34] Orton Clark shares Griffith's impression of the place. "Ship Island is the most desolate and God-forsaken spot upon this footstool. It is situated some twelve miles from the coast of Mississippi, and is seven miles in length, varying from one-half to three miles in breadth. It is entirely destitute of vegetation, for the most part being simply one vast sand-bank." Clark, 45-46.

[35] Ague was a generic term used for any illness characterized by episodes of chills, fever, and sweating, especially malaria. Jeanette L. Jerger, *A Medical Miscellany for Genealogists*, (Bowie, MD: Heritage Books, 1995), 3; and Elizabeth Briggs and Colin J. Briggs, *Before Modern Medicine: Diseases & Yesterday's Remedies*, (Winnipeg, Man., Canada: Westgarth, 1998), 37. "Malaria, popularly known as ague or "the shakes," was distressingly common from the beginning to the end of the war....One out of every four cases of illness in the Union Army was malarial in character." Wiley, 133-134.

children for me, and don't forget me. give my love to all the folks at home.

from your own,

Frank to Thank

(written on top of first page of letter) tell John that I have not heard from him since I left home, and Fay.[36] tell Carrie to write to me, it is so long since I have [heard] from her.

————

Ship Island
Dec 21 1862

Dear wife,

as the mail is going out to night I will just drop a line to you. I am gitting better as fast as can be expected so that I can drill. the doctor thinks I have got the chill fever, but I shall be all right in a few days. Ashley is getting better and if he does not get cold he will get along now. Lon is well as usual and getting fat, he stands it first rate. I do not know where we are going yet but the talk is New orleans so you may look for the next letter from that place. we have not had any news since we left Fort Monroe, so when you write I want you to write me all the news you can git from the papers for we cant get any papers here. I think I shall be home in the spring, if not before, so you must keep up good courage. there is about four thousand troops on the Island now and more coming every day. the probability is that something will be done shortly. there is no news here that I know of to write for I presume you will git both of my letters at once.

give my love to all the folks, and kiss the dear children for me. how I want to see them now. and take good care of your self for my sake. has Albert got home yet? I should like to see him now. write to me often as you can and I will write to you every time I can send a letter. but I shall have to close this for the mail is going.

From your own loving,

Frank

————

[36] Fayette Treat, also from Concord, was married to Frank's sister Martha. See also Appendix A.

24

Chapter 2

"Kiss the children for me"
Carrollton and Baton Rouge, LA, January 1 - April 12, 1863

The 116th New York Volunteer Infantry and other regiments that were part of "Banks Expedition" arrived on Ship Island, Mississippi on December 13 and spent the next two weeks training. The 116th boarded the steamer *North Star* on December 29 for Carrollton, Louisiana, arriving on New Years Eve.

The camp they established at Carrollton was named "Camp Love" after Major George M. Love of the 116th. The month of January 1863 was spent performing routine activities and drilling. On February 2 the 116th took the river steamer *Che-Ki-Ang* up river to Baton Rouge where on the 5th they began pitching their tents at "Camp Banks," located about two miles from the city, and named after General Nathaniel Prentiss Banks. An expedition to Port Hudson was started from this city on March 14. Although the 116th did not partake of any real fighting, they did spend much time on the march, as well as looting all the food and other goods they could find before returning to Camp Banks on March 22.

At the beginning of April a small detachment of men who had remained at Fortress Monroe due to ill health rejoined the 116th. On April 4 they established a new camp in front of the "Deaf and Dumb Asylum" of Baton Rouge. The camp was called "Camp Niagra," and the 116th remained here until May 19, when another expedition was started for Port Hudson.

Frank Griffith discusses a number of these events in his letters, but spends more time expressing his own feelings. First and foremost is the longing he has for his wife, Thankful, and young daughters, Nettie and Gertie, and other family members. Nothing pleases Frank more than to receive a letter from Thankful. Their fourth wedding anniversary on April 6 is tenderly noted. Griffith often mentions other friends and family members, in most cases with loving concern. However, it is apparent that Horatio Hurd, married to Thankful's sister Sarah, has not paid money owed to Frank from a partnership. A man named Ben also owes money, and financial problems continue to be discussed throughout Frank's letters. His interest in money matters extends to frequent mentions of the prices for food and other items.

Griffith's letters home include descriptions of his day to day activities, life in the various camps, and the beauty and climate of Louisiana. In one passage Frank tells of having a young black boy to do chores for him, and uses terms that we consider derogatory today. One must keep in mind that Frank is only using terms that were in common use at the time. The only real breaks Griffith receives from camp routine are when he uses his carpentry skills to fix up stables for General Banks' horses, when he is sick, and when the 116th travels up to Port Hudson.

Frank Griffith wrote to Thankful expressing his true feelings about the Emancipation Proclamation, "I think that it will end the war sooner than we can by fighting for it is taking the life of the Confederacy faster than we can by killing their soldiers. they go and fight while their slaves stay at home and feed th[e]ir armies. take them away and you take away their foundation." He also speaks about the war, "I do not want to come home till this war is settled one way or the other... I would rather lose an arm or a leg than have it said that the great north has had to compromise with traters [sic]."

In early 1863 Frank still expects to be back home by spring, but notes the determination of the southern spirit. He believes that until the people living in the North give their full support to the war, it will continue on. Griffith expresses his disgust with those who make excuses to stay home instead of fighting to end the war, and believes that the Union cause has more to fear from "the rebels at home than those in front." He also has little sympathy for the managers of the war "who are for nothing but promotion and the almighty dollar." Although not sympathetic to their cause, Frank does feel sympathy for the people of the South. "I tell you we talk of making sacrifices to carry on this war, but they are nothing when compared with what the men and women of the south have sacrificed to their Confederacy."

Thankful, despite missing Frank, states, "I am proud of and glad that in my dear husband I have a brave, a noble, a sacrificing Frank." She further comments, "how noble is the cause, how great is the issue. and when the war is over, when peace reigns in the land, when our loved ones are restored to us, then how proud we will be to rank among the defenders of the flag, Frank as a true soldier."

Carolton, Louisania
Jan 1st 1863

Dearest wife,
    I shall have to wish you a merry Christmas and happy New
year all at once, though it does not seem much like New years here.
the weather is most delightful here. it seems like April here, the grass
is green and the gardens are in full bloom, but the nights are cold. I
am well at present and enjoy my self first rate at present under the
present circumstances. we came here yesterday from ship island and
camped here last night. we are about six miles from New Orleans up
the river[1]. it is the most delight[ful] country about here that I ever saw
and we are in a verry healthy place, but I do not think we shall stay
here any time. we shall proba[b]ly go up to Baton Rouge in a day or
two. we have not had any mail since we left Fort Monroe and it is
getting pretty lonesome here I tell you.

Jan 8th

well dear Thank,
    there has been so many rumors about our going away from
here that I have not finished this, and as we are not likely to move for
some time yet I will send it for I know you will be anxious to hear
from me. by the way that I feel it seems so long since I have heard
from you and so much longer since I have seen you that I can hardly
wait till the time comes when I can hold you in my arms again. but
still I know that you love me still and our pleasures will be sweeter in
each others society when we meet again, is it not so <u>loved</u> one? we do
not get any news here but what comes from Rebel sources and they
make out that we are getting pretty badly whiped, but I do not believe
it. I want you to write me all the news so that we [k]now what is
going on at home. Ashley is in the Hospital yet, he does not get along
very fast, but I think that he will get well if he is careful. Lon is
Tough and I think he will go home with the 116th in the spring. don't

---

[1] Carrollton, Louisiana is located about five miles from New Orleans
according to Clark, 48; but it is eight miles according to John D. Winters in *The
Civil War in Louisiana* (Baton Rouge: Louisiana State University Press, 1991) 98,
hereafter referred to as Winters.

you think we shall all be home then?

Jan 12th

Dearest,

I have just [got] the mail and have got six letters from your own dear self and two from home. we have not had any mail before in almost six weeks and you can not tell how glad I was to get a letter from you, it is the next thing to seeing you. Oh dear Thank, you do not know how lonely I get here sometimes. it seems so long since I have seen you. I suppose you will wonder how I can get lonesome here with a thousand men around me and every thing going on, but here I have no one to confide in, no one to sympathize with me, and when the toils of the day are over no one to meet me with a smile and a kiss of disintrested love. Oh, how much I miss your dear presence in these long evenings, it is so lonesome. but then it is not always so for in my dreams you come to me as of old with the same fond caress and feel your warm kiss upon my brow, and I live out those blissful hours again. Oh dear wife, if God in his great mercy should permit me to come to you again may I know better how to value the great blessings he has given me in your own dear self and those darling children He has given to us.

I do not want you to think that we are having very hard times here. I do not think there is a regt in the field that has fared better than we have for we have had enough to eat and wear. we never had to stay out doors all night yet, and to have never been on any long marches. I think we have been favored as a regiment to what some have.

I should like to tell you about the country here and our trip from Ship Island. here it is the pleasantist place here that I have ever been in. the roses are in bloom and the ground looks like spring. there has not been any frost but twice since I have been here. there are lots of Oranges here, 3 for 5cts, and they are delicious. butter is 40cts, eggs 5cts a piece, milk 5cts a pint and half water at that. but I shall have to stop writing. I am going to the city in the morning and I will put this in the mail and write again. you will wonder why I have been so long writing this but the mail boat has not left since we came so I have not sent it. I am well and tough. keep up good courage dear wife and look for me home in the spring. kiss the ba for me, and hug

Nettie for pa, and accept this from your own,
Frank

(at top of first page) Ashley is getting along first rate. take the money
H[oratio] got for the cattle and do what you think best with it.

Camp Love
Greenbelle, La[2]
Jan 13th [1863]

My darling,

I take the present opportunity of writing a few lines to you. I
am well and tough and that is the main thing in war. to night I have
been reading over some of your dear letters and they make me feel as
though I could not wait for the time I shall again hold you in my arms.
oh dear, if I could see you to night I could tell you more than I can
write in a month. it has been more than four months since we parted,
yet when I look back it seems as though it is not more than a week.
and when I think of the three long weary years before I shall be free it
seems like a long time to wait. but then when I think of what we have
at is[s]ue in the final settlement of this war, and the dear brave little
woman at home who has made such a sacrifice, I feel that I should be
a mean coward to stay at home at my ease while other[s] go forth with
their lives in their hands. and when this dreadful war is over and I am
restored to you and the darling little ones I shall not have it to regret
that I have not done my duty in this her hour of need. I know darling
that you are lonely without me, but then you have kind friends that
you can go to, so you must not get discouraged and grow old so fast
that I will not know you when I come home.

I have got a letter from Carrie and Corydon.[3] I think they
might have waited till I come home so that I could help them for I do

---

[2] Why Griffith refers to this place as "Greenbelle" here, and "Greenville"
in the next letter is unknown, as Carrollton, Louisiana is where the 116th established
"Camp Love," the camp where they lived for four weeks. Clark, 48-49.

[3] Frank's sister Carrie was married to the Rev. John Corydon Steele, a
minister of the Free Will Baptist Church, ca. Dec. 1862. See Appendix A.

not think they will prosper getting married when I am gone. I have sent you a present by Express so you may look for it as soon as you get this. I will send it to Springville[4], and I want you to tell me how you like it. but I shall have to stop writing for to night. here is a kiss for you darling.

[Jan 14]

As the mail is going to leave this afternoon I will have to finish this this morning. I am going on guard to day and I shall not have time to write much. It rains here this morning and I think that your humble servant will get wet to day. I have sent Nettie some roses in that box that I have sent to you. kiss the little darlings for me, and give my love to all of my friends. I have had one letter from Sarah Spencer. tell her that I will answer her soon. please write often, and accept this from your own,

     Frank

Camp Love
Greenville, La
Jan 24th 1863

Dear wife,

I received your most wealcome letter this morning and was verry glad to hear from you that you are well. I am well at present and never enjoyed better health than at present. I have been up to the Commissaries to night and I weighed 150 lbs[5], so you see that I do not suffer much for something to eat. I think we have been the most fortunate regiment in the service for we have never had any long marches with our knapsacks. I do not think we have ever carried them over three miles at a time. we have always had enough to eat, and as for clothes we have all we are a mind to draw. my shirts are good yet only they are so short that they do not come down - my socks are good yet. I have not had to mend them yet, but I found a hole in the toe of

---

[4] Springville was one of the largest towns in Concord township, with a population of 953 in 1861, according to J.H. French, *Gazetteer of the State of New York* (Syracuse: R.I. Smith, 1861) 289, hereafter referred to as French.

[5] 150 pounds was a fair weight for a man 5 feet 8 inches tall, like Griffith.

one to night. I have to pay five cts a for washing and do not get them done so nice as you used to do them for me, but they are good enough for a soldier. there is not any thing you can send me that I can think of. it would be more trouble to send to [me] than it would be worth. I would send you some money if I could be sure that you would get it. if you cant get the note of Ben's let me know and I will send you some. get John to see to it for you if he will. what have you done with the grain down to Evans? and will you have enough to last you till next winter?

you want to know what I do to pass the time. we do not have to drill as much as we did when we were in camp Chapin, but we have to go on guard about one in four days and then we have to be out all night. we do not get much sleep. we have to walk post two hours at a time, then we are off four hours. but then it does not rest us much, but when I come home I will tell you all about it.

The news is to night is that the river is clear, that we have taken Vicsburgh and port Hudson.[6] and if that is so I think you will see Frank about next May if I do not have any bad luck. I think that our chance of going to Texas is good yet and I would rather go there than any other place. now I think that the chance of our going into a fight are rather slim, but then we may see fun in a week. every thing is so uncertain in war, but dear, I have a presentment that I shall be home in the spring. don't you think so dear? and there is joy for us in the future, and then, love, I shall know better how to appreciate such a darling wife as you have always been to me, perhaps it will cure me of my pettishnes and impatience. Did you know that you came verry near to me last night in my dreams. I thought that we were at home again in our room and you came and put your arms around my neck just as you used to, and I was so happy. then it seemed as though my troubles were over and I should not start at the sound of the drum. and then I woke and found that it was all a dream. but I believe it is only a forerunner of the happy times that are in store for us in the future. don't you think so dear? but the mail is going to leave in a few minutes and I shall have to close this in haste. please write to me after and keep up good courage and look for me home the first of

---

[6] It was a false report. Vicksburg, Mississippi did not fall until July 4, 1863, and Port Hudson, Louisiana on July 9th.

31

Map of Louisiana showing where the 116th New York Volunteer Infantry traveled, camped, and fought. Produced for this volume by Andrew Serak.

May. kiss the children for me, and accept the love of your own,
        Frank
                To Thank

Camp Love, La
Jan 31st /63

Dearest,

I take the time to write a few words to you to night. I am well
and tough as a Buck, and I hope this will find you the same. I have
received your letter dated the 10th and you do not know how glad I
was to get it, though I was sorry to hear that you were sick. you see
by the date of this that we are still at New Orleans yet, but I do not
know how long we shall stay here. You want to know if my side
troubles me. it does not so much as it used to, it has not been lame
but once or twice since I came from home, but then you know I do not
lift so much as I did when I was there. but when I carry my knapsack
long it swells up some. The climate agrees with me first rate or I
should not weigh 150 lbs. We have not been in a fight yet and I don't
think we shall be very soon for we are here to guard the city. but then
we may [be] ordered of[f] in a week. there are lots of soldiers going
up the river every day and the probability is that there will be
something done sometime.

you want to know if I think of you. yes, dear one, always
when I lay down to sleep at night I think of you and the dear ones at
home. and in my dreams you come very near to me and I seem to live
over again the happy days gone bye. and I know that every night there
are prayers for the absent one that he may be preserved from the
dangers of the battlefield and that I may be again restored to you. oh
yes, dear wife, it is a great blessing to feel that I am thus remembered
by one that I love, even as my own life.

The Country is very pleasant here. there is some of the most
splendid places here that I ever saw. but then the blight of war is over
all. the streets of the city seem like Sunday at the north. but there is
very little done here except in provisions. they do not have any
Sunday here. their shops are all open and every thing goes on the
same on any day in the week. we have a Sunday in Camp for on that
day every body has to fix up in his best and take every thing he has

drawn from Uncle Sam out on inspection, and woe to that unlucky soldier that has not his gun in the best possible order, his clothes clean in his Knapsack, and everything in order. it costs five cts a pair to get our washing done, and indeed every thing costs five cts and upward. they do not have any thing less than five cts. but I shall come in on them now for I have got me a nigger boy to black my boots, wash my dishes and my clothes, and do my house work, so that all I have to do is to go out and drill with the company, and go on guard once a week, eat my salt horse and hard tack, and order my boy round. you did not think that Abolitionists as I am would ever be a slave owner, but I have got a shade and he is one of the pure blood, about the size of Gene.[7] and I think I shall bring him home with me when I come. his name is Mose and he says he run away from the Rebs on the other side of the river. and he may take a notion to run away from me, but then there are plenty more that can be had for th[e]ir board. so you may look for a black cloud when I come.

you want to know what effect the Proclamation[8] will have on the war. well, I think that it will end the war sooner than we can by fighting for it is taking the life of the Confederacy faster than we can by killing their soldiers. they go and fight while their slaves stay at home and feed th[e]ir armies. take them away and you take away their foundation. the slaves have got hold of it and they are flocking to our lines bringing every thing they can steal from their masters, even to their horses and wagons, tools and provisions. and as our armies advance their numbers increase so that they will have to either cultivate the soil themselves or starve. and as soon as we can open the river it cuts their Confederacy in two, cuts of[f] their supplies from Texas. and in the course of a few months they will feel the want of something to eat, and you know that a man cannot work if he does not eat.

---

[7] Frank's brother Marcus Eugene, "Gene," was twelve years old at the time Frank wrote this letter.

[8] Lincoln had issued a preliminary Proclamation on September 22, 1862 giving notice that all the slaves in those areas still in rebellion would be freed on January 1, 1863. On that date Lincoln signed the official Emancipation Proclamation. *Encyclopedia*, Vol. 2, 650-652.

Sunday, Feb 1

well, we have just been out on inspection and Co K has the praise of being the cleanest Co in the Regt, so you can see the Co are not all fools. but the mail is going out and I shall have to close this poor scrawl. I do not know as you can read it for I have to write in a hurry. take good care of yourself for my sake. tell Nettie that pa was very glad to get a letter from his little girl and I will send her one in return. kiss the little darling for me. have you got the box I sent you? if so just tell me what you think of it. give my love to all the folks, and accept this from your own,

Frank

(upside down on top of first page) P.S. this sheet costs 2cts here, cheep enough.
good bye darling, Frank

_____

Camp Banks
Baton Rouge, La
Feb 8th [18]63

My Dear Wife,

I received your verry welcome letter yesterday and now I try to pen a few lines to you to let you know how we get along down here in Dixie. we are all well at present, though there is some sickness here in camp with the fever. the water is verry poor here. it feels in my stomach like a cold potato, but then we have to drink it or go with out. the weather is very warm now, like June there. the trees are all leaved out and everything looks green. and if it was not for the blight of war this would be a verry desirable Country to live in, but every thing looks dessolate, the fences are all torn down and the roads are blocked up with waggons and artilery, and you see nothing but the great prepprations for the coming battle at port Hudson which is but 20 miles from here. I do not know whether we shall be called on to go up there or not, but I think there will be something done in the course of ten days.

Sunday night

well, dear wife, the order was re[a]d on dress parade to night

35

for us to be ready to march at any time, and I suppose that means up the river, so I thought I would finish this poor scrawl and put it in the office for there will be no chance to write on the march. there is about 70,000 men here and more coming. and we mean to make a sure thing of it this time. it is about 30 miles from here to port Hudson,[9] and as that is the first place on the river I expect there will be some tall fighting there. it will take two or three days to go there. we are in Gen Augers division the first brigade.[10] Col Chapin[11] is acting brigadier General, and we are the first regt in the brigade. but then we may be kept here to guard this place, it is very uncertain, but it is best to be prepared for any emergency. there is some talk of our going back to New Orleans to do guard duty in the city, but for my part I had rather go up the river than to go back there this summer for it will be hot there I can tell you. there is lots of gunboats in the river and they will go up and shell them out, and then perhaps we will come in for our share of the fun. now you wont worry about me, will you darling, for I have a presentment that I shall come out all right yet. and if we clear the river it will close the war.

I have just got a letter from John the first one he has written to me since I left home. I think I will answer it in the morning. I have not heard from Jay yet, but I will write him a letter as soon as I get time. tell mother that I am looking for that letter that she was going to write to me. has Gene got the one that I wrote to him yet? where are your folks going to live this summer, and what are they going to do?

---

[9] Griffith was right the first time in preceding paragraph. Orton Clark states they were twenty miles from Port Hudson. Clark, 52.

[10] General Christopher Colombus Augur, was Commandant of Cadets at West Point when the war began. He joined Banks in the Department of the Gulf in November 1862, and commanded the District of Baton Rouge from January 20 to May 20, 1863, and oversaw the attack on Port Hudson into July 1863. Health problems caused by earlier wounds necessitated a change in assignment. From October 1863 to August 1866 Augur commanded the Dept. of Washington, D.C. *Encyclopedia*, Vol. 1, 147-148; *Dictionary*, 34.

[11] Edward P. Chapin was named Colonel of the 116th New York Volunteer Infantry on September 5, 1862 and commanded the 1st Brigade, 1st Division, 19th Army Corps, Department of the Gulf, from February 9, 1863 until his death May 27, 1863 at Port Hudson. *Dictionary,* 140. See also Appendix C.

have you heard from Albert lately? and where is he? I think he has had enough of the war by this time.

it is a splendid night to night, just such a one as I remember once before we were married that I spent in your company when we took a walk down the road. do you remember it darling? we little knew how happy we were then. and then the three short happy years that we have spent together since then. and as I sat down to write to you to night I have laid down my pen and thought of the many happy hours that we have lived since we were married. my heart goes out in thankfulness for the many blessings that I have been permitted to enjoy. and if we are met or permitted to meet again I pray that Heavens choicest blessings may be showered on your dear head. and if it should be my lot to fall in the coming battle, may He in whose hands are the destines of Nations and men watch over you and give you strength to bring up the dear children that He has given us to be a blessing to you, and an ornament to society. tell often of me, and if they are never permitted to know a fathers love, let them know that they had a father who loved them and was willing to stake his life for their future happiness. but I hear the officers call and I shall have to close this letter. I shall write as soon as I get time for I know you will be anxious to hear from me. please write as often as you can, and accept the love of [y]our own,

     Frank
          Direct to Baton Rouge, La
          Good bye, darling

Camp Banks
Feb 9[th] /63

My Darling,

You will see by the date of this letter that we have moved our camp since I last wrote to you. we are now at Baton Rouge in camp. there is about forty thousand troops here so that we can see something of the glori[e]s of war. I do not know as I have ever given you a description of the way that we live here in camp so I will try to tell you something about the way a soldier enjoys life. the tents are pitched in streets, like the streets of a city, by company begining on the right with A, F, D, K, C, H, E, I, G, B. C being the color

Company they carry the flag. and our company is the fourth company and next to the flag. the captains tents are at the head of the streets. the captains and the lieutenants are called the line officers, and the Col and his staff are the field officers. their tents are back of the line officers, and the Cols is headquarters of the regt. and in the night a Camp is a splendid sight with its camp fires and a light in every tent.

and now you will want to know how we live. well, I will commence with the beginning of a day. The first thing you will hear is the drummers call at past the break of day. then all the drummers and fifers have to turn out, and in fifteen minutes they play the Revalie, and then eve[r]y body turn out and form in the company streets for roll call. and every body must answer to his name or be put on guard. then we clean up the street, fix up our tents. then the doctors call, and if any body is sick they must march up to the hospital and be examined. and if he is half dead he will get a dose of salts or quinine and be excused from duty for that day. we do not get any other medicine here no matter what ails us. then the drum beats for breakfast. then you ought to see every body grab his cup and tin plate and rush for the fire to get his coffee and salt horse[12] and potatos, when there is any, and his hard tack.

Did I ever tell you what we had to keep house with? if I have not, then it consists of a tin plate, a pint cup, a knife, and fork, an iron spoon, and these serve to eat our meat, bean soup, rice and homnany. on time we go to our tents and for the want of better accomodations sit down on the ground, hold our plates in our laps, set our coffee on the ground, and go in. after we have satisfied the cravings of nature we either wipe our plates with a piece of paper or turn them over, they seldom see any water, light our pipes and smoke. and those that are to go on guard clean up their guns and brasses and get ready to go on guard. at half past eight the drummers call the assembly, then guard mount till ten. then company drill till noon, then dinner, Bean soup tak[e]n the same way as breakfast. another smoke and we lay around

---

[12] Standard Army fare, salt beef, or pickled beef, was generally called "salt horse" by the soldiers. It was a special product prepared to meet government specifications. Prepared to last at least two years, the beef was preserved in brine so strong that it was often inedible unless soaked thoroughly in water before cooking. *Dictionary*, 719; Wiley, 239; and George Washington Adams, *Doctors in Blue* (New York: Henry Schuman, 1952), 207.

till 2 oclock. then Battalion drill till 4. then we have an hour till dress parade. then supper, rice and mollases, and coffee, another smoke, and then we have our time till nine at night. then the tattoo is played, and roll call. and every time we turn out we have the roll called. so you see what time we have to write, or mend our clothes, or do any thing for ourselves. well, when we come to go to bed we just spread our blank[e]ts on the floor and lay down two on each side of the tent, spread the rest over us, and call each other all the names we can think of, and then go to sleep if we can for the lice and those other <u>varmints</u> which infest the army and mankind generally.

I shall have to tell you how our cooking is done here. we have a camp kettle, made like a tin pail of shot iron. these we hang on a pole over the fire and boil our meat and potatoes, coffee, and rice, and bean soup, or anything else we have to make, and if they are not washed very often it is just as well. so you see we must have some most delicious meals as any body can see. then the water that we have looks like the suds you have to wash your clothes in, good isnt it. say, but then it must be h[e]althy or I should not be so fat. and then you know that a fellow can eat most anything when he is right hungry. so I do not complain as long as I can get enough to eat and an appetite to eat it.

Our Camp is situated on a battle ground of Baton Rouge and we can see the graves of the poor soldiers. it is here that General Wiliams[13] was killed. the rebels lost about sixteen hundred men here[14] and our camp is just beside their graves, and those of our men are farther back in a corn field and in the woods. we can [see] where cannon shots have plowed up the ground and tore their way through the trees. I noticed where a six pound shot drove square through an oak tree two feet in diameter. I think that it would [have] mad[e] quite a prominent bump on a fellows h[e]ad if it had hit him. I saw

---

[13] U.S. Brigadier General Thomas Williams was hit by a minie ball in the chest and died August 5, 1862 at Baton Rouge. Clark, 54; Winters, 118; and Carl Moneyhon and Bobby Roberts, *Portraits of Conflict* (Fayetteville: University of Arkansas Press, 1990), 146.

[14] Griffith was off in his estimate. Confederate losses were estimated as 84 killed, 315 wounded, and 57 missing for the Battle of Baton Rouge according to Winters, 122.

pie[c]es of shells and grape shot scattered on the ground. it looked as if they must had some fun here. there is a grave yard here and there is some splendid monuments and vaults. they bury there dead in vaults here built of mason work above the ground. there is one here that must have cost several thousand dollars, it is built of marble.

but I am afraid you will get tired of reading this long letter, or trying to read it, for I do not think you can read much of it for I have to hold my paper on my knee. and I have been at work pretty hard to day and my hand trembles so that I can hardly read it myself. and if you get tired of it you can throw it away. but I shall have to stop for to night as it is time for the tattoo and roll call. good night darling.

12th

I have just received your very wealcome letter dated Jan 20 and you do not know how glad I was to hear from you, though I am so sorry that you find it so lonesome at home. there, you must not worry so much about me for I came away expecting to endure privations and hardships. but I have always found it much easier than I expected, and others have lived through and come home again and I think that will be the case with me. but should it be otherwise ordered I shall think that I have always tried to do the best that I can for you and the children. and as for our going into a fight, we may be called on in a day or we may not be called on at all. and you know, darling, that I came here to fight and if need be die for the cause. you must cheer up and not look on the dark side of the picture so much for the war will not last always. and then when we are restored to each other we shall be so happy, wont we, dear? and though the time seems to drag so slowly, yet I feel that it will surely come. so cheer up dear and hope for the best, for I believe that your prayers will be answered.

we hear a great deal of war news here, mostly through Rebel sources, but we have got so used to it that we do not think much about it. some of the boys were so badly scared last night. we heard the picket firing about nine oclock and the boys thought the rebels had come down. they were all just loading their guns so as to be ready. well, I suppose you will want to know what Frank done. well, I have got some of Fathers blood in me I suppose for I went down to my tent and laid down and went to sleep. I told the boys if the rebels come to wake me up so that I could see them for I have not seen a rebel soldier yet.

Lon tents with me now. he is well and tough. Ashley is doing duty again, he will be tough now. Birney is at Fortress Monroe yet, so is Loren and May. I am going on picket tomorrow and perhaps I shall have some fun. some of the boys get pict of[f] once in a while by the rebel guerrillas, and they get once in a while a stray pill in return. now you must not fret about me for I do not think they want me yet. we are about 20 miles from Port Hudson on the mississippi river, and if we get into a fight I think that will be the place. but then I shall not write to you what we are going to do for I know that you will worry about me when it will do no good.

I have just had a lame back, well it was some lame I tell you. and then my teeth set in to ache and one of them ulcerated and I went to the doctor and had it pulled out. he did not break it off but four times, and you know that did not hurt much. but he got it out at last and the tooth hole ached more than the tooth, but it is better now and my back is most well. but I tell you dear that I thought if you had been here perhaps you could have sympathized with me if nothing more. we have one cold night since we came here and I thought I should freeze. it put me in mind of a warm bed at home, and a good warm <u>bedfellow</u> too, but as a general thing I enjoy myself as well as I can away from you. but I am afraid you will get tired of this long letter so I will stop writing.

Have you got that money from Ben yet? and has Horatio paid you any yet? I have not had but one letter from him since I came away. I should think he would write to me. do you have money enough and enough to eat? please write to me all about how you get along. have you got the grain home from Evans yet? about the Horses, I do not hardly know what to tell you. if I should come home in the Spring I should not want them to have Colts, but perhaps it would be the best thing that can be done. you must act your own pleasure about that.

Tell mother I have not had an answer from her. has Gene got his letter yet? I have got two from him. tell Him that I have been looking for a letter from him but it does not come yet. and John has forgotten me quite. How does David Griffiths folks[15] get along? I

---

[15] David E. Griffith is Frank's cousin. David's parents are Millicent Beers and Hezekiah Griffith, brother of Frank's father, John Griffith.

heard that Sarah[16] was not expected to live. and Lois, what of her? write me all the news. but I promised not write so long. you cant read this for I cant myself. give my love to all the friends. kiss the darling Children for me. and dear wife, if you should never get another letter from me you mus[t] think that I have always loved you the same. I will send Nettie a picture in this. how I want to see her, the little darling. please excuse all mistakes, and acept the faithful love of your own,

      Frank Jr[17]

Thank,
PS to you dear, that I am going to send you a new name. so I will leave you to wonder till my next.

      FEG[18]

PS ---- Direct your letters to New Orleans

_____

Camp Banks
Batton Rouge, La
Feb 27th /63

Dear wife,

      I take this opportunity to write a few lines to you. I have received but one letter from you in four weeks and I did not know but you was sick or had forgotten me. but I thought that I would write a few lines and see what was the matter. I am well at present and tough, though I do not know how long I shall be so for it is pretty sickly here. while I am writing this there is three funerals going on to the burying ground, and there is more that ar[e] not expected to live, though they

_____

[16] Sarah Ackerson was David Griffith's first wife. She died in 1869.

[17] The terms Sr. and Jr. were sometimes used to distinguish persons of the same name, not necessarily related, by their ages. Paul Drake, *What Did They Mean By That?* [Vol. 1] (Bowie, MD: Heritage Books, 1994), 190; David L. Greene, "What is Genealogical Scholarship?" *New England Ancestors*, Holiday 2000 Issue, 7.

[18] FEG stands for Frank Elnathan Griffith.

are not all from our regt. there is about 40 thousand men here so you see we have plenty of company.

Saturday Feb 28
well dear, this is the last day of this month and it has rained all the fornoon and all night, and thundered an[d] lightened like fun. the weather is warm as it is in may there, and the trees are leaving out. the peach trees are in bloom and eve[r]y thing looks green. we were to be mustered for pay to day, but it is so wet that I do not think we shall now. I have just had my shirt off looking for lice and I only found four. I think some of them are absent with out leave for they had a dress parade on me last night and there was more than a hundred. I think I shall send a patr[o]ll after them. I tell you we have fun hunting for them sometimes.

Do you know, darling, that it is almost six months since I enlisted and yet the war drags along. It seems as though it is no nearer to a close than it was one year ago. sometimes I get almost discouraged when I think of the vast army that we have in the field and so little done, and ev[e]ry day our troubles get more complicated and harder to be settled. we do not get much news from the north and what we do get is not of the most encouraging kind. and the army along the river is laying idle for all that we know. and with two parties at home and rebels here the prospect of getting home is not verry encouraging, but we will hope for the best. Dear wife, you must not think that I am getting discouraged or homesick for that is not the case, for I believe that the right will yet triumph over wrong, that we shall yet live to see the day that our Country will be united and happy. but when you write me such dear letters I know that you try to be brave and keep up good courage, but then the feeling of lonling will come. but my heart goes out to you, and I think what a good and faithful wife you have been to me. I pity your lon[e]lines[s], but then you must keep up good courage.

Sunday March 1st
well dear, the rain did not stop us from having a review and inspection yesterday afternoon so we all fixed up in our best and went out and waded in the water all the afternoon. and as a natural consequence about half of the boys are sick with a cold to day. but then I suppose it is necessary to save the country that we should drill

and parade if it rained pitchforks. Captain Ira Ayer[19] has resigned and is coming home. he will probably be there by the time this letter gets there. he has been sick and is coming home on the acct of his health. if you should go down to Evans you could go and see him. I suppose it would be some consolation to see somebody from the regt. I have got a letter from Dora and one from Sarah Spencer. Dora says that they expect the Indians will trouble them in the spring and wants me to come and help fight them.[20] but I guess we have got all the fight that we want here. I think I will send the letter to you. tell Carrie she need not be so much taken up with being married that she cannot write to me. I have not had but one letter from Horatio since I enlisted. I think he does not care to hear from me. Ashley has got well so that he is doing duty again. Lon is tough and harty. I am going to send you a book with this letter. did you ever get the one that I sent you?

I will give you the price of some things here. Potatoes are worth 10 cts per pound, Butter 60 cts, eggs 5 cts a piece, Cheese 30 cts, milk 10 cts a pint, apples 6 cts a piece, and such paper as this two cts a sheet, envelopes are 3 for five cts, and stamps are not to be had at all. I am going to send you some money after pay day by expres. have you got the box yet I sent you? I have not got but one paper since I have been here so you see it is of but little use to send them. I almost dread to hear from home, I am so afraid the children will get the diptheria. write often and let me know how you get along. and keep up good courage and be a brave little wife, wont you for my sake. here is a kiss for you, and accept the love of your own,

Frank

Direct your letters to Baton Rouge, LA

Baton Rouge, La
March 31st 1863

---

[19] Ira Ayer enlisted at Buffalo, age 59, and was commissioned captain of Company A on September 8, 1862. Ayer was discharged for disability on March 1, 1863. *Registers*, 370. See also Appendix C.

[20] Dora and Charles Cornell live in Maine.

My Dear Wife,

I received your most wealcome letter last night, and one from Yorkshire from your Mother. and you do not know how glad I was to get them, and the paper which you were kind enough to send me. it costs us 90 cts a quiver here, and hard to get at that. and post-stamps are out of the question entirely, so you see we have to frank[21] our letters home. I am well at present and tough, and I suppose that is the most interesting news to you. I think your presentment will prove false as long as Gen Banks[22] has command of this department.

I suppose you have heard of our raid on port Hudson by this time, and if you have not you will have to wait till I get home for one for I never can write a description of it. I had been sick for about a week before we started and I had just began to get some better and I thought that the boys were going to have some fun so I packed up my knapsack and started off for port Hudson[23]. well, we marched about 15 miles before noon and you can guess that I was some tired. it seemed that my knapsack never was so heavy before, and my feet were blistered all over the botoms. well, we stopt and stayed all night and killed all the cattle and sheep and pigs and chickens we could find. I tell you we lived high that night. wel[l], in the morning the order came to fall back so we packed up in double quick time and marched 3 miles in 35 minutes. that is some of us did, but I tell you it was some tough on a fellows sore feet. well, we fell back a bout five miles and camped in a potato field and then it began to rain like the Devil, and then there was fun I can tell you. the water was about three inches deep all over the ground. wel[l], we piled up some rails so as to keep us out of the water and pitched our little tents over them and

---

[21] To "frank" meant to mark a piece of mail with an official signature or sign to indicate the right of the sender to free mailing. *Webster's Ninth New Collegiate Dictionary* (Springfield, MA: Merriam-Webster, 1991), 489.

[22] General Nathaniel Prentiss Banks, although lacking military experience was commissioned a major general at the start of the Civil War. Assigned by the War Department to direct the Department of the Gulf, in Louisiana, November 8, 1862, he developed a reputation as an ineffective commander. Winters, 146; *Encyclopedia*, Vol. 1, 174-175.

[23] They left Baton Rouge early on March 14th and marched twelve miles. Clark, 55-56.

spent a most uncomfortable night. and the next night we went back to Baton Rouge and got on the boat and went up the river to Port Hudson on the other side of the river and stayed there most a week, and took every thing we could find horses, mules, cattle, sugar, and tobacco, and rum, and wine. well, they talk of starving the Rebels out but that is played out. you may just as well talk of starving a mouse in a corn field for every where we have been we have found plenty to eat, Corn and Beef, and they are not very likely to starve on that. you ask when will this horrid war cease. Well, when there are no more rebels to fight then the war will be over for they will fight as long as there is any of them left to fight, and that is likely to be some time yet fhurther carried on.

about that stuff at Evans. wel[l], it makes me so mad to think about it that I can hardly hold my temper to say any thing about it. but I suppose it is all right for him[24] to take the advantage of me when I am gone and cant do any thing about it. I supposed after I had paid him $130 cent, and let him have all the fodder, and all the cows, made that half of the grain would belong to us and then half of those calves were mine. but then he is a Christian and so I suppose it is all right for him to rob us, for I can not think him any better than a thief, nor quite as good for a man that would rob a soldiers wife, would steal the cents off his dead mothers eyes, and then swear because they were not half dollars. get what you can and when I get home I will settle with him.

Give my love to all the folks at home, you have mine always. kiss the children for me, and here is a kiss for you. write often to your own,

Frank

Direct to New Orleans

(*at top of first page*)
Dear Thank, I am writing you along letter on a sheet of rebel paper so you can look out for it in the next mail. kiss the ba for pa. Frank
(*sideways on first page*)
Please put a stamp on this and send it home to your folks.

---

[24] Frank and Thankful's brother-in-law, Horatio Hurd apparently had a business arrangement involving a farm.

(original consists of two sheets of light blue paper, 12" x 18 ½")

Camp Banks
Baton Rouge, La
April 5th 1863

My Dear Wife,

      I have found a sheet of <u>sesesh</u> paper and I thought I would take a week and write you a good long loving letter on it, and if you get tired of reading it you can just lay it up on the table and guess at the conte[n]ts. We are all well at present. I say we, that is Lew, <u>Lon,</u> Hank,[25] Ashley and [this] subscriber, and I suppose that is what you will want to know first for that is of the most consequence to the soldier. for as long as we have our health we can stand all kinds of hardships.

      I shall have to tell you how I came to get this little sheet of note paper. you see I had been sent down to Headquarters to fix up some stables for the Generals horses, and while waiting for some nails to work with I went out reconnoitering and found a little office that originally belonged to some <u>secesh</u> Architect. so I just pried open the door and went in to see what it contained and found a lot of papers and books and maps, drawings and pictures, and all the <u>pomp and Glory and circumstance</u> of a first class mechanic.[26] there was some of the most splendid pictures you ever saw. and among other things I found five [of] the neatest smoke pipes in the Busines. well I just seised and Confiscated them as Contraband of war and gave on[e] to the General, and one to the Adjutant [John B. Weber], and one to the Lieutenant [Warren T. Ferris], and one to the chief butler, and one to

---

[25] Hank may be Henry Shultes, age 20, in Company F, whose family lived near the Griffith's in Concord. *Registers*, 472; *New Topographical Atlas of Erie Co., New York* (Philadelphia: Stone & Stewart, 1866), 39. See also Appendix C.

[26] A "mechanic" is a laborer who is skilled and works with his hands. Paul Drake, *What Did They Mean By That?: A Dictionary of Historical Terms for Genealogists, Some More Words, Volume 2* (Bowie, MD: Heritage Books, 1998), 50. Mechanic can also refer to an "artisan." *Webster*, 737.

Frank, if you know who that is. I think I will send it home by express and then when I get home you will see some of the tallest smoking you ever heard of. they are worth about ten dollars apice here. well, they are some I can <u>tell you</u>.

I think I [s]hall have to write between each line to get it all in to this small sheet, but it is time for roll call and I shall have to dry up for to night. While I think of it I should like to be where I was four years ago tomorrow night.[27] would not you say, darling? well, I shall have to say good night.

I have got a few minutes more to write and I will tell you where our camp is. we have been camped about two miles in the rear of the city till yesterday when we moved down to the city, and now we ar[e] camped on the banks of the river in front of the Deaf and Dum[b] Asylum. it is a great deal more pleasant here than it was up ther[e] where we were before. I suppose you will want to know what we have com[e] down here for. The troops have been moved down the river, I do not know what for. and we have come down here to do guard duty, and garrison the rifle pitts, and do Provost duty, so that we come on guard or Picket once in three or four days. I shall have to tell you what fun we have on Picket sometime but not tonight.

/Here is a <u>kiss</u> for you dear /
April 6th

well dear, I have a few minutes this morning and I will write a few words in my note. four years ago tonight, if I remember, was one of the happiest of my life. do you remember it? say dear, how fast time flies. it <u>does not</u> seem more than one year since we were married. and if the next three years will only pass as happily I shall not complain much.

I want to tell you about the situation of our present camp. We call it Camp Niagra[28] and it is right in front of the Deaf and Dumb

---

[27] Frank Griffith married Thankful Myers on April 6, 1859 in Ashford, Cattaragus County, New York.

[28] Orton Clark stated, "In the disposition of the regiments the One Hundred and Sixteenth found itself encamped on the banks of the river, immediately in front of the Deaf and Dumb Asylum, used... as a hospital. It was the most beautiful ground for a camp we had thus far... We named it, in honor of our noble river at home, "Camp Niagra," and for two months remained there." Clark, 68-69.

The "Deaf and Dumb Asylum" of Baton Rouge, Louisiana was used as a hospital by the Union Army. Frank Griffith and the 116th New York Infantry spent two months camped in front of this beautiful building in the spring of 1863. This building's verandas and yard with flowerbeds greatly impressed Griffith. Courtesy of the Massachusetts Commandery Military Order of the Loyal Legion and the U.S. Army Military History Institute.

Asylum. it is the most splendid building in the city situated on the hill and commands a fine view of the river. the yard is laid out in flower beds and nice gravel walks with rows of hedges and fine shade trees. indeed a yard is not in fashion in this country with[out] shade trees in it. The roses are all in bloom and presents a most splendid sight to the eye. / I don't think you can read what I have written to night for my hand trembles so that I can hardly hold my pen / The building is four stories high and built of brick and plastered on the out side of [it] in imitation of marble. there are verandas running all around of the out side, and that is another peculiarity of the houses here. every house has a veranda on as much as two sides of it. and the houses ar[e] general[l]y but one story high, but the rooms are very high and airy. they look very comfortable and pleasant. there is a few deaf and dumb children here, but the main part of the building is used for the general hospital. and it is here that you see the horrid realities of war in all their ghastly reality. on a cot here lies one poor soldier, who has taken his life in his hand and gone in the name of liberty to defend the spot he calls home from the ruthless hand of a traterous foe, with a leg shot off. another with an arm, one with a hand missing, and others wounded in all imaginable ways, others laid low by disease. and all without a wife, or sister, or mother, or any kind friend to take care of them, and more than all to sympatiyze them in their distress, or give them even a cup of cold water. There is sometimes 15 dead in a day and it seems hard to see the poor fellows taken out and buried without hardly a board to mark their last resting place, or a friend to mourn for them now they are dead. But then I know that far away there is some hearth made dessolate and some h[e]art that groes tired and sick at hope delayed. alas, they will never more be mad[e] glad by the presence of the poor tired and dead soldier. Oh Darling, you little know the horrors and the miseries of a military Hospital and I pray that you never may know by actual experience. I do not know but there is every thing done for the poor soldier, but it seems hard to me to see the government expend milions of dollars on experiments and comparitivly nothing for the poor sick soldiers in the Hospitals. and I hope and pray that I may not be obliged to be the inmate of one.

but I shall have to stop writing for tonight as it is bed time. write and tell me what you are thinking about to night. it does not seem much like four years ago to night, does it darling? here is a kiss for you all. good night.

April 7th

    I am at work down to Headquarters now days and I have just come home and got my dinner. and now I will try and write a few lines in my note. I have just got my fifty dollars state bounty[29] in a check out the Bank and I am going to send it home to you. and if I get my pay in a few days I will send you some more with it. I shall have to get my boots fixed, and some new shirts. my old ones are not near worn out yet, but they are so short that I can hardly keep them in my pants. and then the lice are getting so thick in them that it makes me swear some when they get right busy drilling on my back. it is almost impossible to get rid of them. I want you to send in the receipt that we got of George Kellog[30] for making that ointment we had last winter. what has become of George? I have not heard a word from him in a long time.

    Do you hear any thing said about our being called home in June? we have got a yarn here in camp that if the New England Nine months men are sent home when their time is out that Gov. Seymoar [Horatio Seymour] will call all the men home over the 110 regt for he thinks it will not be fair for New York to furnish all three years men and the New England states fill the quota of nine months men. I hope that he will do it for I am getting tired and Sick of the war. I can not see that all this sacrifice of lives and property is doing any good. and it never will as long as the war is carried on by men who have no love for Country, or honor, and who are for nothing but promotion and the almighty dollar. why, I have even heard men boast of making two or three Hundred dollars in a day out of the Commissary stores, and all this money comes out of the rations of the men in the ranks. it is no wonder that we get tired and sick of throwing away our lives for nothing. and if the managers of this war had it to live on our rations, and take our fare, the war would be settled in double quick time. and now they are going to draft six hundred thousand more men while they do not half feed what they have got, and do not know even what to do with them. It is very easy for men to sit in their easy chairs, and by their comfortable fires, and their well filled tables, to sleep in

---

[29] This bounty was a payment offered to encourage men to join the army.

[30] George P. Kellog was married to Thankful's cousin, Helen Amanda Pierce. Both George and Helen became teachers. *Concord*, 231 & 233.

security in their warm bed, and talk patriotism. but when they come
to take their musket and go into the field and take the soldiers fare
they will find that the theory and practice are two different things.
now, you must not think that I am homesick or that I have lost al[l]
love for my Country, for that is not the case. but when I think it all
over it make[s] me somewhat <u>riled up</u>, and I want to preach to those
patriots who have the rheumatism every time there is a call for more
men. but I shall have to report again now.

Wednesday evening April 7th

well dear, I have a few minutes to night and I have got my
little note around again to write a few lines to you, though I don't
know but you will get tired of trying to read it for it is written so poor
that I can hardly read it my self. I hardly know what to write about to
night. I guess I shall have to tell you about going on Picket. well,
there is a number of men detailed ev[e]ry morning and they have to
take all their traps on his back and go out to the picket line about a
mile from camp. The line goes from the river clear around all the
camps to the river again, which makes about five miles of picket.
there is so many regiments gone away from here now that it takes
about five men from each company now. Well, they are posted three
men on a post, with a reserve about once in a mile. the posts are so
that we can see each other. and the orders are not [to let] any one pass
either way without a pass signed by the General in Command. well,
one man has to keep his gun in his hand all the time, and at night two
of us are on guard all the time. when it is pleasant weather it is not
very hard work, but when it rains it is pretty tough for we are not
allowed to have any fire after dark. and if it rains ever so hard there
we must stand and take it. and now the Rebs have got a notion of
picking of[f] our pickets so that it stands us in hand to keep our eyes
open. but you see they have not got me yet, but I about know how
long it will be before they will. they get our early pickets quite often
for they have go to go out beyond the infantry so that they have a
better chance at them. When I was out on picket the other day a
Lieutenant and a Sergeant and one private went out about a mile b
beyond the lines, and the first thing they knew they were surrounded
and ordered <u>to halt</u>. well, they just turned their horses toward home
and put there spurs to them, and the rebs fired on them and killed the
private and wounded the sergeant. but he rode into the lines so that
we got him. the Lieutenant got of[f] without a scratch, but he had a

narrow escape. his bridle reins were cut almost of[f] just above his horses neck. I believe that he allowed there were twenty five or thirty of them. the Captain of the guard sent twenty of us down to see if we could find the missing man. we went down to the woods and half of us were left there for a reserve while ten of us went on to see where the rebs were. we found the place where the shooting was done, but could not find the man. and out in the woods we found where they had hid and eat their peanuts. If the cowards had stayed there they might have hooked us as well as not, if there were as many as the Lieutenant allowed there were. Ashley was one of the party.

Wednesday April 8th 1863

Well, I have got my little note around to night, but I am so tired to night that I do not know as I can write any thing that will be interesting to you. but if you think as much of any thing from home as I do you will read it if it is not so <u>cunning</u>. I have been down to Headquarters to work again today. they talk of detailing me as Brigade Carpenter,[31] but I do not know as I want the job though it would take me out of the ranks and I should not have to drill any nor do any other duty. and if there is any work to be done I should have a detail of men to do the work and I could sit around and <u>boss</u> the job and get 25 dollars a month for doing it.[32] but then I do not like the Quartermaster[33] well enough to be ordered around by him.

We are at work close by the old State House, but it is in ruins now for the rebs set fire to it when our folks took the place last winter and burned the inside all out so there is nothing but the walls standing to show its former magnifisence.[34] it must have been a splendid

---

[31] Griffith was a carpenter by trade.

[32] This would double Griffith's monthly wage as U.S. Army Infantry privates earned $13.00 per month. Michael J. Varhola, *Everyday Life During the Civil War* (Cincinatti, OH: Writer's Digest Books, 1999), 37, hereafter referred to as Varhola.

[33] Alexander Goslin, from Buffalo. *Registers*, 414. See also Appendix C.

[34] Union forces had re-occupied Baton Rouge in December 1862, and on the night of December 28th the capitol was burned. Charles Robert Goins and John Michael Caldwell, *Historical Atlas of Louisiana* (Norman: University of Oklahoma Press, 1995), No. 38.

Griffith described the Louisiana State House in Baton Rouge in April of 1863 after it had been burned the night of December 28, 1862. He noted that "it must have been a splendid building if we can judge from its present appearances... it was lighted with gass for we can see the gass pipes all over the inside, and some of the most splendid stone cornice around the rooms... but they are all in ruins now, and all blacked with smoke." Courtesy of the Massachusetts Commandery Military Order of the Loyal Legion and the U.S. Army Military History Institute.

building if we can judge from its present appearances. it is situated on the bank of the river and commands a fine view of the river and the city. it is built of brick like the Asylum and plastered on the out side in imitation of marble, and cost the state $100,000. it was lighted with gass for we can see the gass pipes all over the inside, and some of the most splendid stone cornice around the rooms I was in. but they are all in ruins now, and all blacked with smoke and shored timber. the tower is used as a signal station by our forces. but the yard which covers about two acres is the most beautiful place I ever saw in my life. the unusual shade trees abound here in all there magnificcence, nice shady walks, and the most beautiful shrubs and flowers of this southern climate here greet the eye. it is like our May or June here now, only the nights are cool so that an over coat is comfortable soon after sun down, while the days are hot enough to roast eggs in the sun. there were once nice fountain and every thing pleasant here, but it has all been sacrificed to the demen of secession. The city is about as large as Springville. now the most of it was burned when we took the place by our shells, and you can see the ruins of the once splendid stores and palaces of the southern aristocracy. I tell you we talk of making sacrifices to carry on this war, but they are nothing when compared with what the men and women of the south have sacrificed to their Confederacy. The Old State Prison is standing yet, but it is used for the use of the army to hold their prisoners and for military stores. I will write you a description of it ne[x]t if you do not get tired of reading such poor descriptions as I give of places.

but I shall have to stop writing for to night as it is time for roll call again, and my h[e]ad aches so that I do not think I have half written what I have wrote. so I will put up my little note for to night. good night.
Thursday morning April 9th

I have a few moments this morning to pen a few lines in my note. My head feels better this morning after a good nights sleep on the hard boards. if I should ever be so unspeakably happy as to get home again I do not think I could ever sleep in a bed, I should not feel at home at all. my sides and hips have got calloused so that the skin is half an inch thick and I can lay on a board all night as easy as I used to on a feather bed at home. I never slept any better in my life than I do here, only it is so cold nights and you know that it [was] always hard

55

work for me to keep warm when I was at home.

I believe I promised to give you a description of the States Prison here. I[t] is built of brick and is three stories high which would be as high as a four story building there. and the windows are all bared with inch square iron. it is in four long buildings with their ends touching in the shape of a square, and the square contains about one acre of ground, so you can judge something of the size of the institution. on two sides of the square were the workshops, but the machinery is all taken out of them and the lower stories are used for Artilery stables. there is a yard covering about three acres more with a reservor in it to catch rain water in. they drink it here all the time for the water is so poor that a horse would not drink it there. There is a walk on the top of the wall and at each corner there is a watchtower where the sentrys used to be posted. and inside of the wall there is brick machines where they used to make brick, and just outside of the walls are the kilns where they burned them. there must have been a very large engine in the machine shops by the looks of the arches and the chimneys. on two sides of the square there is where the cells are situated. they are about six feet high and five feet square. they are pretty strong looking places and I guess it would bother a man some to get out of them. they are built in the middle of the room with a mile alley all around them so if a man got out of his cell he would not be only half out of prison. but I think I have written enough about that so I will tell you something about our trip up to Port Hudson on the other side of the river.

Well, we broke camp on Monday night [March 16] at dark and marched back to Baton Rouge, about five miles in the night, and got on the boat about midnight and started up the river. we went up five or six miles and tied up till morning and then started on again. I b[e]lieve it is about twenty five miles from here to port Hudson. we got there about nine oclock and landed on the other side of the river. that is the Boys did, for I was sick when we started but I did not mean to be left behind so I stayed on the boat to take care of the knapsacks. Well, they all fell in and went back from the river about three miles and then came back and camped for the night. and the next morning they did the same thing, and so on for five days. I beli[e]ve the Major [George M. Love] allowed they were looking for a <u>north</u> <u>west</u> passage to the Red river or something else. you [know] we privates are not supposed to know what we do anything for. well, the next day I felt better so I made a break for a sugar house that stood back in the lot a little ways from camp. I tell you it takes a soldier to smash things. there was about a hundred barrels of sugar and molasses with their heads knocked in and all running out on the ground. we took what we wanted and the gunboats carried of[f] a lot of it. it was a verry large building and must have cost 25 or 30 thousand dollars, but it will hardly be worth coming back to if we get another chance at it. the man had one of the finest plantations on the river. he had a splendid house, but the boys went in to that and smashed up the furniture and everything they could get their hands on.

we were within three miles of the Fort. I went up so that I could see the rebs at work on the fortifications and could hear them talk across the river. they called us all the names they could think of, and maybe you think we did not answer them. we were camped every night so that the gunboats could throw shells into their works. one day some rebel boats came down to the Fort and our boats pitched some shells into them and they made tracks double quick up the river again. some of the boys found rum and tobacco and preserves and lots of things that they allowed were contraband of war. well, we found lots of beef and horses and mules and chickens and such things. I believe that Gen Dudey[35] allowed if the 116 regt were left there two weeks longer they would steal Port Hudson. The brigade went out almost opposite of the Fort one day and the rebs opened fire on them with shell[s] and wounded one man in Co C. I do not know what his name is, but he is getting better so that he is out around the camp now. I believe a piece of shell hit him in the leg some where.
Saturday April 11th

Well dear, as I have a few minutes time to night I thought I would write a few lines in my little note. I will have to give you the price of some of the necessities of life here in Baton Rouge. For instance Butter and Cheese 50 cts per pound, Eggs 60 cts per dozen, flour ten cts per pound, Pottatoes Irish 10 cts per pound, Cotton cloth 50 cts per yard, boots such as those I got to the station are worth 18 dollars per pair, and such shoes as we used to get for fine shoes ar[e]

---

[35] Colonel Nathan Augustus Monroe Dudley of Massachusetts commanded the 3rd Brigade, 1st Division, 19th Corps, Department of the Gulf from January 12 to July 10, 1863. Stewart Sifakis, *Who Was Who in the Union* (New York: Facts on File, 1988), 119; *Dictionary*, 250.

worth eight dollars a pair, and such a coat as my black coat would cost about twenty five dollars, milk is 10 cts a pint, or I should have said 20 cts for it is half water as the cows run pretty near the river. Dogs there is no end to them. every man, woman and child owns from one to five dogs, all the way from the little lap dog to the big hound, and all yelping and howling for dear life.

You will excuse me if I write the rest of this rather disconected, and pen down my thoughts as they come along. there is a funeral from the hospital almost every day, and some days there are as much as fourteen and fifteen in a day caried to their long homes. the way they bury the poor privates is enough to make one heart and home sick. the other day there was a Captain and two Lieutenants and a doctor all buried in one day. they had a military funeral and our regt furnished the escort which for a capt consists of forty privates, 1 capt and 2 Lieutenants. the men are formed in line on each side of the grave and after the body is let down into the grave they fire three volleys over the hero, and then he is buried and forgotten before we get back to Camp.

There is <u>great</u> <u>excitement</u> in camp tonight. the boys have heard that the regiment is ordered to report in New York the first of June to be mustered out of service as nine months men, but I <u>cant see it</u> in that <u>light</u>. I wish I could though. but then I do not want to come home till this war is settled one way or the other. I want to see the [story] played out to the end of the chapter. I would rather lose an arm or a leg than have it said that the great north has had to compromise with traters, that we have been obliged to yield the great question that americans can not rule America.

I received your ever wealcome letter this afternoon, and you can never tell how glad I was to hear from you that you are well and enjoying your self as well as you do. as long as we both have our health we should not murmur or complain because we ar[e] separated, for as long as we ar[e] well the prospect of a happy union is not far distant. for if the war should last for three years it will pass in reality as fast as the three last have done, though the time may seem long to us. and should we both be spared to meet again we will strive to forget our long lonely separation, and in the happiness of each others society we will strive to spend the rest of our days in peace and love. I do not know but you will think that I am getting sentimental in writing so to you after we have been married four years, but then I

58

love you as though we had been married but this month. and if I write somewhat warmly to you, you must excuse me and tell me so and I will try and do better in future.

You want to know if I ever dream of you. Yes dear, very often in my sleep you are by my side and I live over the happy hours of other days. and darling Nettie, how often I hear her dear voise saying pa come pa come, and I feel the little arms around my neck and the pure innocent kiss upon my lips. and how often I have held her in my arms in my sleep as of old. and when I have waked it seemed so much like reality that I was sorry to wake up, it made me feel so lonesome. and our dear Mother, oh how often have I thought of her when I have been out on Picket. and in my lonesome watch in the night I have thought of her great love and care of her wayward son and how anxiously she has watched and prayed for him, and of the many anxious hours and heartaches I have caused her that I might be something in the world. and I have been ashamed that I have never been a more dutiful son to so kind a Mother. tell her that I think often of her and I will write to her in a few days. tell Father that I have got a pipe that will beat any thing he ev[e]r saw, or heard of, for a smoke. but tobacco is so high that it is worth about 150 cts a pound, and we poor soldiers cannot indulge in the luxury of a good smoke very often.
(written upside down and between lines of first page)

well, as there is a little space in this little note that is not full I thought I would write a few words in conclusion, if you can read it. it is some what [*illegible word*]. You had better get that stuff from Evans for that will all be gone first you know. and when I get home I will talk the matter over with my <u>dear brother</u>. I want to tell you about a flower garden that I go past every time I go to my work. it is in front of a house and the roses are all in bloom, and they smell so sweet that I stop at the gate eve[r]y time I go past to enjoy the sight and smell of them. I will try and get one to send you in this letter, and one to my little girl. I will send her a picture, too. does she think as much of a book as she used to? if I do not get home you must learn her to read so that she can read to me when I come home. have you got the papers I sent you? I got that letter paper that you sent me and was very glad of it. but I have not got any stamps, if you could send me a few. but then it would be as cheap for you to pay the postage there. I will send you fifty dollars when I get my pay. I have got my check for my state bounty which I think I send by expres in a few days, and you can do what you think best with it. I want you to write to me often so that I will [get] a letter every time the mail comes. and I will write as often as I can. but I think if you do not get tired of reading this you can tell me so and I will promise not to do so any more. Give my love to all the friends, and my heart you have already, and accept this from your own, Frank

(miscellaneous phrases scattered on first page, upside down)

Give my love to Carrie and tell her that I will answer her letter in a few days

Hank says tell you to excuse this short letter for paper is scarce here

Lon says I am coming home when the nine months are up

Lew says say anything for me

Kiss the children for me and don't let them forget me, from your own

Please excuse me for all the mistakes both in composition and writing, and write me a note, you know, a little one. F.

East Concord
April 12th 1863

Dear Husband,

It is four years and a few days more since we were united as one through life, and for a week past it has been constantly in my mind the varying scenes we have passed through in those four years. some times I almost or quite murmur at my lot, and then again and more often I am proud of and glad that in my dear husband I have a brave, a noble, a sacrificing, Frank. and the thought gives me new courage to be brave and have a firm heart and even write a cheerier word to Frank, far away suffering so much, for I have heard how fatigued your Regt was on its return from port Hudson. my anxiety for you was great. be carful and take good care of youself. I feel in hopes that in the course of a few months you will be with us again, for it seems impossible for the rebels to hold out much in such a condition as they are. there is a great deal of skirmishing going on all through rebeldom. the fleet have reached old Charleston, and by the time you get this I presume they will be through. and I hope ere long Vicksburg and port Hudson will be reduced, and soon we shall see the (tail of the war).

I shall have to stop writing for to night as I have written two letters and it makes my shoulders ache to write. good night, and may the angels of love and mercy watch over and keep you. here is a goodnight kiss,

from Thank

13th Monday sundown
Loved one,

I am sitting by the window in our dear old cabin, and am going to try and finish this poor line. I have washed and hetcheled about five pounds of flax[36] and so you can guess I am some tired, but never so that if I am well I can write to my dear loved Frank. and sitting where I am to night I am thinking of the scene in this room 31 weeks ago to day. I do not think that I regret the step you then took, for if you had not gone I felt afraid you would be drafted, and it would seem so hard to have you pressed into service, driven to the aid of our loved land by law. how noble is the cause, how great the issue. and when the war is over, when peace once again reigns in the land, when our loved ones are restored to us, then how proud we will be to rank among the defenders of the flag, Frank as a true soldier. I think by the turn things are taking that if port Hudson and vickburg are taken that soon the end will come. and may the God of battles look upon our armies and give victory to the right.

I do not think of much news to write. Coydon and Carrie are going to Attica to live. Allen Bumps wife[37] has been here to visit. Heneriette Killom is married. Nettie talks constantly and Gertie says quite a number of words. if she wants anything she says <u>um</u> <u>um</u>. she grew real poor while she was sick, has got about well. but she wants me to take her so I will finish when the lamp is lit.

Nine oclock

---

[36] Flax was grown to produce linen cloth and flax seed oil. After the seeds were removed from the stems, several steps were taken to break down the stems into fibers. The "hetchel" is where the silken fibers of the flax were combed and straightened in preparation for spinning into yarn. The yarn was spun, similar to spinning wool, and then woven to produce cloth. *Concord*, 128; *Encyclopedia Americana* (Danbury, CT: Grolier Incorporated, 1998), Vol. 11, 382.

[37] Clarissa Bumps, of Concord.

Lydia has just come from Evans in the stage. Mother[38] has got the measles. Sarah and both her babes, and Lydia and Weber have had them, but I have not been exposed to them. I guess you cant read this, but you can write to me just as soon for all that, a good long letter just as you would talk. and ever he assured of the amazing love and trust of your own, to Frank.

Thank

---

[38] Thankful's mother, Mary Peirce Myers.

Chapter 3

"In the lonely watches of the picket"
Real Soldiering, May - December 1863

Since early April 1863 the 116th had been camped at "Camp Niagra" at Baton Rouge. On May 19 the regiment joined another expedition to Port Hudson. They enter into a fight on the 21st which becomes known as the Battle of Plains Store. The 116th had casualties of 44 wounded and thirteen killed. On the 24th Port Hudson is surrounded, and in an assault on Port Hudson on May 27 the 116th suffered the loss of 85 wounded and 22 killed, including Col. Chapin who died from a bullet wound to the head. A second assault on June 14 resulted in 23 more wounded and five more dead.

On July 2 the 116th marched nearly to Plain's Store to reinforce the escort of a wagon train that had been attacked, returning to Port Hudson that evening. Rumors that Vicksburg had surrendered to General Grant on July 4 were confirmed on the 7th, and Port Hudson sends out a flag of truce. The following day Port Hudson surrendered, and early on July 9 the 116th and the 2nd Louisiana march inside Port Hudson to receive the surrender. That evening the regiment boards a boat and moves down river, arriving at Donaldsonville on July 10. By the 13th the regiment is at Bayou LaFourche where they fight in the Battle of Cox's Plantation. In this Confederate victory the 116th had five killed, 23 wounded, and 21 taken prisoner.

On August 1 the regiment boards the steamer *Excelsior* and travels back to Baton Rouge where they remain at Camp Niagra for a week. The 116th then moves to nearby Fort Williams on August 9 for garrison duty. On the 27th of the month they receive orders to go to New Orleans. The 116th boards the steamer *Iberville* on September 2, reaching New Orleans the next day. After transferring to the *Alexandria* they head out on the Sabine Pass Expedition. On the 7th the coast of Texas at Sabine Pass is sighted. Rebel forces fire on the armada the next day, disabling the gunboats, and forcing the abandonment of the expedition. The *Alexandria* is becalmed in the gulf for two days, and the men are put on half rations. Finally, on September 11 a gunboat tows the *Alexandria* to the mouth of the Mississippi. They arrive at Algiers, opposite New Orleans, on the 13th.

On September 16 the 116th boards railroad cars en route to

Brasher City. They cross Berwick Bay to Berwick City on the 17th, where they remain through September 25. On the 26th they march nine miles through Pattersonville and camp at "Camp Misery" on Bayou Teche. Two days later the 116th joins in a short reconnaissance to Centerville, Louisiana.

October 3 finds the 116th on the march past Franklin, and they reach New Iberia on the 8th . The next day they march ten miles to Vermillionville and engage in a skirmish. On the 11th they march fourteen miles to Carrion Crow Bayou where they remain for nine days, engaging in a skirmish with the rebels on the 15th. On October 21 the regiment marches through Opelousas to Bayou Barri Croquet, where they camp until the end of the month.

The first of November finds them marching back to Carrion Crow, and the following day to Vermillionville. After a few hours rest, just after midnight on November 3, they were awakened. In a forced march they travel fifteen miles in five hours to Bayou Grand Coteau to reinforce General Stephen Burbridge's 4th Division of the 13th Corps which had been attacked. The next day the 116th returned to Vermillionville. On November 16 the 116th starts back to Camp Pratt. They reach New Iberia on the 17th and remain there until January 7, 1864.

Frank Griffith spends most of May, June and July at Baton Rouge sick with various ailments. He receives a letter from the "Donation Committee," apparently one of the many organizations formed by the folks back home to provide encouragement, food and clothing for the soldiers. While the 116th is at Port Hudson Griffith works on carpentry tasks at Head Quarters when his health allows, and later serves as acting commissary sergeant. Frank writes Thankful about what he has heard about the fight at Port Hudson, noting that their nephew Ashley Stanbro has been wounded. When Frank learns that Ashley lost an arm in the battle, he goes searching among the wounded until he finds him.

Thankful's seventeen year old sister, Libbie, writes Frank on June 10. Although she tends to ramble, her genuine affection for Frank comes through. It is about this time that the tone in Griffith's letters begins to change. He reflects on the possibility that he, too, could be a casualty of war, while continuing to believe that the cause is one worth dying for.

Money continues to be of concern for Frank and Thankful, and is mentioned frequently. Thankful's brother-in-law Horatio apparently has not settled accounts, so Frank plans to send money. When his money is stolen Frank advises Thankful to sell something to get by.

On September 1 Griffith writes that the 116th is packing for another march. Although no letters have survived from the unsuccessful Sabine Pass Trip, Frank does reflect on the voyage at the end of the year, and states that it "was the hardest time that we ever saw." When Frank writes on September 15 he is ill once again, but is ready to head out to Texas. Despite the rain and the cold Frank feels well, presumably because he has been eating better. Griffith's first personal taste of fighting comes in a skirmish with the rebels on October 15, when a bullet hits about six feet from him. Meanwhile, Thankful's brother Albert had been taken prisoner at Gettysburg. Following his release from Belle Isle Prison in Richmond, Virginia, Maryland Albert writes to her on October 21 from Annapolis, Maryland. Knowing of Thankful's money problems he pledges to send money to help out.

Griffith's health seems to have improved as he was able to march nearly thirty miles during a twenty-four hour period on November 2 and 3. The last six weeks of 1863 are spent at New Iberia, where life in camp, with the lice, is becoming routine. An exception is Thanksgiving Day when most of the officers get drunk. Frank makes it a point to tell Thankful that he did not drink.

Writing in December Griffith expresses dissatisfaction with officers who punish men for trivial offences. Frank also gets riled up over the fact that items sent by the Aid Societies are often taken by others, instead of being given to the hospital patients. He also voices his feelings about slavery and the treatment of the slaves, and in his December 19 letter Frank encourages Thankful to read an article in the *Buffalo Express* that expresses his views on the subject.

Camp Niagra
Baton Rouge, La.
May 12 /63

Dear Wife,
  as I have a few moments leisure to day I think I will try and
write a few lines to you. I have got a hard head ache to day so you
will not exp[e]ct me to write much. I have been sick about a week
with the jaundice and it is not the most agree able condition in the
world I can tell you. but I think that I am getting better now so that I
can do duty in a few days. I have been at work at Head Quarters most
five weeks at my trade, making bird cages for the officers, so you see
we are having a vigorous prossecution of the war down here. but then
we have got marching orders again and perhaps there will be
something done now. I got a letter from the Donation Committee the
other day and I suppose they will look for an answer immediately so
that I shall have to write to them or suffer the penalty of not hearing
from [them] again. that is the second one that I have got from them in
eight months so you see we do not keep up a very furious
correspondence. There is rumors that Port Hudson is being evacuated
and that Fredericksburgh is captured, though I do not know how much
truth there is for it.
  I am going to send you a book with this, and the Children
some pictures, and you must take them in lieu of a long letter this
time. I have got your letter with the stamps and I will send you some
money in a few days by express. eggs are worth $1.00 per doz, butter
.50, cheese .40, flour 25.00, sugar .25 per pound, each fish .15 cts per
pound, crackers .40 cts, and every thing in proportion. give my love to
all the folks, and accept this from your own,
  Frank

———————

Camp Niagra
May 20th /63

My dear wife,
  I received your most welcome letter yesterday and was very
glad to hear that you are all well. the hot weather affects us here
some. the boys most all have the jaundice, or the fever, or the diarea,

or something else, so that there is about twenty in the company sick now. I am getting better so that I can eat some and shall be around in a few days. Lon is sick with the fever, but not verry sick. he went to the Hospital yesterday but he says that he is not going to stay there. the fever that we have here are not dangerous, it is a sort of process of aclimation and when we get over them we are generaly tough and well. but one gets poor here mighty fast. I lost 20 pounds in two weeks, and then we get fat almost as quick. it is some warm here I can tell you. we have new potatoes and cabage and letuce and plums and most all kinds of garden seed, while you have barely planted your seeds there yet.

the regt has gone to Port Hudson again this morning, but the doctors would not let me go, so I sit here in the Majors [George M. Love] tent writing to you while they are marching in the hot sun. it is quite cool here now and it makes me <u>sleepy</u> to write. and you must excuse me if I do not write you a verry long or interesting letter this morning.

about that matter of Horatio. he has got all the advantage of you and the best thing you can do is to get all you can and let him have the rest. and when I get home I will see what can be done, but keep an acct of every thing that you do get and I will make out a bill of what I ought to have and send to you.

May 24

You will think it is a long time since I commenced this letter but I have been waiting for news from Port Hudson. the regt have gone up there and had a fight I think there is sixteen killed and about forty wounded.[1] our regt had the front of the fight and suffered the worst, but they showed that they were heroes for they drove the rebs into the fort at the point of the bayonet. there was not any body that

[1] Port Hudson was the only large rebel stronghold south of Vicksburg. The 116th was traveling with General Augur's troops. On May 21st they fought at Plain Store, four miles east of Port Hudson, at the intersection with the main road between Baton Rouge and Bayou Sara. The 116th lost 13 killed and 44 wounded. Crisfield Johnson, *Centennial History of Erie County, New York* (Buffalo: Matthews & Warren, 1876), 486-487.

you know killed. Fred Hovland[2] is wounded in the shoulder, but not seriously. Birney is here sick, not very. Ashley is at to Port Hudson. Lon is here, he has had the Fever but is getting better now. I am getting some better now, but my side pains a great deal. it is swelled some this morning and is some lame, but then I manage to keep around. I am staying in the Majors tent and acting Commissary sergent while the regt is gone. I think I shall go up there in a day or two. I do not want the boys to go up there and have all the fun to them selves.

but I shall have to close this for the boys are coming for their rations, and the boat will leave before I shall have time to write any more. Capt Ayer is dead.[3] he died of a fever in the quarters. we buried him last Saturday. he was one of the best men that ever lived and we all regret his untimely death, as we would a father.

Write to me often, and accept this poor hasty scrawl from your own,

Frank

PS. I will send you an order in this for three dollars and 20 cts that Riley Blakely owes me and you can get John to get it for you. tell him it is for that money I let him have at Fortress Monroe. I owed him 1.80 cts and gave him a five dollar bill and he could not make the change then, and when we cou[l]d he went home. I guess Mara Sibly will remeber about it.

Camp Niagra
Baton Rouge, La
June 8th 1863

My dear wife,

I will try and write a few words to you to night for I expect to

---

[2] Frederick E. Hoverland, Co. F, from Concord, was wounded in action at Plain Store, May 21, 1863. He recovered and mustered out with the company in June 1865. *Registers*, 426. See also Appendix C.

[3] James Ayer of Evans, mustered in as captain of Company K on September 4, 1862. He died at age 50 of disease May 22, 1863 at Camp Niagara. *Registers*, 370; Clark, 296-302. See also Appendix B.

join the regt in the morning and I do not know when I shall have another chance to write, not till Port Hudson is taken surely. and it is possible that I shall never have the pleasure of writing to you for we can not tell [what] the fortunes of war may be. but then our lives are in the hands of Him who saith all things well. and in any event I shall think that I have alway[s] done my duty to my country. and if it should be my lot to fall as one of the defenders of the principals that I have always advocated, and I shall feel that my life has not been in vain, that I have been the means of doing some little good in this her hour of peril. and if it is necessary that so many precious lives should be lost, no I will not say lost, but sacrificed to sav[e] the best government that ever existed, my life is worth no more than thousands of others that have been laid on the altar of their country. and while I look back on the past four or five years that <u>we</u> have been acquainted I thought that, for your sake, that it were better perhaps if we had never known each other, for your dear sake, for then you would have been spared the anxiety that I know you feel for me now. and then the dear little children. how will you get along with them all alone? if if I had wealth that I could have left for you and them, but in stead I leave you almost nothing. but then we are young, there may be brighter days in store for us. at any rate we will look on the bright side of the picture for I feel that I shall see you all before another year. and then we shall be so happy in each others love. and when this wicked war is over and peace restored to our once happy land we shal[l] feel that we can rest secure.

I have got a letter from Albert which I will send to <u>you in this</u>, <u>take care of it</u>. perhaps it is later than any that you have got. but it is getting late and I shall have to close this pourly writen letter. write to me often. and when we have taken port Hudson I will write again. Kiss the children for me, and here is one for you. and when I get there I will give you another. Excuse the mistakes and ac[c]ept the love of your own,

Frank

_____

Smiths Mills
June 10[th] /63

Dear brother,

as I have not heard from you lately I thought I would just write a few lines to you. am well as usual and hope these few lines will find you the same. have just been writing to Thank, and am living at Smiths Mills in the depot. have not heard from Albert or anyone else in over 2 weeks. Cant think of much to write to night, I am so tired and sleepy. is Birney with the regt now? how do the boys all get along? well, I will finish this in the morning. how is it? are you fighting for the negros or not?

11th

Good Morning, Frank. how I would like to see you this morning. it is very warm here now, but it rains like fun. it is quite pleasant here, but rather cool generally. we had some green peas the other day, but I suppose they are all gone out there by this time. I am 12 miles from Dunkirk, two from Silver Creek, so you see I am not far from Gates. am going down there in a few days. have you been in any battles yet? how does Alonzo like soldering? I have not heard from Thank in a long time. do you ever get homesick down there? when I came home from H's [Horatio's] I stopped at Thanks, and Nettie went and got your likeness and showed me and said that was her pa. Nettie wants to see her pa. but I must stop writing and go to work. write soon and often as you can. and believe me, your friend and sister.

      Lib

direct to
Miss Libbie L Myers,
Smiths Mills, Chautauque Co. N.Y.

Camp Gatt
Baton Rouge, La
June 19th 1863

My Dear Wife,

      I received your kind note yesterday. and you do not know how glad I was to hear that you are well, and the children. I wrote you about a week ago and I do not see what the reason is you do not hear from me oftener for I have written to you almost every week, and I get one from you almost every mail that comes from the north. you must not think that I have forgotten you if you do not hear from me oftener for I shall try and write to [you] as often as I can.

Smiths Mills June 10th/63

Dear brother as I have not heard
from you lately I thought I would just
write a few lines to you am well as
usual and hope these few lines will
find you the same have just been
writing to Thank and am living at
Smiths Mills is the depot have
not heard from Albert as anyone
else in over 2 weeks   ain't this
of mine to write to night I am so
tired and sleepy   is Birney with
the regt now how do the boys all
get along well I will finish this
in the morning   how is it are you
fighting for the negros as not
I   Good morning Frank how
I would like to see you this morning
it is very warm here now but it rains
like fun   it is quite pleasant here
and the cool generally now but
I guess few is it's only but

Libbie L. Myers of Smiths Mills, New York, wrote this letter to her brother-in-law Frank Griffith on June 10, 1863. Griffith Papers, Regional History Center, Northern Illinois University.

I have not been to port Hudson yet and I do not think that I shall go now for Gen Banks has ordered that all convalescents shall remain here to guard this place. and so you see that my chances for getting into this fight is very small. I do not think I am much of a coward, but when I see how the boys are cut up I do not feel as anxious as I did when they went away. Lon has got a ball through his big toe, but it will not lay him up long. Fred Hovland is hit in his shoulder, but he is getting better fast. Ashley has got his right arm off at the Shoulder and a wound in his chin. I have not seen him yet for I can not find him. I have looked all through the city for him. I will write as soon as I see him. I do not think he will get well. it is so hot here that their wounds mortify if they do not have the best of care.

you must excuse me if I do not write a verry long letter. there is so much excitement that I cannot think of any thing. when the siege of port hudson is over I will write you a good long [letter] and tell you all about the battles for they have been fighting for four weeks. you must not worry about me for I am safe for the present. we are expecting an attack on this place eve[r]y night from the Guerillas. they keep firing on our pickets almost every night, and to day there was two men killed and one wounded of the nigger regt. we can hear the firing up to Port Hudson to night quite plain. I am acting commissary sergt for the company, so I do not have to go on guard or on picket now.

it is very warm here now, a great deal warmer than we have it up north. I am going to look for Ashley again in the morning so that I can tell you all about him. I have not had any pay in four months, but I have got fifty dollars of my state bounty. but I am going to lend it to the poor wounded boys that have got no money, for we can not get anything here with out money, and the government does not furnish any thing that any body can eat, and you can get plenty there without it. but I will send you some when we get our pay and perhaps before. don't you think that will be the right way to do? I have not sent you any money since I have been gone, but I have got some and will send it if you want it. please tell me what you think about it. have you got my money from Horatio yet? and that of Ben? I did not sign the allotment roll for I do not think that there is any thing certain about getting the money on it. but it is roll call and I shall have to stop writing for to night. good night.
Frank

Baton Rouge
June 23rd [1863]

Dear wife,

I am afraid you will think I am a long time writing this little letter, but the fact is that there is so much excitement here now that I can not find time to write hardly. and if you do not hear from me so often you must not worry. I have found Ashley. he has got his right arm off at the shoulder joint, but he is doing first rate now. and if this weather is not too warm I think he will get well. but it is a rather a poor site here now. I go down to see him every day and do all that I can for him. he is cheerful and jokes about his short cloak, poor boy. it seems hard to think of.

24th

I shall have to finish letter for the mail is going to New Orleans to night. I received your letter last night and was glad to hear you were all well. I went last night down to see Ashley. he is doing first rate, and if there is no drawback he will be home by the first of September, if not before. I do not think there is any danger between you and me at present, without the things you mention, do you? but we live in hope for the future. please, write to me often and do not get discouraged, but be a brave little wife for my sake.

your own,
Frank

Baton Rouge
July 11th /63

Ever dear and remembered Thank,

I have looked and waited and looked again for the last four weeks for a letter from you but in vain. and tonight after they are all in bed I am going to try and write a few lines to you darling, [and] see if that will bring any news from the loved ones from home. I do not think you can read this, my hand trembles so. I have been at work to day, and that is something unusual for me in this place or any other. you verry well know I am as well as I can expect to be in this hot place. and think I shall go and join the regt in a day or two down to Donaldsonville. the <u>rebs</u> have come back and are trying to blockade the river below us to cut off our communication with New Orleans. but Gen Banks has gone down there and got in their rear, and I think will be able to bay the whole pack at them, at least that is the intention.

We have good news here plenty now. Vicsburgh is captured on the ever memorable forth [4th of July]. they say that Grant has taken 27000 prisoners, 300 pieces of artilery, 80 siege guns, and any quantity of small arms.[4] and on the 8th Port hudson surrendered to Gen Banks with three thousand prisoners, and 100 pieces of artilery, and forty siege guns.[5] and to night the news from below, that they have taken four thousand prisoners and one or two batterys, but I do not know how true it is.[6] so you see that we have not been idle down here all summer. there is a rumor around town that Richmond is taken, and that Lees army is cut to pieces, and that Charleston is in our hands, but I do not credit it.[7] but I sincerely hope that is the case for then we may soon see the end of this dreadful and cruel war. we hear that the rebs have been into Pensylvania again and that they are

---

[4] On July 4 General Grant accepted Lt. General John C. Pemberton's surrender of 2,166 Confederate officers and 27,230 enlisted men, as well as 172 cannon, and 60,000 long arms, many of those Enfield rifles. *Encyclopedia*, Vol. 4, 2026.

[5] Banks troops surrounded Port Hudson, and for forty-seven days the assaults combined to weaken the Confederate defenders through sickness and hunger as well as casualties. Major General Franklin Gardner surrendered to General Banks July 8. Banks report of July 10, 1863 to General H.W. Halleck stated that they had taken "over 5,500 prisoners...20 pieces of heavy artillery...31 pieces of field artillery." U.S. War Department, *The War of the Rebellion* (Washington: Government Printing Office, 1891), Series I, Vol. XXVI, Part 1, 55. Prisoner numbers vary from 3,000 in *Encyclopedia*, Vol. 3, 1549, to 6,340 cited in Winters, 283. As a result of the victories at Vicksburg and Port Hudson the Union now had control of the Mississippi River.

[6] He refers to Donaldsonville, and until July 13 only minor skirmishing took place there. The Battle of Cox's Plantation on the 13th ended up being a Union defeat.

[7] Indeed, just rumors.

getting somewhat waked up there in the north now that their own firesides are in danger.[8] wel[l], I hope it will do them good. I think they need puryfying a little, for instead of going heart and soul into this war they stay at home and enjoy their own firesides and try and discourage the brave men in the field. there is nothing like adversity to bring men to their sences. but it is getting late and I shall have to draw this to a close.

Ashley is getting along first rate, I think he will [go] home in a month. I go down and see him every day and try and keep him cheerful. Lons toe is doing nicely. he will be fit for duty again soon. Birney is not verry well, he has been sick ever since he came here. he gets a letter quite often from your friend Miss Warner.[9] she sends her respects to me.

I have writen so much about this place and everything that I do not know what to write about. but when I get home, which pray God I may soon, we will have such a good visit, say, wont we? and then I can tell you all about every thing so much better than I can write it. and then you can sit in my lap and put your arms around my neck and we shall be so happy. now you wont think that I am foolish or sentimental for writing so to you, or that I am homesick, for I am not. but if you knew how in the lonely watches of the picket when danger and death stares me in the face, or in the wakeful nights of pain and unrest when I have lain on my hard bed and thought of the dear ones at home, and in the feverish dreams of sleep I have felt your dear presence, and I have thought of your dear love and kindness always to me. how in days of sickness you have ever watched and patiently borne my words of impatience and unkindness. and what a poor return I have made for all this great love. and I have thought that if ever I am again permited to meet you that I would try give you back

---

[8] In particular at Gettysburg, July 1-3, where Meade's Union Army of 88,289 suffered 23,049 casualties (killed, wounded, and captured), and Lee's Confederate Army of 75,000 had 28,063 casualties, would have "waked up" the north. *Dictionary*, 339. Noah Andre Trudeau reported a similar figure for the North of 22,813, but stated that recent research indicated the Confederate losses were much lower at 22,874 casualties. Noah Andre Trudeau, *Gettysburg: A Testing of Courage* (New York: Harper Collins, 2002), 525 & 529.

[9] Birney Weber and Amelia Warner were later married, at the end of 1863.

love for love. that my life should be devoted to the solemn promise that I made to you before God at the altar, to make your life as pleasant and happy as it should be. Oh my darling wife, if you knew how much comfort it is to the poor soldier to feel that though surrounded by all the evil and corrupt influences of a soldiers life, to know that far away there is one gentle being who thinks and cares for him, and loves him, and longs for his return to her without a blot on his name, or a stain of dishonor on his caracter, then you would know what your secret influence has been to your unworthy husband.

but it is time for me to go to bed. but if I do not go away in the morning I will write some more if I can think of anything to write. kiss the darling Netty for pa, and Gerty. write often, your own,

Frank

Baton Rouge
Aug 13 /63

Dear Wife,

I have just come in from Picket and I thought I would just write a few lines to let you know that I am in the land of the living. I am well at present and enjoying myself first rate as well as I can <u>away from you</u>. it is awful hot down here now, and try all we can, we can not keep cool in the middle of the day. the boys are all getting along one way and another. Ashley is doing first rate and you can look for him home in the course of a month. his shoulder is most healed up and his discharge is made out. we have just four months pay and I was going to send it home by him, but some infernal scamp has stole my pocket book money and all so that ends that. maybe you will have to sell some thing and get along the best you can till next month. and perhaps we will get our pay and I will not wait for another good chance, but send it by express <u>immediately</u>. I had about seventy dollars that I was going to send you but it seems of ill luck atends our regt. but if I get safely back to you with my life I shall be thankful. we think we shall be home to spend christmas. I hope so, don't you? and then we will not regret this long lonesome year of separation, and we will commence life over again.

Lon is doing first rate and will be fit for dùty in a few days. both of the Negro boys have died from wounds received at

Donaldsonville. Sam had his leg cut off but it did no good for he died the next day.[10]   Milt McCumber is dead,[11] and so is George Hawks[12] of our company. there is no war news that I need write from here for you can read in the papers better than I can write. I suppose that the state malitia are all home again by this time. they must [of] had a nice little trip, but they have never seen the fun that we have. oh, I tell you that w[h]en I get home I will have some nice stories to tell you that [will make you] laugh for a month. Birney Weber is going to have his discharge. he has been sick ever since he came here, and if he stays for two months he never will come [home] alive. I guess he is some homesick and that will never do for a man here if he wants to live. he is having a verry interesting correspondence with your friend Miss Warner, I think, for she sends her respect to me by her letters to him.

The boys have left this morning for Buffalo after the drafted men to fill up the regt. they are to be gone 60 days. but then you know that it never was my luck to have any good luck. and though God knows that I want to see you bad enough, I had rather stay now till my time is out than come home and live in misery all the time in dread of the parting hour. then let us live patiently in hope of the joyous reunion when we shall dread war no more.
(ends abruptly, apparently continued by next letter which was written on same type of stationary)

Fort Williams[13]

---

[10] Probably Corporal Samuel A. Mayo of Concord. He was 27 at enlistment in Company F. Wounded at Donaldsonville, he died August 8, 1863, at Baton Rouge. *Registers*, 444. See also Appendix C.

[11] John M. McComber, age 33 when he enlisted at Colden. A member of Company D, he died of typhoid fever on August 4 in the hospital at Baton Rouge. *Registers*, 445. See also Appendix C.

[12] George H. Hawks, from Evans was 26 at enlistment. He died of disease on July 11 at Baton Rouge. *Registers*, 420. See also Appendix B.

[13] Named after Union General Thomas Williams who was killed in battle, August 5, 1862, Fort Williams was located at the northern edge of the city. Orton Clark of the 116th stated that "during our stay here, a large fort - embracing within its

Baton Rouge, La
17 Aug [1863]

as I have a few moments to spare this morning I will try and finish this as to send it by the mail this afternoon. it [is] raining and it is some cooler, but it is plenty warm enough. now my hand trembles so that I can hardly make a crooked mark. I am getting tough now so that I feel right smart, but I have had the diarea for the last two months, but this is getting better now.

I have not found my money yet, and those pictures that you sent me were in with it. if they pay us next month I will try and send it again. if we do not come home before winter I want you to send me a pair of nice woolen shirts. you can get some cloth, red or blue, and make them fancy. Tell John and Charley[14] to send me some cheese and I will sell it for them, it is worth 40 cts per pound here. they would get 20 cents clear at least. butter is 50 cts, eggs 1.00 per doz, potatoes 10 cts per pound, onions 10, crackers .30, beef steak .40, chickens .50 a piece, water melons plenty .50 to 1.25, news papers .10 to .25, so you see that we have to pay if we have any delcacys. but then I hope the time is not far distant when we can partake of the comforts of life with the loved ones at home. I expect to be home to spend christmas with you.

I have moved my quarters into another tent, and Val Done[15]

---

limits the Arsenal - was planned and constructed, and in honor of the hero of the battle of Baton Rouge, was named 'Fort Williams'." The Union forces began construction of this fortification in August 1862, which encompassed the Baton Rouge Barracks and the Baton Rouge Arsenal, structures originally built between 1819 and 1823 by the U.S. Army. James F. Ryther of Co. H, 116th in a letter dated August 11, 1863 wrote about Fort Williams. "It is a very pleasant place in the fort. It covers about ten acres of ground & is situated right on the bank of the river. There are several very nice large buildings in the enclosure, & there are two rows of large shade trees extending across the Fort..." Original letter held by Gordon G. Ryther, West Oneonta, NY; Clark, 53-54; Roberts, *Encyclopedia of Historic Forts*, 328-329, 355.

[14] Probably Frank's brothers-in-law John Morse and Charles Spencer.

[15] Valentine Doan was 29 when he enlisted at Eden. Mustered in as a private in Co, K, he had been promoted to corporal prior to May 1863, and had just been demoted to private on August 6, 1863. *Registers*, 397. See also Appendix B.

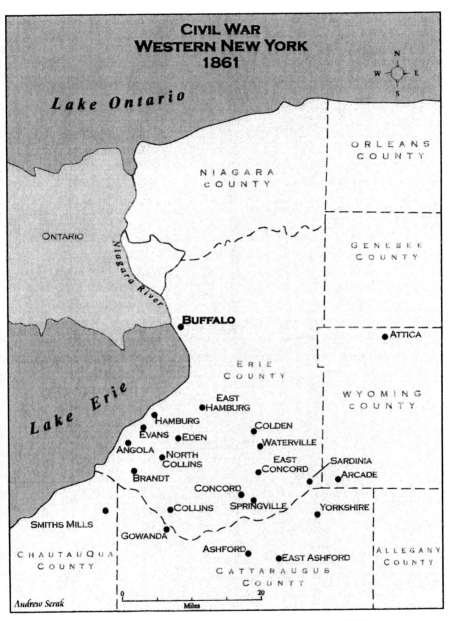

Map of Western New York State showing the towns where Griffith's family
and friends lived and visited. Produced for this volume by Andrew Serak.

say, he boards with me now. he is a bully fellow. but I shall have to stop writing. there is a lot of the boys coming home on a furlough. I think Birney will come, two. and if he does you can go and see him, and he can tell you more than I can write in a week. I have got to write to Carrie this afternoon. Give my love to all the children, and kiss them for Pa. write often, and accept the Love of your own,

   Frank

Fort Williams
Baton Rouge, La
Aug 30th /63

Ever remmembered wife,

   I suppose you have got tired of waiting and thought that I had forgotten that I promised to write once a week, but that is not the case for I think of you most all the time and I have writen once a week till the boys went up to port Hudson, and then I could not put my mind to anything long enough to write anything. I have writen once since we have been in the fort, to you, and once to Charleys folks.[16] I have had but one letter from you since I wrote. you must not worry about me if you do not hear from me again in the next month or two for we are expecting to make another raid somewhere and we cant carry any writing materials with us, but when we get back I will write again.

   Ashley started for home last night. you will see him before you get this and he can tell you more than I can write in a week. I am not very well this summer. my side troubles me a great deal. it is quite sore, but then it is of no use to complain here for there is no one to pity you if your h[e]ad is off so long as you can go. we have to go on guard ev[e]ry other day now and it is wearing me out to be up ev[e]ry other night. and what little sleep we get we have to lay on the ground. it makes me feel old. and then the grub, it makes me sick to think of it. but then I do not mean to complain, for when I think of the end to be obtained it is worth any sacrifice that we may be called upon to make, and that glorious end is almost obtained, do you not think

---

[16] Charles Spencer's parents, Asaph and Roxy Spencer lived in Sardinia, near Concord, New York. *Concord*, 884.

so? and then when this war is over, and the living restored to their homes and loved ones, we shall not have it to say that we have not had any lot in the suffering, and can claim no share in the glory of restored liberty and the blessings of a free government. but my head ackes so that I shall have to stop writing.

Tuesday morning, Aug 2nd [September 1st]

I write a few lines to you this morning in haste for we are packing up our things for another march. I do not know where we are going, but I will write you as soon as we get settled. I got a letter this morning from you, and mother, and was glad to hear from you. keep up good courage for the end is nigh. we have just got the news that Charleston is taken[17] and we feel first rate about it.

I am well this [morning] and tough. have you ever got my pipe that I sent home in the capt[18] things? I sent it in care of Horatio. the box was sent to Mr Black at Evans. I have sent my bible home by Ashley. we are going to leave our Knappsacks and I do not think we shall ever see them again. but I shall have to stop writing. give my love to all the friends, and kiss the children for me. I have not found my money yet.

Direct your letter as usual, and write often. and keep up good courage for the war is most played out.

From your own,

Frank

Algiers[19] opposite New Orleans

---

[17] Just another rumor. Charleston did not fall until February 18, 1865. The Union forces had been attacking Charleston in late August, but Charleston held out. E.B. Long and Barbara Long, *The Civil War Day by Day: An Almanac 1861-1865* (Garden City, NY: Doubleday & Company, 1971), 400 & 640. Hereafter referred to as *Almanac*.

[18] Sent in box of Captain James Ayer's belongings, after his death in May.

[19] The 116th arrived at Algiers on September 13 and remained there just three days. Clark, 128. John William DeForest, Captain in the 12th Connecticut Infantry, in a letter dated September 6, 1863 described Algiers as "a dirty, rascally suburb of New Orleans, separated from it by the Mississippi." DeForest, *A*

Tuesday Sept 15th 63

Dear wife,
     I hasten to write a few lines to you for we have orders to be ready to march in two hours, so you see that I shall not have time to write much. I am not verry well at present. I have just had a twinge of the fever and ague, and [have] taken about a half a pound of quinine, so you see that I dont feel first rate. we are bound for Texas this time. we expect to be gone three months and by that time we hope the war will be done. so keep up good courage and hope for the best. I wish I had time to write you all a good long letter, but you must be content with this poor scrawl.
     I got a letter from Fays folks[20] and one from Mother. tell them that I will answer them as soon as I have a chance, or answer them in person. I have got those pictures you were kind enough to send me, but they were stole from me before I had them two weeks. you must not worry if you do not hear from me in a good while for the chances are poor for sending letters on the march. but be assured that where ever I am I shall ever think, love you the same, and that my thoughts are ever with the loved ones home, and that I long for the time when I shall see you all again. give my love to all the folks at home, and accept this hasty note from your own devoted,
     Frank
write often

Camp Misery
Bayou teche, La
in the mud knee deep and so forth
St Marys parish on the road to Texas
Oct 2nd 1863

My Dear Wife,
     I will try and write a few lines to you this morning to just let

---

Volunteer's Adventures, 154.

[20] Fayette Treat was married to Frank's sister Martha. His parents, John and Eunice Treat, were neighbors of the Griffith family in "Waterville."

you know that I am still in the land of the living, although you will see by the date of this letter not in the happiest circumstances that could be imagined, but still better than two dead men. I have been wet through for two days and nights with[out] being dry in the time. but yesterday I got dried up and last night I slept most all night, and so this morning I am as good as new. we are having first rate living here on the road such as beef steak and sweet potatoes, and ducks, and chickens, any geese, fresh pork, and mutton, and Oranges, nuts, and garden sauce.[21] general salt horse is played out, but we still hold on to hard tack like grim death.

Our regt and the 30 Mass, a detachment of Cavalry, and a section of artilery made a recannasance as far as Centerville last monday. it is about four miles from here on the road to Franklin. we are on the same road that Gen Banks went to Port Hudson last Spring, but did not find any rebs of any consequence. but we got a lot of beef and horses and mules and three or four rebs. we stayed two days and one night. after we had been there three or four hours it began to rain, and it rained you had better believe. and then at night our company were sent out on picket about a mile and a half from the town, and it rained all night. we were in the road and in the lots, right out in the rain. and to cap all not one of us had our rubber blanket with us. and you may guess we were some wet and just a little cold. but as soon as it came day light we caught some chickens and mi[l]ked the cows and the [illegible word] to make us some hoe cake, and to cook our poultry, and fresh pork. and I think if I remember right we had a pretty good breakfast. and when we got back to camp I went and dug about a peck of sweet potatos and boiled them, and fried some pig, and stuffed my shirt with that for dinner. I tell you that those potatoes are a great institution in this Southern Canthievocracy. some of them grow as large as as my foot, and when they are boiled they are dry and

---

[21] James F. Ryther of Company H., in a letter dated September 25, 1863, wrote, "We have plenty of fresh meat and sweet potatoes, and Oranges if we want them....We are encamped right on the bank of a Bayou called the "Teche"....The Bayou....extends from Berwick Bay a long distance into the State of Louisiana and is navigable by river boats in time of high water about 50 miles. The water in the Bayou is salt and we have to depend on cistern & well water to drink and some of the time we have to go two or three miles to fill our canteens." Original letter held by Gordon G. Ryther.

mealy. and if I only had some of that butter, down [in the] cellar in that stone jar, I think I should eat myself to death in a month. but you will get tired of so much talk about eating. but then you must remember that is the most that we look for is something good to eat. and if I do get somewhat enthusiastic over a good meal you must excuse me for it is so seldom that we can get any thing fit to eat.

I do not [mean] to complain, nor have you think that I am discouraged, for that is not the case. I think the prospects of the country are better and brighter ev[e]ry day, and that finaly when the nation is sufficiently humbled, when we are willing to let the world know that we acknowlege that [we] are willing to be governed by the great principals of <u>right and Justice to all</u>, we shall have peace and again be a prosperous and happy nation. and until that time arrives I b[e]lieve that God will let this awful war go on. I b[e]lieve that the responsibility rests with the men and women of the great North, and so long as they are so loth to give the government their support, so long as they are so afraid of their comfort and their lives that they will invent ev[e]ry excuse to get rid of going to the defense of their own lives and liberties, just so long they must see this war go on. I b[e]lieve that if the men of the north would arouse and go forth in their might with the determination to crush out this rebelion at all hazards, the war would be closed in three months, and what there is left of us alive be home again.

we are going through Texas and it [is] currently reported that we have got 90 thousand men. and if we do not get defeated we shall clean out the rebs west of the Mississippi river. the 19th and 13 army corps goes from this way, and then there is a force coming down the red river to meet us, so that if every thing works favorable you may look for some tall running or some hard fighting in this department before long. I will write to you as often as I can, but I have got neither mor[e] emrald pens, nor money with me. all my things were left at Baton Rouge, and it is ten chances to one if they ever are found again.

What you wrote about Dr. Lynde being unkind to the soldiers is hard to connect for he has so many to deal with. but I think that he has been pretty rough with us sometimes. but then it is of no use to complain here or look for sympathy for it is every man for himself. I have not seen Birney in more than a month, his company [Co.F] are detailed as guard for Gen Franklin. Nick is here. he is a bigger old grammy than he was when at home. Lon is here. his toe has got well and he looks tough and fit. but I shall have to close this poor scrawl. I do not think you can read it.

about that matter of Olden. he owes me five dollars, but it was to be paid in logs three years ago and I never have seen any thing of the logs. but then he will not be foolish enough to pay any thing to a soldier or his wife, but you can try him. Mr Tr[e]at owes me between four and five dollars, but I do not suppose he will want to pay it now I have gone to war. and then there ought to be some money coming from the <u>donation committee seeing we did not pay any rent</u>. but if we should ever get pay again, and somebody does not steal it till I can get to the expres[s] office, I will send it to you. I have some hope of getting some of that back that I lent the boys that were wounded at port Hudson sometime, if I do not get killed on this trip. I suppose you have seen Ashley by this time. I should have sent you sixty dollars by him if it had not been stole. but then if you have enough to eat and a good warm place to sleep it is more than I have had since I left you. I sent you fifteen dollars when I sent you that box from New Orleans last winter by express. did you not get that? do the best you can and if I should ever come home we will commence life again. write to me often, and ev[e]r think that you are r[e]mmember[e]d by me. I have written to you almost ev[e]ry week. I do not think that you get all my letters. tell mother and all the rest of them that I will write to them as soon as I get where I can. I have not heard from Dora and Charly in a long time. I got a letter from Sarah when I got your last, but I can not answer it now for the paper that this is written on I had to buy from one of the boys who had forethought enough to bring a little with him. I owe Lydia and your folks a letter, but you can write to them for me.

you wanted to know who our Brigadier was. Col Love of our regt is in command now. we are in the first Brigade, first Division, and the first regt of the 19th army corps, and in the advance, the post of honor and the post of danger. W.T. Ferris[22] of East Hamburgh is Captain of our company now. but when I get home I can tell you all about it so much better than I can write. but I must go and see what I can find for dinner, so I shall have to stop writing for this time.

---

[22] Warren T. Ferris was 19 when he enrolled at Buffalo. Mustered in as second lieutenant of Co. A on August 12, 1862, Ferris was promoted to first lieutenant, Co. K, November 24, 1862 and was promoted to captain, May 23, 1863. *Registers*, 405. See also Appendix B.

kiss the children for me and take good care of them as I know you will. tell all the folks to write to me and not to wait for me to answer all theirs for they do not know how much trouble it is to write here. I am writing this sitting on the engine of an old sugar mill, holding my paper in my hands, so you must not wonder if it is not written very well. tell Carrie I have not forgotten her. and when I come home I will make her an [*illegible word*] if she has got any mince pie. Write often, and good long loving letters as you alway[s] do. and ac[c]ept the love of your own,

       Frank

PS I dreamed of you last night. but I shall not write my dream for it might not please you to see it on paper, and I had rather tell it to you by word of mouth.

In the field 14 miles from
Oppelousas, La[23]
Oct 12[th] 1863

My Dear Wife,

       I will try to write you a few lines to night for I know that you will be anxious to hear from me now that you know that we are in the field. we have marched 80 miles since I last wrote to you and it makes my legs ache some. but I am well and hearty, and getting fat again, and that is all a soldier can expect. we are having pretty good living now. we find plenty of sweet potatoes and fresh beef, and I can tell you that the potatoes ar[e] some. we just go into an old rebs field and dig all that we want and boil them, and fry some pork on a plate, and they are first rate. We are following the rebels as fast as we can and we may have a fight any day, but we are bound to drive them out of this part of the state. and if they do as much on the other side of the river you can look for me home in the spring, so keep up good courage.

       We got paid of[f] last night and I will send you $20 in this

---

[23] On October 11 the 116th reached Carrion Crow Bayou where they remained for nine days before marching on to Opelousas. Clark, 131-132.

letter. you can pay Uncle Archie[24] the interest on that note, and tell him not fret for he will get his pay. if I do not come home, or if he can not wait till I am done fighting for him, he can sell one of the horses for I think I can get another if I live to get home and want one. if those who stay at home and live at his ease think that a man can get rich on $15 a month they are a little mistake[n] when we have to pay 3 times as much for every thing that we buy as you do. I would like to have them live on army rations for a year and see what they would sing. but then I have got enough to pay all that I owe, if somebody does not steal it from me for I do not think it any better than stealing to take the advantage of a man when he is gone to war.

Lon is well and hearty. he sends his respects to all the friends. I have not seen Birney in a long time. his company [Co. F] is detailed as Gen Franklins[25] body guard and we do not see them verry often. the rest of the boys are all well. Nick is here but he is not verry well and he grunts some. I think we shall finally fetch up at Sabine city or Galveston and perhaps both. but I must stop writing. this envelope cost me 2 ½ cts so you see that things are cheap here. write as soon as you get this and tell me all the news in a good long letter. kiss the children for me, and accept the love of your own,

Frank.
Goodnight

(written in light pencil on back of this letter)

Oct 14th 1863
as I have a few moments to night I thought I would write a few

---

[24] This may refer to Archibald Griffith, although I could not verify the relationship. He arrived in Concord township, New York, in 1815. A farmer, he also taught school for a time, was a Justice of the Peace, and became a successful business man. Following the war, in 1867 he made a "liberal donation" to the Springville Academy to pay for free education for poor children. As a result the school was renamed the Griffith Institute. Lillian Geiger, *A History of the Town of Concord*, ([Buffalo]: Buffalo and Erie County Historical Society, 1971), 5; and *Concord*, 370.

[25] Major General William Buel Franklin, was in charge of the Sabine Pass Expedition, commanding the 19th Army Corps, Department of the Gulf. *Encyclopedia*, Vol. 2, 773.

lines for I do not know when I shall have another chance. our regt went to the front last night on picket and to night the cavalry ar[e] skirmishing with one battery. they have kept up quite lively firing since four oclock this afternoon and perhaps we shall go out in the morning and fetch them up with a jerk. I do not think there are many of them. the cavalry brought in the rebel Brigader Gen.[John G.] Pratt last night. I have had a good supper of sweet potatoes and beef steak to night with hard tack soup. I am getting to be a famous cook. you would laugh to see us get our meals. but I shall have to stop writing. hoping to have a chance to write again soon. good night from F.

(upside down on top of page)
tell mother I will write to her as soon as I get a chance. kiss Nettie for Pa

---

Crayon Bayou[26]
St Landrys Parish, La
Oct 17[th] 1863

My Dear Wife,

    I rec[e]ived your most wealcome letter last night dated Sept 24, and was verry <u>Glad</u> to hear from you that you are all alive yet. I am well at present and that is the most that a soldier can hope for. It must be verry lonesome now at Horatios now and I feel sorry for them. has Sarah got any better yet? and how does she bear her gr[e]at affliction? but then God orders all things for the best and it may be for the good of the children to be called this early to the grave. it seems as though ill luck has always attended Horatio from the first, but he does not seem to proffit by his sad experience.

    I sent you $20 dollars by Lieut Erwin.[27] have you got that yet? we expect to get our pay again in a few days and then I will send you some more if I can get a chance. it is not safe to send any thing by

---

[26] Carrion Crow Bayou, see footnote 23 in previous letter.

[27] First Lieutenant Edward Erwin of Company I resigned October 14, 1863. Clark, 341. *Registers*, 429, lists him as Irwin, and age 24 when he enrolled in the116[th] at Buffalo. See also Appendix C.

mail from here for it has to go overland 70 miles and the rebs are all around here. I do not think you can read this for I have to write sitting on the ground and hold the paper on my knee, and you can see what work I make of it.

You will want to know where we are. well, we are on the road to Texas and about 15 miles from Oppelousas. day before yesterday we had a right smart Skirmish with the rebs here. they came down to see where we were, and I gues[s] they can tell by this time. but if they have gone all the time as fast as they were going the last that I saw of them they must be about 150 miles from here by this time. there was nobody hurt on our side or in our Brigade, but the Cavalry had four officer[s] wounded, but the bullets whistled in rather close close proximity to our ears. one struck about six feet from me as we were laying down and some of the boys picked it up. but when the battery on our right began to pitch quoits at them you had ought to see them skedadle. and I think myself that it was rather an uncomfortable situation for them. there was perhaps 1500 of them in all. yesterday the cavalry went out and captured their commissary store and some prisoners. I do not know how many. we shall probably move again in a day or two as far as Oppelousas. I do not think we shall go much farther. We hear that Bragg has licked Rosincranse [Rosecrans] in Tenes[s]ee badly but no particulars.[28] I hope it is not so.

I suppose George[29] and Nell are so proud of their girl that they do not show it for common, but you can tell them for me I do not think it is such a great thing after all. and if they can get time they may just write me few lines by way of remembrance. I wrote to Dora and Charley the other day but have not got an answer yet. they are most scared to death for the Indians. tell Fays folks that I will write to them soon. tell them not to wait for me, but write often. did Charlie

---

[28] Earlier, on September 18 Confederate General Braxton Bragg defeated General William Starke Rosecrans at Chickamauga Creek. Bragg hoped to get between Rosecrans and Chattanooga, but instead the defeat caused Rosecrans to retreat into Chattanooga on September 20. On October 17 Bragg was actually in Georgia, Rosecrans was still surrounded at Chattanooga, Tennessee, and Secretary of War Edwin McMasters Stanton gave General Grant orders in which Rosecrans was to be relieved of command of the Department of the Cumberland. *Almanac*, 421-424; *Dictionary*, 78 & 708; *Encyclopedia*, Vol. 1, 267.

[29] George Myers is Thankful's brother.

S.[30] pay the 300 or did he go to war? I think he could better afford to pay than go. and if he knew as much about war as I do he would pay quicker than lighting. but then we have a good deal of fun here after all and when I get home I will draw you some vivid pictures of camp life for your amusement.

the weather is very pleasant here now, though the nights are cold. and I think of the good warm fire at home, and the nice <u>clean</u> bed, and the good warm meals at the table, and more of the loving hands that will be held out to meet me when I come. and [I] pray that it may not be long be delayed. let us keep up good courage and hope that our dear land may not long be cursed with this cruel war. Lon is well and sends his love to all. Andrew Coak[31] is here and fat as a pig. send me a letter by Birney when he comes back. did you get my big pipe when you went to Evans? but it is most dinner time and I shall have to stop writing for the present.

Oct 18th

since writing there has been no chance to send this letter so I thought I would write a few words to night. we expect to move again in the morning and I do not know when I shall have time to write again. the weather is cool and pleasant and it is a good time to march. I think by the signs of the times we shall be back in Baton Rouge in a week or so and then I will write you all the particulars of this trip. take good care of yourself for my sake and do not get discouraged for the time is not far distant when, if we both live, that we shall see each other again. do you not think so? you need not send me those shirts till I write again. I have worn one pair of those socks you sent me last spring ever since I got them and they have not got but one hole in them. they are worth a dozen pairs of army socks. they will last me two months yet. the other pairs somebody took while I was gone to Donaldsonville. I laid it to Elder Sawdy,[32] but he denied it. I had not

---

[30] Charles Spencer did not pay the exemption fee or go to war.

[31] Andrew Cook, enlisted at Evans at age 18, and was in Company A of the 116th. *Registers*, 390. See also Appendix C.

[32] "Elder" may refer to his age, William H. Sawdy was age 44 when he enlisted at Evans in August 1862, or to his membership in the church. Sawdy was a

worn them but once. have you seen Ashley yet? and have you got my bible and pistol? I sent them home for I could not take them with me and I did not want to lose them for it is a chance if we ever see our things again.

do you have any apples this year? if you do just eat some for me, Just a few, for you know that I do not like them <u>much</u>. and you can get Nettie to help you for she is pa[']s own girl. they do not have any such thing down in Dixie, but then they [have] almost every thing else. I will tell you the names of some of the good things they raise here, figs, and I tell you they are <u>good</u>, Oranges, lemons, melons, Peaches, plums, Bannanas, Gumbo, Egg plants, Persimmons, Walnuts, Chestnuts, and every other kind of nuts, but they cannot raise wheat here. I wish you could see some of the sugar plantations and Cotton fields. and a cotton field in bloom is a splendid sight. the cotton is ripe now, but there is no one to harvest it. if I could see I would get some Cotton seeds and send you. there is about $1000 worth of cotton where we are camped, but it has never been gined or baled and the soldiers are taking it for beds. There is some talk of our being mounted, but I guess it is all talk. but I shall have to close this for my candle is most gone. don't forget to write often, and accept the Love of your own,
Frank

Tell nettie that pa wants to see his little girl, and kiss her, and have her <u>sleep,</u> for she must be a great deal of comfort to you, is she not? you must make her mind you at all times and be a good girl.
Good night for the present. here is a kiss for you all.

Collage Green Barracks
Annapolis M.D.
Oct 21st 1863

Ever remembered Sister,
I received your very welcome letter by due course of mail & hasten to answer it. You said your health was not very good this

member of Company A. *Registers*, 467. See also Appendix C.

summer. you must not think of trouble & make yourself sick. I am as well as could be expected after loosing 38 lbs. I have been here three weeks & I just had a good ague chill, so you see I cant feel very gay at the present, but I hope I shall feel better after I get some of the lost flesh made up.

Well, I was taken prisoner after dark on the night of the 2nd of July [at Gettysburg] after firing 70 rounds of Uncles pills. our Brigade fought & whipped [Maj. Gen. Edward] Johnsons Division, killed Generals, rebs Agt Genl, a[nd] captured 4 battle flags. I was marched five days on a pint of flour. we had to march 170 miles to stanten [Staunton, VA] & then jam[m]ed into a hog car & sent to Richmond & put into the Tobacco house where were all robbed of every thing we had. they even took my shoes from me. they took $35.50 cts and 80 cts worth of postage stamps from me & that was not all. they took Lydias likeness from me. they said they wanted a yankees girls picture to look at. then I was sent to that little Hell called Belle Island.[33] there we got a half a pound of bread each day & 2 ounces of meats. sometimes we got it in meat & some times in bones. I was kept there 10 weeks with nothing to sleep under or nothing to eat & nothing to do but kill lice & drink muddy water. but I have got one more year to pick bones with them & if I ever take a prisoner I shall take every thing from him he has got & if I don't want the things I will burn them up. then if he gives me any of his lip I shall feed him a death pill sure as life, for they shot three of our boys in cold blood on Belle Island.

well, thankful, you say you do not know what you are a going to do this winter as Frank had such bad luck with his money. now you try & get along untill I get my pay & I will send you some money if I get it before Frank does, for I never can see a sister of mine that has done as much for me as you have, I never can see them hard up if I can help it. do you know that living with you one summer learnt me how to get along in the world more than all the time I ever lived at home. perhaps you did not know that Frank neve[r] scolded me one

---

[33] Belle Isle was a Confederate prison located on an island in the James River at Richmond. Used only for enlisted men, during the summer of 1863 Belle Isle's average occupancy was double its 3000 man capacity. There were only 300 ten-man tents, and the remaining men slept in the open. Living conditions and food shortages made disease common. *Dictionary*, 57; *Encyclopedia*, Vol 1, 206-207.

single word while I was there. I don't know whether I satisfied him, or whether he thought it was not best to scold me, but I know I tryed to satisfy him in every thing I done. while I was at Horatios I was scolded all of the time & after I went home from there I was scolded all of the time. I never was scolded after I went from your house home. now I can lay it to nothing else only being from home & being in a place where I was not scolded that I got along at all. you know I never could stand scolding at all.

I pity Sarah for the loss of her children.[34] it seems so they are not permitted to enjoy life in that family. but I must close so don't get downhearted. if I get paid before Frank does, which I probbaly shall, I will assist you. please wright often. Accept this from your loving brother,

Albert

Vermillionville, La
Oct [Nov] 6, 1863

My Dear Wife,

as I have got a chance to send home by G Ferrin[35] I thought I would write you a few words, but I shall have to do it in a hurry for he is going right off. he has got his discharge from the service, and you will have to see him for all that I do not have time to write. I am well at present, though awful tired for we have just had a fast tramp after the rebs. we went up to Oppalusas [Opelousas, La.] and then came back here, leaving the thirteenth army Corps at Carrion Crow Bayou. and the rebs pitched on to them and we had to go back after them. but when we got there the rebs had <u>retired</u>, so we had a march of 29 miles for nothing.[36] they got about 300 of the 13th that were out on picket,

---

[34] See Frank's letter of October 17.

[35] William Augustine Ferrin, of Concord, was 19 when he enlisted. A musician in Company F, he was discharged October 29, 1863 at New Orleans. *Registers*, 404. See also Appendix C.

[36] The 116th broke camp to go to Opelousas on October 21, and had returned to Vermillionville on November 2. About 1 a.m. on the 3rd they began a

93

but when they came up to the camp they met some grape and canister that gave some of them their everlasting discharge. they left over 100 of their men dead on the field and some of their wounded. we got about 60 prissoners and they are a hard looking set I can tell you.

We have lots of fun down here. the day before yesterday [November 2] I went out with a foraging party after potatoes and we kept going till we found ourselves about six miles from camp. the rebs had been prowling around all day and they had got one of our waggons. but we went out for potatoes and we were bound to have them, and we went into a field and went at it. there was 11 rebs in the house when we went in to the field, and I can tell you they got on to their mules <u>right</u> <u>smart</u> and got out of the way in double quick time. but we got our potatoes and got back to camp all right, about nine Oclock at night, tired and hungry. went to work and got my supper, and by the time I got ready to go to bed it was 11 Oclock. laid down and fought my lice for an other hour, and then the order came for us to go back to Carrion Crow. so we turned out and got our breakfast, struck our tents, and started at half past one. we went 12 miles in 5 hours and a half, and that made 24 miles that I had marched since 2 Oclock in the afternoon.[37] so you can see that [I] must have felt first rate tired, but I shall get rested now and then I will be as good as new.

I do not know but that you have forgotton that there is such a chap as F.E.G. who looks for a letter every time the mail comes, but does not get one, or has not got but one in six weeks. but then I shall keep writing just as thoug[h] nothing had happened. I do not think that you got all of my letters for I have written almost every week. have you got the money that I sent you? just drop me a line and let

---

march which covered 15 miles in five hours, but the battle was already over at Bayou Grand Coteau. General Stephen G. Burbridge leading a division of the Thirteenth Corps had been ambushed by two brigades of infantry and cavalry led by Thomas Green. The Union lost 25 men killed, 129 wounded, and 562 captured out of 1,625 men, plus weapons and camp equipment. The rebel losses were slightly less, with only 53 men missing. The 116th spent November 3 burying the dead and moving the wounded. They left at daybreak on the 4th and returned to Vermillionville. Clark, 132-134; Winters, 298-299.

[37] Griffith underestimated the distance, according to Clark it was "not quite fifteen miles, and it was traveled in less than five hours." Clark, 133. See footnote 36.

me know if you think of it and I will send you some more in a few days, if we get our pay. but I shall have to stop for my time is up. Lon is laying here. he is well and fat, but tired. he sends his love to all the friends. Geo Carr[38] is my chum. he sits here looking at his wifes picture, and he says tell them he sends his love. he is the fife major and a chap after my own heart, neither true nor honest. he says that he is comeing up to see us when we get through and bring his pail and show you how to cook. well, he gets up some pretty tall stories anyway.

I want you to write me all the news. Lon got a letter from John[39] and he never said a word about you, nor our folks. I guess he has forgotten them, or you are all dead. you will please excuse all mistakes and write me a good long wifely letter. be careful of yourself and the children, and keep up good courage for the good time coming. here is a kiss for you, and Mother, and Nettie, and the ba.

God Bless you all. good bye from your own,

Frank

Vermillion Bayou
Oct [Nov] 8[th] 1863

My Dear Wife,

I read your most wealcome letter last night, and you do not know how glad I was for I thought I should never hear from you aga[i]n. I have not had a letter from home in five weeks. and last night when the mail came there was only one that read FE Griffith on it, and I thought you had put your threat in execution, or else had forgoton me entirely. but there is no certainty about the mail, and perhaps I have not got all the letters you have sent. I had rather believe the latter supposition than the others.

the weather is very fine at present, though the nights are rather cool and they make me think of the good warm cheerful fire and the nice clean bed, and more than all the good bedfellow at home. can

---

[38] George W. Carr, from Evans, now about age 25, was a musician in Company K. *Registers*, 386. See also Appendix B.

[39] Griffith's brother-in-law, John Morse.

you guess who that is? I think that I will. you would like to know what kind of of a bed your corrispondent sle[e]ps on. well, I have got a rubber blanket that is about four feet wide and six long that I lay on the ground, and then I have got about 2/3 of the woolen blanket that I had at home to put over me, and lay my head on my cartridge box, shut my eyes and go to sleep (if I can). but I tell you it takes a good deal of turning over to get a little sleep. but my shoulders and hips are getting pretty tough so that I can sleep almost any where. there is one thing that I forgot to mention and that is the <u>lice</u>. we have to turn them over as a prelimmary before we think of doing anything about sleep. I think I will send you a specimen of our <u>body guards</u> if you will keep them corked up in a vial. for if you should hapen to get one on you he will be a great grandfather in two hours and you might as [well] try to get rid of the <u>seven year itch</u> as to get them off again, so be careful.

I never have felt better in my life than I have on this march. I sent you a letter by Augustine Ferrin. have you seen him yet? They say that this expedition has been entirely successful and that we are going back to New Orleans to winter. I do not know what was intended in the first place, neither the what was the result to be obtained. but I do know that the rebs are following us up, and that it is not safe for a man to go 2 miles to the front unless he wants to be Gobbled up by the rebs. we went out after forage to day and I do not think that we went more than 1 ½ miles from camp and there they were loading corn. but we drove or rather they run off and we went to loading corn ourselves. the cavalry went after them and a little skirmish, but they don't like Uncle Sams pills first rate. and I do not think they are good for the disease we call <u>white liver</u>. I have never got a shot at them yet, and I am not over anxious to have them try their skill on me, but if I do get a chance at them I mean to make them think of the time that I used to shoot wood chucks up on Johns hill. we were out on picket yesterday and about daylight they came down to see us, and the boys gave them the hand of friendship in the shape of some blue pills which they did not seem to like for they went back with their coat tails sticking out straight behind. I do not think there is much of a force here and they are all mounted so that it would be useless to follow them for when we got where they was they are not there. but I think we are setting a trap for them and the first thing they know uncle sams boys will come down on them short.

I am afraid you are getting discouraged for you do not write as cheerful as you used to. you must keep up a good strong heart for that is more than half of the battle. and then we have the most cheering prospects now before us. Rosincranse [Rosecrans] holds the key to the rebellion, and if he can get men enough to crush out the army of Bragg, or even hold his position this winter, the rebels will be whiped and the war closed.[40] and the government should make everything bend to strenghten the army of the Cumberland.

Oct [Nov] 9th

my light gave out last night and so I had to stop writing. I am very sorry to hear that the ba is not well. I do not know what you can do for her. but I should think that Mother would know. if she does not get any better you had better see the doctor. take good care of her and not let her eat much sweets. Tell Albert that there is such a fellow in Co A as Wayne White[41] that married his Cousin Jane. he is the Commissary of that Company. if you get a chance to send me some Gloves, I should be verry glad of them. the boys are all well. Lon is tough yet. have you seen Ashley yet, and got my Bible and the other things? and is he comeing back again? but the mail is going out this after noon and I shall have to hurry up. keep up good courage for the end is near. and then if we are both spared we shall meet again in joy. write often, and be assured of the love of your own devoted,

Frank

(upside down on top of first page)

Tell Sarah that she owes me one. has Charley gone to war yet, or has he [*illegible word*] over? you will have to pay the postage on my letters for we cant get any stamps here. I will send you some money in this to pay with. tell mother to write to me. kiss the children for me. and here is one for yourself. tell John that I have never had but one letter from him yet.

---

[40] Griffith is unaware that Rosecrans has been relieved of command. See footnote 28, letter of October 17.

[41] Horace Wayne White, was 23 years old when he enlisted at Hamburg. He was promoted to sergeant in Co. A on November 9, 1862. *Registers*, 495. See also Appendix C.

Camp on Vermillion Bayou, La
Nov 11th 1863

My Dear Wife,

as the mail is going out in the morning I though[t] that I would write a few lines to you to let you know that I am still in the land of the living, and that I am in good health and spirits though I am aweful sleepy. we were out on Picket last night and it was so cold that I could not sleep. it froze ice 1/4 of an inch thick and we are not allowed to have any fire in the night, and with nothing but our shirts and blouses an[d] pants and drawers you can imagine how much fun it is. and w[i]th the cold and standing on our feet all night you can guess we are some tired. so if I do not write a verry interesting letter you must excuse me, or if I write too often you can tell me for this is the third letter that I have written this week, and for all that I know it may be the last.

there was one division of our army went out to day on a scout with the cavalry and they had a right smart little fight with the rebs. first our men drove them and then they drove us from Carrian Crow Bayou to this place, about 14 miles, but they have gone back again to night[42]. I do not know how many men we lost, but I saw one old reb that they got somewhere. I do not think that they will attack us here for we are in too strong a place and they might get a cleaning out here. but we may go up there again, and they have got as good a place to fight in as we have here. the Cavalry says they think that there is from 8 to 10,000 there so you see we are like to have a great time with them sometime, though I do not know when. The niggers have dug a rifle pit in front of our camp to day about a mile long. and they are cutting down the timbers all around so that we can have a good range for our cannon. and if they do think best to try us on here we will treat them to a little grape and cannister a la port Hudson, to say nothing of some of Uncle Sams blue pills. if we can manage to gobble up the whole nest of them here it will end the fighting on this side of the river for I think they have got all they can get together to offer us here.

---

[42] Orton Clark also mentions this event, and the earthworks erected to protect the camp. Clark, 134.

and if we can hold our ground till the forces of gens. Herron[43] and Wasburn[44] and Banks get in their rear we can pretty effecually squelch the rebelion west of the mississippi. and if the army of the cumberland can gain a victory over Bragg at Chattanoga you may look for me home by the first of April, if not sooner. that is if there is any thing of me left after this campaign is over. so keep up good courage and hope for the best.

I have never felt as though the rebs were going to lay me up on the shelf yet, but if it is my lot to be killed or wounded I shall feel as though I have done my duty to my country at least. and if the men of the north would turn out in mass with and lay aside all their old party hatred and quarrels and take up their muskets and go to quarreling with the rebels this war might be ended in thirty days as well as in three years. I tell you my darling that when I read of the excuses and the inventions and all the ways that men will try to go [to] keep their skins whole and stay at home at their ease it makes me <u>mad</u> and ashamed. and I want to live long enough to come home and call them by their right names. I would tell them that their lives are of no more consequence than ours, and if they were not all a pack of cowards they would not sell their shirts to raise the 300.[45] I would like to have Gov Seymour[46] and all his sympatizers in their right places so that we

---

[43] Brigadier General Francis Jay Herron, at this time he commanded 2nd Div., XIII Corps, Division of the Gulf in Texas. *Dictionary*, 397-398.

[44] Major General Cadwallader Colder Washburn, commanded 1st Div., XIII Corps, Division of the Gulf in Louisiana. *Dictionary*, 892.

[45] A number of historians have argued that the Civil War was a "rich man's war and a poor man's fight." Adrian Cook in *Armies of the Streets: The New York Draft Riots of 1863*, noted that the three hundred dollar exemption fee represented approximately a laborer's annual wage, thus making the above charges "all too convincing, and it was bitterly resented." James W. Geary, *We Need Men: The Union Draft in the Civil War* (DeKalb: Northern Illinois University Press, 1991), 106.

[46] Governor Horatio Seymour of New York, a Democrat, objected to the draft on constitutional Grounds. On August 3, 1863 he asked Lincoln to suspend the draft in New York. Lincoln refused and debate between the two on this issue continued for several weeks. Seymour was nominated for President in 1868, but lost to Grant. *Dictionary*, 733; *Almanac*, 394-396, 398; Geary, *We Need Men*, 108.

could fight them as we do the more honorable rebels. I think that we have more to fear from the rebels at home than those in front with their arms in their hands.

but I shall have to draw this letter to a close for it is most <u>roll call</u> and then I want to go to sleep. and the mail leaves at five in the morning and you know that I am not notorious for getting up in the morning, so this will have to suffice for the present. write to me often and tell me all the gossip at home. and I will try to write as often as you do, for if you like to get letters as well as I do you will not forget me, will you? tell Nettie that pa says she must be a good girl, and kiss ma for me. how I do want to <u>see</u> <u>them</u> <u>and</u> <u>you,</u> but I live in hope. if you find this a dull letter please excuse it, and be assured that my last thoughts at night are of the dear loved and lovely <u>one</u> at home. give my love to all the friends. here is a kiss for you all.

From your own, F.E.G.

<u>write</u> <u>often</u>

_____

Biviouac of the 116 regt on the
Bayou Teche La near New Iberia
Nov 24th 1863

My Dear Wife,

another mail and no letter for Frank Griffith. well, I guess that you have all forgotten there is such a <u>chap</u> as Griff that sometimes looks for a letter from home when the mail does come. but I have made up my mind that it is of no use, so I shall have to content myself with writing to you though it makes me feel lonesome to see some of the boys get 3 or 4 letters ev[e]ry time the mail comes and there is none for me. but then I suppose that you are all so happy ther[e] that you have no time to think of anybody else, or perhaps you are all dead or moved off. but then you might just drop me a line when you left so that I might know what was the matter. but then I shall keep on writing till I have <u>orders</u> to the contrary.

The weather is rainy, and the mud, well such mud you never saw in New York State. and I hope you never may for when we put our feet down into it once, if we do not slip down, we get stuck fast. and if by chance we do take our feet up again they take a quarter section of mud with them. so you see that locomotion is not the easiest thing in the world. they can make brick any where here. all they have to do is to wet up the soil, mold, and bake them. they make mud houses and mud chimneys that answer first rate. lumber is scarce and I have not seen a stone that grew in the state of Louisiania yet. there is a salt mine[47] about 8 miles from here, but I have not been there yet.

it is healthy here. the regt never was in better health since we have been in the service. I have never had better health than since we left New Orleans. I weigh 156 lbs, so you see that I have not grown poor. now my side troubles me some lattely, but it is not so bad as it is sometimes. but my hair is all coming out and I think I shall have to have it cut off close to my head to keep from being baldheaded. they have sent to Baton Rouge this morning after our blankets and over coats. and I think we shall be more comfortable when they get back, that is if they have not all been stole.

the boys went on picket yesterday and it rained most all day. and last night it just <u>poured</u> and such a looking set you never saw, wet cold tired and hungry and cross. I tell you that this picketing is no fool of a job, for there you must stand no matter how hard it rains or how cold you are. but then the boys are in good spirits and take it cheerfully, hoping for the end, and that they live to reap the benefit of all their toil and suffering in land of peace and liberty. hoping for the speedy overthrow of our enemies both in the field and at home, for we have more to fear from our enemies at home than those that are in armies in front.

The boat has just gone down to the Bay with the mail and a lot of Gray backs (rebs) that the boys have gobled up around here. they are taking them to New Orleans. I tell you they are a hard looking set, the cavalry went out the other morning and they got 140 of them on the ground where we camped the night before. we had only one man hurt by his horse falling on him. there was some of the rebs killed and more wounded, I do not know how many. they say that the Cavalry got over 100 the day that we went foraging, but I do not know how that is. The talk is now that we shall stay here all winter now, but there is no telling what we shall do. I suppose it all depends upon

---

[47] The Avery Island salt works were located ten miles southwest of New Iberia. This valuable mine was taken by the Union forces led by William K. Kimball in April 1863, the buildings burned and equipment destroyed. Winters, 232.

what is done on the other side of the river. I do not know as you can read this for I have got the worst pen that you can imagine, and have to set on the ground and hold my paper in my lap, and you see what work I make of it. but if you cant read it you can guess. there is nothing verry bad in it, and then burn it up. perhaps that is the reason that you do not answer my letters. if so please tell me and I will try and do better.

is Birney coming back again, or will he go into the Invalid Corps? has Ashley got his discharge yet, and how does he get along? what has Sarah named her Ba[48]? and Em and Helen, you have never told me yet. and Carrie, how does she get along, and why don't she write to me? and Marth and Fay owe me a letter or two. I have given up all hope of hearing from John, only by the way of Lon, he gets a letter from him once in a while. Lon is well and fat as a pig. Nick is still in the land of the living yet, though he is the oldest Granny in the regt. he is not verry well and he thinks he is most dead. the boys hector him most to death and you can imagine that he has a splendid time of it. but my space is most overcrowded.

(*at top of page one*)

I shall have to close this poor scrawl. please to write if you ever get this, and let me know if you still live or not. Please excuse this poor writing, and accept the Love of your own,   Frank

---

Bivouac of the 116th near New Iberia
Nov 26th 1863.

My Dear Wife,

To day is Thanksgiving and I thought I would write a few lines to let you know how we spend it in the army. In the first place I am well and that is of the most consequence in the army. We have been fixing up our camp today. we had to take our tents down and put them in a line. I went to the woods and got some poles and raised our tent up about a foot from the ground so that we can stand up almost straight in the peak. it is just wide enough for three to lay down spoon

---

[48] Frank's sister Sarah and her husband Charles Spencer named the baby, Arthur.

fashion, and when one turns over we all have to do the same. it is done in true military stile, one gives the command to right or left flop and we all flop at once. we lay on one side till our backs get cold and then flop over to get it warm. and we generally flop the blankets all off the outside one, and it takes a great deal of fixing before we get settled again. the front of the tent is all open so that our feet stick out and I recken they get some cool some of these cold nights. I have not had my clothes off to sleep in over three months. I do not think I should know how to go to bed like a christian. and if I did I could not sleep like one for I should be getting up at all hours to <u>fall in</u> or to <u>Reville</u> or some other roll call. but then it is all for the good of the country.

Well dear, I set down to tell you how I have spent to day. well, after we had got our tent fixed I set down and <u>mustered in</u> my <u>lice</u> and they were all <u>present or accounted for</u>, the larger share being present. I tell you there is nothing that makes me so homesick as it does to take off my shirt and find a dozen or fifteen lice on it. oh, will the time ever come when I can get home and put on clean clothes and [not] feel the <u>devilish</u> lice crawling over me. there is nothing in the known world that will kill them but to boil all our clothes at once. and then we would not be rid of them but for a few days for they are all over camp. and all the way that we can get along is to kill all we can find ev[e]ry day. I gues[s] you would laugh to see the boys strip off their clothes and hunt them, some laughing, some mad, and some swearing, and all making fun of each other. but I am afraid you will get tired of reading about them so I will tell you what I had for dinner, <u>Chicken soup</u> and it was first rate. George Carr made it and I got the chick, or rather old hen. I suppose you will want to know where I got her. well, we went out about 12 miles foraging yesterday and when we came back we had to walk so I came across by an old rebs house and there was lot[s] of hens and chicks that refused to take the oath of allegience, so I just knocked an old hen on the head and brought her into camp and she made a good supper for the three of us, and soup enough left for breakfast in the morning. I tell you the sesesh hens and sheep and pigs and such things have to swear allegience to uncle Sam or be confiscated, and that does not always save their necks. I have never captured but two yet, but now I have got a taste of them they will have to keep out of my way or suffer the consequences. I went out the other day on my own hook with one of the boys and we found a <u>bee tree</u>. but it was so late that we did not have time to eat it, and I do not know as we shall be able to get it for it is out side of the Pickets and it is not verry safe to go far. but we have got plenty of sugar so that we can make all the candy that we want, and that is no small amount.

The mail has just come, but no letters for me. well, I guess you have all forgotten me or you dont want me to write any more, or else are all dead. I shall have to hunt up another correspondent that will write at least once a month so that I can find out when the war does <u>let out</u>, if that happy period does ever arrive. I answered Corrydons letter more than a month ago. if he can read it he can do better than I could by all of his. did you ever see any of his writing? if you have you can gues[s] what a job he had of it for I wrote it full as bad as he did, if not a little worse. and perhaps that is the reason you do not write that I write so poor that you cant read it. I do not know what to write, but it is getting most time for Tattoo and I shall have to finish this hasty scrawl. the officers have celebrated today by getting gloriously drunk, from the General down to little Leroy Russell the drummer boy[49]. and having a good time generally running horses, and eating ro[a]st goose has been the order of the day among the big boys. So you see that we have some amusement and a great deal of fun down here. now you must not think that I get drunk or that I even drink for we privates get nothing but quinine and whisky, and that [not] very often. and if you ever tasted any quinine you can guess how good it is.

but I shall have to close for to night. Lon sends his respect to all. he is well. do write once in a while, and acept this poor letter with the love of your own devoted,

Frank

Bivouac of the 116th Regt NYSV
Near New Iberia, La
Dec 2nd 1863

---

[49] Leroy J. Russell was age 14 when he enlisted August 30, 1862 at Evans. He served as a musician in Co. K. *Registers*, 466. See also Appendix B.

My Dear Wife,

Well, I have got a letter at last and you can never guess how glad I am to hear from you once more. I am well, or nearly so, for I have just had one of the <u>jofiredest</u> <u>biles</u> [boils] on my <u>rear</u> that you ever heard of a poor fellow having. I could neither stand up, lay down, sit up, or walk much. all the way I had to do was to lie flat on my <u>belly</u>, if you know how that is. and you may <u>reckon</u> that I <u>grunted</u> some, but it did no good. well, yesterday I got Carr to open it and he opened it till I yelled like Blazes. but I think it did some good for I make out to sit up some to day. and if I do not write a verry long letter to day you must excuse me, with the exception of that I am well.

we got our pay yesterday and I am going to send you 10 dollars in this, ten in the next. we shall get our pay the first of next month and I will send you 20 more, take good care of it. I think if you turn over what stuff I left to Popple[50] I shall owe him $25 or 30. you can pay him 25 and then I will pay the rest when I get home. John has the papers so that you can tell pretty near. I would not pay more than that now. have you got any wheat left? and do you have enough to eat? make yourself comfortable first, and then if there is any thing left do as you think best. Pay Uncle Archie the interest for another year if he wants it. I am sorry to hear that the <u>ba</u> is sick all the time. I dont see what the matter is with her. take good care of her and Nettie. you dont know how bad I do want to see them. but then I think that whoever lives to see spring will see the close of the war. send me some stamps for we cant get any here. please excuse me for not writing more for this time and I will try and do better in future when I dont have a bile on my ___. please to write often, and tell me all the news, both social and war like, in a good long cheerful letter. how does the donation Committe get along? I have had but one letter from them in more than a year. has Birney gone back to the Regt yet? and did you send me any gloves? they would come right handy now these cold nights. but I shall have to stop writing for the present. From your own,

Frank

---

[50] Possibly A.W. Popple who lived in North Collins and was a farmer according to the 1855 New York Census.

105

Sunday Dec 5th [1863]

Well, my Dear,

another week has past and to night I am going to try and write a few words more. I don't know but that you will get tired of reading such long letters, and if you do just let me know and I will make them shorter. I do not think that I can write any thing to night that will be interesting for I am <u>mad</u>. yes, that is the word, and I want this war to close before another month or I shall get madder yet. and now I suppose you will want to know what has happened to so excite my usualy mild disposition. well, I will try and tell you. it is on the account of the style that our <u>whiskey</u> officers put on today. they have had a man standing on a barrel all day in front of the Majors⁵¹ tent for some trivial offence. and tonight on dress parade the Major called a man out for just turning his head on one side a little. and tonight he stands in front of the majors at <u>attention</u>, and perhaps he will have to stand there half of the night. they will punish the men for the same things that they do themselves. they can get <u>drunk</u> and make all the noise that they are a mind t[o], there is nothing said about it. but if one of us should get a little too happy, we go into the guard house for four or five days. well, I have never been punished for any thing yet. but they are putting on so much style lately that I expect ev[e]ry day I shall be caught winking once to[o] much, or swear more than nine times in a day, and be paraded up before the majors tent for half a day or more. and you need not be surprised that next letter that you get to see is dated from the guard house or Ship Island.⁵² but I shall have to stop writing for to night, or I may say something disrespectful of my superior officers.

8th

I think you will think it takes me a good while to write a letter, but then we have so many orders and so much style that we have to write fast as we can catch it. we went out foraging yesterday. we

---

⁵¹ John Mappa Sizer, was 22 when he enrolled at Buffalo. A captain of Co. G, Sizer was promoted to major on September 14, 1863. *Registers*, 473. See also Appendix C.

⁵² Ship Island, Mississippi, where the 116th spent two weeks in December 1862, was also used as a "jail," for punishing both soldiers and civilians.

went about seven miles to an old secesh planters and took what corn and chickens he had. the 13th army corps had been there the day before and took all their mules and horses, so I reckon that he will not have much to come back to. the owner has gone to Texas and took all the best of his darkies with him, but I do not think they will do him much good there for they are all running away and going to Gen Banks. we do not hear much from Gen Banks or his expedition. but the last that we did hear he was enlisting men at the rate of two hundred a day, so that Gen Dick Taylor[53] will soon find a force of his own men in his rear that will make him howl.

    I was verry agreeably surprised to find a letter from you and mother and Gene when I got back last night. and am glad to hear that you are well and keep up good courage. I am so continually interupted that I shall have to finish this letter and begin another. I will send you some money in this and some in the next. keep up good courage, and write often. tell mother I will answer her letter in a few days. tell marth that I am looking for a letter from her every day. I dont know but she has forgoton me. write often, and accept the love of your own,
    Frank

Bivouac of the 116th
Near New Iberia, La
Dec 13th 1863

My Dear Wife,
    I recd your most welcome letter last night and you dont know how glad I was. I got one from Dora at the same time, they are all well and prospering finely. I am not verry well at present. I have got another bile on my back, but that is getting better now. I have had the

---

[53] Richard Taylor, son of President Zachary Taylor, had moved to Louisiana in 1849 and established a sugar plantation. In June 1861 the 9th Louisiana Infantry elected Taylor its colonel. Taylor was promoted to major general in July 1862 and ordered "to enroll and conscript troops in the District of Western Louisiana of the Trans-Mississippi Department....and to command all troops south of the Red River." He arrived in Opelousas on August 20, 1862. Moneyhon, *Portraits of Conflict*, 161; Winters, 152.

diarea for the last week so that I do not feel quite so keen as I did the last time I wrote. but then it is nothing serious and I shall be all over it in a few days and be all the better for it.

I am glad that you have got that money that I sent and am sorry that there was not more of it. I have sent you ten dollars more and will send you some more in a few days. if we do go back to New Orleans, which we expect to in a few days, then I will send it by express. I am going to save a little for Christmas, if we are in any civilized place, so that we can have a dinner. you must take care of your self and the children first, and then if there is any left it will be time enough to pay. for folks that owe me are in no hurry to pay me now that I have gone to fight their battles for them, while they can stay at home and grow rich on the necesities of the war. yes, they can stay at home, out of the way of danger, and have enough to eat. that they can eat and [have] a good warm place to sleep, and then they think that we can live on Government rations of hard tack and Salt Horse, sleep on the ground in the rain, stand guard or picket in any kind of storm, and then ev[e]ry thing that we do buy pay four times what it is worth. and yet we can send home our 20 or 24 dolars a evry two months, for the government furnishes us rations and clothes and evry thing that we need. well, if any body thinks they can get rich on $13 dolars a month in Louisiana I just want they should just try it for one year as I have, <u>that is all</u>.

I have had a benefit from the donation Committee just recd for which I shall owe them an eternal debt of grattitude. and what do you think it was or rather is for I have got it yet. well, I have a great mind to let you guess, but as it would take you four months to find out whether you guessed right or not I will tell you at once. wel[l], they sent me in a box of Robt Woods of Co A,[54] a can of Nice Butter and a can of Honey, like that can that you sent me at Baltimore, and a bag of dried Cherries and some tea and some currants. was not that <u>Generous</u> of them. well, I think so and I am going to write them a letter of thanks this verry day. have you got my Pipe that I sent home last spring? I sent it in the box with the captains, that is captain Ayers. they were sent to Mr Blacks at Evans Center in care of

---

[54] Robert H. Woods was 18 when he enlisted at Buffalo, August 4, 1862 as a private in Company A. *Registers*, 500. See also Appendix C.

Horatio. I have never heard from it since I sent it. if you have not got it I wish you would see about it the first chance that you have for it is worth ten dollars to me.

the talk is now that we are going to New Orleans to do Provost duty. and if that is so I want you to send me those shirts as soon as you can. send me some nice ones with good long <u>tails</u> so that I can keep them in my pants, for I would look bad parading the streets of the Crescent City with my shirt tail streaming in the wind. I think that your Aid Society would do as much good in that way as giving to a set of great lazy louts who ar[e] to[o] lazy to work and to[o] mean to give anything nice sent to the Hospitals to those who real[l]y need them, but appropriate them to their own use while those in whose behalf they were sent suffer for the need of them.[55] but if one half of the things sent ever reached those in whose behalf they were sent I would give you my heart and hand and go with you in the noble work. but as the thing is carried on in all the Hospitals that I have seen, your money and time are worse than thrown away, or they go to a pack of thieves.

but I shall have to close for to day as I have got to write to dora and the committee. so you will please excuse me for this time. write after and tell me all the news about home. and dont write such verry sanctimonious letters that make one have the blues, but write something cheerful and more hopeful and full of fun.

(top of first page)
tell mother to look for a letter from her soldier boy soon. I am going to write to your folks in a day or two. where is Albert? I want to write to him.

From your own,

Frank

---

[55] The Waterville Aid Society made clothing and food items for the soldiers in the hospitals. The *Buffalo Express* listed the items received by the U.S. Sanitary Commission for the week of November 27, 1863 from this organization: 116 lbs Dried apples, 22 ½ lbs mixed dried fruit, 1 sheet, 1 pair pillowcases, 4 pairs socks, 4 towels, 8 forks, 1 quilt, 21 papers, ½ lb bandages, 10 lbs cheese, 2 firkins pickled cabbage, 5 bush potatoes, 1 bush beets, 1 ½ bush apples, 2 galls pickled onions, 4 lb linen and cotton." Frank's comments reflect the fact that often these items did not reach the soldiers, but were instead taken by others higher up whose duties involved caring for the soldiers. *Buffalo Express*, 1 December 1863.

Bivouac of the 116th Regt
Near New Iberia, La
Dec 19th 1863

My Darling Wife,

I received your most wealcome letter last night on Picket, and you can guess how glad I was to hear from you that you are well and in good spirits. I am well and I suppose that is the thing that you want to hear the most for that is the most essential thing for a man in this country. We are having a cold snap and it is cold enough for the sun[n]y South. it freezes ev[e]ry night but we have got plenty of blankets and some hay to sleep on, so that by spooning we manage to sleep first rate, that is Carr, Lon and your humble servant. but then I think of the good bed, and more of the good dear bedfellow at home. but then I try to be patient hoping for the best and looking for a Glorious peace, though it is secured by the blood of our brave men in the field and the sorrow of the dear hearts at home, a peace that will secure for us and our children the blessings of freedom. and I am one that believes that though it [is] gained through the loss of our dear ones, yet in the end, it will prove a blessing to the country. for in proportion to the sacrifice so shall we have gained in the purification of the country from that great curse of all nations, Slavery. I came from home an abolitionist and the more that I see of this land of slavery and oppression the more am I strengthened in the belief that it has proved their ruin. but the time has come when the bou[n]d shall go free, and I for one glory in it.

I have just bought me a new gold pen so you may look to be pestered to death with letters, that is if I can get the time to write them. but if you do not want to read them you can give them to the children to play with. I r[e]ad a Thanksgiving Sermon last night in the Buffalo Express preached by the Rev Mr Wilcox, and it is the best thing that I have read in a long time.[56] and if you have not read it I

---

[56] "A Sermon Preached in the LaFayette Street Presbyterian Church on the National Thanksgiving Day, November 23rd, by the Rev. G.W. Heacock, D.D." In this lengthy sermon Heacock explained that Thanksgiving originated after periods of trouble, when hope was needed. The current war gives men a reason to think. He believed that there are evils greater than war, such as slavery. Man would, without God's intervention, settle for a bad peace rather than fight for justice. "God

want you to get the paper and read it for it is the truth, it is my views precisely. and I only wish that I had the eloquence of that man, or the command of language, I could write you a letter that would be worth reading.

This is one of the richest districts in the whole South. and if we can believe the stories told us by the slaves it must have been one of the most toil and suffering. it is no uncommon thing to see these poor black men with their backs scared by the lash of the driver. and on ev[e]ry plantation we can find their implements of torture, the stocks and the whipping post and the whip. and by these cruel means the wealth of these great lords of creation have lived and grown rich on the blood and tears wrung from these poor slaves. but that is past now and these poor men can assert their manhood, while their once rich owners, now poor and made so by their own folly, will have to earn their bread by the sweat of their own brow. and even now the federal army has to feed them. but this war will inauguerate a new system here. these large farms will be divided between the brave men who have fought the battles of this war. and in a few years of peace the South will take her place in the wealth of the nation.

it is so cold that I have had to go and warm my hands. we are going to move up to New Iberia in a day or two. the 13th army corps goes to Franklin to day, and we are going to take their place. I do not think we shall stay here long. the talk is that we shall go to New Orleans in two or three weeks. have you heard from Albert yet, and where is he? I have written to Lydia and will send the letter in this, and you can send it to her for I do not know where to direct. Lon is not verry well at present though nothing serious is the matter. when is Birney coming back? about that pistol, I want you to keep it till I get home, it is worth $20. it is one that I captured. We have drawn some flour and had a mess of pancakes and butter and molasses of our own manufacture, first rate. but I shall have to close this. write often, kiss

---

compelled us to the war by the stern obligations of patriotism and of national duty....Let us....sincerely, thank God that he has given us an honest and righteous war, instead of a lying, unrighteous, deadly peace." He also stated that both free blacks and slaves should be allowed to fight for this just cause, and that at the end of the war the Constitution should be amended to outlaw slavery. Quoting the whole of Lincoln's Gettysburg Address, Heacock concluded by saying that, "War will have taught us a heroism which will illustrate itself in missionary and philanthropic labors all around the world." *Buffalo Express*, 30 November 1863.

111

the children for me.

     Frank

Bivouac of the 116th Regt
Near New Iberia
Dec 22nd 1863

Dear Heart,

    I am tired and lonesome to night and so I thought that I would write to you. I was on Picket last night and that is the reason that I am tired, and why I am lonesome I cant tell. I am well and tough and that is the most that a soldier can hope for. it rains and is cold, but I dont think that it will snow for it never does that here.

    I had a very interesting talk with the officer of the guard. he is a democrat and I, well you know what I am. well, we talked the thing over from the beginning of the war till the present time in all its bearings upon the destinies of both the present and future generations. he in favor of Slavery and I aga[i]nst it. I cant see how a man who loves his country or has even the common feelings of humanity can advocate the doctrines of proslaveryism and more especial[l]y in this country. and I believe that in proportion as we are guilty of the crime of slavery so in proportion are we punished. the north have grown rich from its spoils. and the Aristocrats of [are] the richer out of its toils and groans and pray[e]rs, and they are being terribly punished for it. their homes destroyed, and their fenses taken for wood, their horses, mules and cattle taken for the use of the armies. it is no uncommon thing to see the once rich slaveowner coming into town take the Oath and draw rations from the government to keep soul and body together. oh I tell you, <u>they</u> are getting enough of the war and are glad to have peace on any terms. the north are being punished by the loss of her dear Fathers, Husbands, Brothers and sons sacrificed on the altar of civil war. and when we are sufficiently humbled then, and not till then, may we hope for peace. and we are fast approaching that happy period in our nation, and may God speed the time.

    But you will get tired of such dry and perhaps uninteresting letters. and perhaps it is not best for me to write to you when I am in the mood that I am in tonight, for I do sometimes get lonesome even in the army, and long for some one that I can talk the feelings of my

heart to in confidence, and hear the fear at the utterance of some unpopular sentiment. and sometimes when I have seen the boys abuse and curse these poor ignorant people for being black and ignorant I could stand it no longer. I have cried for shame and taken their part. but then it is not always so and ther[e] are some who can sympathize with them. and there are some pleasant r[e]colection of happy days past in the service of the country. and if I should live to come home to you again, I for one shall not regret the hardships nor toil of the years spent in the service of my country. but then I am so far away from all good influences that I am afraid that I shall need civilising befor[e] I shall know how to behave in decent society. and I am afraid you will be ashamed of me. but I will stop writing for to night before I get ashamed of myself for writing you such an uninteresting letter. please excuse me this time, and here is a kiss for you. how I wish I could give it by the word of <u>mouth</u> instead of sending on paper.
23rd

Today is Inspection and ev[e]ry one has to come out with his best bib and tucker or get <u>jessie</u>. and that is what we don't like, so we all go to work cleaning our guns and straps, blacking our shoes, brushing our clothes, and fussing about generally. but it rained and I think that hurried up matters so that they did not find much fault, only with Poor Nick. he has got so home sick that he dont care wheather school keeps or not. I guess his girl has gone back on him for he never gets a letter from home, nor any where else. you should just write him a line once in a while for you dont know how much good it does a fellow to get a letter once in a while.

The boat is going by for the bay so I shall not have time to get this letter in today. it is clearing off and is going to be cold as ice again. but then we are pretty comfortable for tents and blankets so that we shall not suffer much if we stay in them. the ground is as slippery

[*missing next page of letter*]

———————

Bivouac of the 116th Regt
Near New Iberia, La
Dec 24th 1863

My Darling Wife,

as I am on picket for my Christmas I thought that I would write a few lines to you just to wish you a merry Christmas. and while I am about it I may as well wish you a happy New Year too. and I hope that the next anniversary of this holliday may be spent in your dear society in a land blessed with peace and liberty. that I am well you guess or I should not be on picket on Christmas. and as long as I am well I shall be satisfied.

we have got a new excitement in camp. there was an order read to us on parade to night that all who will enlist in the regulars will have thirty days furlough at <u>home</u> and will receive $750. in bounty in three years. and as it will be only sixteen months longer that I have yet to stay dont you think I had better enlist again? I dont think we could [make] 750 dollars any easier. what do you think about it? I want you to write and tell me just what you think about it. by the time that my time is out we shall get so used to living alone that we will not mind it so much, will we? but I shall not commit myself till I hear from you. but it is time for roll call so I shall have to stop for to night. here is a good night kiss, but how unlike those that I remember of old.

Christmas morning.
Good morning Dear,

I am not on guard duty today so I am going to write you the begin[in]g of the day. there was an order last night suspending all military duty today except what is necessary for our defence and that is the reason that reason that I am not on duty. it rains and is cold, just such a disagreeable day as we have at the north in November. Well, for breakfast we had Coffee, boiled salt pork, and hard tack and butter. I have got some butter left that the <u>Donation Committee</u> sent me yet but it is most gone. but what we shall have for dinner I dont know. we have just drawn some flour and meal and we might have a Johnny Cake if we had some nice little <u>woman</u> that I know to make it for us. but as that cannot be to day we shall have to fuss it up the best way that we can. and I hope that by the next Christmas I shall be where that same little woman can cook for me to my hearts content. There is an extra ration of whisky to day and you can see, or I can see, the effects of it already. two Corporals drunk already and more that are already in a fair way to be so. but I do not class myself with either class yet though I dont know what will happen before night. and I

114

think I shall try and keep sober enough to finish this letter to night.

one year ago today we were on Ship Island and such a time we had there. I think that I told you about it in the time of it. Well, since that time there has been some changes in our regt. Our Capt has died, the <u>Father</u> of <u>this</u> <u>company</u> and I believe the <u>best</u> man in the regt.[57] then the siege of Port Hudson where many of the brave boys laid down their lives in their Countrys cause.[58] and then the battle of Donaldsonville, another bloody fight.[59] and then the lingering death of those brave men that were wounded and whose constitutions were not strong enough to bear the hardships of war. and the death of Lieut. Cottier,[60] a man whom we all loved as a brother. then the voyage to Sabine Pass.[61] and that was the hardest time that we ever saw, with nothing to eat and such water as we had to drink. I tell you

---

[57] James Ayer, see letter dated May 24, 1863, footnote 3.

[58] The 116th was involved in two assaults on Port Hudson. On May 27 the regiment lost 22 killed and 85 wounded. The second assault on June 14 resulted in five more deaths and 23 wounded. *Memorial Services in Memory of Ira Ayer, Capt. Co. A, 116th N.Y. Vols.* (Buffalo: Webster Brothers, 1890), 54. Hereafter referred to as Ayer.

[59] The Battle of Cox's Plantation, near Donaldsonville, July 13 was a Confederate victory with General Thomas Green's force of about 1,200 men defeating a Union force three times larger with only three killed and 30 wounded, although six died later. Union General Grover lost 56 dead, 217 wounded, and 186 missing or captured, plus equipment, ammunition, and provisions. Winters, 293. The 116th lost five killed, 23 wounded, and 21 prisoners. Ayer, 55.

[60] Elisha B. Cottier was 31 when he enrolled at Buffalo. Mustered in as a second lieutenant of Co. K, he was promoted to first lieutenant May 27, 1863. Cottier died of malaria at Baton Rouge on August 21, 1863. *Registers*, 391. See also Appendix B.

[61] Led by Major General William Buel Franklin, the expedition to Sabine Pass, Texas began September 3 at New Orleans. It was a disaster which cost the Union two gunboats, 350 prisoners, and 50 killed or wounded, in addition to the 200,000 rations and 200 mules tossed overboard from the grounded federal gunboats. The Confederates claimed not to have lost a man during this action. Franklin's retreat down a storm tossed river, men seasick and on half rations, ended when they landed at Algiers opposite New Orleans, on September 13. Winters, 294-296; Ayer, 55-56.

if we had stayed on the ship another week your Frank would not [have] been writing to you to day for I was the sickest chap that you ever saw and I only weighed 118 pounds. so you may guess that I did not have a first-rate time on that trip. I had the chill fever and took 90 grains of quinine in two days, but that is all past now and I weigh 156 to day.

well, we have had some pancakes for dinner and they were put up in butter and sugar just as you used to fix them at home. I superintended the

[*missing next page of letter*]

(*on top of first page, written upside down and along edge of paper*)
I am going to send Nettie some more pictures in a little while.
Please accept it with the love of your own.
has mother got her letter yet? and do you know where Albert is?
Give my love to all the friends, my heart you have. Frank

Chapter 4

"We have been fixing up our camp"
Winter Quarters, Franklin, LA, January - March 1864

For the greater part of the first two months of 1864 the 116th was camped at Franklin, Louisiana. They had left New Iberia on January 7 and arrived at Franklin on the 9th. However, after a few days they moved to better ground at "Camp Emory," where they remained through March 4. Little war activity took place in Louisiana during this period. On February 5 the 116th raised a flag pole, and on the 9th all the companies of the regiment worked on decorating their sections of the camp. Frank Griffith apparently was in charge of the decorating for Co. K, and writes Thankful about his handiwork. By early March the men know that they will soon see some action, but are unsure where that action will take place.

Griffith starts the year numbering his letters to Thankful, presumably so she will know if all of Frank's letters have been received. In addition to missing Thankful and his daughters, Frank's letters for early 1864 contain a number of other repeated concerns. Frank's side continues to bother him. Although Frank does not know the cause of his discomfort it is likely that Griffith suffered from amoebic liver abscess.[1]

Frank frequently comments about other family members. Although Thankful has received some "presents" from her brother-in-law Horatio Hurd, that does not compensate for what he has taken from Frank. When Thankful's parents go to live with Horatio it is obvious that Frank does not believe it would be a peaceful place to live. On the other hand, Frank is quite interested in hearing about Thankful's brother Albert who is home on leave from the war.

Surprisingly, Frank starts mentioning Southern women occasionally in his letters, and in glowing terms. He mentions receiving a letter from his cousin Nettie Sanford, and he even tells Thankful about a woman with a small child that looks down upon his bed. I suspect he is probably just describing a photograph of Thankful in order to make her jealous, and perhaps all mentions of other women may just be a ploy

---

[1] See letter dated February 2, 1864 footnote 18.

to encourage Thankful to write more often.

Griffith also seems more concerned with religion. The 116th did not keep the Sabbath as Frank would like. He would like to attend church services, but the regiment often had to undergo extra inspections on Sundays. Frank is proud of his wife for becoming president of the local soldier's aid society, but is discouraged with the course of the war, and the lack of action to help out the war effort by others on the home front. Such words as "altar" and "sacrifice" appear more often. As author Steven Woodworth states, when the word sacrifice was "used in connection with the concept of an "altar," the word had a much stronger religious connotation. Things sacrificed on an altar were offered directly to the deity whose altar that was, for the purpose of propitiating that god or atoning for wrong doing....Thus, for people of the Civil War era, most of whom were familiar with at least the terminology of Christianity, to say that a soldier was a "sacrifice upon the altar of his country" was to give that soldier a special place in a new theology in which country, not God, occupied the position of deity."[2]

In one notable letter Griffith writes about slavery. His use of the word "nigger" and his descriptions are painful to read today, but understandable when put in the context of the times. He goes on to curse slavery and express thanks to God that the war will end the practice.

---

[2] Steven Woodworth, *While God is Marching On*, 106.

No. 2
Bivouac of the 116th Regt
Near Franklin, La
Jan 10th 1864

My Dear Wife,

I recd your most wealcome letter to day and you do not know how much good it done me. I was glad to hear that you and the children are well and I hope that you may always be so. I am well at present though my side has troubled me some lately, but it is better now. you will see that we have moved since I wrote last and we had a tough time of it. It rained and snowed all day and night before we left New Iberia [January 6] and then it froze so that it would almost hold us up. so you see that it must have been nice traveling. we stayed one night [January 7] in a sugar mill and one night I was on guard. but the boys put up their tents and slept on the ground. it was as cold as greenland, but then I had a good fire and plenty of coffee so that I managed first rate. and yesterday we came here and we have been busy evey [ever] since so you must excuse me for not writing before.[1] I went out with the boys last night and shot some beef so that we have plenty of beef steak, but no bread. to day it rains and is cold enough to make an over coat feel good. I have got those gloves and I think they are nice [in] this cold weather.

I think it would have been a good time for you to have the measels and I don't see the reason you did not catch them for you catched the itch once if I remember right. and I don't think the measles can beat that much, do you? I suppose that Albert can tell you some thing about war and camping out. does he look tough? and why don't he write to me? you can just believe any thing he tells you. I should like to see him and compare notes. I suppose that Horatio thinks he can buy us with some little present so that we cant remember any of his old tricks. well, perhaps they can you, but you

---

[1] Orders to move were received the evening of January 5, but after packing up on the 6th a countermand kept the 116th at New Iberia until the morning of the 7th. The frozen roads soon turned into a "vast bed of mud" and only ten miles was covered. The evening of the 8th found the 116th camped at Harding's plantation, ten miles distant. They arrived in Franklin about 11 a.m. on the January 9. Clark, 136-138.

just wait till I get home and I will read them a chapter that they cant find in the Bible. and if I had been in your place I would have told them they could go to the <u>Devil</u> with their presents, for they will be telling how much they have done for us. and if you cant get enough with out accepting presents from them sell the horses and waggon and harness and ev[e]ry thing that I have got, and I will live on hard tack and salt horse till I die, and send you all the money that I earn here before I would acept any peace offering from them till he is ready to do the right thing. I do not know but their family alter is well enough, but I do not for one want to be sacrificed on <u>it</u>. I think the girls are some on names. but I read a book the other day and the Heroines name was Leealine. don't you think it is a pretty name? I like it. I think your folks will have nice times living with Horatio. they will do so <u>much</u> for them, that is if he has got any thing left that he can cheat him out of.

I think that Birney had rather report to [the] Alter any time than to the regt.[2] but then I do not blame him much for I know a place that would suit me first rate to report to. and I sincerely hope that I shall be ordered to do so before long. I am sorry that you have so much to do that you cant find time to write but one sheet once a week. but I do not know but that is a hint to me not to write such long letters. why don't Lydia write to me? I have written to her twice since I got a letter from her.

Jan 13th
I have been so busy that I have not had time to finish this poor scrawl till now. the mud is A--s deep all over camp. well, you can guess what I mean. and it is rather dangerous navigating the streets. we have got some bricks and have built us a fire place in our tents so that it is verry comfortable now. but it rains ev[e]ry day so that we do not have to drill any now. the talk is that we are going to move again in a day or so. I saw in the Buffalo paper that Sol Stocker[3] and L M Charchel are married. I think that she must have been <u>cramped</u> some

---

[2] James "Birney" Weber married Amelia Warner, see letter dated January 20, 1864.

[3] Possibly Solomon Stocker, a farmer from Evans, age 25 in the 1855 New York State Census.

where, don't you? well, I will have to dry up for the present. write often and tell me all the news. kiss the Babies for me, and accept this from your own,

       Frank

Camp Emory[4] Near Franklin, La.
Jan 17th 1864

My Dear Wife,

       as the mail is going out in the morning I thought that I would write you a few lines to night, although I have written twice since I have heard from you. and I thought that perhaps you might find time to read a letter if you could not get time to write one. I am well and that is about all the news there is to write at present.

       we have moved our camp about half a mile nearer Franklin to a nice grove and we have got a splendid place to camp now. we have fixed up our tent and built a fire place in one side so that we are verry comfortable now. the weather is cool and rainy so that a fire is comfortable and nice. and we have nice times frying beef and Pancakes, and I tell you they are nice, we put butter and sugar on them just as I used to at home though the butter [is] fifty cts per pound and not very good at that. I think that if I stay three years in the army that I shall get so that I can cook my own grub, and wash and mend my clothes, and keep house for myself, and then if you dont like your soldier boy, well, I wont say what for. I dont know but I shall like you just enough to keep hanging around till I shall forget all that I know.

       but I shall have to stop writing such nonsense or you will not write to me at all, for you always write such matter of fact letters that I am afraid that you dont like to have me write such nonsense to you. but if I should set down and write any thing so matter of fact I should get the blues so that I could not write at all, so I do any thing to keep up good spirits for I b[e]lieve that our lives depend a great deal on the state of our minds. and there is many brave boys died whose death

---

    [4] Named after General William Hemsley Emory who was now commanding the 1[st] Division, 19[th] Corps since General Weitzel's return to the North. It was Emory who selected the site for the new camp. Clark, 138-139.

was hastened by the neglect of the dear ones at home to write often such long, loving letters and encourage him to hope for the best. for when we do not get any letters from home it seems as though they had forgotten us, and then we get lonesome and melancholy, and then is the time that we get sick. and when one is sick here is the time that [brings] the longing for home and the sympathy of some dear one, for sympathy is [one] thing that we do not get here. and if one is sick he bears to suffer in silence till he gets so that he cant help himself any longer. then he is sent off to the hospital to die. oh, if those that we have left at home only knew how much good a letter does a poor soldier they would write ev[e]ry day. and if they wish to see their sons, Fathers, and brothers, husbands come home to them men and not brutes write to them such good long loving letters as you write to your own unworthy Frank, My darling. and I hope the time is fast coming when we can lay aside the slow medium of pen and paper and talk our thoughts to each other. is not the case with you?

but I shall have to finish this poor scrawl for it is most time for taps, and then we must all go to bed. how does the children get along, and are they good? do you make them mind you? does Nettie sing any yet? I want you to learn her to sing if you can. I will send them each a picture in this letter. how did Nettie like her letter?

Please to write often, and tell me all about yourself just as though I was there. do you ever dream about me?

Give my love to Mother and all the rest of the folks at home. Good night.

        Frank

Camp Emory Near Franklin, La
Jan 20th 1864

My Dear and ever remembered Wife,

here is a sheet of paper that Dora sent me from Maine, and I am a going to answer you[r] letter of Dec 27. which I received to day. so you see that I do not wait till Sunday, and in Church at that, to answer your kind letters. but then I am glad to get a letter written at any time. I have written to you once before this week, and one to Ma and one to Pa, so you see that I do not forget you. I am well at present though my side troubles me some. I found 8 stamps in your letter which are verry acceptable for we cant get any here, and paper is 90 cts a quill, and envelopes 25 cts a pack. I have got a lot of paper at Baton Rouge. I cant get them here.

I have been at work at Brigade Headquarters to day and my hand trembles to night so that I cant write verry wel[l]. and if you can read this you will do well. we have not had any sleighing here this winter, but rain and mud enough to make bad enough going. how does Albert look? has he grown any, and why dont he write to me? and Lydia, I think it is about time she was writing to me and giving an account of herself. and Nettie has she forgotten me? how I do want to see her, the little chick. I think that if I could just have one good <u>train</u> with her I would not be lonesome again in a month. but the time is fast coming, I b[e]lieve, when if I am spared I shall see you all again. I cant see what ailes the ba. you must be careful what she eats and not let her eat too much. I think that her stomach is weak and that she eats too much. I am glad to hear of your [friend] Amilias good fortune, that is if a soldiers wife can be called so. and I hope that they may be blest till their cup of bliss runs over. I shall be glad to see Birney back again, but sorry for her. and I sincerely hope they may not be parted as long as we have. give her my best wishes. I think that if we ever get home again there will some visiting all around. perhaps you and I will not have one good visit, perhaps not.

you ask if I remember New Years five years ago. yes, I do remember it verry well. but it does not seem more than two years. and now I think that I was too happy when I was with you to note how fast the time passed. I am glad that you have got the money that I sent you, and we are expecting to get our pay eve[r]y day when I will send you some more. I think that I will send you $30. and you can do what you think best with it. I wish you would go to Mr Wards[5] and get me a good gold pen worth about 2.80 and send me if you can. you can send it in a letter. I got one here but it was not good for any thing and so I sold it again for what I gave for it. I think some of going to headquarters as a clerk, and I shall have a great deal of writing to do.

---

[5] O.S. Ward was listed under the Merchants and Traders of Concord. *Concord*, 188, 191.

I suppose that they have some tall singing in church[6] now, but I do not think that I should go to church to hear you sing for I used to think you could sing to me the best at home. dont George Newton say any thing about writing to me? or do they think that I do not care to hear from them. but I shall have to close for to night for it is Tattoo and then the lights have to be put out. but I['ll] try and finish this in the morning.

[Jan. 21] morning

it is pleasant this morning and I am going down to head quarters to day. I had a most delightful dream last night. I dreamed that I was at home and that the war was out and such a happy time as we had.

You want to know who this Geo Carr is. Well, he is a cappital fellow. he is fife seargent of the regt. he used to live in Evans and he has got a pretty wife [Hattie] and he writes to her almost every day, and I guess that she writes to him ev[e]ry hour by the number of letters that he gets from her. they have got a boy that Geo has never seen, but it is a most wonderful baby if you can believe the stories that she tells tells about it. I am going to write to Mr. Ward to send me a doz Gold pens and cases to sell on Commission. I can sell them in one day. Please to write often, and good long letter[s]. tell me all the news. and accept this from your own,

Frank

PS Oh, I forgot to tell me who my other tent mate is, Eb Ames.[7] He

---

[6] Most likely the Free Baptist Church of East Concord.

[7] Apparently Acil [also recorded as Ashael] Ebenezer Ames remained Frank Griffith's friend for life. Ames was born at Poultney, Vt. on August 14, 1835 and at age four moved to Hamburg, New York with his parents. A farmer in Evans, he was 27 when he enlisted. A member of Co. K he was wounded in action, May 21, 1863 at Plain Store, LA, and mustered out with regiment on June 8, 1865. Following the war Ames worked as a carpenter and millwright in Angola, NY. In April 1868 Ames and his family moved to Somonauk, IL, where he found employment as a farm laborer and carpenter. In 1876 Frank Griffith moved to the nearby town of Sandwich. They were both charter members of the Sandwich G.A.R., and were buried not far from one another in the Oak Ridge Cemetery in Somonauk. In June 1892 Ames went before the Notary Public to verify Griffith's military service for a pension claim. *Registers*, 367; Henry F. Kett, *The Voters and Tax-Payers of DeKalb County, Illinois* (Chicago: H.K. Kett & Co., 1876), 194;

is a jolly good fellow and such times as we have would make a deacon smile. he has gone out chopping wood to day. George sends his best wishes and hopes to make your acquaintence. he is a good singer and I think you would like him. I have written to John and Eva, and if they don't answer that they will catch it next time. hoping this will find you well, I remain your Devoted,

    Frank

(on back of this letter)
To my little Nettie,

    Good morning Nettie, I am going to write you a little letter on this side of this paper. then you think that Pa would give about four dollars for you. I would give that to kiss you once. I sent you and the ba pictures. do you like them? Just tell me what you think of them. can you sing any yet? you must get ma to learn you some little song so that you can sing to me when I get home. learn to read and then you can read me such pretty stories, and I can get you such nice books. be a good little girll. love ma and the ba and pa. and when I come home we will have such nice times.

    Good bye, and here is a kiss from your
        Father

No. 5 I forgot to number the three last letters. please excuse me for it.

Camp Emory Banks, La
Jan 22, 1863 [1864]

My Dear wife,

    I set myself down to write you a few lines to night. I am well

National Archives. Pension Records, Griffith, Frank E., C-2509-042 (hereafter referred to as Pension); National Archives. Pension Records, Ames, Acil E., SC-181,242; National Archives. Military Records, Ames, Asahel E., Co. K. 116 N.Y. Inf.; "Taps for Aged Veteran," *Sandwich Free Press*, 30 November 1916; *Sandwich Free Press*, 25 November 1915; William S. Ames (great-great-grandson of A.E. Ames) e-mail to author, 22 October 1999; Bureau of the Census, DeKalb County, Sononauk Township, 1870 & 1880. See also Appendix B.

To my little Nettie

Good morning Nettie I am going to write you a little letter on this side of this paper then you think that Pa would give about five dollars for you I would give that to kiss you [once] I sent you and the [cashmere picture] do you like them just tell me what you think of them can you sing any yet you must get ma to learn you some little song so that you can sing to me when I get home learn to read and then you can read me such pretty stories and I can get you such nice books be a good little girl love mamma the ba and pa and when I come home we will have such nice times

Good bye and here is a kiss from your
Father

Letter written by Frank Griffith to his three and a half year-old daughter Nettie, on January 20, 1864. Griffith Papers, Regional History Center, Northern Illinois University.

and tough and hope this will find you the same.

Evening. [Saturday, Jan. 23]

Well, I am going to try and write some in this to night for I have been so busy to day that I have not had time to write any since I commenced it. I have been washing my clothes to day and after I got through with them I went into my tent and Ames washed my back and then I washed myself all over and so I feel real clean to night. The weather is most delightful to day just warm enough to be comfortable, but I think that it will freeze some to night. but then we do not have any such cold weather as they do up north. We have just got a story in camp that the rebs have got Jeff Davis under arrest for trying to run away from the Skedadeleracy. there did you ever hear that word before? I found it in a paper the other day and I think it is expressive. and if that is the case their concern must be about played out. do you hear any thing about it, or perhaps it is only a camp story.

I hear that G. Ferrin has bought out the Herald and that he is going to change the name and run it on his own hook.[8] I wish him all the success in the world. I think I shall send for the paper and perhaps write to him occasionally if I see any thing of interest. please send me a paper if you can.

We have been fixing up our camp and we have got a splendid place now, but perhaps we shall not stay long to enjoy it. I believe that I have never written any thing to you about the trees in this country. there are not any very fine looking forest trees here, but the Orange trees are splendid, and the magnolia is the most common shade trees here. the cypress looks at this time like a dry hemlock. then the cotton wood like o[u]r baswood and is about as soft. the trees are all covered with what they call southern moss. it grows on the limbs and looks like evergreens only it is a good deal lighter colored. it is the stuff that they get to stuff sofa cushions with and we

---

[8] See letter of November 6, 1863. Ferrin, who had formerly assisted Mr. Saxe editing the *Herald,* returned to Concord in January 1864 following his discharge from the army due to disability. He leased Mr. Saxe's office and started the *Chronicle,* "a seven column Republican sheet," which he published until March 1865. Ferrin then went to work as City Editor of the *Buffalo Express,* and later editor of the *Cattaraugus Republican. Concord,* 267; H. Perry Smith, ed., *History of the City of Buffalo and Erie County* (Syracuse, NY: D. Mason & Co., 1884), 638.

buy for hair matrasses. and when it is cured it makes a good bed, but it has to be cured something like we cure flax there. I wish that you could see an orange tree. about six weeks ago then the oranges were getting ripe and some were green and some just turning yellow. I tell you it is a splendid sight to see an orchard at that time of the year, but they are most all gathered now. there is plenty of them between Franklin and Brashear City, but they are not verry plenty[ful] above here. the leaves are green the year round. there are some of the most splendid places along the Bayou that I ever saw in my life, and before the war the owners must have been immensely rich. I have not seen many of the southern Ladies for they keep shy of the soldiers, but now and then we are blest with the sight of a beautiful little secesh and I tell you that some of them are handsome enough to make a poor fellow think of <u>home</u>.

I wish that you could be in camp for a week just long enough to see how we do things. for instance about this time, that is about Eight Oclock in the evening, the tattoo is being played in about a dozen regiments, now while I am writing. and such a racket of fife and drum, you can hear them in all directions. then in the morning, about sun rise, it is the same at reveille. it then [is] the police call, that is to clean up the streets. then the breakfast call, then the doctors call, then drill, then recall from drill, dinner, the drill in the afternoon, then dress parade, then retreat at sundown, then tattoo, then taps. there, if that is not musick enough, and every day it is the same. I wish you could hear it for a week. we are drummed up in the morning, and drummed to everything till we are drummed to bed and to sleep. but I am afraid that you will get tired of so much of our camp life so I will go out to roll call and then try and write something else.

I b[e]lieve that I have written to you about everything that I can think of and I do not know what to write next. dont you get tired of reading the same thing over so much? and then I write so often I dont know but that I had better stop writing for a month or so till I think of something new to write about, or wait till I get home and then you can tell me what to talk about. our life is so much the same every day that if I were to write the incidents of the day it would be of so little interest that it would not be worth while. George Carr is writing away for dear life and perhaps if I had his fertile brain I might think of something that would be worth writing. Ames is reading a novel and he is so interested that he would not hear it thunder unless it struck our chimney, but he says that he can hear the scratch of our pens. he sends his best wishes to you and says that if we should be so happy as to get home again he should be happy to make your acquaintance. he is a pretty good fellow and is some on <u>the talk</u>. We have got the name of being the civilist company in the regiment, but we can [make] some noise when we get loose.

Tomorrow is sunday and we are going to have an inspection in the morning. there is no sunday in the army.[9] Oh, how unlike the quiet sabaths that we have spent together at home. how often I have wished that I could have one sunday where I could be quiet and go to church like a civilized man and get away from all this noise and confusion and have a time for sober thought. I tell you my darling that this mode of life is not to my taste at all, and in no other cause but that of my country would I for a moment be a <u>soldier</u>. there is no money that would tempt me for I can tell you that in the army there is no influence that will make a <u>man</u>, but all the worst and basest pasions of the heart have full play. and it does not matter what we do so long as we do not get caught at it. and if it was not for the dear mother and sister and <u>dearer</u> Wife that I have left at home I do not know what I might not do. but the thoughts of you, and the thought of the confidence that you have in me, have been my shield so far. I and I would come home to [you] with a name that you would not blush to hear. how often I have thought of your love and devotion to me, unworthy as I am, and prayed that I might be more like you and more worthy of the love of you and my <u>mother</u>. Oh, I never half realized the how much I should miss her counsels and advice till I was deprived of them. but then I do not think that all her love has been thrown away for I often think of how much she expects of her soldier boy.

but I shall have to stop writing for it is time to go to bed. if you get tired of reading such long letters just tell me. write often and

---

[9] Steven Woodworth stated in his book *While God is Marching On*, that the reason soldiers so often mentioned the lack of Sunday observance was because they were so accustomed to keeping the Sabbath. Not only were church services rare, but extra activities such as dress parades and inspections were often held on Sundays when soldiers expected to have a day of rest without the usual work activities. Steven E. Woodworth, *While God is Marching On: The Religious World of the Civil War Soldier* (Lawrence: University Press of Kansas, 2001), 79-81.

tell me all you think just the same as you used to talk with me when I was at home. kiss the children for me. Give my love to mother, and reserve as much for yourself as you think will be sufficient. tell me all the news, and please dont wait till you get to church to write to me. Lon is well and that is all you care to know of him. Nick is the same old <u>grany</u> yet.

From your own,

Frank

(sideways on top of first page)

I will send this in a franked envelope for I want to use the stamps on other letters.

No 7

Camp Emory near Franklin, La

Jan 25th 1864

Dear Wife Mine,

I received your most wealcome letter to day and I am going to sit right down to night and answer it. it is the one that you were going to send by Sergt Weber.[10] he has not got here yet so you see that I got it quicker by mail than if you had not made that <u>aweful</u> mistake that you seem to feel so bad about. altho I cant see any thing to worry about in it and I do not see any thing to cause you so much trouble about, and do not think that you need keep awake nights on account of any unpleasant consequences that may arise from any such mistakes. but then I will make all suitable appologies to him when I see him.

I have got the blues to day so you will excuse me if I do not write a verry interesting letter tonight, though I cant tell what makes me have them. and with that exception I am quite well. The weather is verry fine at present and the mud is direct up in the road. We are to have a grand review of all the troops in the 19th army corps. I expect that we shall have a fine time and I wish that you could see it. it will be a splendid sight to see, fifteen or twenty thousand troops pass in review, and one that you will never witness in your life, though it will

---

[10] James "Birney" Weber had been home on leave, and married Amelia Warner.

be nothing new to me for I have seen the whole army at Baton Rouge last spring. I will tell you more about it tomorrow. but you know that I am not verry good at a discription. but I shall have to close for to night.

26[th]

Well, we have had a splendid review to day and a splendid day to have it on. I think that I never saw a nicer day in my life. it was just warm enough to be comfortable and every body was in fine spirits, and ev[e]rything passed off in fine style. we formed in line at ten Oclock and marched to the parade ground and formed in line by Brigades, and as we are the first Battalion, first Brigade, and first division we were in front and passed in review first. in passing in review we march at a Company front, that is in two ranks in a line (I could tell you a great deal better than I can write it) and march at a shoulder arms past the reviewing officer. all the artilery and cavalry not on duty were present. Brigadier Gen Emory reviwed the parade. we had a nice place, level ground, and indeed there is no other here. I wish you could see it.

There is some talk of our coming home in the spring on furlough as a regt to recruit by request of Col Love,[11] but I do not know how true it is. I hope so at least, dont you? I think that I will send you a plan of our camp so that you can see how we are situated and I will tell you who the officers are.[12] Col Love commands the Brigade; Lieut. Col [John] Higgins Commands the Regt; Maj [John Mappa] Sizer and Lieut J[ohn] C Nial acting adjt; Surgeon C[hauncey B.] Hutchins; assistant Sur. John Coventry; Hospital Steward C[harles F.A.] Nickel [Nichell]; first Lieut [George W.] Miller, Co. D. acting

---

[11] George M. Love, mustered in as major of 116th on September 4, 1862. Previously he had been Captain of Co. A, 44th N.Y. Infantry. Love was wounded in action at Port Hudson on May 27, 1863. He was commissioned a colonel the next day, May 28. He mustered out with the regiment in June 1865. Love was awarded the medal of honor for capture of the battle flag of the 2nd South Carolina at Cedar Creek, Virginia on October 19, 1864. *Registers*, 440; Frederick Phisterer, *New York in the War of the Rebellion 1861 to 1865*, 3rd Ed., (Albany: J.B.Lyon Company, 1912), Vol. 4, 3363. Hereafter referred to as Phisterer. See also Appendix C.

[12] For information on the long list of officers of the 116th which follow, see Appendix C. The men of Company K will be found in Appendix B.

Quartermaster; Quartermaster A[lexander] Goslin is acting Brigade Q
M; M[ichael] Mc Danner [Danner], Q M Sergeant; W[arren] K
Russel, Commissary Sergt; Lieut J[acob C.] Newton, Com Co A;
Capt [Wilson H.] Gray, Co B; Leut Geo N Brown, Co C; Leut J[ohn]
H Rowen, Co D; Leut [Henry A.C.] Swarts [Swartz], Co E; Leut
C[harles S.] Crary, Co F; Capt J[ames S.] McGowan, Co G; Leut
[John G.] Woenhardt [Woehnert], Co H; Leut [William J.] Morgan,
Co I; Capt W[arren T.] Ferris, Co K; and Geo H Shepherd, Co K. the
rest of the line officers are on detached service or at home on
furlough. first Leut O[rton] S Clark, is on Col Loves staff, Capt
[Charles F.] Wardsworth [Wadsworth],[13] is at Washington, both of Co
A. I ca[n]t tell you all of the Non Comisioned officers, but I will tell
you who they are in Co K: D[aniel] C Conger, on furlough, wounded
at Port Hudson, Orderly; C[harles] H Ballard, W[illiam] C Ewers,
A[lbert] D Prescott, and E[lijah] P Smith, sergts; V[alentine] Done,
H[enry W.] Eno, R[ichard] H Avery, H[orace A.] Paxon, wounded at
Port Hudson and on furlough, J[ob] B Sherman, D[avid] Wissinger,
A[ustin] Riefel, and H[arvey] M Crawford, Corporals. we have got
about forty men for duty. We have had sixteen die since we left
Buffalo,[14] and the rest are sick in the Hospitals or on Detached duty. I

---

[13] On June 16, 1863 "Captain Wadsworth left under orders to report to
Washington and subsequently resigned." Ayer, 54. The resignation took place
August 18, 1863, and Griffith is obviously unaware of his resignation. See also
Appendix C.

[14] The dead men were: Captain James Ayer, May 22, 1863, of disease; 2nd
Lieut. Elisha B. Cottier, August 21, 1863, of malaria; Corporal Frank M. Judson, of
wounds at Plain Store, May 23, 1863; Bela Crawford, October 27, 1863, of disease
at New Orleans; Charles Bremiller, of wounds received at Port Hudson, August 23,
1863 at Baton Rouge; Ariel Evans, January 11, 1863 of inflamation of the bowels at
Carrollton, La; James H. Fales, November 11, 1863 of disease at Evans, NY; Lyman
M. Frary, November 21, 1862 of typhoid fever at Fortress Monroe; Milton H. Hill,
of wounds from Port Hudson, June 1, 1863; George H. Hawks, July 10, 1863 of
disease at Baton Rouge; Charles E. Kingsley, July 26, 1863 of disease at Baton
Rouge; George N. Ostrom, December 16, 1863 of disease at New Iberia, La;
Theodore Slater, September 9, 1863 of disease at Evans, NY; John A. Thomason,
July 18, 1863 of disease at Baton Rouge; Wendell Tice, December 1, 1863, of
disease; Horatio G. Whittemore, December 30, 1863 of dropsy at Baton Rouge. See
Appendix B for more information on these men. Clark, 310-348; *Register*, 484;
Concord, 737; and Military Register, Company K, 116th Regiment, New York

b[e]lieve that I have never written to you any thing about our Co before and if it is not interesting you need not read it.

We are going to have a meeting to night and an address by one of the Christian Commissioners from Buffalo and I think that I will go. I went to church last Sunday night and heard a verry good address by the Chaplain of the 161st Regt NYSA. his subject was the responsibility of man to his God, and he handled it in good language though I do not agree with him in all of his views on the subject. there is quite an interest felt in religion in that regt.

Well, I have just come in from meeting and we had a very good address from the agent of the United States Christian Commission,[15] or rather an exalation. he spoke of what they were trying to do for us while we are away from home and the loved ones, and said that though we were so far away from home and friends and though we might feel that we were forsaken and alone, yet there were loving hearts and hands that were stretched out to us. and though we have offered ourselves a willing sacrifice on the altar of our country and homes, yet there were loving ones at home who were praying daily for us that we might be spared to them, and when this scene of war and dessolation was ended that we might return to them and enjoy the blessings of peace and a land of liberty. and while the Government was trying to clothe and feed us so that we might be prepared for the duties of the field, the Commission were trying to furnish us with Good books and paper and trying to feed and clothe our souls with the bread of life and prepare us for the fortunes and vicissitudes of war, and that we might be prepared to meet death in all its horrors. He looks like Elder Ball, but I do not know what his name

---

Volunteer Infantry. This item belongs to Esther Williams of Middleton, WI, and resembles a large colored poster and includes a small tintype of her great-grandfather, John Dibble, in one corner. It lists all the men, officers and staff of Company K, 116th, as well as the engagements they participated in. Hereafter referred to as Military Register.

[15] The U.S. Christian Commission, organized in November of 1861, "was a national agency in which evangelical Christians from various denominations across the North could unify and coordinate their efforts to minister to the Union soldiers in an orderly, methodical way." Woodworth, 167. Griffith provides a good description of the mission of this organization. See also Griffith's letter dated February 17, 1865 for an example of the stationary provided to soldiers.

is, but he is smart and a good speaker.

I wish that we could have a meeting here every Sunday, it [would] seem more like civilization. but we do not have any Sunday here. all is bustle and hurry though we do not have any drill on that day, yet there is a guard mounting and inspection and dress parade so that it takes up most all of the time. and then one hears nothing but cursing and swearing from morning till night. no good examples and less precpts. I can tell you, my dear, that the army is no good place for a man to cultivate either virtue or religion. and in no other cause would I for one moment be a soldier. but I have never been sorry that I have taken up armes in the defence of my country. and I never mean to have it said that I did not do my duty to her in this her hour of peril. so much as [I] love you and our dear children, I am willing to sacrifice all my comfort that you may enjoy a land of peace and liberty. and when this fearful struggle is over I do not mean to be ashamed to have the question asked me, "what have you done for your country, what did you do towards the accomplishment of this glorious peace?" I think that I could point them to the march, the nights on picket in the rain, the fever, and the sun, wind, and ra[i]n, mud and water, the skirmish, the bloody battles with all its attendant horrors. Oh yes, I can tell you of days and night of hardship, sickness, and danger such as these that have never

[*next page missing*]

No 8
Camp Emory near Franklin, La
Jan 30[th] 1864

Mien Leiber Frow,[16]

I feel pretty well to night and so I just thought that I would commence a letter to you, although I have written once before this week. but I have nothing else to do so I thought that I would talk to you a little before I went to my virtuous couch. Carr is writing as usual to his Hattie, Ames is reading a novel, and you can see what Griff is doing. I have just laid one down to commence this letter, so

---

[16] "Mein Lieber Frau" is German for "My Dear Wife."

you see that I care more for you than I do for a <u>love</u> story, unless it is one written by you. and they are about as interesting to <u>me</u> as any I have read in a long time, though I do not know how it will end. well I hope, and that pretty soon, for I am in a hurry to see the characters happily <u>married</u>.

We are having most splendid weather here now, just warm enough to be delightful. it rained yesterday, but it has been verry pleasant to day. I have been at work all day fixing up the camp, and making bunks, and cleaning up my musket, and washing my face, getting <u>showd</u>, went on dress parade, eat my supper, and commenced a letter to you. there, havent I been busy? I want you to send me your likeness again for the one that I have <u>carried</u> in my <u>pocket</u> <u>so</u> <u>long</u> that it has got spoiled. the glass is broke and the pictures are faded. get one in a case with a looking glass in one side if you can, for it would be handy and then I can see how <u>we</u> look side by side in mineature, if not in reality. and I will [be] verry much obliged to you. but I shall have to go out to roll call now for the tattoo is being played. After roll call.

There is going to be preaching tomorrow at the church in Franklin and all who feel disposed are invited to attend. I think that I shall go if we get through with our usual Sunday morning <u>inspection</u> in time, for it is so seldom that we have a chance to go to church that I do not know but I have forgot how to <u>act</u>, and that is about the last thing that I want to forget. And now I want to ask your advice about a certain matter that lays on my mind. There is a certain <u>Cock</u> that has got the very bad taste, and against all military rules and regulations and to the great annoyonce of all peaceable disposed soldiers, of making the night hiddeous with his nocturnal crowing. and he has pitched his tent next door to our verry quiet house. and in the small hours of the night when all should be sleeping the sleep of innocence, Leo the <u>Cock</u> doth crow, and such an unearthly crow. Well, now what I want to know is this, We, that is Carr, Ames and Griff have have got a little kettle and a nice fireplace, plenty of wood, and water, and some flour and hardtacks that would make a nice soup. do you think that if this same cock should find himself suddenly seized some dark night and before he knew what was the matter find his head in one place and his body made into a nice soup by some skillful hands, and thus made to help put down the rebellion, would it not be better than to have him waking up Uncle Sams camp and doing nothing for the

135

good of the country? I shall anxiously wait for your advice in this most important matter. and now I think of it I do not know but that it would be best to anticipate your advice before some body else gets so disgusted as we are and we lose the soup in waiting for you to tell us what to do in the matter. but I shall have to close for tonight for it is time for Taps.

Sunday, Jan 31st

Well, we have had our usual sunday morning Inspection and I have just taken my ration of bean soup and hard tack. and now on a full belly (excuse the word I ment stomach), I set myself down to talk with you, or rather finish this letter, so that I can read a story in the New York Weekly called the neglected warning.[17] I could not read verry well with this half finished letter before me and knowing that it would do your lonely self more good to read it than it would me to read a dozen stories. so I have taken your likeness and set down to talk with it. Carr is reading a story, Ames a novel, and I am looking at your dear picture and trying to write to the original. Say, you dont believe what George said about my not half loving you, do you? for if I did not I would not write to you twice to your once and rack my brain trying to think of something to write.

I did not go to church to day for we did not get through with inspection in time. I do not think that the Officers wanted us to go for they had the inspection an hour later than usual. I think on purpose. I do not want to complain, but I think that as a nation our regt has got the meanest set of Commissioned officers that ever cursed the army. I would like to tell you what the boys call some of them privately for we have to show a propper respect for our superiors. for instance, they honor the Adjutant with the appellation of Lord Christ Nial. but some of them partake of the brimstone order and so I refrain. but perhaps if your imagination is fertile enough you can guess what they are. I pity some of them. if we ever get to be equall I think that some of them will get a shanty built over their eye.

Birney has not got back yet, but they are looking for him every day. I would not like to have been to his wedding you know, oh no.

---

[17] "The Neglected Warning or Trials of a Public School Teacher" by Mrs. Mary Kyle Dallas, was a serial novel that ran for seventeen weeks in the *New York Weekly* beginning January 21, 1864.

but if I had been obliged from the present circumstances to attend that trying Ordeal I would have kept as still as a mouse, oh yes, oh Lord, yes (in a barn). and you can tell Amelia that she has lost half of the fun by not waiting till the war was out so that she could have had plenty of help. I think that I will give Birney a private lecture on the duty of husbands, for you know that I have had some experience in that line myself and I could give him some good advice, though it would be hard for him to put it in practice here.

I want you to write to me often and write just as you used to talk with me, for I read you letters and then I have to burn them up for I have no place to carry them, and then if I were to loose them somebody might find them. or if I left them in the tent after I have answered them they might get read by some one besides my self. so after I have answered them I burn them up. and I want to hear all about you. tell me all you think of, and what you do, just the same as if I was there. I would do the same, but there is so many to read my letters and I might write somethings that you would not like to have them read. and then it is so dull and lonesome here, I want something to stir and cheer me up. we should have confidence enough in each other to have no secrets from each other. and when I get home I can tell you fun enough to make you laugh for a month. but I shall have to close this for this time. Oh, I had forgot to tell you that there is some talk of our comeing home on a furlough in the spring to recruit, but I cant see it yet. I will write you more next time. Give my love to all, and kiss Ma and the children for me.

Frank

(*sideways on top of first page*)
PS dont forget about the likeness

No 9
Camp Emory
Feb 2nd 1864

Ever Remembered,
My Dear Wife,
I recd you most wealcome letter last night with the greatest pleasure. and if you know how much good it does do a poor fellow to get a letter from his wife you would not content yourself

with writing just one sheet of paper once a week. but then I do not know but it is a hint to <u>me</u> not to write such long letters ev[e]ry day or two. and then I do not know as I write any thing worth the postage, so I think that when this paper is gone I will follow your example for a while and take to reading <u>novels</u> for the want of something else to do. then paper is forty cts a quill, and envelopes 1 cent a piece, postage 3, so that ev[e]ry letter costs about six cts, and I do not believe that any thing that I can write <u>is</u> <u>worth</u> <u>the</u> <u>money</u>. if you think different please let me know and I will keep on writing.

I am well as usual at present. my side troubles me some lately. it acts queer, then will come a sore spot on my ribs about half way from my arm down, and that will be so sore that I cant bear to touch it for a few days, and then there will [be] a bunch on my side where it used to swell when I was at home, only a great deal larger, and then it will get well again for two or three months. I do not know what makes it, but I am not worried about it any for it does not hurt me much and is not lame.[18] I was verry sorry to hear that Mr Treat is dead. it must be verry lonesome there now. I suppose that Fay will live there now.[19] but there goes that everlasting Tattoo and I shall have to turn out to roll call. goodnight.

Wednesday, Feb 3, Evening

Well my dear, I find myself trying to finish this letter to night for I have had no time to write to day. I am at work at the Brigade Headquarters again, though I do not know how long I shall stay there this time. we are going to have soft bread again, and I have been fixing up the bakery and laying floor in the Cols tent. it will seem more like living again if we can have good bread again, but then butter is sixty cts a pound now so we shall have to eat it dry. The

---

[18] Bruce Kenamore, M.D. of Wilmette, Illinois is an internist, and formerly specialized in infectious diseases. He believes that Frank suffered from amoebic liver abscess. In future letters Frank will mention other symptoms such as chills, fever, and also jaundice, and the fact that quinine made him feel better. Letter dated March 6, 2000, from Kenamore to the author. Hepatitis, an inflamation of the liver, generally characterized by jaundice, liver enlargement, fever and malaise, is another possibility. Jerger, 61.

[19] John Treat, father-in-law of Frank's sister Martha, died January 10, 1864 on his farm at Waterville, not far from the Griffith homestead. It is not known if Martha and Fayette moved back to the Treat farm. *Concord*, 500.

weather is verry fine now, just cool enough to be nice. the boys go out and play ball ev[e]ry day.[20] it is cool tonight and I think that we shall have a frost, but we have got such a nice little fire in our tent that it is very comfortable. I do not think that you did wrong to let your folks have the team. but I do not like to have you let them go much. I suppose that Father thinks that if he takes care of them that he should have the controll of them and it is no more than right. I told him when I come away that I wanted him to take care of them just as if they were his and that I did not want ev[e]rybody to have them, but that you were to have them when it is necessary, and if any body wants them just refer them to him. I do not think that he will hurt them, but you know that they are high [*illegible word*] and that a hired horse has to earn his money. I had rather they would be sold than to have them hired out to ev[e]rybody.

about enlisting again. I do not think that you understand arithmetic well enough to enumerate the sum that would be any temptation to me to enlist for three years longer. I could give you my reasons if I thought best, but there is no use for me to tell you for you have enough to worry about now. but I do think that if a man has served his country faithfully for three years he has done his duty. and when they have <u>all</u> gone to war for three years, then I am ready to go again and not till then. no, I love my wife and children too well to sacrifice their comfort for the sake of others.

Well, about that chewing tobacco. I have got so that I like it pretty well, and as I am not where you can kiss me now why tobacco is the next best thing, so I will take a chew and then we will talk about it. I suppose that you will let me kiss you once just once when I get home if I do not have any in my mouth at the time, wont you? and then perhaps I will want you to kiss me so bad that I shall leave it off entirely. and then when I want a chew you can kiss me, and perhaps that will do as well. I will try it for a while and see how it will work. but I have never been so well as I have since I commenced using it. the doctor told me that I had better chew for we would not be so apt to have the fever in this country. and I find that those who do not use it are sick the most. the water is verry poor and rain water is the best

---

[20] "Baseball....appears to have been the most popular of all competitive sports" among the Union Soldiers. Wiley, 170.

that we can get. ev[e]ry house has a cistern that will hold from one to two hundred barrels, and they use that in place of well or Bayou water.

I am verry sorry that you have broke my pipe for I thought a great deal of it, but I suppose that you did not think that it would brake so easy. and then it was through no carelessness of yours that it got broke, so you need not feel bad about it for I could forgive you if you had broke it all to smash. I do not know what you will do with those cold feet of your[s] unless you put a hot brick to them nights or leave them by the fire. I have put a brick to my feet two or three nights, but it made me luke cold and so I lift it off. oh dear, will the time ev[e]r come when I can take off my clothes and go to bed like a Christian? I have not had my pants off to sleep but twice in six months, and that was to wash them and they did not get dry in time. we have to keep ourselves in readiness to turn out in a minute all the time. and a part of the time we have had to sleep with our straps on and our gun where we could lay our hand on it at any time for we do not know when the rebs may take a notion to make us a v[i]sit and we want to be ready to pay them our compliments at any time.

Well, about this body guard of mine. they are not so numerous lately for I have given some of them there descriptive lists, their final statements, paid them off, and discharged them. but some of them have become so attached to me that they refuse to leave the service. I hope that they will get enough of the war before I come home, oh Lord yes, for I should hate to come home to you without a rag of clothes on. you know that I am naturaly a verry modest man, and I supposed that you were a modest woman too, and this Idea of comeing home sark naked after I have been gone so long is shocking to my weak nerves. please to reconsider that order and see if you cant let me wear a shirt or something, wont you please.

Yes, I got your letter about that note of Uncle Archies and I have written to him about it. I am very much obliged to him for his kindness, but I think that if I should happen to get rubed out that there will be enough left to pay all my debts and something more. I got all the stamps that you have sent me, but some poor soldier has seen them and borowed four or five of them on his own hook and forgot to bring them back. I don't know but he thought that they were his. they get such notions here sometimes.

I should like to see the children cut up sometime, I think that

Nettie could do something at it by this time. learn her to read if you can, and to sing, too. does Girtie get any better? I think that it is time that I had a letter from Dora by this time. but I said that I was not going to write such long letters any more, but I dont know when to stop. Avery[21] got one from his wife with 12 sheets in it. if I should got such a one from you I will bet that I would wag my tale once. Just try it once and see.

(*top of first page*)

but I shall have to close her[e] to night. give my love to all. and write me a good, long, <u>confidential</u> letter just as you would talk to me if I was there. and rest assured of the love of your own,

Frank

Camp Emory
Feb 4th [1864]

I did not finish my letter last night so I am going to write a few lines this morning. Nick got the letter that you sent him and you dont know how much good it seems to do the poor fellow to get a letter once more. he says that is the third one that he has got since he came away from home. he has written you an answer and if you can read it you will do better than I can. I will send it in this for I forgot to put it in the other and so I will send it in this. you can write to him again for I do not think that I shall be jealous. Carr says that <u>he</u> is going to write to you and tell you just what kind of a chap you have got for a <u>Husband</u>. I told him to do so and I expect that he will set me out in flying colors for he has got a good command of language and can write any thing that he has a mind to. you must not let him know that I have said one word to you about it, but you can write him an answer that will make him howl for I shall catch <u>Elie</u> when his wife writes to me for she is a regular blue <u>stocking</u>. now dont be afraid to write for he is one of the best fellows and it is all in <u>fun</u>.

There is some talk of our coming home on furlough in the

---

[21] Probably Edwin Avery, who was 24 when he enlisted at Evans, and a private in Co. K. Richard Avery was six years younger and had been promoted to corporal by this time. *Registers*, 369. See also Appendix B.

spring, but I dont know whether we shall or not, but the Col says that is [if] we cant have it now we shall have it on the end of our time, and that will amount to 120 days, so that we would be home four months before we can be mustered out of the service. I think that we shall stay here all winter for we are fixing up our camp verry nice and perhaps the war will be out by that time. I think that you had better, if you have got any thing to send me, to send it by post for it is doubtful whether Birney comes back here. you and John might send in a box if you think best. The mail has come. I wonder if I will get a letter this time. I have written to Sarah this week. Horatio has never written to me but twice since I have been here, but if they dont want to hear from me they need not write. You have never told me how <u>Mina</u> gets along and whether that was so about her. what has become of Orlando?[22] does he stay with Olden[23] yet or did he have to go to war?

but I shall have to close this for it is time to go to work. I am going to work for Col Love to day fixing up his tent. They are having Guard mounting now and the Band are playing <u>Home</u> <u>sweet</u> <u>Home</u> and it makes me think of my own home and the dear ones there. when will I ever see them again? you can just put these two letters together and then tell me if I have not written you a good long letter. dont forget <u>the</u> <u>likeness</u>, <u>will</u> <u>you</u>? Now please to write me a good long letter. I would fill this sheet out if I had time. I have got but one more sheet of paper here, but we are going to get our pay this week and then look out for some money and a good letter.

So good bye for this time, and acept the love of your,

Frank

_____

Camp Emory, Franklin, La
Feb 7th 1864

_____

[22] Probably Orlando Wheelock, who was about age 26 at this time. The Wheelock family lived near the Griffith's in East Concord. In the 1860 Census the Wheelock's are dwelling 180, family number 174, and the Griffith's are dwelling 181, family 175. 1860 ~~Federal~~ Census. Concord, Erie County, New York, June 22, 1860, by enumerator Thos. W. Fowler, 322. Reel #751, Buffalo & Erie County Public Library, Buffalo, New York.

[23] Possibly Enos Olden, schoolteacher in Concord. *Concord*, 234.

Ever Remembered,

I recd your most welcome letter yesterday of Jan 17th and now I set myself down to write you a few lines. I am glad to hear that you are well and that Girtie is better. I am better than I was when I last wrote to you, my side is better now. it has not been verry bad this time and perhaps it will not trouble me again in three or four months. we have been fixing our tent to day and it is real nice now, high enough so that we can stand up in it in the center. and I have made me a bunk and am going to christen it to night, and if I dream any thing I will tell you what it was. the weather is verry fine to day, just cool enough to be nice. We are going out foraging tomorrow with two days rations in our haversacks. I do not know where we are going, nor what we are going after, but I think if there is any <u>chickens</u> they may get <u>transfered</u>. I will tell you when I get back. but I shall have to close for to night for it is after Taps and we are not allowed any light after that.

Monday 9th [8th].

It does seem so strange that after all the good advice and all the fearful examples that the <u>poultry</u> of this country has had that they should still adhere to the foolish and wicked notion that the <u>Conthieveracy</u> is an institution and is destined to be a success. Well, we went out foraging yesterday and we went about twenty miles into the country after corn and cotton.[24] there was 135 wagons in the train and four hundred men. we saw a few <u>rebs,</u> but they run as if the <u>old boy</u> was after [them] when they saw us. all went well till we came to a plantation where we were going to load up and there we found about 200 chickens, ducks, turkeys, and geese and they imitated the example of the rebs by trying their legs. but we made a charge on them and the result was a complete victory on our side. and the consequences are <u>first</u> <u>the first thing they knew they did not know anything</u>. and second, that after we, that is Ames, Carr, and Griff had a chicken soup

---

[24] John D. Winters states that "The desire for cotton played no small part in Banks's decision [to proceed with the Red River campaign]. He learned that tens of thousands of bales of cotton were stored in western Louisiana and that for a price he could pick up this cotton and ship it safely to New Orleans. If he helped to relieve the cotton famine in New England, influential textile-mill owners would be more ready to support him politically [in a run for the Republican nomination for president in 1864]." Winters, 325-326.

for supper last night about midnight, for we did not get back till nine Oclock last night. and for supper we have just had a <u>pot pie,</u> homemade of course, but it was good. and you will allow that I am a judge of such chicken fixings. we got some eggs and honey and sweet potatoes and some of the boys <u>mustered in</u> some <u>pork</u> so that we shall live pretty high for a few days, <u>Oh yes.</u>

I had almost forgot to tell you that I saw <u>one</u> of the <u>prettyest girls</u> that I ever saw in my life out there. I did not have time to talk to her much but I told her that she was handsome enough to be a <u>soldiers wife.</u> she <u>smiled</u> and said - well, I guess that I will not tell you what she did say for I did not get <u>rich</u> at it, and besides it might make a hardness, you know that would not be pleasant. but she was pretty, <u>yes, oh Lord yes.</u> If all the southern ladies are like her they could make the southern Chivalry do most any thing. now dont be jealous now will you, for if you are I shall not tell you anything more of the girls down here.

I got a letter from you dated Jan 29th at Evans, and one from Horatio. but I shall have to answer both of your letters on this sheet for it is all that I have got to night, and then it is as large as two of your letters. I do sincerely hope that your folks will have <u>fun</u> living at Horatios for as you say it is time that they had a home to go to. but then that is the last place in the world that I should go for a quiet, <u>peaceful, happy</u> home. but I wish them all the happiness in the world, and that they may not loose the rest of their goods, if your father should be drafted and did not have the <u>rhuematis</u> so that he could not go to war.

I b[e]lieve that the preacher was right when he said that they did not know how much good it done the soldiers to get a good long cheerful letter from home. and if their Husbands and brothers should come home the wreck of humanity they will be the ones that are to blame in a great measure. for when a man thinks that they have forgotten him at home, or have ceased to care for him, he loses his own self respect. and you can imagine what will because of him in the army then, Oh yes. write often to those who have gone from the good influence of home if you would save them from every thing that is bad. but then I do want you to write me any thing that happens to you or any thing that you think, for I do not want you to have any troubles that I cant share with you.

I suppose that you have had the coldest winter there that has been in a good while, while we have had but little weather that we needed our coats on. it has [been] just as pleasant as it can be for the last two weeks, Just like April weather there. I do not think it is possible for you to wish for the war to close more than I do so that I can be home again. and I think that it is altogether likely that it will be over before another winter.

I got verry well acquainted with H G Whittimore.[25] he was a pretty good fellow, but he was no soldier and never would be if he had lived a hundred years. he was a corporal, but was reduced to the ranks for inefficincy. he leaves a wife and two little children to mourn the loss of a father and a patriot.

Well, I suppose that Albert has got back to his regt by this time. why dont he write to me for I have written to him twice since I have had a letter from him. I am glad that we did not get into the army of the Potomac for we have easy times here comparatively, but it is hard enough any where. I have just got a letter from Carrie and Corydon. I wrote to her and give her some for getting married and having that baby when I was gone. and she has told me all about it. she said that I might name it now if I wanted to so bad. I will send you her letter if you will not let her see it. it is time that I had a letter from Mother. tell her that I am waiting with all the Patience in the world. If I ever do get home I shall go and see Carrie and then wont we have such a visit.

but it is getting late and I shall have to close this letter for to night. kiss the children for me and write me a good long letter. Carr and I have had a fuss to night about the way to spell a word, and he says that I had better ask you befor[e] I call him a fool much more. he said that the way to spell Receipt, that is a compound of medicine, is recipe, and I say receipt. now which is right?[26] Ames sayes that I may

---

[25] Horatio G. Whittemore died December 30, 1863. (Mentioned in footnote 14, letter dated January 25, 1864). He was 33 when he enlisted at North Collins. Due to illness he had been transferred to the Veteran Reserve Corps, November 14, 1863. He was 35 when he died of dropsy [edema, retention of water] at Baton Rouge, LA. *Register*, 496; Joyce S. Jewitt, comp., *Some Deaths in Erie County, N.Y. 1863* (Hamburg, NY: Joyce S. Jewitt, 1984), 8. See also Appendix B.

[26] According to Michael J. Varhola, receipt is a period term for recipe. Varhola, *Everyday Life During the Civil War*, 95.

tell you that he has his hands full to keep us two fellows from fighting and that if it was not for him we would be building <u>shanties</u> over each others eyes every day, a la Henan[27]. Well, it is a good thing to have one peace maker in the family, but I <u>reckon</u> that he has his hands full sometimes to keep the <u>shanty</u> from his own eyes. but as A Ward[28] says, that is sarcastical. There, Carr has got his fist doubled up to fight somebody, but he has subsided and gone to hugging Ames, a la accepted lovers.

     Frank

N. 12
Camp Emory, La
Feb 12th 1864

My Dear Wife,

     I do not know but you will think that I have <u>spread</u> myself on the commencements of this letter, but then I felt just so. and if you do not like the looks of those flourishes why just tear them off and give it to Girtie to play with, or take it to Mrs <u>Janses</u> with you some night for I <u>could</u> <u>not</u> <u>help</u> <u>it</u>. and besides I have answered all your letter and this is <u>extra</u>, so that if I do cut a flourish on it it will not be on the old <u>debt</u>.

     I have got an <u>alfired</u> cold and I feel some cross and tired to night, but not <u>sleepy</u>, and so I am going to write to you a little. I have written to Horatio and another to my <u>Cousin</u>. I dont think that I had better tell <u>you</u> who for you might be jealous and say that I am writing to all the girls. but the[n] I write to <u>one</u> <u>woman</u> on an average twice a week and I am determined to have much as one letter ev[e]ry time that we have a mail. but I think that I will just tell you the initials of her

---

[27] John C. Heenan was a famous heavyweight boxer who was born in Troy, NY. On April 17, 1860 , in what was billed the "Fight of the Century" Heenan fought Thomas Sayers in England. The fight went 41 rounds, and by the end Heenan's eyes were so badly swollen that he was unable to see. The fight was declared a draw and both men received championship belts.

[28] Possibly "the Honorable Arunah Ward." *Concord*, 227. Ward is mentioned again in a letter dated February 17, 1865.

name, they are Nettie Sandford.[29] I dont think you ev[e]r saw her, nor I either, but then there was a time once when I used to get some <u>nice</u> letters from her and I hope to get more.

I am just about sick to night, my side pains me a great deal lately and my head aches so to night that I dont know what I am doing half of the time, but that is the effect of my <u>cold</u> I think. Oh, if I could only be at home with you to night and have you bathe my poor head just as you used to, and then put your arms around my neck and sing me to sleep once more and have just one nights good sleep. it seems as if I could come back and stay another year contented. I do not know but that I am getting homesick, but I do want to see you again so bad that it seems of if I could not wait another year and a half before my time will be out. but then it is possible that we may be home in the spring on a furlough, but I do not have any hopes of it.

there is some talk of our going to New Orleans in a few days, but I do not know how true it is. We have got the best camp here that I ever saw any where and we are fixing it up nice. ev[e]ry Co are making some kind of an ornament at the and of their Co street.[30] I have been at work all the week making an arch in our street. there is the letter of our Co on the top and under that 116, and then in the arch I took some vines and made this sentence, "Our Country and Our Flag." it is all trimed with moss and is high enough for the Co to march through. I heard the Col say that it was the neatest thing he has seen yet. there, is not that complimentary? but then I dont feel verry

<hr>

[29] Frank's mother was Harriet Sanford. I was unable to discover the name of Nettie's father. Nettie lived in Brunswick, Rensselaer County, New York.

[30] Camp Emory was located on level ground with a few scattered trees, according to Orton Clark. He states it was the way the different companies of the 116th decorated the camp which attracted attention and visitors to the camp, and quotes from the record of the 114th N.Y.S.V.: "The camp of the One Hundred and Sixteen New York was a place of especial resort, being regarded as one of the greatest curiosities in the army. Situated in a very romantic spot, its inmates had, with a great amount of pains and pride, enhanced the natural beauty of the location. By the use of moss and evergreens, they constructed arbors, bowers and arches, resembling architecture of every kind. Their grounds were laid out with exquisite taste. Flower beds, miniature forts and monitors, rustic seats and shrubbery, every where met the delighted eye. In the evening, when the camp was lit up by the fires the effect was perfectly enchanting, resembling one of the fabled scenes of oriental magnificence." Clark, 139-141.

proud of it myself for I have had all the Co mad at me all the time that
I have been at work on it. We have got our Oven done so that we
have soft bread now. and if I only had some butter I could live, but
that is sixty cts per pound and I cant afford it.

does Lydia stay with you yet? if she does, I tell her that if she
could not stay away from Wheelocks She could not stay there, for
when once the tounge of slander is let loose on her, her character is
gone forever. and that in all her after life She can never regain what
she may loose in an hour. and I pray that you will do your whole duty
to her. I should like to have her stay with you, but not if she cant stay
away from there.

but I shall have to close this poor scrawl for to night. and as
the mail is going out in the morning I shall not be able to write any
more in it. but be assured that I shall write often. and if I am spared
to meet you again I pray that I may not forget the hand that has led me
through all my wanderings, nor the Eye that has watched over me and
mine. pray for your unworthy husband that he may be prepared for all
the vicissitudes of life. and if we are never permitted to meet here
again that we may meet wher[e] partings will be no more.

Please except this with all the love of your own,

Frank

here is a kiss for you three, my darlings

No 13
Camp Emory, La
Feb 14th 1864

My Dear Wife,

what do you think of that? well, if I had not plenty of ink I
should not be so lavish with it, and it only costs ten cts per bottle.
Well, I set down to tell you that we have had a grand review to day
before Col Love. the weather is verry fine and we had a nice time.
after the review we marched down to Franklin to show ourselves. we
performed all the evaluations in tip top style. you know that we are
noted for putting on style. we saw Gen Franklin and all the pretty
girls in the place, and some of them are pretty enough to make a
fellow cry or something else. I dont know what you women folks do
call it. and they seem to know that they are just as pretty as they can

No 13

Camp Emory La

Feb 14th 1864

My Dear Wife
                                        what do
you think of that well if I had not
plenty of ink I should not be so
lavish with it and it only costs ten
cts per bottle. Well is set down to tell
you that ive have had a grand review today
before Col Leove the weather is very fine and
we had a nice time after the review we
marched down to Franklin to show ourselves we performed all the evolutions in
tip top style you know that we are
noted for putting on style we saw Gen
Franklin and all the pretty girls in the
place and some of them are pretty enough
to make a fellow cry or something else I
dont know what you women folks do
call it and they seem to know that they are

Frank Griffith wrote this letter to his wife Thankful on February 14, 1864
from Camp Emory, Franklin, Louisiana. Griffith Papers, Regional History
Center, Northern Illinois University.

be and show themselves just to tantalise us. but I dou[b]t that I had better tell you any more about the Southern beauties for fear that you will be jealous, and that would be unpleasant now. but then you know that I am notorious for telling the truth, and I, so I have to write to you Just as I see things.

Well now, I have got a confession to make to you and I expect that you will give me fits when you get this letter. Ev[e]ry morning when I wake up there is a woman at the head of my bunk, and she looks down and smiles on me just as you used to in the times long ago. I dont know as you will like to hear of this, but it is a great comfort to me, and sometimes I think that she looks just like you. and there is a little one to[o] that sometimes comes too and looks on with big bright laughing eyes, like one that I left at home. now I expect that you will just give me Elie, but I could not sleep well nights till I had made a clean bosom, or breast, of it and told you all. and you know that we solemly promised not to have any secrets between us. now dont get crazy about it for I dont think that it will do any good. now I suppose that you will acuse me of making love to her and all that, but I tell you it is no such thing for when I talk love to her she says never a word and makes of[f] if she did not hear me. so you will hold her guiltles[s] of any wrong. well now, I suppose that you will want to know her name, but I think that I will wait a while and see how you feel about it. Just Please to write and tell me if I have done right.

It rains to day and I dont think there will be any drill so you may look for a good long letter this time. it is getting warmer fast here now and I dont think that we shall have any more cold weather now. has Birney started for the regt yet? I am sorry that you made me those shirts now that it is coming warm weather for I shall not get them till it will be so hot that I cant wear them. I thought when I wrote to you about them that I could get them by the time it was cold enough to need them, but then I have not suffered much for the want of them. I dont think that it is of any use for you to try to send me any thing from home for I can get along some way and then you can use the money for yourself. it is so far to send any thing that it is most spoiled before it gets here. we have not got our pay yet, and I dont think that we shall before the middle of March now, and then we will [get] four months of pay. It has stopped raining and I shall have to go and drill.

Feb 16th

Well, I have just got your most wealcome letter of Jan 31st. I am verry glad to hear that you are well. but I cant say that I like to have you stay there so long with the children and I <u>wonder</u> that you go there at all after they have done what they have.[31] and besides they have got the scarlet fever in Evans and the children are dieing off there. it seems so fatal, almost ev[e]ry one that has it dies, and yet you take the <u>little</u> <u>ones</u> there in the middle of it as though they were impervious to disease. and as though Horatio's folks had not lost both of their children by it. it seems like presumption almost, and then you know

[*next page missing*]

No 14
Camp Emory, La
Feb 19th /64

My Dear Wife,

I do not think that I owe you any letters, but I feel so lonesome to day that I dont know what else to do. and still I know that I ought not to write to you when I have the <u>blues</u> for I may write somethings that you ought not to know, or at least would make you feel unhappy. but I try to write cheerful letters, but if they do sometimes take their tone from the heart I pray that you will excuse me for it for I do not mean to write any thing that will give you pain.

we are having a <u>cold</u> <u>snap</u> now and I believe that I suffer more from the cold here than I ever did in the north. the wind seems so penetrating here that it chills one through in a short time. it snowed a little yesterday. The 30th Regt of Mass Volunteers started for home on furlough yesterday. They have but one year longer to stay, but they have all but about twenty re-enlisted and are going home to recruit and see their friends. We cant enlist till we have been in the service two years and that will be next September. I do not think that there

---

[31] Thankful apparently went to visit her sister Sarah and brother-in-law Horatio Hurd in Evans. Frank's letters have implied that Horatio has not been fair in handling a previous business deal between them.

are many here that will go for three years more. The Brigade turned out and escorted them down to the boat and we made quite a show. the boys looked as if they felt glad that they were going home, and I think that I know of a few more men that would be glad if they could be escorted home about this time. I am glad to hear that you feel so encouraged about the war, but I think that all you [will] see of me in less than Eighteen months will be on furlough or discharged for some of inability, or I shall have to <u>run</u> away. and in that case you may make up your mind not to see me till my time is out.

I think that there is an other expedition fitting out here and perhaps for Texas or the Red river country. and I think that we shall start about the first of April or sooner, and there is no knowing when we shall sta[r]t. I b[e]lieve that the rebs are determined to fight it out to the bitter end. and I believe that they have the ability and the means of carrying on the war for three or four years longer, although I do not have any fears for the result. but I am so tired of this everlasting drill, drill and <u>style</u>. it seems as if the officers racked their <u>brains, if they have got any</u>, to see how we will stand and to see what they can make us do. and I have got so sick of it that sometimes I wish that the war would close so that my <u>commission</u> would date back as far as theirs so that I could pitch into them and either give them an alfired thrashing, or get one myself. but then it is of no use for me to complain to you for it will do no good. and if I ever live to come home I can tell you all about it.

my head aches so to night that I can hardly see. I think that I must have taken more cold or else I am going to have the fever again. I felt so bad that I have got excused from dress parade to night and so I am going to try and write a few lines while the rest of the boys are out. but if I could see <u>you</u> I could talk so much faster than I can write.

We have had some pretty warm discussions in our <u>tent</u> lately on the subject of <u>religion</u>. Well, I suppose that you will think that is a rather <u>curious</u> subject for <u>Soldiers</u> to talk about, but then you know that we must do something and so we have got to talking about that. Carr is a <u>mongrel</u> between Spiritualism and universalism, and Ames is an old professor, but I think that soldering has been too much for him and he is somewhat backslidin, but he is honest. wel[l] Carr and I are opposed, and ames does not say much. but I say things that you do not suppose I ever thought of. I contend that a change of <u>heart</u> is necessary, and that we are to take the bible just as it reads, and that if we are ever saved it will be through the atonement. and if we believe their is a Heaven for the blessed and Redeemed, there is also a Hell of the lost and damed. that there is no intermediate state of existence between the grave and our final reward or punishments. but as the Savior said to the Thief on the cross, "This day [thou] shalt be with me in Paradice," so also shall we go to our place of eternity at death. but then my doctrine and practices are sadly at variance with each other. Oh, if I only had the true moral courage to live *(on top of first page)* up to the light of my concience. I do not know as I can tell you what Carr does believe or affects to for I do not know, nor do I think that he believes it himself. and perhaps you will think that this is of no consequence to you and perhaps will not thank me for writing it to you.

[*next page missing*]

———————

No 16
Camp Emory, Franklin, La
Feb 27th 1864

Dear Wife Mine,
    The Niggers[32]
    In my last letter I promised to tell you something about them and as I have got a few spare moments this morning before we go foraging I thought that I would commence a letter to you, but I do not know when I shall finish it. Well, the niggers, and here is where you will find the genuine pure and unadulterated black nigger, though there are some that have been galvanised by the process of amalgamation till they are of all shades from the blackest to the fair and beautiful Octaroon, but the real genuine simon pure nigger is a character of himself. I do not think that you have ever seen one for all of those that come North are of a higher order, and only those who have any feelings of manhood and are of a higher order of intelect that are smart enough to get away. They are of three classes. the first are

———————

[32] Although the term "nigger" is viewed as extremely offensive today, in Griffith's time the word was commonly used. The descriptions that follow not only show Griffith's feelings about those in slavery, but reflect common prejudices of that era.

the field hands and they are a great stout healthy looking animal, a cross between the man and the monkey, lazy and dirty. all they care for is to get rid of work and to get enough to eat and to sleep. they do not look as if they possessed the reason of a hors[e], and some of [them] look realy hedious.

the second class are of a higher order. they possess some intelect and are sharp and cunning. and it is this class that suffers the most for they are the most to be feared by their masters. and as a class they are the confoundest liars in the world, but this is not to be wondered at for they are brought up in deception and it comes natural to them. they are constantly under the eye of the overseer and the least departure from duty is visited with the <u>lash</u>.

the third class are the house servants, and they are petted and clothed and spoiled by their masters. they are of all shades from the blackest to the whitest and they are a saucy, independent and tyranical to their inferiors. and it is with this class that the sin of slavery exists. the most beautiful woman that I have seen in this state was a <u>slave</u>. and such are slaves in two ways, Slaves to work and slaves to the passions of their masters. for with this accursed institution the masters has unlimited control and he can do as he pleases with his <u>property</u>. but you knew all this before so perhaps you will not thank me for writing it to you. if I could see you I could tell you more than I can write for you know that I am a poor hand at a discription and there are some things that I cant write about [to] you, or at least perhaps you would not like to have me. but Slavery is done for in this country. and these scenes ar[e]to be witnessed no more, and I thank God for it. and if this [*interrupted by visit of Lt. Shepard*]

Lieut Shepherd[33] has been down to see me to night and we have had a good visit, ta[l]king our old times of our boyhood days. he is a capital fellow, but he got the blues to night and came down to have me cheer him up. when I get home and he gets him a wife we will go and make them a visit.

Well, we got [back] from our foraging expedition last night about midnight tired and hungry and dusty. we went about twenty

---

[33] George H. Shepard was 30 when he enlisted at Evans. He mustered in as a private in Company K, but by the time the war ended he had been promoted to captain of Company A. *Registers*, 471. See also Appendix B.

miles with about 200 waggons and got corn and hay for the teams. some of the boys got a few chickens, but they are about played out and ther[e] is nothing much to get now. I got about half a bushel of sweet potatoes and about twenty pounds of sugar. but we have to get things on the sly now for we are forbidden to forage on our own hook any more. The corn that we got belonged to a girl from Maine who is down here teaching School. she has got a sister here and that is the reason of her being here. I b[e]lieve that she took the corn in pay for some debt in stead of Confederate money and sells it to the government. that is we give her a receipt for it and the government will pay her when the war closes. I believe that she gets $1.00 per bushel for it. the boys went into the school house and got some books and letters that belonged to her. I think that I will send you one of them if I can get it. it is a good letter and good writing, dont you think so?

Well, I suppose that before you get this letter we shall be on the march again. I think we shall go onto the Red river this time, a march of about two hundred miles. I do not think that we shall have any fighting till we get to Opelausus,[34] and probably not till we get to Alexandria on the Red river. there is a large force of caval[r]y coming here, probably about eight thousand. and fresh troops are coming every day so that we shall have a large force. the 29 and 30th maine are here now. they are mostly raw recruits and they are green enough, regular yankees, and we have fun enough with them. we are in the 3rd Brigade now under the command of Col Lew Benedict,[35] and Col Love is coming back to the Regt and I am glad of it for he is the best man that we have got here. Gen Emory was out to see our dress parade to night and had a lot of the genrals with him. I think that he has some tall times here, and it must be a fine thing to be a Gen here.

my side aches so to night that I think that I shall have to stop

---

[34] Opelousas, Louisiana, was located northwest of Vermillionville. It served as temporary state capitol in late 1862 and early 1863. Winters, 165.

[35] Colonel Lewis Benedict was an attorney and politician in New York before the war. On February 19, 1864 the troops were reorganized and the 116th was transferred to the Third Brigade, First Division, under Colonel Benedict. However, the officers of the 116th did not like this change and in early March the 116th returned to the First Brigade. *Dictionary*, 58; Clark, 141.

writing and go to bed. it is so quiet here to night. Ames is on Picket, Carr has gone down to the Bakery to get us a swe[e]t cake. there don't that sound well for a soldier. and I am alone and trying to write to you to pass away the time till he gets back. Oh, we have got such a drive on Corporal Eno.[36] I believe that I will tell you if you wont be mad at me for writing it to you, but we do have much fun with him. he is a pretty smart fellow about
[*next page missing*]

No 17
Camp Emory Near Franklin, La
March 4th 1864

Dear Wife Mine,
I recd your verry wealcome letter of Feb 11th with the greatest pleasure, and was glad as I am always to hear from you and to hear that you are well. but I feel so bad about Father.[37] I am sure that I do not know what you will all do this summer. I have written to John and I told him that he had better take Gene this summer and let him come home and do the spring work. but I do not know whethe[r] he will think that he is called on to make any sacrifice in this war, or that he can spare him for he can not Get so much work out of Gene and consequently will not make so much money. I do not think that he has any claim on him, or not so much as father has at least, and if I was in fathers place I would have him now at any rate for John is able to hire some one to do his work and father is not.
you will please to excuse me if I do not write verry plain to night for I have been on Brigade drill this forenoon and on company drill this afternoon and I am tired to night. and my side aches so to night that I can hardly sit up, and my lips are all raw so that they bleed. I think that I shall have to go to the doctor in the morning if I dont feel better.

------

[36] Henry W. Eno was born in England, and was 18 at the time of his enlistment at Brandt. *Registers*, 401. See also Appendix B.

[37] Frank's father has cancer on his lip.

I got those papers that you sent me all right, and I thank you for them. I am very glad that you did not wait till Sunday and in church at that to answer my letter, and I shall not scold you if you do for I am so glad to get your dear letters at any time. and I am verry sorry that you thought that I must to scold you in what I said. I hope you will forgive me and I will promise not to do so any more. it does not seem as if your conscience need to trouble you so as to keep you awake nights for that.

Well, I suppose that you have seen that <u>wonderful</u> baby of Carries. perhaps the next edition will be larger. is she the same Sister Carrie that she used to be before she was married? I expect that the great Rail Road excitement will turn out just as it did before to be a humbug. I am sorry for Father and I do not know what advice to give him from here. I think that he had better get to Buffalo and see dr Hamilton before he goes to doctoring it.[38] if he does not get it cured it will kill him in the end, and it will be so awful that I can not bear to think of it. I know a woman in Collins that had one on her lip so and it eat her throat all out till she died. he can not doctor it too soon if there is any thing that can be done for it.

Well, I suppose that I shall have to address you after this as Mrs <u>President</u>[39]and be verry obsequious and take of[f] my hat and salute you when I want to say any thing to you. I suppose that you think it is all verry fine and a great honor to fill the highest office in the gift of your Country women. yes, it is a noble effort and it shows the goodness of your hearts. and there is many poor fellow[s] that will rise up an[d] call you blessed, men, who in the lonesome hospitals who have no one to care or sympathize with them in th[e]ir sickness and wounds, who will be cheered and comforted by the little comforts and delecasies that you can send them. and as you can not go into the field and fight, you can by your influence at home, cheer

---

[38] Dr. Frank H. Hamilton, was an original member of the medical faculty at the Buffalo School of Medicine, and a medical pioneer. He performed the first successful skin graft in 1854, was the first in the area to use ether as an anesthetic, and was the first to do plastic surgery in western New York, and the only one prior to the Civil War. Jane S. Woodward, *Men of Medicine in Erie County 1821-1971* (Buffalo, NY: County of Erie Medical Society, 1971), 27.

[39] Thankful was chosen president of the Waterville [Soldiers] Aid Society.

and comfort many dark and lonesome hours. yes, it is a noble work and does credit to your hearts.[40]

I do not think that I have se[n]t you a plan of the camp, please excuse me for my thoughtlessness and I will send you one in this if I can get time to make one. I think I will send you some poetry composed by W K Russel[41] of this regt, and he is fool enough to think that they are a great litterary effort. perhaps they are, but I cant see it in that light. I believe that he is engaged on another work to appear about the first of next September to be entitled "I faced the mule drum, the Yankees, and the Gurrellas." I suppose that it will be a great effort and will astonish the Natives. I think that I shall have to prevue a copy and send you if you want it.

after reading the Christmas story I do not believe that you would like to take a sleigh ride any more than I should. but then don't mention it to me again for I cant bear it. perhaps that I shall be ther[e] to read with you by another winter. Well now, if you don't want to have me hang around you when I do get home again I shall have to hunt up somebody else for I am bound to hang on to some _feminine_, so you will have to be careful how you lecture me. I am sorry that you did not send those shirts to me by mail in the first place, but I cant see that you are any to blame about them so you need not worry about them any more. and if you have not sent them I think that you had better keep them now till next fall and then send them so that I will get them about the first of October, for it will [be] so warm now that I

---

[40] The women at home did much to support the war effort. Typical were the women of Erie County, New York who organized the "Ladies' General Aid Society" which became a branch of the United States Sanitary Commission, and whose mission was to provide articles and services to the soldiers which the government could not. It is reported that between 1861 and 1865 that the women of Buffalo and the surrounding communities cut and sewed 30,060 shirts, knitted 9,380 pairs of sox, collected 86,495 hospital supply items, made 5,588 pounds of bandages, in addition to preparing and shipping great quantities of food. They also sponsored fairs which raised funds for the war effort and relief for soldiers families. Richard C. Brown, _Erie County and the Civil War_ (Buffalo, NY: Buffalo and Erie County Historical Society, 1973),15-16; "Niagra Frontier Women's Part in War - Work, Work, Work," _Buffalo Evening News_, 9 November 1963.

[41] Warren K. Russell was 42 when he enlisted, with his son Leroy, at Evans. A member of Company K, he was promoted to Regimental Commissary Sergeant October 1, 1863. _Registers_, 466. See also Appendix B.

shall not need them this summer. and now we are going to march again and there is no knowing when I would get them. I suppose that we have got a hard summer campaign before us, and how many of us will come out of it alive God only knows. I do not know where we are going yet, nor when we shall go, but perhaps the next letter that you get from me will be written on the march. and I mean to write to you ev[e]ry week and p[e]rhaps oftener. I will try and keep a journal of this march so that we can refer to it after I get home, and I will try and give you a history of all our doings and the sights that I see.

There is two regts of Maine men here and they have come in a bad time of the year for them. there is about 200 men sick in the 30th now and they have been here only two weeks yet, but they have got the measels so that will make some difference. Carr is writing to his wife, and Ames is on guard, and you can see what I am doing. and if I do not write you a verry good letter to night you will please excuse me for I have written it with a acheing head and a terrible pain in my side. Oh, if I could only be at home with you to night my darling and have you bathe my burning brow, it seems as I could forget my pain and go to sleep once mor[e] and sleep a good refreshing sleep. but as that cant be I shall have to lay down on my hard board and do the best that I can. but I do not mean to complain for I came knowing that I should have to endure hardships that I have never been used to at home. and if I live to see you again I shall not think that I have suffered any more than my share. but I shall have to close for to night for it is after Taps and we shall have to put out our light. Good night.

5th

Good morning Dear,

I have got time to write you just a few lines this morning. I feel some better than I did last night. we expected to get another mail this morning, but we have got news that the mail carrier died very suddenly in New Orleans so that we shall have to wait till another goes down and gets it. he is going this morning and I will send this by him. Give my love to all. kiss the children for me, and be assured of the undying love of your own,

Frank

Chapter 5

"Still in the land of the living"
Red River Campaign, LA, March - April 1864

The Red River Campaign began for the 116th New York Volunteer Infantry on March 15 at 8 a.m. when they began marching up the Opelousas Road from Franklin. After five days they were allowed a day of rest on Sunday, March 20. They continued north until they reached Alexandria, on the Red River, on the 25th, where they rested for two days. Frank takes the opportunity to write Thankful on the 26th. He described the expedition to that point from the diary he had been keeping, which was lost soon after.

On March 28 the troops start up the Natchitoches Road, and reach Natchitoches on April 2. From the 3rd through the 5th they enjoy a well deserved rest. The march resumes on April 6 and they reach Pleasant Hill on the 7th. On Friday, April 8 the 116th goes up to Mansfield. It was here that the 116th took part in the Battle of Sabine Cross Roads. The regiment lost two killed, nineteen wounded, and one missing. The next day was sunny and warm, a day that tired men would have preferred to enjoy.[1] Instead, they marched ten miles back to Pleasant Hill, where they fought in the Battle of Pleasant Hill. Two more men of the 116th were killed, and ten were wounded, including Frank Griffith.

At 2 a.m. on Sunday the 10th, the troops retreated 21 miles to Yellow Bayou. The following day they march 14 miles to Grand Ecore, where they remain for the next ten days. Frank writes from here on April 13, telling Thankful of the fighting he has seen, describing his minor wounds and the retreat to Grand Ecore. He writes again on the 19th as the 116th guards the pontoon bridge.

The 116th left Grand Ecore on April 22 at 4 a.m. and marched until 1 a.m. on the 23rd, stopping at the Cane River, a distance of 45 miles in 21 hours. They were in time to participate in the Battle of Cane River (Monet's Ferry), and had one man wounded in the fight. Griffith did not travel with them due to his wounds, instead he takes a boat down

---

[1] Curt Anders, *Disaster in Damp Sand: The Red River Expedition* (Indianapolis: Guild Press of Indiana, 1997), 66.

river to New Orleans. On April 24 the regiment heads back to Alexandria, reaching that city the following day. The 116th moved their camp closer to Alexandria on the 28th and remained there until May 13. Meanwhile, Frank Griffith arrived at New Orleans on April 30, taking up residence in the Marine Hospital.

Thankful writes two letters to Frank during this period which show her continued concern for Frank's health and welfare, not knowing at the time that Frank had been wounded. Her life is full of work and worry, not only for Frank, but also for her daughters and for Frank's parents.

This was General Banks second Red River expedition. The failure of this campaign resulted in his removal from command. Its purpose was to capture Shreveport, the Confederate capital of Louisiana, giving the Union forces a base to move into Texas. The campaign had been planned in Washington, and Lincoln and his advisors were aware that a successful campaign would also result in the acquisition of cotton which would benefit the North.[2] Water also played a part in the failure of the campaign. The Red River was extremely low which prevented Admiral Porter from bringing his ships to a location where they could help. In addition, at Pleasant Hill there was little water for the men to drink, much less the horses and mules.[3] With little chance of support arriving Banks' order to retreat seemed the most prudent thing to do at the time.

---

[2] Capers, *Occupied City*, 116.

[3] Brooksher, *War Along the Bayous*, 141.

Bivouac of the 116th at Alexandria, La
March 26th 1864

To the Hon, The President of the Soldiers Aid Society,
Mrs F E Griffith,

Dear Madam,
    I take my pen in hand to write you a few lines to let you know
that I am well, and hope these few lines will find you enjoying the
same great blessing. We arrived here last night safe and sound after a
tramp of 11 days through the best part of the state of La. and I can tell
you that we passed some nice places. Birney came here last night and
brought me two letters, one from you and one from mother, which
were most welcome for we have not had any mail in two weeks. we
had a rest to day but there was no letters for Griff and I could not see
the shirts that you sent me so I cant tell you how well they do fit me.
did you ever read the life of Solomon Northup or twelve years a
Slave?[1] if you have I have been through the place where he lived on
Bayou Beauf [Boeuf][2]. but I think that I will copy from my diary as I
agreed before we started, so I will commence here.
Tuesday, March 15th 1864. I left Camp Emory this morning at 6:50

---

[1] *Twelve Years a Slave, Narrative of Solomon Northup, a Citizen of New
York, Kidnapped in Washington City in 1841, and Rescued in 1853, from a Cotton
Plantation Near the Red River in Louisiana*, was first published in 1853. After
Northup returned to his family in Glen Falls, New York a local lawyer, David
Wilson, arranged to publish his story. It was "an immediate success; the first
printing of eight thousand copies was sold within a month." The narrative continued
to be printed through 1856, with over 30,000 copies sold. While it did not achieve
the popularity of Harriet Beecher Stowe's fictional *Uncle Tom's Cabin*, this
autobiographical tale was one of the most popular of it's genre. Solomon Northup,
Twelve Years A Slave, ed. by Sue Eakin and Joseph Logdon (Baton Rouge:
Louisiana State University Press, 1968), ix, xii-xv.

[2] "Bayou Beauf - pronounced Beff - is a stream of water 3 or 4 hundred
yards wide and about 12 feet deep.... The country is low and almost perfectly level
and the current is so slow as to be almost imperceptible," according to George A.
Remley of the 22nd Iowa Infantry. He goes on to say that mosquitoes, "crab fish,
gars and alligators are some of the luxuries of this country." Julie Holcomb, ed.,
*Southern Sons, Northern Soldiers: The Civil War Letters of the Remley Brothers,
22nd Iowa Infantry* (DeKalb: Northern Illinois University Press, 2004), 88.

and marched on the road to New Iberia 16 miles and Bivouaced for the night across the road. Weather clear and cold. there was a frost last night.

16th. Left Camp at 7 this morning and marched to camp Pratt on Lake Tasso.[3] very tired to night. had to fall out half a mile from camp, feet blistered and lame. there was one man died to day out of one of the Maine regt on the road. had some Chicken for supper that Ames bought, verry good. got a mail to night, one letter from home. went to bed early.

17. started at 6 this morning and went to Vermilion Bayou.[4] feet very sore. the boys are all verry tired and lame. nothing of any consequence happened to day.

18. Left camp at 5:30 this morning. got my knapsack carried on one of Co F waggons. stood the march good to day. went 9 miles beyond Carrion Crow Bayou and Bivouaced on the old battle ground.[5] we wer[e] all called out to night by a company of Cavalry firing off their guns, thought that it was the rebs, we fell in double quick time.

19th. Left camp at 5:30 this morning and marched through Opelausas. saw a lady with the stars and stripes, the first that I have seen since we left New Orleans. the boys all cheered her as we passed along. came to Little Washington and Bivouaced on the Bayou. Here is where the Rebs built their Gun boat Cotton [J.A. Cotton]. it is a town as large as Springville.

20. We have rested to day and some of the boys went out on a scout and got arrested, were let off cheap. the 13th army corps passed us to day. it rained all night and the roads are muddy.

---

[3] Griffith's diary entries closely match those of Clark's official history of the 116th. Clark states that they marched sixteen miles, Camp Pratt being four miles beyond New Iberia. It was a former confederate training camp, established in mid-1862 on Spanish Lake and named after Brigadier General John G. Pratt of the Louisiana Militia . Clark, 134 & 145; Roberts, *Encyclopedia of Historic Forts*, 349.

[4] Vermillion Bayou was reached about 2 p.m., after a march of fifteen miles. Clark, 145.

[5] This twenty-one mile march ended at Bayou Grand Coteau, where November 3, 1863, Green ambushed Burbridge's Union troops. Clark, 145. See letter dated November 6, 1863.

21st. marched 15 miles to day.[6] it rained some in the day. went on picket. rained all night and cold.

22. left at 6 this morning and came as far as Homesville on Bayou Beouf and camped for the night near the Bayou. cold and clear.

23. Today we passed the plantation of Edwin Epps, the scene of Solomon Northup life when he was a slave in La. passed the plantation of Gen Dick Taylor to day. it is a splendid place. Bivouaced on the Bayou near Cheneyville.

24. marched 16 miles to day and Bivouaced near the plantation of Lieut Gov Wells,[7] 13 miles from Alexandria on the red river.

25. Arrived at Alexandria to[day] at noon. it is quite a nice town of perhaps 2000 inhabitants. the Refugees are coming in from the swamps to get away from the rebs. Birney came to the Regt to night and brought me some letters from home. he is looking first rate.

26th. we are resting to day and getting ready to march again.[8] the boys are looking very well. went into the town saw the cannon that

[*next page missing*]

East Concord
April 10th 1864
Sunday evening

Beloved one,

    I am again seated to write to you, the dear object of my love. It rained all the forenoon so we did not go to church. and if it had been pleasant I should not have gone for Gertie was sick so that I had to hold her all the forenoon, but before night she was playing around about. well, nothing but worms I guess.

---

[6] They marched eighteen miles according to Clark, 146.

[7] Governor James Madison Wells' plantation was reached after a march of eighteen miles according to Clark, 146. Wells was a Union sympathizer. He was against secession and organized a "guerrilla campaign against Confederate authority in Louisiana." *Encyclopedia*, Vol. 4, 1998.

[8] Two days were spent resting at Alexandria, where the combined army of 13th, 16th, 17th and 19th Corps now numbered about 40,000 men. Clark, 148-149.

The evening is a most beautiful one. the clouds are nearly passed away, only a few broken fleecy ones remaining, and the young moon in all her beauty is shining mildly down upon the earth. oh, how little does it seem like this same night five years gone. Then you was here and we little dreamed of war and life of seperation. But God who knoweth all things from beginning to end has wisely hid the future from our eyes. Then we were happy in each others society. and are we not happy in each others love made stronger by absence and by the dear letters we each recieve from the other bearing words and thoughts of love and constancy to us from the one on earth we love the best. oh happy thought, oh blest assurance, that though apart we are not forgotten. is it not so dear one? But I have written my thoughts just as they presented themselves to me without regard to your feelings. if I have done wrong and wounded them do forgive me for when I am in such a lonely mood as I have been today it does me good to confide in some one, and who is there but you to whom I can go.

Hem has been here to night, has just gone home. How is your side, does it get any better? I feel so anxious about you that I can hardly rest of nights. be careful as you can for your own sake and mine. We have got two lambs, found them this morning. Our Nettie, you never saw her equal in your life, always ready for a scrape and to notice what is going on. to day she got a piece of cloth and cut it about square and said she was going to pick for the <u>shoulers</u> [soldiers], so she pulled the threads out and laid them down as she had seen us do and said she wanted me to put it with the lint.[9] Her Bounty lays and she looks for eggs and brings them in as much as she ever did. the other day she brought one and said she would save it for pa. when I told her you did not want it saved she wanted to know if pa

---

[9] Women who belonged to various Soldiers' Aid Societies often gathered lint which was sent to the hospitals for dressing wounds. The lint was obtained by scraping with a knife or picking apart old woven linen. The lint was usually applied to a wound wet, covered with cheesecloth or muslin and held in place with adhesive plaster. Sometimes it was used to pad around a splint or to wipe away puss. Lint was abandoned when it was discovered to increase the potential for infection, rather than aid in healing. Jeannie Attie, *Patriotic Toil: Northern Women and the American Civil War* (Ithica, NY: Cornell University Press, 1998), 35; Stewart Brooks, *Civil War Medicine* (Springfield, IL: Charles A. Thomas, 1966), 86; Adams, *Doctors in Blue*, 116-117, 125.

had <u>hens</u> to war. and she asks questions all the time from morning till night.

Has Birney got there? Have you got those socks yet? Do you chew that nasty weed yet, or have you given it up like a sensible man, for you know you cant help me if you chew tobacco. Do those hive trouble you much as ever? I will send those shirts soon as I get money so that I dare spare enough. I dont want to get out [of money] for fear the children should be sick. Keep up good courage for the time is passing as fast as it can, and we are not suffering for the great want of anything, only your own dear self. and oh, may God in mercy give us strength to outride the trials and sorrows of this life, and lay up treasures above, is the daily prayer of one who will ever love the sound of your name and who ever looks and longs for the time when we shall be again united.

your own,

Thank

(*upside down on top of this page*)

I shall have to get some more paper before I can write again, so please excuse this short letter [*letter was written on a sheet of paper that had a portion cut off*]

(*upside down on top of first page*)

oh, write often

Grand Encore [Ecore] on the Red Rv., La
April 13th 1864

My Dear Wife,

I am going to try and write you a few lines this morning though I do not know as you will be able to read them. I am still in the land of the <u>living</u>, though not verry well. I have had some fever for the last few days, but I am some better this morning and I think that I shall get a long now well enough.

Well, we have had a pretty rough time of it the last six days.[10] we have marched 102 miles and fought two big battles in that time,

---

[10] The Red River Campaign, in particular the Battle of Sabine Cross Roads on April 8 and the Battle of Pleasant Hill on April 9.

lived on half rations, and if we get two hours sleep in 24 we done well. well, in the first days fight the rebs had the field and gave the 13th army Corps fits, Captured 22 pieces of artilery and about half of their waggon train, perhaps 150 waggons, and the whole of their force was only saved by the 19th Corps coming up in time to cover their retreat.[11]

Well, we retreated that night to Pleasant Hill, sixteen miles, and the rebs followed us up and about 3 Oclock in the afternoon they pitched in for a fight. and I think that they got about all the fight that they wanted that time for we had the choice of the ground and were fighting on the defencive.[12] We lost in both days in killed wounded and prisoners and missing 5,000.[13] I do not know what the rebs loss is, but they must have lost heavy for we have some 4 or 5000

---

[11] This was Sabine Cross Roads, also called the Battle of Mansfield. "Nimb's [Ormand F. Nims] Sixth Mass. and the Chicago Mercantile Batteries, together with the supply train were captured." Clark, 155. "Banks lost a score of artillery pieces and 175 wagons." James G. Hollandsworth, Jr., *Pretense of Glory: The Life of General Nathaniel P. Banks* (Baton Rouge: Louisiana State University Press, 1998), 189.

[12] At Pleasant Hill the combined Union force was 18,000 versus a rebel force "nearly a third larger....which was flushed with the victory of the previous day." The 116th was on the extreme right of the line, "its right resting on a deep ravine," and in front of them a crude fortification of fence rails. Six times the rebels charged the position and were repulsed each time. Clark, 159-162.

[13] Griffith overestimates here. At the battle of Sabine Cross Roads Winters stated the Union lost 115 killed, 648 wounded, and 1,423 captured, for total loss of 2,186, and at Pleasant Hill the Union lost 152 killed, 859 wounded and 495 captured for a total of 1,506 out of about 13,000 men for total Union losses of 3,692 for two days. Winters, *The Civil War in Louisiana*, 347, 355. Brooksher reported similar statistics with 113 killed, 581 wounded, and 1,541 captured at Sabine Crossroads for a total of 2,235 out of 12,000. At Pleasant Hill he lists 150 killed, 844 wounded, 375 captured for 1,369 of 12,000, giving a total of 3,604 for two days fighting. William Riley Brooksher, *War Along the Bayous: The 1864 Red River Campaign in Louisiana* (Washington: Brassey's, 1998), 105, 135. The losses of the 116th in the two battles was light, at Sabine Cross Roads two were killed, nineteen wounded and one missing; at Pleasant Hill two killed and ten wounded. Clark, 163.

prisoners, and the dead were pilled up three deep in some places.[14] out of a whole brigade of rebel cavalry that made a charge on us there was only one man seen to get back alive. the rest were either killed or wounded. the fight lasted till dark and we held the field all night, and the next morning we came back here for supplies. we are receiving reinforcements and supplies by the way of the river so that I think that we shall be ready to make another advance in a few days. Darling, I don't want you to ask me to describe a battle to you nor the field after the battle is over, it is too horrible to think of. I can hear the groans of the poor fellows when there could nothing be done for them, and I cant get it out of my mind.[15]

Well Dear, I suppose that you will want to know how I got through the fight, and I suppose that I shall have to tell you or some one else will and make it worse than it is. now you must not worry nor fret about me for it will do no good. the first fight I was not in at all. I had been sick for two days and that day the Dr put me in an ambulance to ride, and our Division stoped for dinner about six miles this side of the battle field. and when the Division moved on I was left there, so I got out of that fight. but about midnight we had orders to fall back and so I went back on foot. the regt overtook me in the morning [Saturday, April 9]. well, I was tired, but when the boys formed a line just out of the woods I fell in with them. I thought if there was to be a fight that day I was bound to see it.

---

[14] Griffith overestimated here, too. Winters reported a two day total of 2,500 killed, wounded and missing out of just over 12,000 men for the rebel forces. Winters, *The Civil War in Louisiana*, 347, 355. Brooksher's totals were 2,626 killed, wounded and captured out of 12,500 men. Brooksher, *War Along the Bayous*, 105, 135.

[15] The wounded men were left on the battlefield because Banks had sent the ambulances off with the retreating wagon train. Hollandsworth, *Pretense of Glory*, 193. The 114th fought near the 116th in both battles, and after Pleasant Hill it was recorded that "they saw sights and heard sounds that will always remain in their memories....The air was filled with groans, and shrieks, and delirious yells. Such touching appeals for pity; such earnest prayers...." Harris H. Beecher, *Record of the 114th Regiment, N.Y.S.V.: Where it Went, What it Saw, and What it Did* (Norwich, NY: J.F. Hubbard, 1866), 324. "A fresh battlefield was always a frightful and sickening place, but the one at Pleasant Hill seems to have impressed the soldiers as one of particular horror." Ludwell H. Johnson, *Red River Campaign: Politics and Cotton in the Civil War* (Kent, OH: Kent State University Press, 1993), 164.

well, we laid there an hour or two and then moved back about half a mile and formed another line and stayed there till the fight commenced. well, in the afternoon my fever came on again and I went to the Dr to get something to take. he said that he did not have anything that he could give me but told me to take my things and go to the rear, but I could not see it. then in a little while the shells began to come over where we were right smart, but they did not hurt any body. but I can tell you that it is not the pleasantest noise that you ever heard. we formed a line across the road and lay down behind the fence and thought that we were all right, but the darned rebs got a cross fire on us from the right, and I can tell you that they came like rain. there was but four of the boys hit, not so many as I should have thought there would have been, only one in our company besides myself, and he only slightly. I got hit in both legs, but they are only flesh wounds and not much at that. on my left leg the ball made a mark across the top and just above the knee about half an inch deep and struck my right in my thigh. but the ball was so near spent that it did not go in much and only made me some lame. but I think that I shall be all right in a few days. I came a great deal nearer getting killed getting off the field than I did in the fight. the shells were bursting all around me and over me and the bullets, well, I dont care to run that chance again. a piece of shell hit me on the calf of the leg and wounded my pants pretty bad, but not my leg. one ball went through under my arm and one through the cape of my over coat. but I think that I got off cheap enough for I am better now than forty dead men in a fight. I walked three miles the night that I was wounded and helped the doctor dress some of the wounded men. and the next day I limped off twenty two miles, but it made me some tired.[16] the next day I got a ride in an ammunition waggon that brought us here. I do not know what we shall do next, but I do not think that we shall stay here long.

---

[16] "A hard retreat it was. Through a bitingly cold night... The army pushed hard for twenty miles, then halted at Bayou Mayon in the afternoon of the tenth. They rested there overnight and at sunrise on the eleventh pushed on to Grand Ecore." Brooksher, *War Along the Bayous*, 144-145. "About noon on the 10th, we halted at Yellow Bayou, a small dirty stream, which refreshed us amazingly." Clark, 163.

The boys are all well. Lon is here and tough as ever. Nick is all right and the same old granny that he always was. Birney is here but his Co are Head Quarter guard for Gen Franklin, so they were not in the fight, and of course are all right. I have got two letters from you since I have had time to write to you, but I will try and write oftener now till we go on the march again. but if you do not hear from me verry often you must not worry for there is a thousand things that may happen so that I cant write. but you must think that ev[e]rything is all right till you hear to the contrary. I would not have told you any thing about my being wounded, but I know that you would hear of it some way and then would worry so I thought that I would write to you how it was so that you might know the truth of the business. I have not been to the Hospital and I do not think that but I shall yet. our Co is down to the river guarding the pontoon bridge and I am sitting on the river bank writing to you. but I shall have to close this for I have got lots of letters to answer, one from the donations Committee, and one from Cousin Nettie. I think that I will send it to you. please to write often, and keep up good courage for the end is coming. how is Father and is [he] able to do any thing? and does mother get any better? kiss the chldren for me, and accept this from you own,

   Frank

I sent you some money from Alexandria, have you got it yet? I would send you some more if I knew how long I should be getting well, but I do not like to be sick here and be out of money for we do not get any thing from the Soldiers aid Society here, and ev[e]ry thing that we have to buy is so high. and if I should send home for any thing I would not get it till my time was out, if it is as long coming as those shirts.

Bivouac of the 116th Regt
Grand Encore, La
Apr 19th 1864

Dear Wife,

   you will see by the date of this that we are still here, and I do not know how long we shall stay here. Our Co are detailed to guard the Pontoon Bridge across the river and we have pretty good times now, no picket and only have to go on guard four hours in a day. I do not know how long we may be here, perhaps all through the march. I am still with the Co., my legs are getting well fast as can be expected. I can go any where I please so you see that I got off cheap enough. the Dr said this morning that I would be well in two weeks and I think that I shall be before that time. my <u>side</u> is better now than it has been in two months. I think that I shall be all right soon. the boys are getting rested and are in good spirits. there is a rumor that we are going back to the mississippi river, but I do not believe it yet. but when they come to figure it all up I think that this expedition will prove to be a <u>failure</u>.[17] we have lost a good many men and about 200 waggons so that we had to fall back to the river for supplies.

the weather is very fine, but it is dusty. the sand blows all over ev[e]ry thing, gets into our eyes and ears and makes us look as if we had been thrashing. I got a letter from Carrie and Corydon, they are all well, and one from Sarah Spencer, and one from the donation <u>Com</u>, they were all well. but We're in a peck of trouble about that saw that I got down to Gowanda.[18] well, let him sweat. I have been just so myself and I know just how to pity him. Lon is well and tough. he is hustling [more] than he ever was at home. Nick is all right yet. there is no news of any consequence to write from here. and you must excuse me if I do not write very long letters at present, though I will try and write often. give my love to all the folks, and dont worry about me for I shall come out all right in the end. I have lost my diary so that I cant send you any more. the rebs got my

---

[17] Historians agree with Griffith. Johnson held that the retreat to Grand Ecore ordered by Banks turned the Battle of Pleasant Hill from a victory to a "strategic defeat." Ludwell Johnson, *Red River Campaign*, 165-166. According to Winters "The retreat from Pleasant Hill to Grand Ecore was a serious error on Banks's part....A drive against Taylor's demoralized forces after Pleasant Hill would have led him into Shreveport. Banks military ineptitude, [Frederick] Steele's case of the "slows" and his failure to co-operate with Banks, the falling river, the difficulty of sending supplies for great distances, [David Dixon] Porter's anxiety for the safety of his fleet, the imminent departure of Smith's troops - all of these things added to the final failure. Banks had little or no control over some of these factors, but he failed to do all that he could have done" and many held Banks responsible for the failure of the campaign. Winters, 378-379.

[18] The "we" is probably Horatio Hurd and Frank. Gowanda was a small village near Collins, in Erie County. French, *Gazetteer of the State of New York*, 289.

haversack and all my Grub and <u>Tobacco</u>, knife and plate and spoon, and all my kitchen gear, but I can skirmich me some more.

April 23

I thought that I would try and write a few lines this morning and put them in the mail when we get to Alexandria. I am going to ride down on the boat, but it is so crowded that there is hardly room to stir. my leg is doing nicely now, and I think that it will be quite well in a week so that [I] will be able to pitch into the rebs again if we have a chance. the flag of Truce boat went up the river yesterday to exchange prisoners and has not got back yet.

Did you know James Frost?[19] well, he got asleep when we were coming back from Pleasant Hill when we stoped to rest and got left, and the rebs Gobbled him up. we have not seen him since, but perhaps he will be exchanged to day. he belonged to our Co and is the only one missing. the rest of the boys are all right, but some of them had a pretty narrow escape. they are still Guarding the Pontoon Bridge and perhaps will through the Campaign. if they do we shall not see any more fight. I think that the army will fall back to Alexandria and perhaps to the Mississippi river. and when we come to figure up the results of this Campaign it will amount to a <u>Failure</u> as far as the object for which it was planed amounts to. but we have got any quantity of cotton, perhaps enough to pay us for coming up here. I believe that the reason that we do not go on to Srieveport [Shreveport, La.] is the river is so low that the Gun boats cant go up and we cant Get supplies. there is no prospect of any rise in the river at present so we are obliged to go back.

The Rebs say that we whiped them bad at Pleasant Hill and if we had followed them up the next day we could have captured the whole of Dick Taylors army. and that the last charge that they made on us was to cover their retreat. I think that the first days fight was the worst managed of any thing in the war, and if the 19th corps had not come up in time the rebs would have captured the whole of the 13th. they say that they fought the rebs all day by <u>detail</u>, that is one company at a time. the rebs say that they captured 2 waggon loads of

---

[19] James M. Frost was 19 when he enlisted at Evans in Co. K. No date is given for his return to the regiment, but he did muster out with the company in June 1865. *Registers*, 408. See also Appendix B.

paper dollars marked Gen Dudly[20] and one load of protection papers that Gen Banks had sent ahead to the rebs. I do not know how it is, but I for one am fast losing confidence in Gen Banks. I do not believe that the rebs can be conquered on this side of the river by kindness, and I wish that we had old Gen Butler[21] here. the rebs hate him and he hates them. they are afraid of him and he is not of them. I do not think that he is the man to charge on the enemy with his supply train or send a load of protection papers ahead of the army. the rebs say that Gen Banks is the best Commissary that they have got in the Confederacy and they would not take him prisoner if they could. all that we want is some man to lead us that we have confidense in and we are ready to go ahead. and I for one had rather have my leg shot off then to turn my back to them now and give up whiped.

but I shall have to close this poor scrawl for my head aches so that I can hardly see. and when we get to the Hospital I will write you often and a good long letter. I shall get rested and something to eat. I have had nothing but Hard Tack and coffee for the last three days and I am getting rather hungry. keep up good courage and we will hope for the best. I have stood it first rate for 18 months, and if we get a furlough at the end of our time we have only one year more to stay. Col Love says that if we cant get it now we will have it on the last end of our time.

(on top of first page)

There is a boat load of sick and wounded men and it makes me sick to look at the poor fellows with no one to take care of them. one man died last night and he is out on the bow of the boat, and ev[e]ry one stepping over him, and it is a wonder that any of them lives. but I think that we shall go to day and then we will get where we can be

---

[20] Colonel Nathan A.M. Dudley. See footnote in letter of April 5-11, 1863.

[21] General Benjamin Franklin Butler, had occupied New Orleans beginning May 1, 1862 as military governor, but was recalled December 16 of that year due to severe criticism. He became Governor of Massachusetts in 1883. *Dictionary*, 109. "By subduing its [New Orleans] defiant residents and taking other steps to improve the safety of Federal troops, he made possible the combat missions of his successor in 1863." Gerald M. Capers, *Occupied City: New Orleans under the Federals 1862-1865* ([Lexington]: University of Kentucky Press, 1965), 114.

taken care of. I am verry thankful that I can help my self. and we should thank God that I am as well off. write to me often any thing that you think of, and I will try and write you a more cheerful letter next time. and dont worry about me for I shall do well enough. kiss the children for me, and tell my little <u>Boy</u> that I shall be tickled most to pieces to see him when I get home.

      yours in love,
        Frank

East Concord
April 19th 1864

Beloved one,

      After the manner of women I seat myself to write to a man I love. now if you know who that is you are happy, or miserable as the case may prove to your own mind (dont look at these crooked marks). It is very pleasant to night and as I am going to the village tomorrow, <u>the</u> <u>Lord</u> <u>willing</u>, I thought I would write a word or two.

      Our folks start to morrow for Attica to see a man that cures cancers to see if there is any help for pa's, but I am afraid it is of no use for it is so large and begins to run. If it can be cured they will be gone some weeks. oh how I dread it for there will be no one but Gene here to stay with me and see to things & it will be so lonesome. when I think of it, it seems as though I could not live another week and you gone away. oh God, give me strength to bear all things with patience that I may not complain when others are so much less favored than I am. Dear Frank, if you pray, oh pray for me your unworthy wife.

      I am going to give you an account of one weeks work commencing with yesterday. in the morning I <u>dressed</u> myself and babies, put the breakfast cooking, eat, put the water over to wash, then offer prayer, went to working, got that out and mopped the kitchen floor, Hetched three lbs & quarter of flax, got supper, washed the dishes, milked the cows, helped dig up some currant bushes, sewed in the evening, and went to bed. so much for so much. This morning got the breakfast, mopped the floor, baked some indian bread, spun a skein or two, and this evening have ironed. oh, I got supper, and done up the work for mother was gone, and milked the cows, too. The weather is very pleasant, only a little to cold, there is frost every night.

Thankful Griffith wrote this letter to her husband Frank from East Concord, New York on April 19, 1864. Griffith Papers, Regional History Center, Northern Illinois University.

I have just got four papers from the Aid society at Buffalo to night. have not read them.

Well, I think I will close for to night and eh so, more in the morning. good night dear one, may angels guide and keep you is the prayer of your own,

Thank

Morning.[April 20th]

it is cloudy this morning and looks like rain, but I am going to Springville because I cant go often. our folks are gone and we need some oil and candles, and I am going to get this bill changed and let them have some money. you know you never paid grandpa for the oats you had of him so we owe him eight dollars and the interest on it. and I am going to pay him part or part as I can as so to not be dunned for it. Gene has gone to harness the horses and I have got to comb my hair and dress so I will have to cut short. oh dear, Gertie and Nettie do plague me so that I cant half write. Write often as you can and keep on writing a diary. do not forget your own wife amid all the bustle of marching. and ever know that you have the I ove and prayers of your unworthy,

Thank

New Orleans, La
May 1st 1864

My Dear Wife,

perhaps you will think that I have been a long time answering your kind letters but my excuse is that I have had no chance to send a letter and no chance to write one either since I wrote last. but now I hope to have more time to write. I am in the Marine Hospital.[22] We got here last night and had a good wash and got on clean clothes and I

---

[22] The Marine Hospital was located just west of the city of New Orleans, occupying land bounded by South Broad on the east, Common on the north, South White on the west, and Cravier on the south, or front side of the building. E. Robinson and R.H. Pidgeon, comp., *Atlas of the City of New Orleans, Louisiana* (New York: E. Robinson, 1883), plate 5. See Griffith's letter of May 8, 1864 for a good description of this building.

feel like a new man. My leg has got most well and is so that I can walk around <u>right</u> <u>smart</u>. and I think that I shall be all right and ready for the rebs to <u>pop</u> <u>away</u> at again in a week, that is if I get ov[e]r the Fever and ague in that time. I will bet that you would laugh to see me shake it down ev[e]ry other day. I can tell you that it is fun, and then the nice little fever that comes after. I can tell you that it is nice. But then I shall get ov[e]r that soon now.

Ev[e]ry thing is so nice and clean here. and then I have got such a nice bed to sleep on. I tell you that last night was the first time that I have undressed and went to bed in a year and a half, and it <u>felt</u> <u>so</u> <u>good</u> that I could not sleep but had to stay awake to enjoy it. I shall get rested now and get fat again.

We were a week coming down from Grand Ecore to New Orleans. and there was where we saw hard times. we were fired into twice on the Red River by the Rebs, but there was no one hurt. there is no news to write only what I wrote you from Grand Ecore. the Army have all fallen back to Alexandria and perhaps will come back to New Orleans, and perhaps go on to Srievport [Shreveport]. I do not know what they will do, but I had rather be shot again than to <u>Give</u> <u>up</u>. so The Regt had another fight at Kane [Cane] River when they were comeing down to Alexandria, but there was only one man hurt and that was in our Co. he had his arm shot off and died after it for the want of care I suppose.[23] there is more die of that than any thing else here. There was more than half of the wounded men left on the field at Mansfield and pleasant hill and they fell into the hands of the rebs. it seems as there might have been better management, but I do not know but it is a military necessity to treat brave men in that way, but I cant see it.

I wish that I could be at home to day and have a good visit. there are so many things that I want to say to you and ask you about, and I cant write for my head aches and I am tired. if you could only

---

[23] The injured man was William Tromler who was 25 when he enlisted at Evans. A private in Company K, he was wounded in action on April 23, 1864. Griffith was wrong in his prediction as Tromler lived and was discharged for disability May 17, 1865 at Willet's Point, New York. *Registers*, 486; Clark, 348. The 116th performed well at Cane River. On General Emory's urging they were the first regiment to cross the river and occupy the position formerly held by the rebels. Clark, 171-172; Brooksher, *War Along the Bayous*, 181.

just comb my hair once just you used to, it seems as though it would do so much good. but as it cant be at present we shall have to live on the hope of the good time comeing. but you know that the saying is that Hope defered maketh the heart sick. but I do not think that I am heart sick nor body sick much for that matter. if you can send me some stamps, but then I can get them here now.

I do not think of any thing more that I can write to day, but when I get settled you can look out for some old <u>setters</u> for I shall get my <u>Ideas</u> together and can write. but you can write to me and tell me all the news and all that you think of. and above all dont worry about me for I have got a nice place here and ev[e]rything is nice and clean. and I am only just <u>comfortably</u> sick, dont have any duty to do, and nothing but just get well and enjoy myself. give my love to all the folks, and write often. kiss the <u>Babies</u> for me, and I shall have a kiss for yourself when I get home. Direct to the regt as before.

> Yours in love,
> Frank

Chapter 6

"Inmate of the Hospital"
The Marine Hospital, New Orleans, LA, May - August 1864

Due to injury and illness, Frank Griffith had been sent to the Marine Hospital in New Orleans, arriving the evening of April 30. Meanwhile, the 116th New York Volunteer Infantry was still up north working on the "Red River Dam," which eventually raised the water level sufficiently for Porter's Union fleet to move down river. They continued to skirmish with the rebels, seeing action at the Battle of Mansura Plains, on May 16. Following that they marched to the Mississippi River and camp at Morganza until July 2, when they board the *Colonel Cowles*. The 116th arrived in New Orleans on the 3rd, and the next day transfer to the ocean vessel *Mississippi*. On July 12th they reach Fortress Monroe, Virginia, where they receive orders to proceed to Washington, D.C. President Lincoln and Secretary Stanton are at the landing when the 116th arrives at 7 p.m. on the 13th. For the next several months the 116th serves with Major General Philip Sheridan's Army of the Shenandoah on reconnaissance in Maryland and up and down the Shenandoah Valley of Virginia. They participated in several battles including Opequon Creek on September 19 and Cedar Creek a month later where General Jubal Early's Confederate troops were defeated.

Griffith is apparently not only suffering from the pain in his side, but also from malaria. His bed in the Marine Hospital gives him a good view of the city. While he is in the hospital he receives a letter from Thankful's Uncle Gifford Peirce. Peirce wishes Frank improved health and God's blessings on the Union Armies. He also receives letters with similar sentiments from his mother and cousin Nettie. Now far from the 116th, he is without his friends and isn't able to receive much mail, which makes Frank miss Thankful even more.

Thankful, as president of the local Soldiers Aid Society, would like to visit Buffalo to see how their society operates. Frank encourages her to go if she will be going with someone, for he fears that she could end up in a dangerous part of the city if she isn't careful.

On June 20 Griffith is officially transferred from the 116th to the Veteran Reserve Corps, an assignment for soldiers not healthy enough to participate in combat duties. He is now quartered in the *Picayune Cotton Press* building. As a member of the V.R.C., Frank spends most of his time on guard duty, or helping watch over "our sick boys" in the hospital. He is also doing some barbering on the side, earning a little extra money for milk.

Near the end of August Thankful received a letter from her brother Albert. His unit, the 78th New York State Volunteer Infantry, was combined with the 102nd on July 2, 1864. They were part of General William Tecumseh Sherman's army that was besieging Atlanta. Albert sends money to Thankful to help support her and her family through the hard times, a very generous gesture. By the end of August Frank writes that his unit has orders to go to Washington, and he believes that he will finally get paid and be able to send money to Thankful.

Marine Hospital
New Orleans
May 8th 1864

My Darling,

I have written a letter to you to send by Mr McClure.[1] but as he is not going till the last of the week, and as I am lonesome here in this crowd with <u>nothing</u> <u>to</u> do, I thought I would write you a few lines though I have written four since I had one from you. I am getting along first rate now. my leg is most well, only a little stiff. but I think that I shall be ready to join the Regt next week if my side was only well. I should think that I was all right but that pains me almost constantly lately, but it is not swelled much yet. I spoke to the Doctor about it the other day and he said that he could do nothing for it only that I must be careful with it. but when I am on duty I have to do as much as any one, and on the march I must go as far as the rest and carry as much load. so you can see how well I can be careful of it. but then there is only 16 months more and I can stand it the rest of the time as well as I have the last year. and then you will let me rest and have something to eat besides Salt Horse and Hard Tack, and then I shall get well again. but the time seems so long here with none that I am acquainted with, and no letters from home, and nothing to do. and now the Red River is Blockaded so that no boats can go up to the army so I can not get my mail for all the letters have to go to the Regt and then are sent back here again. and as I have been here but a week there has been no time for letters to come.

The army was still at Alexandria the last that we heard, but they may make a move at anytime. but there are a number of the Gun boats above the rapids and as they are the best in the fleet they will have to wait till the river raises or they can build a dam and get them down.[2] they are the two Monitors that were built at St Louis, and the

---

[1] A shoemaker by trade, Julius A. McClure was 42 when he enlisted at Concord. He served as a private in Company F, and was discharged for disability on May 10, 1864 at New Orleans. *Registers*, 445; 1860 Federal Census, Concord, Erie County, New York. See also Appendix C.

[2] Lt. Colonel Joseph Bailey, an Army engineer on General Franklin's staff suggested constructing dams to back up the water to allow the gunboats to pass. On

Essex No 2, the Layfayette, and two others that I have forgotten, all iron Clad.[3] but then I think that the army is safe and that the rebs will soon get cleaned out down below so that there will be no trouble.

The <u>Marine Hospital</u> is about a mile and a half from the river, or the city, on the west side of it and is a large Iron Building, or rather three buildings, and is very pleasantly situated near the canal that goes from the river to lake Panchertrain [Pontchartrain] eight miles from the city. I think that I told you about going out on the <u>Shell road</u> to the lake when we were at Carolton [Carrollton]. it is verry still and quiet here. and although it is May the weather is cool so that one wants on a coat, and the nights are quite cold. there is about five hundred patients here now, but as I suppose that you have never been in a Hospital, although <u>President</u> of the Society, I shall have to tell you something about it. it is divided off into rooms and each room will hold from forty to one hundred beds. the beds are 6 ft long and 2 wide. each man has his bed and if he is able has to make his own bed and keep it clean, though he does not have to wash his clothes. each room is a <u>Ward</u> and they are lettered off commencing with A. our ward is M and is on the Second floor, and I think is the pleasantist in the Hospital. my bed is next to the door and I can look out all over the city, if there was <u>not</u> <u>so</u> <u>many</u> <u>houses</u>. each room has a ward master and as many nurses as we need. and they live on the good things that are furnished by the Aid Society and the Sanitary

---

May 5 the 116th New York Volunteer Infantry was sent to work with 3,000 men from other Maine and New York units and some from the 13th Army Corps on constructing wing dams at the rapids on the north bank near Pineville. Work on the Alexandria side was performed by two Negro regiments commanded by George D. Robinson, and 400 men from Dickey's colored infantry brigade. Trees were cut and stone quarried, and some men worked up to their necks in the river. After many days of intense labor, the dam proved effective, and fleet was able to pass through to the deeper water. Anders, *Disaster in Damp Sand*, 126; Clark, 174-175; Winters, *Civil War in Louisiana*, 369.

[3] The term "ironclad" did not appear in print until 1867. During the Civil War, Northern gunboats covered with armor plate to just below the waterline were often referred to as "monitors." Varhola, *Everyday Life During the Civil War*, 147. On May 9 the *Lexington, Neosho, Fort Hindman,* and *Osage* came through the dam. They were followed by the *Mound City, Chillicothe,* and the *Pittsburg* on the 11th, and the *Carondelet, Ozark, Louisville,* and two tugs on the 12th. Anders, *Disaster in Damp Sand*, 133-136; Clark, 175-177.

THE MARINE HOSPITAL, NEW ORLEANS.

The Marine Hospital, corner of Common and Broad Streets, New Orleans, Louisiana, where Frank Griffith was sent in May 1864 to recover following the Battle of Pleasant Hill. Original lithograph, 1873. Courtesy of The Historic New Orleans Collection, Accession No. 1974.25.3.342, The Williams Research Center.

Commission. and then if there is any thing left we get it. But then the Sanitary Commission is a good thing, and I say God bless them, for if it had not been for them we should half of us died coming down from Grand Ecore to New Orleans. they Gave us clean shirts and drawers and something to eat.

Sunday afternoon. [same day, May 8]

I have been to church this afternoon and now I am going to try and finish this poor scrawl to you. it is quite warm and looks like rain. We have had news from the red river. some of the boys have been down in the city and they say that our army are all surrounded, the river is Blockaded, and that the army will have to cut their way through, though I do not believe it all. the rebs have sunk one Transport, and two Gun Boats in the river, and the folks are getting somewhat <u>scared</u> here. but then I do not feel much frightened yet. All eyes are now turned to <u>Gen Grant</u>, and I think that the results of this years campaign all depends on his Success. if we are defeated in the move about to be made on Richmond the end is a long way off, but I do not think that the Goverment will give up the war if we should meet with a defeat there.[4] no, we can never give up this war till the <u>Flag</u> floats over ev[e]ry boat, of the soil of our <u>once</u> <u>Glorious</u> <u>Land</u>. and I am looking anxiously to the great battle soon to be fought in Virginia. The troops are fast losing confindence in Gen Banks as a General, though I think that he is a true Patriot.

There was about forty Sick men came to the Hospital to day, but none from our Regt that I know of. there were most of them from the 8th Vermont, none wounded that I know of. I b[e]lieve that I have written about every thing about here, and as I have not been down to the city yet I am about <u>played</u> <u>out</u> for any thing to write about. I am taking <u>Quinine</u> now for the chill fever, and I can tell you that it is nice stuff to take, bitter some <u>aint</u> <u>it</u>. one man died to day in our ward of the Chronic Diarhea. he has been sick a long time. it is a hard thing to cure in this climate. I do not know what Regt he belonged to but he was a fine looking fellow. There was one of Co F boys died here

---

[4] The Armies of Ulysses S. Grant and Robert E. Lee faced each other in the Battle of the Wilderness in Virginia, May 5 and 6, both sides suffering heavy losses. On the 7th Grant's army proceeded to Spotsylvania Court House, where fighting took place from May 8 to 19. *Almanac*, 492-505.

yesterday, a Tyre from Gowanda.[5] I do not know what was the matter with him.

It is allmost Supper time and so I shall have [to] close this. write often, and tell me all the news and any thing that you think that I care any thing about. don't stay with one sheet, but write me something funny. tell me all about your self, all that you think. I dream about you almost ev[e]ry night. and when my side gets so that I can sit down and write for half a day I shall write you some of the letters that we read of but seldom see. kiss the children for me, and when I get home I will kiss you if you will let me.

Applesauce Bread and Tea for supper, and I have just come back from eating it. I feel so much better to night that I think I shall tell the Dr in the morning that I want to get back to the Regt. it is so lonesome here without any mail. Do you want that I should try and get a Furlough for 60 days and come home? I should like to see you so much, but then I had rather stay now till my time is out for I would only just get home before I should have to come back again. and the Sorrow of parting would be just the Same as it was when I came away. no, I think that I had better Stay now and then when I do come our joy will not be clouded by the thought that we shall have to <u>part</u> so soon. So keep up good courage and be brave for my Sake. Give my love to Mother, and tell her I have not forgotten her, and that I have *(on top of first page)* written to her. write often, and accept the love of a heart all your own,

　　　　Frank
Direct to the Regt

Springville
May 16th 1864

Dear Nephew,

After a long delay I again take my pen to let you know that I have not forgotten you entirely. My health is good and has been, and I have no excuse for not writing sooner only the indisposition to begin.

---

[5] Hiram A. Tyrer was 18 when he enlisted at Collins. A private in Company F, he died of chronic diarrhea. *Registers*, 487; Clark, 334.

I indeed work hard every day and tired at night, so I put it off untill the next night, and then the next and so on. I am at work in the pump shop this spring making pumps for 50 cts. apiece, make about three in a day. I have made 83. I do not keep house at present but hire my board of Mrs. Stroup who hires my house for the summer. I think probably Geo. a[nd] Helen[6] will move here in the fall, if so I shall board with them if I stay here.

We are having very cheering news of late from Virginia. Grant is pressing Lee with almost continual success, our hopes are high, as we know God is just and our cause is just. we expect success in due time when we are sufficiently chastised for our national sins and humbly acknowledge our dependence on him.

I have not heard from you since I heard you was wounded. I have not seen Thankful in some weeks. I mean to go and see her soon. I know she must be anxious about you since the unfavorable news we received from your expedition. it is sad indeed to think of the amount of property, but more especially of the many precious lives sacrificed. but we hope the end will come and then it does seem we shall know how to prize liberty, peace and prosperity. We feel here but little yet the effects of war but taxes, and prices are getting pretty well up, brown sugar at least 20 cts loaf 28, molasses nearly 1.50 I dont know exactly, and other things about in proportion.

Spring is rather backward. we have had a good deal of cold rain until about a week past. it has been and still is quite warm, things are growing quite fast, plumb and cherry trees are just beginning to blossom. I guess there is little or no planting done as yet except in the garden. Our soldiers aid society are still trying do what they can, and now since the fighting in Virginia are making extra effort. there is to be a concert of vocal an[d] instrumental music at the Baptist church on Friday evening of this week for the purpose of raising funds for the society.

I guess I have not written much news and did not expect to when I begun, but I thought a few lines from some friend besides your wife might be acceptable. I hope to hear soon that you are again able to perform the severe duties to which your country has called you, and

---

[6] His daughter Helen Amanda Peirce and her husband George P. Kellog. See Appendix A.

that in so doing God will bless you and all our armies and give us final and complete victory and peace, and prosperity be again enjoyed throughout our whole land. For this let us labor and pray.

Yours with esteem,

Gifford Peirce[7]

Marine Hospital
May 16th [1864]

My Darling,

I have just time to write you a line this afternoon to send by McClure as he starts for home at five Oclock. you will see that I am still here and am like to stay for a spell as the River is blockaded so that I cant get to the Regt if I was ready. and then I have got the Ague and fever like fun. I think that you would laugh to see me shake it down ev[e]ry other day. if I had my discriptive list[8] I think that I would try and get a furlough and come home a few days, and perhaps I may come at any rate, but then you must not look for me till I come.

We are getting good news from the army of the Potomac, and I think that if Gen Grant is successfull it will end the war. and then you may look for me home sure. there is no communication with Gen Banks so I cant get any letters now. I have not had one in four weeks and it is getting aweful lonesome. you may Direct just one letter to the Marine Hospital if you can this month, but not after that for I do not think that I shall be here after that time. but I will write you often so that you may know how I get along. write me often so that I will have lots of letters when I get back to the Regt. write me all the news and ev[e]rything that you can think of. give my love to all the folks at home. If you Direct a letter here don't put the Regt on it for it would

---

[7] Gifford Peirce is Thankful's uncle, the brother of her mother Mary Peirce Myers.

[8] Griffith's military records contain a page which states, "Frank E. Griffith, Co. K, 116th Reg't N.Y. Infantry. Appears on Company Descriptive Book of the organization named above." I believe this is his "descriptive list." It lists his vital statistics and when he was sick or absent from the regiment. National Archives, Military Records, Griffith, Frank E., Co. K. 116 NY Inf.

have to go to the Regt and then come back here, and if you get this before the first of June you can send one here.

> Direct to US Marine
> Hospital Ward M
> New Orleans

I shall have to close this for I suppose that he is ready to go. accept this with all the love of your own,

> Frank

Marine Hospital
New Orleans, La
May 19th /64

My Dear Wife,

I do not know but you will get tired of my writing to you so often, but then I have nothing else to do. and if you do not want to read them you can just lay them by till I get into the field again and do not have a chance to write in two or three weeks, then get one and read it. you see that I am Still here yet, but I do not mean to stay any longer than I can help. I suppose that you will have seen McClure before you got this and he has told you all the news. but as I am tired of reading and lonesome I am going to write. I do not know but I shall have to lay this by and have a shake this afternoon for it is my day to have a shake down. the last one that I had was a tough one and I had to lay abed all the afternoon. but I have been taking lots of Quinine[9] and <u>Whiskey</u> and I hope that it will break it up, but it makes me so weak that I can hardly go up and down stairs. I am in hopes that I shall get well before it comes on hot weather. I have not heard a word from home in four weeks and it is getting awful lonesome here. I am afraid that I shall get homesick here if I have to stay all summer. You do not know how much I want to hear from you. it does not seem as though I had any patience left, but then I try to keep cool and not fret. my leg is almost well now and if I was only over this Fever I

---

[9] "Quinine was the "wonder" drug of the war and the most sought after pharmaceutical in both the North and South....its prime use....was in the treatment and prevention of malaria, commonly in combination with a shot or two of whisky." Brooks, *Civil War Medicine*, 65.

should post off for the Red river country on the double quick.

I wish that you could see the sight that I can see from the window where I am writing. the great Crescent City is spread out in all its glory. I can see the boats going up and down the river, the canal that goes to the lake, the Jackson and New Orleans Rail road, Carolton where we were in camp before we went to Baton Rouge, the city of Algiers, and the cars on the N.O. and Brashar City road, the Gr[e]at Shell road, the fashionable drive for the elite of the Crescent City, and back of here the Market gardens and the cotton and cane fields. the corn is up knee high here now. Oranges are as large as plums, and the figs will be ripe next month. I was going to give you a discription of the inside of the Hospital, but I do not think that would be best now so I will wait for that till I get home. This building was used by the Rebs for an Arsenal, and there is several cords of large shells for mortars piled up in front, but I do not think that they will ever have a chance to use them.

there is Glorious news from Gen Grant and Gen Banks. so the news is [Banks] has left Alexandria and has got his army and boats back to the Mississippi all safe. I b[e]lieve that the Rebs allow that Gen Banks is the best Commisary that the Confederacy have got and I begin to think so myself.

I want you to tell me all about yourself, the children, and ev[e]ry thing at home so that when I got back to the Regt I shal[l] have lots of letters. and do not worry about me for I shall come out all right. I shall have to close this to be in time for the steamer in the morning. give my love to all the folks at home. have you got the money that I sent you from Alexandria when we went up?

Please accept this with the love of your own,

Frank

May 30th [1864]

I do not know but I have written more in this letter than you will care to read already, but as I have nothing else to do this morning I thought that I would write a few lines more.[10] I feel pretty well this

---

[10] This appears to be a continuation of a letter that has not survived.

morning and if I do not have any more <u>Shake</u> I think I shall get all right in a few days again. You asked what I thought about your going to Buffalo to see how they done things there in their Society. I should like to have you go verry much if there is any one going that you are acquainted with that you can go with, and think that it would do you good. but it is not a verry good plan to go alone there unless you know the <u>ropes</u> for you might get lost and the first you fetch up on <u>Canal Street</u>.[11] but then you can do as you like about it.

There was a man died here in this ward yesterday of the Typhoid fever. he had worm fits too, I think that he choked to death. there is another one that has got it in here and he is crazy. he gets up on his bed and thinks it is a horse and will make some of the funniest speeches, but I do not think that he will get well. you know that I told you about a man getting hurt at New Iberia last winter by a tree falling on him, he is here but his back is lame yet I think [he] will get his discharge. and that Mrs. Helmes[12] that that came from Buffalo with us is here nursing. she get $12.00 per month and makes 2 or 3 dollars more sewing in a week. but I would not have <u>you</u> here for $100 a month. Now I do not want you to worry any about me for I have got a good place here and all the care that I need, and perhaps will do better than if I was at home. and I b[e]lieve that I shall be at home this fall if not before.

there is good news from Virginia up to the 23 of May.[13] but I

---

[11] Canal Street, which ran parallel to the Erie Canal, was located in a disreputable section of Buffalo. It was here saloons and brothels thrived, and where "illicit commerce....crammed every nook and cranny with vice." Michael N. Vogel, Edward J. Patton, and Paul F. Redding, *America's Crossroads: Buffalo's Canal Street/Dante Place* (The Heritage Press: Buffalo, NY, 1993), 31.

[12] Possibly Mrs. Morris Helm, 153 N. Divisio, Buffalo. *The Commercial Advertizer Directory for the City of Buffalo* (Buffalo: R. Wheeler & Co., 1861), 181.

[13] The news was not good. In battles at Spotsylvania which ended May 19, the Union troops under Grant had suffered heavy losses, around 18,000 out of 110,000 men. The Confederates had around 50,000 engaged and lost about 12,000 killed, wounded or captured. The following days Grant and Lee spent moving troops. On May 23 the Battle of North Anna began. Lee continued to block Grant, although Grant retained the offensive. *Almanac*, 505-509; *Encyclopedia*, Vol. 4, 1841.

will have to close this for it is most time for passes and I want to go down and see George[14] off. write often and tell me some of your good dreams. tell me all the news, and believe me your most obedient,

 Frank

Kiss the children for me, and tell Nettie that Pa would be glad if he had her.

Marine Hospital
June 2nd /64

I will write you just a note this afternoon so that you can see how I am getting on here. the steamer goes to New York in the morning with the mails and I am going to send you one by ev[e]ry boat that goes. I am better to day of my fever, but my Side pains me all the time. the Dr says that it will get better when I get over this Fever, but he thinks [it] will never be well again and I am half amind to believe him myself, but it is not so bad as it has been sometimes.

I got your letter of may fourth and was verry glad to hear from you. I have written to you two or three times a week since I have been here and you see that I have run out of any news to write. the weather is verry warm. it is raining to day and I hope will cool off the air. oh, I shall have to tell you that I have got to getting up early in the morning just sunrise. aint you tickled? but then it will not take me long to lay a bed till noon when I get home, so don't feel too good about it for I am obliged to get up here, and I suppose that is the reason now. At the most there is but fifteen months more befor[e] our time will be out, but I think that I can get a furlough for sixty days. do you want that I should? I do not think that I shall be fit for the field in that time and perhaps not in all summer if I stay here. if I can be well I had rather stay here if I do not get my discharge.

that Poetry that I spoke about I have lost and if I had I do not think that I would send it to you for it was not fit for the Pres of the S.A.S. to look at, so please excuse me. there is no news to write from here. I have not got my descriptive list yet and the Capt says that he

---

[14] Griffith's friend George Carr was discharged May 18, 1864. *Registers*, 386; Clark, 346.

will not send it till the Surg[eon] in charge of the Hosp sends for it, so there is an end of it.

Please to write often. I want to hear from pa often. tell mother that I shall write to her as soon as I can. I have written to Dora this afternoon. give my love to all the folks at home. how does Harry Segaciate now? kiss the Ba for me.

Frank

Waterville
June the 7 [1864]

My Ever Dear Child,

I imbrace this opportunity to answer your kind and welcome letter sent by Mr. McClure. we got them Saturday. I went to Springville that day but did not see him. I am glad to hear that you are geting better for you can never know how I felt when I heard you were wounded and sick far away from home and friends. I feel very thankful that it was no worse. May Gods protecting care still be over you is the prayer of your Mothers heart. may your trust be in him who is able to keep you through all the danger incident to Soldier life. it is 21 months tomorrow since you went away. I begin to count the week[s] that you will have to stay.

I suppose you want to know what we are doing to day. well, I will tell you. pa is sick today and [I] have been vineeing yarn. Gene has been to work on the road. Thank has gone to help for the church for the exhibition. Sarah had a letter from Dora. She says Charlie consented to let her come home this summer if she think best. I do hope she will [think] it best to come. we expect Carrie home next week. Corydon is sick, or was when Carrie wrote last week. She was afraid he had got the ague and fever. Carrie's baby is very pretty. She is such a litt[l]e mite you can almost put hir in your pocket, She [is] very sprightly.

I expect you will want to [know] how the exhibition goes off. they think that they [will] have a grand time. I hope they will. I want to go, but pa is sick and cant go and I shall have to stay with him. you wanted to know how the horses look this [spring]. they look better than they did when we got home from Atica. Gene did not take very good care of them while we were gone. nell has got a very pretty little

194

Waterville June 7 [?]

My Ever Dear Child

I embrace this opportunity to
answer your kind and welcome letter sent by
Mr. McIvorI [?] We got them Saturday I went to
Springville that day but did not see him I am
glad to hear that you are getting better for you
can never know how I felt when I heard
you were wounded and sick far away from
home and friends I feel very thankful that
it was no worse May Gods preserving care still
be over you is the prayer of your Mother heart may
your trust be in him who is able to keep you
through all the danger incident to Soldier life
it is 21 months tomorrow Since you went away
I begin to count the weeks that you will have to
stay I Suppose you want to know What we are
doing to day well I will tell you pa is sick to day and
have been winning [?] yarn Jane has been to work
on the road Frank has gone to help fix [?]
church for the exhibition Sarah had a letter

Letter of Harriet Griffith to her son Frank, June 7, 1864 from "Waterville"
[East Concord], New York. Griffith Papers, Regional History Center,
Northern Illinois University

colt, black as a mink. but I shall have to close for I have got alot of work to do this afternoon. write often and excuse all mistakes. and accept the love of
> your Mother

Marine Hospital
June 8th /64

Dear Wife,
>Still here and as lonesome as ever, but as the boat goes out in the morning I am going to <u>try</u> and write you a line so that you may know how I am getting on. I am a little nervous this afternoon and you will please excuse me if I do not write verry well. I think that I am getting better of my fever for I have not had a <u>shake</u> in 3 days, and then not much of a one. my leg has got well and my side is no worse that I know of. and if I do not have any more chills I shall get well now soon.
>It has rained here ev[e]ry day this month and is raining now, but it is <u>aweful</u> <u>warm</u> here. the mail has just come in but no letter for me, but I think there will be one the next boat that comes down from the Regt. I do not know of any news to write. it is just the same here ev[e]ry day so you see that I cant have much to write about. it is just possible that I may get a furlough yet, but I do not make any calculations on it yet. I have been taking <u>Quinine</u> ev[e]ry day and to day the Dr ordered a dose of <u>Calomel</u>,[15] but I do not think that I shall have to take it.
>I suppose that you have seen Mr McClure and he has told you

---

[15] Calomel, or mercurous chloride, was a widely used as a purgative, or laxative, and was also used as an intestinal antiseptic. It was also believed to cure such ailments as gastro-intestinal problems, yellow fever, cardiac dropsy and syphilis. On the other hand, excessive use could cause mercury poisoning or mercurial gangrene, and loss of teeth. In May 1863 U.S. Surgeon General William A. Hammond issued Army Circular No. 6 which banned the use of calomel. Unfortunately, this order was disregarded by most army doctors. Brooks, *Civil War Medicine*, 64; Adams, *Doctors in Blue*, 38-39; Briggs, *Before Modern Medicine*, 146; Jerger, *A Medical Miscellany for Genealogists*, 20; Drake, *What Did they Mean By That?* [Vol. 1], 31.

all the news. and then I sent you a letter by Frank Shulters,[16] and George Carr you may see him yet for he said that he would come and see you. How does Martha get along? Dora said that she was sick but she does not write to me lately and you do not say any thing about her.

but I will close this poor letter. write and tell me all about the Folks at home and if you have done any thing about my Discharge. now dont tell any one that I have said any thing to you about it, but it seems as though I had ought to be there if Father is so that he cant do any thing. but then you can do as you think best about it. I think that Uncle A[r]chie would be the best man to do any thing about it. now do not think that I am getting homesick or that I am not Patriotic, but I think that after two years in the service I can do as much good at home as here if I am no better. give my love to all the folks at home. kiss the children for me, and acept this with the love of your

Frank

———————

"When absent far from home and friends
  Is there no charm, the heart to fetter &
  As time rolls on and still one rove
  Is there no care? O Yes! a letter."

Brunswick
June 12th 1864

Dear Cousin,

Perhaps you have wondered ere this why your letter has not been answered? certainly not because it was not a <u>welcome</u> missive for I had been waiting anxiously to hear from you for a long time. but from the fact that letter writing of late has become a great undertaking and I put it off just as long as conscience will permit. I am sure Frank you will pity instead of blame, and forgive your negligent coz. I was sorry to hear of your being an inmate of the hospital from (honorable) wounds and hope you have fully recovered also that you may have the

———————

[16] Franklin C. Shultes was age 18 when he enlisted at Concord. A private in Company F, he was discharged for disability, May 1, 1864 at Alexandria, La. *Registers*, 472; Clark, 334. See also Appendix C.

satisfaction of dispatching rebels enough to avenge your wrongs. Probably <u>you</u> are enjoying very fine weather while here it is very cold and unpleasant, remarkably so for the season of the year. it is seldom that a fire is necessary for comfort the middle of June, but for the past few days it would have been uncomfortable without one. Vegetation is very backward and the force of Nature wears a gloomy look.

I thank you very kindly for your offer to assist me in that <u>dangerous</u> undertaking of name changing. I am sure I would need some friendly advice if I had the subject in contemplation, but I have about concluded to settle quietly down without assuming the responsibility of another name; however I shall wait until you can assist me verbally (if it is not too long). About my photograph which you requested in my next. I am sorry that I haven't one to send you now but will do so the first opportunity, and yours would be gladly received. I believe you promised it to me years ago. I think it is time the promise was fulfilled with the addition of your family.

How long have you to stay in Dixie? I am flattering myself that we will not always be such strangers, that you will some time make us a visit. I would really like to visit my Erie Co. relatives and hope I may. I am writing with a faint heart Frank as there are so many changes in the army of late I hardly knew what to do about writing fearing you had changed your position since you wrote; therefore will submit but these few common place remarks for your consideration.

Hoping to hear from you soon.
I remain affectionately,
Cousin Nettie

(upside down)
– All unite in regards and well wishes. N

Marine Hospital
June 14th /64

My Dear Wife,
You will please to excuse me for sending you this sheet that has been written on but it is the only one that I have that is ruled and my hand trembles so that I cant write straight on the othe[r]s, and I guess that you will think that I cant on this. But I thought that perhaps you might like to know how I get on here so I am going to write you

twice a week. I am getting <u>better</u> fast now only my <u>side</u>, and that is no <u>worse</u>. my <u>back</u> is some lame, but that will get well now. I have got over my <u>fever</u>. I have not taken any Quinine in three or four days and I begin to have a good appetite for my <u>grub</u>, so I think that I shall <u>do</u> <u>now</u>. I suppose that I have been transfered to the <u>Invalid Corps</u>.[17] we had an examination to day and they put me down for that so that I expect to go to Washington soon, but I do not know for certain yet. I do not think that you had better write to me any more here till you hear from me again and then I will know more about it and will tell you where to direct. I have not had a letter from you in two weeks and it is getting lonesome, but I suppose that they are up to the Regt for me.

the weather is getting pretty <u>hot</u> here now, but it has rained ev[e]ry day this month till to day. you never saw any thing grow so fast as the corn does here. some that was just planted when I came here is all silked out now and is higher than any man can reach. and some that was sown last week came up in two days. but the grass does not grow verry fast here. they have all kinds of fruit in the market now. I saw new potatoes three weeks ago as large as eggs, plums and peaches and bannannas and all kinds of tropical fruits, but they are verry high. how I should like to have a dish of good bread and milk for my supper to night. but I think I will make up lost time when I do come home.

The news from Gen Grant is most encouraging and all ar[e] looking for the close of the war this <u>summer</u>. there is no news that I can write you from here that I know of. we had an Emancipation

---

[17] The Invalid Corps was established April 28, 1863 as a way to utilize disabled soldiers discharged from the hospitals in such non-combat duties such as clerks, cooks, nurses, orderlies, and police in hospitals, garrisons and prisons. It was renamed the Veterans' Reserve Corps in March 1864, and included men whose enlistments had run out. In the summer of 1864 nearly all able-bodied. "soldiers had been sent to reinforce the Army of the Potomac. The infantry on guard duty in the city [Washington, D.C.] was composed of the semi-invalid Veteran Reserves." Wiley, *The Life of Billy Yank,* 342; Adams, *Doctors in Blue,* 187-188; Brooks, *Civil War Medicine,* 61-62; *Encyclopedia,* Vol. 2, 1035; Margaret Leech, *Reveille in Washington 1860-1865* (New York: Harper & Brothers, 1941), 332. Griffith was transferred from the Marine Hospital in New Orleans to the Veterans Reserve Corps (VRC) 10th Co., 1st Battalion on June 20, 1864, however the official records give the date as January 10, 1865. *Registers,* 416.

celebration here last Saturday [June 11] when all the Darkies turned out in their strengt[h]. I did not see it. you can read all about it in the papers. it is just possible that I may be home this summer, but I do not have much hopes of it, and you must not make any calculations on it.

But I shall have to close this. Give my love to all the folks at home. kiss the children for me. I hope that it will not be long till I can kiss them for my self. and sometime I will tell you all about Hospital life. please excuse all mistakes and accept this from,

Frank

New Orleans
July 24th 1864

Dear Thank,

I b[e]lieve you will be glad to hear that I have been to a Soldiers pray[e]r meeting to night and that I was asked to express my mind on the subject of religion. but I told the chaplain that I felt as if I would be out of place in such a place as that and beged to be exempted. and I am almost ashamed to write it to even you, but you know that I have got a notion of telling you ev[e]ry thing that I know so I have written it to you. I am well as I expect to be in this war and I am getting <u>fat</u> again and feel first rate, all but my side and that is getting better so that it does not pain me as much. you know that it used to swell up and be a bunch on there. now that has all gone away and more too for there is a hollow place that you can lay your hand in. but it is better so that I do not mind it so much now.

I am on guard at the Baracs Hospital this week, and the <u>Skeeters</u> are trying to eat me up so I have lit my pipe and are smoking them out and writing to you all at the same time. I suppose you will want to know where I am and what I am left here for when the <u>regt</u> have gone to Baltimore. well, I shall have to tell you some time and I may as well out with it now as any time. I have been transfered to the <u>Invalid</u> Corps or as we are more delicately styled the Veteran <u>Reserve</u> Corps, and are to do all sorts of guard duty in all the cities that we happen to be sent to. and we expect to be sent to Washington every day, and we may stay here all next winter. but I suppose that we shall know in a few days where we shall go and then I will write you. If we stay here the next month I had rather stay all winter.

there is not much news to write from here. they have all the news in Washington now. I have written to you so often lately that I am played out for any thing to write about, and do not think that you can read what I have wr[i]tten. It is verry hot here, but the city is verry healthy at present. We have not been paid yet but I have got my descriptive list so that I can get my pay and then I will send you some money. I have not got the socks that you sent me and I guess that they are <u>gave up</u> now. I will try and write to mother in a day or two. I am staying with Sandy to night and we shall have to go to bed. kiss the children for me. give my love to all the folks. and I will send you my address as soon as I find out where it will be.

Good night

Frank

25th

I have just been to supper and I had some of the best bread and milk that I have since I left home. I took supper with <u>Sandy</u> and now I will have to finish this for I have to go on guard, so good bye for the present. yours in

love

New Orleans
August 1st 1864

My Dear Wife,

I am to sit up with one of our sick boys to night and so I thought that I would try and write you a letter. and I have taken a good large sheet and am going to write you a good long letter and tell you what I think, if it will be of any interest to you. I am well at present, only my side is some sore yet, but that is getting better now and I think if I am careful I shall be all right by the time that I get home. we are having some hot weather here now, but I believe that the worst part of the season is over as far as the heat is concerned, but I suppose that the sickly season is to come this month. There has been some cases of Yellow Fever, but that has subsided now and some case of the Small Pox among the soldiers, but they ar[e] all sent down to the Baracs Hospital as soon as they are taken down with it so that it does not spread much.

The soldiers are having a hard time up to Morgansie [Morganza,]. they [say] it is aweful hot there and the water is so bad that they all have the Diarea and there have been several cases of sunstroke.[18] There has been an order is[s]ued by Gen Canby[19] that all of the Citizens of this Dept shall be enroled in the state Malitia. and you can hear some tall swearing in the streets now and some threats. but we have got them where the <u>hair</u> <u>is</u> <u>short</u>, and if they want to raise a mob there will be some tall fun in this place. I think that there would be some of the Rebs cleaned out or at least battle scared, and for my part I am glad of it for then we shall know who our enemies are and how to deal with them. but I will send you a paper with the Order in and then you can read for yourself.

The 116th have gone to Baltimore and I hear that they have had a fight there.[20] Well, I suppose that I shall have to stay out of the fights after this unless it is some street row for our corps will be detailed to do guard duty in this city or some other till our time is out. Last week I was on guard ev[e]ry other day, and this week it will be no better, so that it will [be] as hard as it would be in the Regt only we shall not have any marching to do. and then we will have better Quarters but no better fare. but then I can stand it for I have got me a rasor and a pair of shears and can make enough in one day to buy me a

---

[18] Morganza, Louisiana is on the Mississippi River. Although Banks' troops constructed shelters from the sun, the heat and excessive rain resulted in epidemics of chronic diarrhea, scurvy, swamp fever and smallpox. Winters, *The Civil War in Louisiana*, 390-391.

[19] Major General Edward Richard Sprigg Canby, relieved Banks on May 18, 1864 to command the Military Division of Western Mississippi. Canby was preparing to move on Mobile, but Grant's heavy losses in the Wilderness campaign caused Grant to order Canby to send the 19th Corps to Hampton Roads, Virginia without delay. To replace the men sent to Mobile and Virginia, and to provide local protection, Canby issued an order on July 30 for "all able-bodied males, between the ages of eighteen and forty-five within the lines of occupation in the Department of Arkansas and the Gulf and the district east of the Mississippi River "to enroll immediately in the militia." Ibid. 378, 391-392.

[20] The 116th left New Orleans on July 5 on the *Mississippi* and reached Fortress Monroe on July 12. They arrived in Washington, D.C. on the 13th and went on to Frederick, Maryland and Harper's Ferry, (West)Virginia. By August 1 the 116th was back at Frederick, but had not seen any fighting. Ayer, 59.

pint of milk and that is five cts. I have got about $20.00 dollars owing to me that I have earned since we have been here waiting for pay day. I made two dollars last week in half a day down to the Baracks and have got me a gold pen so you can look out for lots of letters now. we have not got our pay yet though we expect it ev[e]ry day now. we signed the pay rolls three weeks ago but then we may not be paid till the first of Sept and then I will have eight months pay $116.00 and I can send it all to you and perhaps more. I know that you must need some by this time, but I could not send it to you. but if you have had enough to eat and enough to keep you warm it is more than I have had for nearly half of the time since I have been gone. but then I am not going to complain to you, but I have seen the time when Hardtacks were worth .50 cts a piece, and none to be had at that. and that after we had marched 20 miles in the hot sun and the dust so thick you could not see across the road. I should like to have some of those who stay at home and cry hard times come out and take a Soldiers fare for one year. I do not think that you would hear them whine about hard times after that. When they have to pay ten cts apiece for eggs, .80 cts for a pound of cheese, and 60 and 1.00 for butter, 3.00 for a plug of tobacco, or 10., 20 cts for a pound of flour, and then sleep on the wet ground with a brick for a pillow, with nothing but the heavens for a shelter and the rain pouring down on their face they may begin to cry hard times.

I b[e]lieve that I said in one of my letters that I would tell you what I thought and as I shall have considerable time to spare to night, for it is only half past eleven, and I have to stay awake till five in the morning, I will try and tell you privately what I think of, have thought of sometimes with in the last four weeks. and in the first place I will tell you something about where we are. our Quarters are in the Picayone [Picayune] Cotton Press on the bank of the river in the lower part of the city. Now you know what a temperment I have and I will tell you some of the temptations there are in my path. in the first place there is a Saloon in this block a few yards from our door and we can get all the beer and Whiskey that we may want to pay for. and then across the street there is a beer garden and dance house where they have a dance ev[e]ry sunday night and wh[e]re all the young ladies of that delectable street called Basin street come to display their charms. where it cost us the sum of fifteen cts to go in and five dollars to get out again. and then ev[e]ry other house has from three to ten girls of <u>both</u> sexes who will politely ask you to come in and see the Pictures with them. then there is the ball alley, the billiard table, and the card table, the Theatre and all the Places of amusement that the fertile mind of man can invent.[21] and these are in our path ev[e]ry day. and then we are a lot of men by our selves removed entirely from the influence of any virtuous female society with the influence of drunken officers from the Brigadier General down to the Eighth corporal. and where you will hear little else from morning till Taps but cursing and swearing, and see but little else day after day but card playing and gambling.

and when I tell you that this is the kind of influence that constantly surrounds the soldier you can form something of an idea of the amount of moral courage and self denial that one who tries to live so that he will not be ashamed to come home, if god should spare his life, has to posses or rather excercise. I can not say that I always done the best that I could do, but I b[e]lieve that I have always kept from doing any thing that I felt would be a disgrace to you my dear wife, or to the mother that I love. and now you can easily imagine the effect it would have on one situated as we are here, if the ones that we still love and have left to fight the battles of our country for should they be guilty of the sin that of all others we have to fight the hardest. or do you think that I could ever come home to the wife who had dishonored me to come home to a ruined hearthstone, one from which all the love and confidence had gone out forever to live a continual hell upon earth. No, it would be better that we never see each other here again, for if we can not be true to each other in these three short years of our countri[e]s peril we can never be true in the long years that it may please God to spare our lives. now I do not want you to think that I write this because I think that it will be likely to happen to us, but you said in
[*next page missing*]

---

[21] New Orleans had "dives" all over the city. For example, 45 places sold liquor on Charles Street in the six blocks between Canal Street and LaFayette Square. The police seemed to ignore organized gambling and racing as well as prostitution. Capers, *Occupied City*, 204-206.

New Orleans, La
August 6th [1864]

My Dear Wife,

you will think perhaps that I am writing verry often lately or
that I have got something new to write. Well, I plead guilty to the first
but not the latter. but the trouble is that I am watching with that sick
boy again to night and am lonesome, and so I am going to write to you
again to night to pass away the time. this makes the fourth night this
week that I have been up all night with him and I am getting tired and
sleepy. but I have to keep awake and see that he does not get up and
take cold for he is crazy all the time, poor fellow. I do not think there
is much chance for him to get well. it seems so hard for one so young
as he is to die here away from his friends, but such is the fate of war.
and we shall all be called upon to die sometime, and I do not know as
it will make any difference where we die if we are only prepared for
the last great change that awaits us all. and I believe that Heaven is
just as near to the Hospital, the Hovel, or the battlefield as it is to the
Palace. and I have sometimes thought it was nearer to the soldier than
any one else, and certainly it should be dearer.

It seems to me that if there is any thing that a man can do to
mitigate the punishment of the sins of the human family it is the man
who goes forth in a war like this in the defence of his country. one
who of his own free will takes his life in his hand and goes to the field
to face death in a thousand forms, leaves his home with all its pleasant
associations and all the comforts and coviniences of this life to take
the chances of the bullets of the enemy, the hardship and fatigue of the
march, and all the diseases that can be brought on by sleeping on the
wet gro[u]nd, exposure to the weather, and allmost ev[e]rything that
will make life seem hardly half worth the living.

But I will not write you any more on this subject but try and
write something more cheerful for fear that you got the <u>blues</u> reading
it, if you read it at all. I do not know but what you get tired of such
long letters so often and do not care to read them. if so please to let
me know and I will try and find some other way to pass my lonesome
hours.

well, we have not gone to washington yet but the talk is that
we shall go next week, but I guess it is all talk. and if we have to stay
here the next two weeks I had as leave stay all winter for by that time

the hot weather will be over and the winters are verry pleasant here. I believe that I should like to live here if I were a citizen, and not a reb, and in times of peace. but I should not like to bring you here to live for you might not like to get aclimated. the first year is always the worst. but then this country has its drawbacks. here they do not raise apples, but then there is plenty of oranges and p[e]ach[e]s and plums and figs and mellons. I b[e]lieve that I told you last summer how good the figs were. well, you see they are as good this [year]. I dont know you ever saw a quin[ce] and so I write tell you how they look. they are shaped like a pear only not so large, about as large as an egg, and they are sweet as sugar, hence I like them. the meats are like a strawberry full of little seeds.

I should like to tell you something about the City, but I think that I will wait till I get home and then I can tell you more than I can write in a month. There is no excitement here at present only that there has been a big fight at mobile[22] and that two of our gun boats had run the Blocade and gave up to the city, the Hartford and another.[23] the Hartford is the one that run the blocade at port Hudson last spring a year ago. and the next news will be that Mobile is taken. I expect that this year will end the war and then for home. but I will close this for to night.

give my love to all. and I hope by the next time that I write I can tell you where to direct.

Frank

[Missing previous page/s, the following letter was written on the same kind of paper as the one dated 12 August 1864 from New Orleans. The events mentioned would place the letter in early August]

---

[22] The Battle of Mobile Bay began the morning of August 5. Admiral David Glasgow Farragut led the Union fleet of eighteen vessels which took control of the bay by 10 a.m. Closing the port led to the surrender of Fort Gaines by Colonel Charles D. Anderson on August 8. Fort Morgan fought on until August 23. Mobile remained a Confederate stronghold until April 1865. *Almanac*, 551-553; *Encyclopedia*, Vol. 3, 1342-1345.

[23] The *Brooklyn*.

.....breaks their constitutions and ruins them for life. it takes the strongest men to endure the hardships of war and only in the defence of my liberties would I go to the field. Ev[e]rything seems to be going on bravely and I am in hopes that this summer will close the war. we have the news that Gen Sherman has captured Atlanta with from Eight to twenty thousand Prisoners.[24] That Grant with his Pigheaded obstinacy is at Petersburgh [Virginia],[25] as the Rebs call him. and they begin to think there is a chance of his taking Richmond yet. and it seems that the Great Raid into maryland is likely to prove a serious affair to the Johnny and has only resulted in a big scare to our northern Cowards.[26]

Billy is crazy and is calling for his mother, so you see what is uppermost in the poor soldiers mind when he is sick. as long as we are well, well we can take care of our selves. when we are sick then the thoughts of the Wife and mother come to us in our helplessness, and we long for the soft cool hand to smothe the pillow and sooth the burning brow. but I have written till I have got lonesome.

it is half past two and if you was only here so that I could visit with you I think that the time would pass of[f] more quickly. do you remember when we used to sit up with Lydia at Evans? the nights did not seem so long then as it does to night. but then never mind, only one year and one month and then I will [be] at home again if my life is

---

[24] General William Tecumseh Sherman and his troops had been fighting in and around Atlanta since May 1864. On August 9 they began intense bombardment of the city. However, the Confederates under Lt. General John Bell Hood did not evacuate the city until September 1. The Union troops entered the following day. *Encyclopedia*, Vol. 1, 128, 145-146.

[25] Petersburg had been under siege since mid-June. On July 30 the Union Army failed to take the city by blowing up its defenses, "due to Confederate resistance and some Federal ineptitude." Grant waited two weeks before beginning his next offensive. Petersburg did not fall until April 2, 1865. *Almanac*, 548; *Encyclopedia*, Vol. 3, 1494, 1499.

[26] On July 29 the Confederate cavalry of General Jubal Anderson Early entered Maryland. They "destroyed property, held small towns for ransom" and successfully battled a Union force under General Lew Wallace. Other rebel units skirmished at Harper's Ferry, Hagerstown, and Clear Spring, Maryland, giving rise to panic by many Northerners. *Almanac*, 547; *Encyclopedia*, Vol. 3, 1259.

spared till then. and then we can have such a visit. and I shall have ev[e]r so many stories to tell you and the Children. I have got a lot of clothes to send home when we get to Washington, if we ever get there. we are expecting to go there ev[e]ry day now and when we get there I want you to write me such a good long letter that it will make up for the four weeks that I have not had any.

Have you seen Geo Carr yet? I suppose that he has got home and is having such a good time, and that puts me in mind that I must write to him. I can't write to anyone but you for I can't tell them where to direct so that I can get them [the letters], for if we should go on to Washington they would have to come here and then go back there, and that would take Six weeks, so I [think] that I shall wait till I know where we are going and then I can get them. and I will write you as soon as I can tell you where to direct.

I tell you I want to see my little Nettie so bad. there is a little Girl here that is about as large as I suppose she is, and she is real pretty. I have tried to make friends with her, but have not succeeded verry well yet. but I am afraid that you will get tired of this lazy letter so I will dry it up. give my love to all who may enquire for me. and accept this with the love of,

Frank

Soldiers Sittress
The mail The mail
And Sunburned cheeks and eager eyes
Come crowding round the Captains tent
Each out stretched hand receives the prize
For fond perusalment
Unless distressing news be told
These letters naught of pain coming
For friends at home forbear to scold
The lad that is far away
The mail The mail
And toil stained partners are closing thus
How rough how verry coarsley moulded
On dainty missives fresh and fair
B[y] Silly fingers fakeled
[*Next page missing?*]

———————

New Orleans
Aug 12th 1864

My Dear Wife,
        You see that we are still here, and I do not know but we shall
stay all winter. and if we have to stay this month out I had rather stay
here than to go north for it is verry pleasant here in the winter. I am
not verry well this week. I guess that I am going to have the jaundice
again for I want to sleep most all of the time. we have not got our pay
yet and I do not expect it now till next month and then I shall [get]
eight month pay due me. I have got my discriptive list so that I think
that I shall get it then. and I have got about thirty dollars owing to me
that I have earned since I have been here so that I can send you all of
my pay and something more. I shall have to keep a little to buy me
some milk and some stamps and some shirts, but then I can make all
that I want to spend, and more too. the boys are all out of money now
so that I cant get any now, but then I manage to keep out of debt here
and get me a quart of milk a day so I think that I shall manage to live.
        what do you think about getting my discharge now? it will be
time to do something about it by the time you get this letter. you will
not need my descriptive list only say that I am needed at home an[d]
tell a good story. you will have to say that I was transfered to the
V.R.C. 10th Co., 1st Battalion, June 20th 1864 from the Marine
Hospital New Orleans, La and that I belonged to the 116th N.Y. If you
want that I should come home, and think that I have done my duty to
my country, I think that you can get my discharge. if I was able to go
to the field again I would not want it, but if I have got to stay my time
out in this corps I think that I can do more good at home. but then you
can do as you think best about it.
        They are having some fun at Mobile now, and I think that the
Rebs are getting fits.[27] there was three boat loads of prisoners come
here befor[e] yesterday and more are expected to day. we are
expecting orders to go to Washington next week and then I hope that I
can tell you where to direct.

---

[27] Following the surrender of Ft. Gaines on August 8, the Union Army
concentrated its efforts on Fort Morgan, cutting it off from Confederate held Mobile.
Almanac, 553.

There is some cases of Yellow Fever here now and we are having verry sickly weather, cool nights and wet days. it has rained ev[e]ry day this month, and the citizens say that if this weather continues it will be verry sickly next month. but I hope that we shall be gone before that time. I do not want to have the fever I can tell you. you have a pain in your head and back, and then if there is not something done immediately you are a <u>gonner</u>. there is not one in ten that has it that makes alive of it, and we might as well be in a fight ev[e]ry day as to stay here. but then you must not get scared about me for I believe that I shall live to come home again.

I do not know of any news to write from here. you can be writing me a good long letter so that when you send it, it will be enough to make up lost time. I have not had a letter in six weeks and I am getting hungry for one. write me all of the news and tell me all about yourself just as you would talk if I was there. give my love to all who may care enough to enquire. kiss the children for me, and acc[e]pt the love of your own,

Frank

I shall have to <u>Frank</u> this as my stamps are played out

---

Camp of the 102nd
Before Atlanta, Ga
Sunday, August 21st 1864

Dear sister,

as The railroads have been cut the mail was stop[p]ed and so I have only just received your letter of the 8th which found me well. well, I think that the wheelocks[28] would want to go west before the draft takes place. the weather is wet and warm. we have not got Atlanta yet but are fighting on some parts of the line every day.

I got a letter from a cousin that I never heard of before and I never knew that there was such a person in the world, she signed her name as "<u>Louisa Myers</u>." did you know that we had such a cousin? I

---

[28] Orlando and Albert Wheelock, neighbors of the Griffith's, would have been eligible for the draft as according to the 1860 Census Orlando Wheelock was 26, and Albert Wheelock 21. 1860 Federal Census. Concord, Erie County, New York, 322.

got a letter from Aunt Add, and one from the above named cousin, she was living at Aunt Adds. now who is her parents and who is she? she stated in her letter that that she had never seen any of my folks but Father.[29]

well Thankful, now I dont want you to bother or worry about that money, but when you want to use it just take it and use it. all I ask is to have you send me such things as I write for and then I am satsfied. I sent it for you to use and now I want you to use it.

well, my time is drawing close to an end, but I will not get home before winter. how many apples are you going to have this season? how is the fruit generally in that part of the country? you said you had heard from Frank. is he still in the Hospital yet? is Gene going to school this season? is william comeing home to live in the spring? tell Grandma Griffith to make Nettie learn those large letters that I tryed to learn her last winter.

My Regt has been consolidated and are now called the <u>102d Regt NYSV</u> and now you may bet that I am glad I have not long to serve for they have humbuged the veterans the worst kind.[30] I suppose you have got my last letter by this time, but I must close. give my respects to all who may inqire, write often, Excuse mistakes and poor writing, and allow me to subscribe myself your brother,

A E Myers
Direct Co. G. 102d instead of 78th

New Orleans
Aug 29 [1864]

My Darling,
I am going to write you just a word to day, and this is proba[b]ly the last one that I shall write to you from here as we expect

---

[29] Jacob Myers was the father of Thankful Myers Griffith and Albert E. Myers. See Appendix A.

[30] "The gallant 78th Regiment, decimated in a score of battles, has at last been consolidated with the 102nd N.Y. of the same brigade..." on July 2, 1864. *Courier & Republic* [Buffalo], 22 July 1864. Dyer, 193. Albert mustered out December 24, 1864.

to go to/<u>Somewhere</u>/ in a day or two, and the most common talk is <u>Elmira</u> N.Y. we have got orders to go to Washington as soon as we can get ready and that will be this week. we shall be mustered for pay tomorrow and then we expect to go the next day. I will have eight months pay then, 114 which I can send to you and perhaps more.

there is no news of any consequence to write from here that you have not read in the pap[e]rs. I am as well as common, only tired for I have been on guard for nine days in succession. and you will excuse me if I do not write verry well. but when we get settled I will tell you all about the trip and all the news that I can think of. get me a good long letter ready so that you can send it as soon as you know where I am. kiss the children for me, and ac[c]ept this with the love of your own,

Frank

I will send this with one that I wrote a week ago but did not know whether to send it or not. excuse me for not sending it before, and tell me what you think of it.

Chapter 7

"On to Washington"
Veteran Reserve Corps, September 1864 - March 1865

At the end of August 1864 Frank Griffith was ordered to Washington, DC. Leaving New Orleans in early September by ship, Griffith arrived in New York City on September 14th. He spent four days at Battery Barracks and arrives in Washington on the 24th, where he is assigned to the First Battalion of Veteran Reserve Corps at Cliffburne Barracks. Five days later Griffith is transferred to Company I, 9th Regiment, VRC, at Fry Barracks, where he remains until he musters out. Meanwhile the 116th is still on reconnaissance in Virginia.

Health problems continue to plague Griffith. On the days when his side (liver) pains him, Frank fears "that in the sacrifice that I have made for my country I have ruined my health," and that in the future he will have to earn his living not with his hands, but with his head. With constant doctoring, by the end of March 1865 he is feeling much better. Frank does some barbering, but for the most part works as a cook, first for the non-commissioned staff of three regiments, then for the band, and lastly for a military hospital.

Thankful's brother Albert writes from Atlanta, Georgia. He continues to see action and is anxious for his enlistment to end. Lincoln is up for re-election and New York was one of the states that arranged for soldiers to vote from the field. Griffith writes Thankful to make sure his vote goes to Lincoln, and not for the "Copperhead" ticket. Frank mentions writing and receiving letters from many family members, including his cousin Nettie. The letter from Frank's fourteen year-old brother Eugene and his mother is an example of their continuing love and concern.

John Griffith, Frank's father, is suffering from the cancer on his lip. Life is hard for the family as John's inability to work puts more burden on Frank's younger brothers, and on Thankful, who Frank wishes to remain with his family to help out his mother. Frank has vowed to take care of his parents as long as they live. Thankful is anxious for the time when she and Frank can make a life for themselves, presumably in a place far away like Minnesota.

On Christmas Eve Frank writes Thankful a long, loving poem. The winter months of 1864/1865 are very cold and rough, in both

Washington, DC and western New York state. With Frank's life becoming rather routine as a cook, Frank has little to write about. One evening, in an offhanded way, Frank asks his bunk mate, Arthur Lester Wilkinson, what to write. Wilkinson, checking Griffith's response takes pen in hand and clarifies the situation for Thankful.

Since his enlistment, Frank has strived to live so as not to disgrace himself or his family. He and Wilkinson both joined one of the many temperance organizations that were thriving among the military in Washington, DC. They were members of the Sons of Temperance, Circle Division No. 17, and Wilkinson became the "Worthy Patriarch" of their Division. Frank becomes increasingly involved, and starts a "newspaper" called the "Strength of the Circle." Only one copy is made of each edition, which is handwritten by Frank and then passed around. Frank asks Thankful to contribute articles to this paper. Griffith also acts as secretary of the group. His involvement includes introducing two women to the group, but some members object. Frank believes that if women want to be "shielded from temptation" then he will aid them in that cause. Thankful agrees he is doing the right thing. A controversy arises, in part because there are so many prostitutes in the Washington area, and that a woman's character is often questioned if she is in the company of a soldier. By February 10, 1865 Circle Division No. 17 has 140 members, all soldiers, and about fifteen lady visitors. Frank asks if Thankful would like to become a member by proxy. In addition to attending the meetings of his Division, he begins attending the meetings of other Divisions, resulting in less time to write to Thankful.

Frank mentions the Hampton Roads Conference of February 3, 1865 where Lincoln met with several Confederate representatives in an effort to end the war. Since the Confederates wished to remain independent and retain slavery, while Lincoln insisted on the restitution of the Union without slavery, the meeting failed.

As Frank's time left to serve approached six months, both Thankful and Frank start looking toward the future. Thankful's brother Albert had mustered out of the service on December 24, 1864. He apparently wants to start farming by his parents, and Thankful asks about going to live with him. Frank doesn't refuse, but rather reminds her of his commitment to his parents, and the fact that the little money he is able to send home helps them all. He also doesn't want Albert or her parents to use his horses. In addition, for some reason, he doesn't want his children under the influence of Thankful's mother.

Frank and Thankful discuss what Frank might do for a living and where they will live. Although he mentions studying law with Arthur Wilkinson and moving to Kansas, all he can say with certainty is that he plans to make an honest living, and provide a humble home for Thankful.

Due to his father's declining health Frank is anxious to get a furlough, but doubts this will occur before April. He and Wilkinson have also given up chewing tobacco. (Perhaps tobacco was a possible cause of John Griffith's lip cancer.) Problems never cease for the Griffith family. For good reason the area of Concord township where they live is known as "Waterville," as following the harsh winter, the melting snows cause flooding in March 1865.

New York
Sept 16th [1864]

My Dear wife,

I have just time to write you a line this morning to let you know where I am and how I am. we got here on the 14th and have just come on shore. I am as well as usual and I want to hear from you awfully. if you get this in a day or two send me one letter here. we expect to go on to Washington in the next week and then I will write you a good long letter and tell you all about it. we have not been paid yet, but I think we shall when we get to Washington. I have got a lot of clothes that I want to send home. tell me if you can pay the freight on them if I send them from her[e], and get those shirts ready to send to me as soon as we get settled again for I have not got any. I think that we shall go to Elmira this winter and then I am going to come <u>home</u>. write me all the news, and ac[c]ept this short note with all the love of your own,

Frank

Direct your letter to: 10 Co 1st Batt
                           VRC
                           Battery Baracs
                           New York City

but write <u>immediately</u>

Washington
Sept 24th /64

My Dear Wife,

I am going to try and write you a few lines to night just to let you know where I am and what I am doing. We have just got into quarters on a hill near the city to day and a verry pleasant place it is.[1] I do not know how long we shall stay here perhaps a long time and

---

[1] Griffith is at Cliffburne Barracks, which was located on the north side of Washington, D.C. on Meridian Hill out 15th Street. Marcus Benjamin, ed., *Washington During War Time: A Series of Papers Showing Military, Political, and Social Phases During 1861 to 1865* (Washington: National Tribune Co.,1902), 205.

perhaps not a week. I am well and feel first rate. I have not been sick so as to take any medicine since I left the Marine [Hospital] though my side troubles me a good deal. I have not heard a word from you since I left New Orleans and you do not know how hungry I am for a letter.

We stayed in New York four days and I went most all over the City. they gave me a pass ev[e]ry day and we had a fine time, but I cant tell you in this letter to night anything about what I saw. I think that we shall get our pay in few days and then I will send you some money for I know that you must kneed some bad. write and tell me how you get along and how ev[e]ry thing is. I got a letter from my old friend Ames to day and he said that Lon was not verry well, but he thought he would be aro[u]nd in a few days.

I have not got any news to write for I have not heard much. I want you to tell me what you have done about my discharge, if any thing. we are going to have an examination in a day or two and then I suppose we shall know what we are going to do.

you may get me a box ready to send if you can. send butter and some fruit. tell Charlies folks to send me some honey and some cheese. I do not think John could spare me any. and I want some socks and those shirts. do not send any cakes or any thing that will spoil for I may not get them right off. send me a towel if you can. just get them ready and I will tell you where to send them in my next letter. if you cant get them ready or do not intent [intend] to send them I can draw them of the government, but they do not last half as long as those you make for me. I have got my dress coat and a jacket and the pants that I had on at Pleasant Hill and some other things that I am going to send home for I cant take care of them and I cant wear them here and they will be good to wear if I should ever get home. I will send them by express.

You will please to excuse me if I do not write a verry long letter to night for I am tired and then we have not fairly got settled. I have not been in the city yet, but when I do go I will tell you all about it. I cant tell you what the prospects are for getting a furlough yet, but I do not think they are verry bright at present, and I do not think we had better make any lot of it. but I will close this for to night and go to bed and write again in a day or so. wont we have good times writing now. it will not take two months to get an answer to a letter.

217

please excuse my poor writing and accept this with the love of your own,

<u>Frank</u>

Direct to: 10th Co 1st Batt VRC

        Cliffburne Baracks

        Washington D.C.

Write as soon as you get this and tell me all the news.
have you got the letter that I sent you from N.Y.?

                                          F

Brunswick
Sept 25th 1864
Sunday P.M.

Dear Cousin Frank,

      I have just returned from church and the thought of an unanswered missive from a far off cousin has presented itself to my mind, and as short credits make long friends I concluded to while away an hour in chit-chat with my pen, with the confidence that you are a ready listener if not engaged with those nearer than an unknown cousin. however, I will proceed and take my chances and turn.

      This is one of the most disagreeable of Fall days, it rains one moment and sunshine the next. You have one advantage over us while sojourning in the sunny South that of avoiding extreme cold Winter weather which of all seasons I most dread. I would willingly dispense with "winter sports" if thereby Jack Frost would keep at bay. By the way I am keeping old maids hall at present and am having a delightful lonesome time of it here all alone, so much so I am almost tempted to say that I will take my name off the list and put it with the list of candidates. but on taking a then second thought it is considered most advisable, that of two evils to choose the least. So I think I will not trouble myself but change the subject to fruit, of which a dish of excellent pears and apples are standing with in reach and to which I most cordially invite you to help yourself. or are you having plenty nearer by?

      Well Frank, what do you think about the war? It seems to me if we were to exchange places with the rebels it would look rather dark: only give "father Abraham" the chair, and <u>Grant</u> a few more

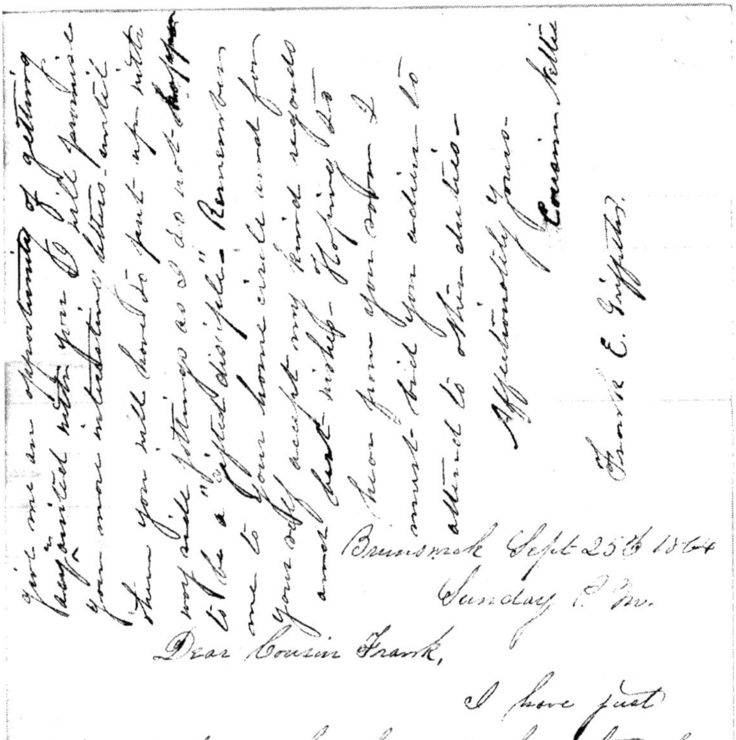

Brunswick Sept 25th 1864
Sunday P.m.

Dear Cousin Frank,

I have just
returned from Church and the thought
of an unanswered missive from a far
off cousin has presented itself to my
mind; and as short credits make long
friends I concluded to while away an
hour in chit-chat with my [pen]
with the confidence that you are a
ready listener if not engaged with
those nearer than an unknown cousin

[The following text is written sideways in the left margin and upper portion of the page:]

[...] are an opportunity of getting
acquainted with you I will [embrace]
you more interesting letter [...]
then you will [...] to part upon with
my [...] [things] as I do not [...]
to be a "[...] disciple." Remember
me to your home circle and do not [...]
your self accept my [...] [...]
a most ardent wish. — [Hoping] to be
then from you soon I
must bid your adieu to
attend to other duties —

Affectionately yours
Cousin Nettie —

Nettie E. Griffith?

Letter from Nettie Sanford, of Brunswick, New York, to her cousin Frank
Griffith, September 25, 1864. Griffith Papers, Regional History Center,
Northern Illinois University

victories. methinks "our brave soldier boys" might soon return to their homes and friends; then I presume you would make us that long promised visit and tell us all about the life of a soldier in New Orleans. but send that picture as soon as convenient so we will recognize you. I had a dozen card photographs taken a short time ago and I designed one for you, but before I was aware they were all gone. I may try it again before long. You asked for the _news_ in a cousinly way. I really would like to grant your request, and after you give me an opportunity of getting acquainted with you I will promise you more interesting letters. until then you will have to put up with my side jottings as I do not happen to be a "gifted disciple."

Remember me to your home circle. and for yourself accept my kind regards and best wishes. Hoping to hear from you soon, I must bid you adieu to attend to other duties.

Affectionately Yours,
Cousin Nettie

Frank E. Griffith
(_on back of paper, in another handwriting– Mr. Jay Boughton, East Nassaw Co, Rensler_)

Camp of the 102nd Regt NY Vols
Atlanta, Georgia
Sept 26th 1864

Dear Sister,

Never do I get tired of reading your letters and as I have just read one of your welcome Epistles. I thought that if I was only where I could have a visit with you without the aid of the silent pen it would be much plesanter. I am well and tough now while we are lying still, but I expect to be sick again if we have to march for I cannot stand marching at all. since I was at "Richmond"[2] my constitution is to[o] much broken, but I only have a little more than two months longer to stay and then I think I shall bid farewell to the soldiers life if I can find a place to live, that is to make it my home. But if I cannot find a home amongst my friends (if any) why I shall have to soldier it longer.

---

[2] See Albert's letter to Thankful dated October 21, 1863.

You asked me where we will go next now since "Atlanta is ours." well, have you forgotten that there remains to be taken yet Macon, Andersonville, Savanah, Charleston and various other places, but Macon is the next place for offensive opperations. Has Franks wounds got well yet? We had a Division review yesterday by Gen Sherman and Macomb.[3] Who is "Drena" going to get married to, and who has Miss Pakers for an elbow part?[4] I have not heard from Evans in quite a while. I have got that Tobacco and spoke of it in my last letter, have you not received it yet? but I must close. asking you to excuse poor writing and short letters. Please write often and remember your brother.

    A. E. Myers

P.S. I send you an Atlanta *Intelligencer* that I captured in the City

---

Washington
Sept 29th /64

My Dear Wife,

    This is the fourth letter I have written since I have had one from you, but then I have been <u>bobing round</u> so much lately that I expect that is the reason. I am going to write you a line to day to let you know where I am and se[e] if I can hear from you now. I have been transfered to the 9th regt and am going to do duty in this city, and I expect that I shall stay here till my time is out. we have not got any pay yet and I do not expect to now till next month now.

    I am well only I have got an awful cold, but that I shall get over in a few days. If you can send me those shirts now I shall be much obliged to you for I have got only one that I can wear. there is no news that I can write from here. I want you to write me a good long letter now to make up loust time. and then I am going to tell you all about the city and what we have to do. we have got a nice place to stay in now, and I think that we shall [have] nice times this winter.

---

[3] William H. Macomb was a Union Naval Commander. Just over a month later, on October 31, 1864, Macomb with seven vessels took Plymouth, North Carolina on the Roanoke River. *Almanac*, 591.

[4] Also referring to marriage.

give my love to all the folks at home, and kiss the little ones for me. and accept this from your own,

Frank

Direct to:

Co I, 9th Regt VRC

Fry Baracks,[5] Washington D. C.

Washington
Nov 3rd 1864

My Dear wife,

This is the last letter that I shall write to you if you dont write to me. this is the third one that I have written since I have had one from you and I begin to think that you do not care to hear from me so often. I am well, only I have eat so much supper that I have to set straight up in my chair. I had warm biscuit and butter and tea and Mince Pie for my supper so you can guess whether I eat any thing or not.

I am cooking for the Non Commission[e]d Staff of two Regts while their cook has gone home on furlough. the barber has got bett[e]r so that he can work again and so I had to get out of there, and the boys wanted that I should come in here and cook for them. I have got a good stove and two rooms and have got a big bed so that when you come to see me I will have some place for you to sleep.

has Father got my Vote yet? I sent it to him more than a week ago. if he has I want that he should take it and go to a magistrate and have it opened and see if the whole of the Union ticket is in there. If there is a Copperhead ticket in it tell him to burn it up so that no one can vote it, but if Old Abe's ticket is in there to Vote it Strong for me.[6]

---

[5] Fry Barracks was also known as Martindale Barracks, and was located at the intersection of Pennsylvania Avenue, New Hampshire Avenue, and 23rd Street, extending to 22nd and I Streets. Benjamin, *Washington During War Time*, 206.

[6] The Republican ticket of Abraham Lincoln and Andrew Johnson was opposed by General George B. McClellan and George Pendleton on the Democratic "Copperhead" ticket. Copperheads were, for the most part, Northern Democrats

There is no news that I can write from here for I have sent you two papers to day. The weather is rainy to day and verry unpleasant. but I have writt[e]n more than I intended when I set down. now remember that I am just going to answer your letters after this, so you can have off writing all together if you like. that is if you do not care to hear from me for I am getting tired of doing all the writing myself. so I may as well bid you good bye. I will send you just one kiss on this paper and you can take it or throw it away just as you please.

Frank

Washington
Nov 27th 1864

My Dear Wife,

I did not get any letter from you to day, but you can see that it does not make any difference to me for I have set down to write to you though I do not know what to write about. I am about the same only my side is getting worse all the time. I went out and cut some wood to day and to night it aches so that I cant hardly sit still, so if I do not write you a verry interesting lett[e]r you will know the reason. I have not been to the doctor since I have been here, but if I do not get any better I shall have to go soon. I think that my liver has grown fast to my side for when I lay on my left side it feels as though there was something pulling down on the other, and there is a hollow place so that you can lay your hand in, and my walking around so much keeps it iritated and sore all the time. but I hate to make any fuss about it for the boys will say that I am playing off for my discharge, so I let it go and only complain to you for you are all the one that will sympathize with me or cares any thing for me. and I do not know any reason why you should care for me when I know that I am so unworthy of your

---

who opposed the Union's war policy and favored a negotiated peace. Leech, *Reveille in Washington*, 348-349; *Dictionary*, 175. "As a sign of protest against Lincoln's suppression of civil liberties, Peace Democrats wore pennies with the head of "Liberty" emblazoned on them. This practice gave rise to the term "Copperheads," though Republicans equated them with the poisonous snake of that name." *Encyclopedia*, Vol. 1, 443.

<u>love</u> or care.

      Say <u>darling</u>, dont you sometimes get tired of my dry and poor letters and wish that I would not write to you so often? and when I write you such lett[e]rs as I did the other day I am afraid that you will learn to <u>hate</u> me more than <u>love,</u> and that you will despise me for giving you so much trouble. but if you will forgive me the past I will try and be more worthy of your love in the future. and if our lives are spared to see each other again I will try and provide a <u>home</u> of our own so that we may live more for ourselves. and that we may be free to bring up our darling little ones more as we shall want them to be. I was so disappointed to day when there was no letter for me from home, and I have been so lonesome ev[e]r since the mail came. I used to think if I could only get a letter once a week from you, but now I look for two as much as I did for one. I have [been] writing twice a week since I have been here, but then I suppose that I have more time to write than you do and so I shall not complain if I do not get them so often. as I write the church bells are tolling, but I think that it will do you more good to get this letter than it does me to go to church here. and I am all alone to night so I think that I will stay at home and write if I can think of any thing to write.

      we have not had any snow here yet but it has rained most ev[e]ry day and the streets are muddy. Oh, I forget to tell you that I am <u>cooking</u> for the <u>band</u> now and shall have nice times this winter. they go out <u>Serenading</u> most ev[e]ry night or to one of the <u>Theatres</u> to play, and I can go with them so that I can see all of the sights and it does not cost me any thing. and tomorrow night we are going to the Paymaster so I think that we shall get our pay soon. I am going to see about my furlough this week so that I will know whether I am coming home or not, then I will not worry about it any more. I could get one but we have got a regular <u>Sour</u> <u>Krout</u> for an officer and he does not like me so I think that my chances are small, but then I can stand it for nine months more and then I will not ask any adds of any of them. I have not been out on a <u>pass</u> but once since I have been in the city and then I went on business so I have not had much chance to look around. I have not been to the capital yet, nor to the Treasury, nor to Washingtons Monument, but I am going before I come home so that I can tell you all about them. The Treasury is the most splendid building that I have ev[e]r seen on the outside. I think it is about 400 feet long and perhaps 100 wide and is built of marble and Iron.

I believe that you said that you had got that bundle that I sent and wanted to know if that coat was a Reb. no it is one of the Massachusetts Infantry Coats, but they would not let me wear it here so I sent it home. I want you to keep thos[e] clothes till I come home if you can. you was right about that being a Mosquito bar,[7] and if it had not been for that I should have been carried off by them in New Orleans last summer.

I have not got Netties likeness yet and I am going to write to her once more about it before long. I sent her our Netties and told her to send it back to me, but she has not written or sent either yet. I have yours yet though and I look at it ev[e]ry day. it seems as though you looked larger or more fleshy than you did when I came away, though your face looks natural. I hope that you are not going to be big like your mother, dont you, for I do not like big women.

you said that you was glad that I was having to do work and cook so that I could help you when I get home. well, I hope that I can be of more help to you, but I am afraid that I shall get so lazy that it will be more work for you to get it out of me than it will be to do it your self. but I will close this for to night and go to bed, or read, or something else. write often and ac[c]ept the love of,

Frank

Washington
Dec 8[th] 1864

My Dear,

I recd your most wealcome lett[e]r yesterday, but I had to go to Temperance meeting last night so that I could not write and so I am going to do so to night. I believe that I owe you two letters, or at least I have had two since I wrote. but then I sent one the same day that I got yours so that will make me about even with you, but still I do not mean to be anyways Pot billied about it. and so if I get a fit on and write you three or four in a week you must excuse me if I do sometimes let a week go with out writing to you. I do not have any

---

[7] "Protection was offered against both flies and mosquitoes by mosquito nets draped on frames over the beds in most hospitals, but without any realization of the role of these insects in carrying disease." Adams, *Doctors in Blue*, 170.

time only nights to write and then there is almost every evening some place to go to so that it takes up all the time.

I am not verry well this week, my side is so bad that I had to go to bed one day but it was on the account of my mopping the floor that made it worse. but it is better now and I am in hopes that I will not have another such a time.

They are having a <u>fair</u> here now in aid of the Protestant Orphan Asylum and our Band goes down there to play. and I have been down and it is in the Odd fellows hall, and I can tell you that it is a nice thing. there is all ways to make money and in a bar room I should call it Gambling, but I suppose that it will not do to apply so harsh a term to any thing that so benevolent Society does. but I have no reason to complain for they done a fine thing for me. the band had a splendid supper, a Turkey and all of the goodies that the Ladies know so well how to fix. there was lots of pretty girls there and they had a plenty of chances to show off their <u>charms</u> to the best of their ability.

I have had only one lett[e]r from you in a week, but I suppose that you have been busy so that you do not have time to write. but if you can find time to write to me twice I will try and answer you. you can take one ev[en]ing in the week and one on sunday and I will take time to write you as often. for if I cant get a chance to come home this winter we can write often so that the time will not seem so long.

You asked me what I think of the war and for an answer I can tell you to read the Presidents Message.[8] I think that is as good an answer as I can give you. I think that the war will be closed when those in rebilion [rebellion] lay down their armes and submit to the authority of the Government and not till then. and how long they may be able to carry on the war is more than I can tell. perhaps with the capture of Richmond the war will cease and then the rebs may perhaps fall back to some other place, but where is more than I can tell. but I think that with any reasonable amount of success this winter will close the war.

I am going down to the Capital some day to see how they do

[8] In his message to Congress on December 6 Lincoln asked for reconsideration of the amendment abolishing slavery, and also stated that "the war will cease on the part of the government, whenever it shall have ceased on the part of those who began it." *Almanac*, 606.

business in Congress and then I will tell you all about it. we have not had any snow here yet but it is cold enough to snow to night. it rained last night and then turned around and froze so that it is real cold. I had a letter from Nettie last week but she did not send her likeness. I think that I will send you her lett[e]r in this. I do not know but that you will be jealous of my correspondence with her, but I cant help it now if you are, so long as I send you all of her letters. and if you dont like it you can just write to her and tell her to quit from me and I think that will close the matt[e]r. I am going to send her your likeness in my next lett[e]r so that she can see what a brave, good little woman I call wife. I think that I will try and come home sometime this winter to see how you are getting along and see what I can do with my things there.

you said that you thought that we had better go to Min.[9] well, if it was not for my father and Mother I should think so to[o]. but my mother has always been a mother to me such as but few have, and it seems as though it would not be acting the part of a Son to leave her now that she is getting old. I never knew how dear to me was a mother till I come into the army. and often when I have faced my lonely post at night and thought of all her great love for me and how unworthy I have been, and how much sorrow I have caused her till (and I am not ashamed to confess it to you) I have wept. and I have resolved that if God should spare my life that as long as I can be of any comfort or assistance to them I will nev[e]r leave them. they have always shared their bread with me and why should not I mine now with them. No, we will make us a little home of our own somewhere where we can see and take some care of them. and though we may not be rich in this worlds goods we will be at least happy in each other. I do not know but you will think that I am asking too much of you in this, but I can nev[e]r do anymore than my duty to them.

I am lonesome to night and the words of that beautiful song keep running through my mind to day, "Do they miss me at home, do they miss me?" Oh, how I would like to lay my head in your lap to night and hear you sing that song. do you sing as much as you used

---

[9] It is likely that Thankful mentioned moving to Minnesota. In other letters both Frank and Thankful have expressed the desire to leave Concord, NY after the war, and get away from the people who have been taking advantage of them.

to? I want you to get your <u>harp</u> in tune by the time that I come home so that you can sing to me. There is a little girl lives across the street, four years old, and I fancy that she looks like our little Nettie, and she and I are getting to be great friends. her name is Cornelia. I do not know the oth[e]r name. she is real keen and we have just such times as Nettie and I used to have to play. she comes ov[e]r here and stays with me half of the time.

but I shall have to close this sheet for to night. Please write often, and accept this with the love of your own,

Frank

I have got a lett[e]r from Carrie, and one from Dora, but none from Em, Marth, or Sarah.[10]

Washington DC
Dec 18[th] 1864

My Dear Wife,

I recd your most wealcome letter to day, and you can guess how glad I was when I tell you that the last that I got was dated Dec 9[th]. but I had two to day so I suppose that any of them got stuck on the road. and I had began to think that there was something the matter or that you had forgot to write. My side has been getting better of last week so that I feel first rate and I am in hopes that it will get well now.

The snow has most all gone off, but the mud has not begun to go off yet. and it rains ev[e]ry day so that the prospect is not verry good for it to go at present, but it does not make much difference to me for I do not have to go out only to get water and wood. but I think of the boys that have to go on guard in the rain and mud. but I believe that I have served my time at that business, and I think that I will try and keep in out [of] the wet this winter at least.

Yes, I think that if you can sell of[f] our cow[s] this winter you had better do it, that is if you will have to buy fodder to winter them. I

---

[10] Since Carrie (Caroline Steele), Dora (Cynthia Eudora Cornell), Martha (Treat), and Sarah (Spencer) are all sisters of Frank, Em is most likely his oldest sister Catharine (Stanbro), as Griffith refers to his younger sister Nancy Eveline (Morse) as "Eva."

do not know what to write about to night for there is no news that I can write from here that you have not heard already. The news here is now that Sherman has Captured Savannah with 11000 Prisoners, that the Charleston and Savannah rail road is in our possession, and that the rebs in charleston ar[e] in a sweat to know what he will do next.[11] it is one of the greatest feats of the war or in the world. and it only proves the rotteness of the Confederacy that an army of only forty thousand can march through the heart of an enemys country with so little resistence.[12]

I believe that you have nev[e]r told me who Mina was married to, and I can not make it seem to me that Rena is old enough to be married yet for she was only a little girl when I came away. I have sent Nettie your likeness just to let her see what a good little woman I have got, and I expect to get hers this week and then I will send it to you or come and bring it my self. I think that I shall be home next month sometime and perhaps Nettie will come with me if I can come that way, that is if you want her to. I asked her if she would come if I came that way, but have not had an answ[e]r yet. have you got a stove for our room yet, or don't you think it is best? does Will go to school this winter? and who teaches the school? how is fathers lip, has that got well yet? and is he well so that he can do anything yet? and does Hem take care of the Horses? What has become of Orlando?[13] and How does Harry get along? you see that I want to know all the news. I have not had a letter from Sarah in a long time, and Lib has forgotten me all together. but I shall have to close this and go to bed. write

---

[11] Griffith's information was a bit premature as the Union army did not occupy Savannah until December 21. The Union troops moved against the Charleston and Savannah Railroad on November 30 and again on December 6, but they did not take it. Sherman's army arrived at Savannah on the 10th, advanced around it to get supplies by sea by the 16th, and the Confederates evacuated the city on December 20. *Almanac*, 603, 607-613.

[12] Sherman actually had well equipped forces of 55,000 infantry, 5,000 cavalry, and 2,000 artillerymen. The Confederates only had 13,000 men available. Between November 15 and December 10 Sherman's army had marched 285 miles from Atlanta to Savannah. *Almanac*, 608; *Dictionary*, 509; *Encyclopedia*, Vol. 4, 1769.

[13] See footnote in letter of February 4, 1864.

often, and acc[e]pt this from,
       Frank

―――――――

[*fragment. if letter of Nov. 27, 1864 was "nine months more," eight months would place this letter near the end of Dec. 1864*]

....it but then I had rath[e]r do this than to do duty in the Company. or rather I can do it a great deal easier for it hurts my side so to walk around so much and carry a musket. but then I have a great deal of lifting to do and that keeps it sore all the time. you will ask me why I do not go to the Doctor and get excused. well, I did go once and he told me that I would have to go into the Hospital for two or three months and keep quiet or he could not do any thing for me. well, if I should go there I would not have any thing to do only to lay around and how could I pass the time? I should die of <u>Ennui</u>,[14] of having nothing to do, while here I can keep busy and the time passes off more quickly. I have had all that I want of the Hospitals. and if I can only worry my time out only a little more than eight <u>months</u> now, and then get home out of all this noise and excitement and have <u>you</u> to take care of me, I think that I can get well. Now you will want to know why I do not get my discharge and I shall have to tell you that they do not discharge men here till they are ready to die, and I am not so bad off as that yet. if a man goes to the doctor here that can <u>walk</u> they tell him that he is <u>playing off</u>, or that he is an old <u>beat</u>, so I keep away as long as I can <u>wiggle</u>.

One of the boys has just got back from a furlough to night. he went home to get married and we have had a great time with him, but he is a fine fellow and will make some woman a good Husband. he belongs to the Sons of Temperance.[15] Say dear, are you glad that I

―――――――――

[14] Griffith defines ennui quite well. It is defined as boredom in *Webster's Ninth New Collegiate Dictionary*, 414.

[15] The Sons of Temperance was one of the early major temperance organizations. It was founded in 1842 by two New York City businessmen, and its members were mainly middle class, and of "fair moral character." John J. Rumbarger, *Profits, Power, and Prohibition: Alcohol Reform and the Industrializing of America, 1800-1930* (Albany: State University of New York

have joined them? I have not drank a drop of anything but water in three months and I do not mean to drink any in the next year. and that puts me in mind that I have to make a <u>speech</u> tomorrow night. I wish you was here to help me. I think that I could talk so much bett[e]r if you was here so that I could look into your face and catch your inspiration. and that puts me in mind to ask you to write a piece for our Paper. we are to have one next quarter and the ladies are going to edit it. I will give you a subject, or an idea, and that is how the wives of the soldiers feel on the Temprance cause in the army. you know that there are lots of soldiers here who instead of sending home their money spend it for drink while their families at home are suffering for the need of it. god grant that <u>you</u> may never know by <u>experince</u>. I know that you can

[*next page missing*]

Washington DC
Dec 24[th] /64

My Dear Wife Mine,

The boys are going out to play to night and I did not feel like going with them. I thought that I would pass the time till bed time more pleasantly writing to you than I would in any oth[e]r way so I have just set down to have a good long talk with you. I have been most sick to day with my side. I have been to the Dr and he is giving me some powders for it. he wants that I should go to the Hospital and have it blistered,[16] but I do not know whether I shall or not. perhaps the medicine that I am taking will help me so that it will not be necessary, but I have been worse to day than I have for a long time

---

Press, 1989), 29-30. "In the spring of 1864 a temperance movement originating in the Fifth Maine Regiment was said to have spread to numerous other organizations of the Army of the Potomac. But these and all other attempts to curb drinking among the soldiers appear to have been of little avail." Wiley, *The Life of Billy Yank*, 254.

[16] Blistering involved applying irritants to the body in order that internal diseases would be brought to the surface of the body from deeper, diseased organs and then dispelled. Jerger, *A Medical Miscellany*, 14.

before. the boys all say that I will get discharged on the account of it, but I do not have any hopes on that score for I am not near enough dead for that. but if I do not get better this winter I shall begin to think that I never will be.

Christmas Eve.

Tis just three years ago to night that we went to Evans to live. and how much has transpired in the three years that has just passed, and how much will happen in the next three years to come. I was sitting here to night and thinking of the folks at home and what they would be doing. and I thought that you would write me something to night, and so I thought that I would write too, though I hardly know what to write. I was thinking to day of the time when, if God spares my life, I should come home again. and how I should feel when I saw the dear ones aga[i]n. and these lines come into my mind, and they are so expressive of my thoughts I can not help penning them down.

> Three Years Oh beloved Wife
> My heart is with the[e] oer the seas
> I did not think to count another
> Before I wept upon thy knees
> Before this scroll of absent years
> Was blotted with thy streaming tears
> My own I do not care to check;
> I weep about here alone
> As if I hung upon thy neck
> As if thy lips were on my own
> As if this full sad heart of mine
> Were beating closely to thine own
> Three weary years how looks she now
> What light is in her tender eyes
> What trace of time has touched the brow
> Whose look is borrowed of the skies
> That listened to her nightly prayer
> How is she changed since I was there
> Who sleeps upon her heart alway[s]
> Whose name upon her lips is worn
> For whom the night seems made to pray
> For whom she wakes to pray at morn

Whose sight is dim whose heart strings stir
Who weeps these tears to think of her
I know not if my Darlings eyes
Would find me changed in slighter things
I have wondered beneath many skies
And tasted many bitter springs
And many leaves once fair and gay
From youths full flower had droped away
Dear Wife dost thou love me yet
And am I remembered in my home
When those I love for joy are met
Does some one wish that I would come
Thou [*illegible*] I am beloved of thee
But as the schoolboy numbers oer
Night after night the Pleiades[17]
And finds the stars he found before
As turns the maiden aft her taken
As counts the Miser aye his gold
So till lifes silver cord is broken
Would I of the fond love be told
My heart is full mine eyes are wet
Dear wife dost thou love thy long lost wander yet.
Oh when the hour to meet again
Creeps on and speeding are the sea
My heart takes up the lengthened chain
And link by link draws nearer thee
When land is hailed and from the shore
Comes off the blessed breath of home
With fragrance from my mother dear
Of flowers forgoten when I come
When port is gained and slowly now
The old familiar paths are passed
And entering unconcious how
I gaze upon thy face at last

---

[17] Pleiades, a conspicuous loose cluster of stars in the constellation Taurus, named after the seven daughters of Atlas which were turned into a group of stars in Greek mythology. Webster, 903.

And run to the[e] all faint and weak
And feel thy tears upon my cheek
Oh if my heart break but with joy
The light of Heaven will fairer seem
[*next page missing*]

Washington
Jan 8th 1865

My Dear Wife,
    I am going to try and write you a few lines to day though I am afraid that I shall miserably fail of writing any thing that will be interesting. I am not verry well to day, my <u>side</u> pains me a great deal although I think that it is better than it has been for the past week. I have recd one letter from you in the week and I accept your excuse for not writing more and shall have to ask the same of you. I have had another letter from Cousin Nettie and I will send it to you as soon as I can answer it, also one from Cousin Ann.[18]
    We are having rough weather here at present. it has rained and snowed and froze and the wind has blew and has been generaly disagreeable all the last week, but it has cleared off to day and is quite pleasant. though it is quite cold, the snow has nearly all gone from the streets. we have had one or two days of rather good sleighing, but I did not get a chance to have a ride.
    Well, we had the installation of officers in our Division last Wednesday night and all passed off verry pleasantly. and at the close of the Ceremonies we were called on for a few remarks to which we responded, though with what elaguence or effect I can not tell, and I leave you to judge. but you know that speech making on the subject is about <u>played</u> <u>out</u> as ev[e]ry thing that can be said on the subject that can be said, and it is only repeating one what we all knew before. I am glad that you are going to write for our pap[e]r and hope that you will write often.

---

[18] Possibly Thankful's cousin Ann H. Peirce, a teacher in Ashford, New York. *Concord*, 233, 428.

Now I have [hope] that you will excuse this random lett[e]r for as you will see I am not in the mood of writing letters to day. but when I do feel the spirit I will try and make up for the deficiency. I did not get any lett[e]r to day but hope to soon. I do not think that I shall be able to come home this month, but it is not certain yet. I shall probably know by the next time that I write. if I do not come now I do not think that I shall befor[e] next spring. There is no news of any importance at present.

9th

I am going to try and finish this this morning and send it to you, but I do not know but what my next may be mailed from Savanna, or Port Royal, or somewhere else. there is on order here for 10,000 men to garrison Savannah and perhaps we may be sent, but I hope not for I have been south all that I want to at present. but if it is so ordered I shall have no choice in the matt[e]r, but then I shall have only eight months to stay and perhaps they will pass off more quickly with the change. I am better of my side this morning and I feel in hop[e]s that I shall get well now.

Give my love to all the folks at home. kiss the little ones for me, and accept this short lett[e]r with the love of your,

Frank

Waterville
January 8th/65

Dear brother,

i have not written to you for i have bin wating for the letter you owe me, but i see i shall have to write to you first, So i Shall not grumble. i wrote to dory[19] last night and i have to write to you and tell you the news. netty says She wants a sugar hors[e] and gurty says she wants a sugar tail. Albert has got home.[20] I was wish[ing] I had a gun for i could shoot a fox about evry day. albert shot one three times and

---

[19] Griffith's sister Cynthia Eudora Griffith Cornell, who lives in Maine.

[20] Thankful's brother Albert E. Myers was mustered out of the 102nd NYSV Infantry on December 24, 1864 at Savannah, Georgia.

the seckond time he shot he bled him. will[21] lays on the lounge a grunting with a soar leg and he says he will write some time. Thank is getting gurty to sleep, and netty is coming around like satun. pa's canser is growing worse all the time and i think he will not live long. it has snowed all day and the snow is so deep that we can hardly get out doors at all.

guess I shall have to give up writing to night for i have got out of writing timber, so good bye for to night. i put some ashes in the Smoke hous[e] yesterday and last night about 4 oclock it was all a fire and i run out barefoot. we thought the pig would burn up. netty said she looked out of the window till she almost cried. i must stop writing for ma says she wants to write some in here. i shall not write to you again till i hear from you. write often to your brother,

Eugene Griffith.[22]
Good bye for this time.

———————

Feb [Jan] 9
Waterville

My Ever Dear Son,

it a long time since I have written to you, not because you are forgoten, you will always have a place in your Mothers heart. Thank writes so often that you hear all the news. Carrie has gone home, Will went with them. he came home Tuesday. has been sick ever since he got home, is better to day. pas lip is very bad, it runs and smells very bad. I cant bear to look at it. I do not think it can be cured. it seems so aweful to think he must die by inches, that he must suffer so much and nothing can be done to help him, but so it is, and we must try to be reconciled to the dispensation of our heavenly Father for he doeth all things well. we cannot always[s] see why we are afflicted, but it is for some wise purpose. Will is not as well to night as he was this morning, I am afraid he is going to have a fever. Eugene is not very

---

[21] William Henry Griffith, was nine years younger than Frank.

[22] Marcus Eugene "Gene" Griffith, was fifteen years younger than Frank. He was only fourteen and a half when he wrote this letter.

well to night. he took cold in his raid after water bare foot last night. it was amusing to see him perform. he was so excited he did not know what he did.

I am glad to hear you are geting better. I have been afraid your side was past cure. I had a letter from Dora a few days ago. She said she had not heard from you in a long time. She would write but did not know where to direct. Martha[s] health is very poor this winter. this is the most unpleasant winter I ever saw. it storms five days ev[e]ry week and has since the middle of September. I hope you will be home before another cold winter, seven months more. dear me, how long the time seems to wait before I can see you. if I could see you I could say in half an hour [more] than I can write in all night. the stage has just come up. I dont believe they can get through the drifts. Fay started for Springville to day and could not get there. I dont know what we shall do for wood if will is going be sick. it is all we can do to get along if we are well. pa cant do hardly anything. we are short for fodder. if it is an early [spring] we can get along.

you will find plenty of mistakes in this. I will not bother you to read eny more this time, So good night.

except this from your loving Mother

[sideways on top of first page, by Eugene's hand]
I will write agin when I hear from you. the snow is 15 inches de[e]p. netty is stringing beads to wear around her neck. well, thos wrote to carie to day. i have to walk [to] the myers so I shall quit writing for this time. January 11[th] 1865

Washington
Jan 12th/65

My Darling,
I was most agreeably surprised to get your lett[e]r yesterday for I did not look for one till to day. I do not know as you can read this for I have one of those good old head aches this morning so that my hand is not steady at all. I went to the Dr yesterday and he put three cuts on my side so that it is verry sore this morning, but I think that it helped me for it does not pain me so much this morning. It is one of the most beautiful days that you ever saw, just warm enough to

be comfortable, the sun shines so beautiful and bright. and the streets are all froze up so that the wagons have worn them down smooth, and you could see long trains of army wagons at almost any time of the day.

Has Birney got home yet? I heard that he was discharged last fall.[23] and Lon, do they hear from him? I have not since I have been here. and now while I am asking questions I may as well ask you all that I want to know. How is fathers <u>cancer</u>? is it any worse or bett[e]r, and how does it look? Have you got enough to eat and wear? and who teaches the school this winter? Does Fays folks live where they did? and where is Lib[24] this winter? I think that she has forgotten that she owes me a letter, but I think that I shall have to write to her again. have you heard from Al yet, and when is he coming home? how does Weber like soldiering? and where is Gene and what is he doing this winter? and Ashley, where does he live and what is he doing? and what of Orlando and Sue? you wrote to [me] that she was sick but have nev[e]r said any thing since.

Sergeant Wilkinson says give her my <u>love</u>. he is one of the Sardines, a regular pill. I will tell you more of him sometime. he is the W[orthy] P[atriarch] of our Div[ision] S[ons] of T[emperance] and my bunk mate. He is corresponding with a <u>lady</u> who he hopes to make his wife <u>when</u> <u>this</u> <u>cruel</u> <u>war</u> <u>is</u> <u>over</u>. and he thinks that he has got her where the boy had the School Marm, where <u>the</u> <u>hair</u> <u>is</u> <u>short</u>. He says that he is going to stick to her like a sick kitten to a hot brick.

Madam: your leige lord invites me to add a word in this communication; and first I must disclaim some of the above remarks which he has attributed to me. With the <u>sang</u> <u>froid</u>[25] which is so common among soldiers, when he signed forth that he could hardly determine "what to write," I suggested laughingly that he might "<u>send</u> <u>my</u> <u>love</u>" and he took me at my word. his subsequent remark was wholly original with him self, however, as probably your common sense would have informed you. trusting therefore that you will

---

[23] It was only a rumor, "Birney" Weber remained with the 116th and mustered out with regiment June 8, 1865 at Washington. *Registers*, 492.

[24] Thankful's sister Elizabeth Myers. See letter dated June 10-11, 1863.

[25] "Sang-froid" means self-possession or imperturbability. *Webster*, 1041.

devine therefrom no unfavorable opinion of me, I recline into the obscurity of my signature. A. Lester Wilkinson[26]

I hope that you will not be offended because I have let my friend write you a line in this, or think that I show our correspondence, for such is not the case. but as he was standing by me, or rather writing to her, I said to him "what shall I write next?" and hence you can see how it has all happened. He has told me something of his lady and how their correspondence commenced, and shown me her likeness. she is handsome and intelectual, and I think that she loves him hartfully, and I am sure that he does her. and perhaps I had bett[e]r tell you more of him here. he is good looking and has a good education of the first class, a christian, and a gentelman in ev[e]ry sense of the word. and as a friend and associate I like him for I can sit down and talk with him on any subject and not be gretet [greeted] with any of those low vulgar expressions so common with the soldiers. honest and candid in the expression of his sentiments. I can assure you that we have some most interesting discussions, to me at least. he holds the highest office in our Div of the Sons of Temperance, and I can assure you that he fills it with honor to himself and the Div. and he is one of the few that I shall remember with friendship when we are separated. and with this I shall close this subject.

Now in regard to your communication for our pap[e]r. I thank you for it and hope that you will continue to write for the pap[e]r. but I hope that you will find it conveni[e]nt to write your communication on a s[e]parate pap[e]r, for you see that I should have it all to copy off before it can be read, and then be more careful to write it plain and not erase so much of it for it looks bad, and you know that I have a good

---

[26] Arthur Lester Wilkinson, was 22 when he enlisted October 12, 1862 as a private with the 7th Michigan Cavalry (which were assigned during their entire time of service to the famous Michigan Brigade under Brigadier General George Armstrong Custer). He was promoted to Sergeant Major January 23, 1863. Like Griffith he was now a member of the Veteran Reserve Corps. Wilkinson was the "Worthy Patriarch" of the Sons of Temperance. After the war Wilkinson eventually settled in Centralia, Illinois. Michigan Cavalry, 7th Regiment, *Roster of Survivors of the Seventh Michigan Cavalry and Muster Out Rolls of the Regiment* (Ann Arbor, Mich.: Register Pub., 1895) 23, 35, 59; "7th Regiment Michigan Cavalry 1862-1866" http://members.aol.com/_ht_a/dlharvey/7thcav.htm; Ancestory.com.

deal of pride in this matt[e]r. the subject mater is excelent, but you can use a little better <u>Grammar</u>. Now do not be angry with me for saying this and not write any more for I shall then be sorry that I have writt[e]n this.

and now about our discussion. I can not write well enough to day to answer it, but will in the course of the week. but just now I have a great deal of writing to do for the Div, so you see that my time is pretty well occupied at present. but that must not make any difference with you, I want you to write to me often for you have more time than I do at present. but I shall have to close this for the present for I have got 24 more to write this week beside one to Cousin Nettie and one to cousin Ann. Give my love to all the folks at home, and accept this with the love of your own,

Frank

PS. this letter is unsatisfactory to me and I am afraid that it will be so to you, too. but please excuse me for this time.

―――――――

Washington
Jan 16th 1865

Dear Thank,

I recd your most wealcome letter to day and I am going to try and write you one in return to night. but I am afraid that you will fail to read it, my hand trembles so and I am so nervous. I have been writing most all day to day for the Div, and to night my side aches so that I can hardly stand it. I have been excused from all duty for the last week, and if I do not get any bette[r] I shall be for the week to come, and then I hope that I shall have time to write to you oftener. I have had a mustard plast[e]r on my side two days and it has made it sore so that I can hardly bear my clothes around me. and perhaps when that gets well I shall be better. but if I do not get better soon I am going to be examined for my discharge, though I do not have much hope that I shall get it for I am not near enough <u>dead</u> for that. When I go to bed at night I generaly lay awake till one or two and sometimes three in the morning before I can get to sleep. and then when I get up in the morning my side aches so for two or three hours that I just walk the floor all the time, and then it will be easier till I lay down again. and it has been so that ev[e]ry time that I change my position it will pain me so. the Dr says that I have got the Liver complaint very bad[27], but he says that he thinks that he can help me. and he said that he would do all that he could for me. and so if the course of treatment does not help me I shall probably get Discharged. I told him that I wanted to get well or so that I could do my duty, and if he could cure me I had much rather he would then to discharge me for I wanted to go home when my time was out as good a man as I was when I left home. No, I do not want to come home to you to be a burden on your hands the rest of my days. but I am afraid that in the sacrifice that I have made for my country I have ruined my health, and that in the future, if <u>God</u> spares my life, that I shall have to seek some other means of livelihood than the hard labor of my hands. but then thanks to that dear Mother and Father I believe that I have a liberal Education at least so that what I fail to accomplish with my hands I may make up with my head. and it will not be as bad for me as it has been with thousands of others who have lost hands and legs and healt[h] in this war, who have no other means of a livelihood than the labor of their hands. and we should be very thankful that my life even has been spared this far.

Yes, I am glad that you have got so that you can eat Oyster soup, and I hope that you will get so that you can go [get] the animals for they are my favorite dish. only I do not think that the cooking improves them for I like them <u>raw</u> best, and then we can get such nice ones here, or could if we had any money to get them with. but we live in hopes that we shall get our pay soon and then I shall treat my self to at least one mess. I should like verry much to take you out to ride on some of these pleasant evenings, but we have no snow here at present. I am sorry that you was disappointed in not getting a lett[e]r from me last week, but I have writt[e]n to [you] one a week all the time, and sometimes more. but you must excuse me if I did not write more last week for I was nearly sick and I knew that I could not write you such a lett[e]r as I want to always, but I will try and write often in future.

Now in r[e]gard to the discussion that I proposed to you. I do not see how I can take your last lett[e]r as a commencement for I can see no point of arguement in it, and I only look on it as an excellent exhortation to me. and as such I thank you for the interest that you

---

[27] See letter dated February 2, 1864, and footnote.

have always manifested in my future welfare. but I can see no debatible ground in it unless I were to take the position that there was no hereafter, or that of the Universal doctrine that all will be saved in the end, which I do not <u>bilieve</u> and therefore I do not like to talk about it. but in the Question of the two distinct attributes of our being, the heart and the spirit, as to be a little plainer on Spiritual Heart and our Intelect I will take sides with you and see what we can say on the subject. I shall contend that when the Bible speaks of the heart of man that it means our Emotions such as Love, Charity, Benevalence, Sympathy, anger, Hatred, revenge, and the like. while the soul means that our life as the body Spiritual. that the heart is to the soul what our natural hearts are to our earthly bodies. Or take any other Question that you think b[e]st.

I was very glad to get your communication for our paper and I shall copy them off for the pap[e]r next week. I want you to keep on writing for us for this pap[e]r is one of my own suggestion and I do not want it to [be] a failure. and I expect that in the cours[e] of a few weeks that I shall have to take my turn at reading it.

You will excuse me if I do not write you a verry long letter to night for I shall have to stop for to night. do you show these lett[e]rs to all the folks at home? I would not if I were in your place for if they want to hear from me let them write to me and then they will get a lett[e]r of their own to read. I had a letter from Uncle Gifford last week but have not answered it yet. and I have to write to Cousin Nettie yet, but shall this week and then I will send you her last letter. write often and acept this from your,

Frank

Washington
Jan 20th/65

Dear <u>Thank</u>,

I am thinking of the good visit that you are going to have to day and wishing that I could be there to enjoy it with you. but as that is impossible to day I am going to do the next best thing and that is to write you a lett[e]r. It seems as though I could see you all gathered around the fire and enjoying the serenity of the dear ones at home, and I wonder if I am missed from that circle or if they will miss me or talk

242

of me, or will their thoughts be only of those present. and will they place me a chair at the table and look for the absent, and sigh that I tarry so long. Yes, I know that there is <u>one</u> that will miss me, and <u>one</u> that longs for the time to come when I shall be with you again.

And to day my brother will come to the years of <u>manhood</u>.[28] it seems only a little time ago that he was a mere boy and I can hardly realize that he is 21 to day, or that in a few days I shall be 30 years old.[29] it seems but a year or two since I was only 21. and now one half of my life is gone, and perhaps with it the strengths and vigor of my life. Oh, can it be that in giving three of the best years of my life to my Country I have given my health also. and that if my life shall be spared for the next 20 or 30 years I shall live in this constant pain and misery. but I suppose that I should be verry thankful that my life has been spared while so many have been cut down. My side is no better than it has been, and I think if any thing it is worse. I do not do any duty at present and I do not know as I shall for the next month to come. I presume that I shall have an examination next week and then I shall be able to tell you more about it. Now I do not want you to feel worried about me, or think that I am going to die here for I do not think so. I can go around where I please and have a fair appetite so that I can eat almost anything. but I am nervous as you will see by this writing and do not sleep good at night. there is hardly a night that I can go to sleep till after midnight and sometimes not till 2 or 3 Oclock in th[e] mor[n]ing.

Oh, I must tell you that I have got myself into rather a delicate position in the Division of the Sons and now I want to ask your advise. On last wednesday ev[e]ning I had the pleasure of introducing two ladies into the Div. and as I supposed that they were ladies in <u>fact</u>, I have only a short acquaintence with them, have only spoke to one of them but once befor[e] last me[e]ting night, and the other I have met at the house of a friend Occasionally, and she asked me if I would take her down to the Div and I told her that I would. and then she said that her friend would like to go also. and so I Introduced

---

[28] William Henry Griffith, was born January 20, 1844.

[29] Frank must mean "a few months" rather than "a few days" as he was born April 26, 1835.

them to the Div and some of the members have took offence at it and are going to call me to an account for it. Now, I have the assurance of at least one of these ladies and I have not seen the other yet, that she wished to join the Div for her own good that she might be shielded from temptation, and that any stories about her are false as far as her actions or <u>crime</u> is conc[e]rned. And now what I prop[o]se to do in the case is to sustain the position that I have taken in the cause, and even though she has <u>sinn[e]d</u> yet if she repent and stretch out her hands to us for aid and assistance, to become a virtous woman, that it is our duty to give that aid. do you think that I am right in this? I think that I shall prepare myself to speak on the subject next meeting, and if you can get me a lett[e]r by that time do so. but I have got sev[e]ral other letters to write to day, and as I have had tw[o] lett[e]r from you this week I shall close this hoping that you will not forget to write often to me. and as the mail is about going I will stop.

     Frank

Washington
Jan 26th 1865

Dear Thank,

     I recd two letters from you to day, and at the first moments of leisure I am going to try and write you one in return. I have been verry busy this week for I am cooking in the Hospital now and have to work most all of the time. I can tell you that I shall get to be a famous cook by the time that I get home, though I do not know how long I shall stay here for I am afraid that I cant stand it to work so hard all the time. my <u>side</u> is a great deal better than it has been in a month before and I feel in hopes that it will get better now, though it pains me a good deal yet. the Dr is going to give me some linament to put on in the morning so as to take the sorness out of the flesh.

     I feel so anxious about Father that I can hardly wait till I can get home to see him. it seems so dreadful that it could not be cured and that he should suffer so much with it. I am going to try and get a <u>furlough</u> in the spring aga[i]n and come home and see him, but I do not know as I shall succed in it. It is quite cold here now and the streets are all ice so that it is awful bad getting around. it has been cold now for a week or more and the ice in the bay is nearly one foot thick so that they are cutting it up for the Ice houses.

we have not been paid yet, and I do not think that we will be now till the first of March. I am sorry for I know that you must need some money by this time, but I cant help it now. I cant send you a copy of our paper for it is to be a written one and there will be only one copy of that, but I can tell you all about it. we have got some poets in the Div and they have composed some songs for us to sing and I will copy some of them and send them to you. I have not got them here to night so I cant send one to night but will try and send you one the next time that I write. I had a lett[e]r from Carrie to day and she told me all about Wills birth day. you must have had a fine time of it. and I thought about you all day and wished that I could be there, too. and so I wrote you a letter on that day as the next best thing to being there. I have not got Netties likeness yet but am looking for it ev[e]ry day now. I do not think of much news to write for you will get that in the papers before you can in this lett[e]r.

The Smithsonian Institute was burned here yesterday.[30] I did not go to the fire but some of the boys did and they said that almost ev[e]ry thing was lost. I b[e]lieve there was no other buildings burned but them. I have not had time to go to Congress yet, but I mean to go before long. Is Albert going to stay with you this winter? I suppose that he has grown to be a man now. and is he satisfied with what he has seen, or do[e]s he think of enlisting again?

but I shall have to close this for to night and go to bed for I shall have to get up Early in the morning to get breakfast. and I have got 25 lett[e]rs to write this week besides one to Carrie and one to Uncle Gifford. The Dr has just been in here to see me and I have been telling him about Fathers lip. he thinks that it will nev[e]r be any bett[e]r. the Dr is a fine old man and I think that he looks like Pa only he is not so tall. he and I have some first rate visits together. I do not know as you can read this, but you can guess at what you cant read.

Frank

---

[30] The fire on January 24, 1865 "destroyed the roof, all the insides of the upper story of the main part of the building, and the interior of the two large north towers and the large south tower" of the Smithsonian. Oehser, Paul H., *The Smithsonian Institution* (Boulder, CO:Westview Press, 1983), 149.

East Concord
Jan 27th 1865

My dear Husband,

to night after doing the ironing I am going to write to you in answer to yours of the 16th & 20th as we have just heard from the [post] office to day for the first time this week. There has been the worst storms I ever saw. it snowed and blowed the hardest it could & was cold as Greenland. to day it calmed down a little so there has three or four teams been past yesterday, and day before there was no teams along. and the roads are completely blocked up & it is, and has been, the lonesomest time I have known since you left home. It was so cold we could not keep warm in the house and a hot fire for the wind crept in at every crevice. I will to talks of something else.

I was glad to hear from [you] again as it was over a week since I had heard from you. Am very sorry your side is no better and I feel very much troubled about you. I think if you could only be at home a while we could doctor you up so that you would get well. do not go on duty again until you get a great deal better than you are, but keep quiet as you can.

And now about that cause you are to advocate or give up. I will say this much, if you have good assurance that the ladies are in earnest in the step they prevailed on you to take, and mean to try and better their conditions by joining your society, by all means maintain them in it for if one sins and afterwards repent and try to renew their lives by doing all in their power to repair the wrong done, then should we lend them a helping hand. but I will close this for to night and go to bed for it can not go out until monday and I will write more tomorrow night.

29th Sabbath.

There is no meeting to day and our folks have all gone down to Fays but the children and me. I am going to finish this to you by way of passing the lonely hours more pleasantly for it is very lonely to me this winter, [*illegible word*] more than common, I can not tell. However, I am going to try and be happy and cheerful as [I] can for Mother. It is sober and silent all the time that it casts a shadow over our lives that are with her. I do not wonder she is so for ev[e]ry day it becomes more apparent that <u>our</u> Father has an awful life to live while

246

he lives and death to die. to be eaten up by a cancer is dreadful, is it not?

we have had the worst storm the past week I ever witnessed. it began to snow & blow Tuesday morning and grow cold and it continued until last evening. the roads are impassible in a great many places and nearly so every where. Will and I went to the village yesterday and we had an awful time getting along but did not tip over at all although we came very near it several times.

Now, I do not want you to be angry with me, but I wish to be excused carrying on a discussion for I am not competent to the task which better it is written when I have [not] got the blues so. but if it makes you feel as though you had rather not get any thus such tell me and I will never write such a letter again. but I must go and get the supper cooking. write often as you can, and I ever do with this. I am ever your own, Thank.

Thank
[*upside down, between lines*]
don't you think I improve in writing compositions

Washington
Feb 3rd 1865

Dear Thank,

I recd your most wealcome letter of Jan 26 yesterday but have been so busy that I have not had time to write before, so you will please to excuse me this time. I am cooking in the Hospital and I have charge of the kitchen so that it keeps me busy all the time, only ev[e]nings and then I go out to Division meetings sometimes so that I do not have so much time as I did to write. but then I like it here for the time passes so much faster when I have some thing to do. I am a great deal better now than I have been since I have been in the city. and I think that my side is going to get well now if I am careful and do not get hurt again, but I cant bear any thing on it yet, neither can I lift any thing heavy. and it makes it ache to go up and down stairs, but then I am going to be verry careful now. the Dr is going to give me some liniament to put on which he says will take the sor[e]ness out of it, and I am so much bett[e]r now that I feel encouraged much.

They say that we have had the coldest winter here that has

been known for a long time, but I have not felt it much for I have been fortunate enough to be in the hous[e] all the time. I have [not] been on duty, that is <u>guard</u>, in nearly three month[s] but once, and then it was not very cold.

And now about that <u>case</u> that I wrote to you about, those Ladies. the subject was brought up in the Div and a vote was taken on their case, and I made a <u>speech</u> on the subject. one of them was retained in the Div and the other expelled. and I am not very sorry either. and now I am going to tell you something in <u>confidence</u> that is up in the Div and is likely to make us some trouble. and I only wish that you was here so that you could go too and then you would know more about it. I have been opposed from the first to the admission of <u>Ladies</u> into our Order for I did not think that any <u>real</u> Lady would join a Soldier Div of the Sons of Temperance as there are but few of the soldiers whose <u>wives</u> are here. and you can think what the state of things are here when I tell you that in the city of Washington there are 15,000 <u>prostitutes</u> who are <u>supported</u> mostly by the Soldiers.[31] so that it is about all a <u>ladies</u> character is worth to be seen in the streets with a Soldier. and it is with shame and sorrow that I make this confession unto you. well, as I was going to tell you that in our Div there is about 15 Ladies, and among the rest the Sister of our <u>Past</u> <u>Worthy</u> <u>Patriarch</u>, the highest office in the Div, and she one of the lady officers. well, the <u>story</u> is that she is in the way, or as the saying is, in an <u>interesting</u> <u>Condition</u>. and she being an <u>unmarried</u> Lady, the <u>Committee</u> on the good of the <u>Order</u>, of which <u>I</u> am one, thought that we must look into the merits of the case. and so we had a Committee meeting to see what should be done in the case. but the story got to the ears of her brother and at the last meeting he had to make a fuss about it. so we called a special meeting and then we had such a time. my <u>friend</u> made a speech, and he made a speech, and <u>I</u> made a speech, and several

---

[31] Griffith over-estimated the number of prostitutes. After an investigation in 1863 *The Evening Star*, a Washington newspaper, estimated there were over 5,000 prostitutes in the city and about 2,500 in Georgetown and Alexandria. Thomas P. Lowry, *The Story the Soldiers Wouldn't Tell: Sex in the Civil War* (Mechanicsburg, PA: Stackpole Books, 1994), 68; Leech, *Reveille in Washington*, 261. Varhola's claim is similar: "In Washington, DC, in 1863, there were more than 450 brothels employing more than 7,000 prostitutes." Varhola, *Everyday Life During the Civil War*, 110.

others made a speech, and then we adjourned. I do not know what will come of it, but I think that she will be expelled from the Div. and her Brother says that he is going to commence an action against <u>us</u> for <u>slander</u>. I think that we will have some fun at any rate. but I will keep you advised of the proceedings. now this is a secret and you must not say one word to any one about it for if it should be found out that I have said any thing they will expell me, too. but you know that I have got in the way of telling you all that I <u>know</u>, and I look to you for <u>advise</u>. and if it shall be proved that this thing has happened to her before she became a member of the Order I am going to take her part and try to have her <u>retained</u> in the Div for I think that there can nothing be said against her since she has belonged to the <u>Order</u>. and I am not the one to hinder any one from making any <u>reformation</u> in their lives, and as I told them the other night I am one to <u>lend</u> a helping hand to any one that may need my assistence.

My <u>Darling</u>, only seven months more from to day, and then if my life is spared I shall be free to come home to you. I know that the time seems long to you, but it will be only a short time, after all the days pass off one by one. and I now begin
[*next page missing*]

———————

Washington, DC
Feb 5th/65

Dear Thank,

I am going to try and write you just a word to night as I have got to sit up and <u>bake</u> some buns for breakfast, so you see that I am making my self useful yet. but I do not know but it is foolish of me to let you know that I can do housework, cooking, and the like, for when I come home you will be wanting me to get up and get breakfast and I shall not have the excuse that I do not know how. I have to get up in the morning at 5 Oclock and I suppose that is what you will be glad of if I can only get in the habit of it. but I am going to tell you that when I do come home I am going to have you cook me five days <u>rations</u>. and I am going to take them to bed with me and then I am going to have one good sleep without being waked up by the <u>ev[e]rlasting</u> drums and having to get up to <u>roll call</u> in the morning, or having to wa[i]t till nine <u>oclock</u> to go to bed. I believe that I have told you that we have to be drum[m]ed to bed, and then drumed up in the morning, drumed to breakfast, dinner, and supper, to drill, and dress parade. and I am getting so tired of this ev[e]rlasting drumming.

I am so much better then I have been, and I feel so glad of it that I hardly know what to write. my side does not pain me now so much as it did, and I can go to bed now and go to sleep with out having to lay awake half of the night. I did not get any letter from you today, so you can see that I do not have much to write about. I think that if it had pleased you to reply to the lett[e]r that I wrote you in regard to the discussion of that subject I could have written about that. I have made out the minutes of the last meeting of the Div and done some other business, and I feel some in the writing mood to night and you will excuse me if I do not Wait for your lett[e]r before I write you.

have [you] heard before this of the Rebel Commissioners coming to Washington to see if they could arrange any terms on which the war could be settled? Well, Father Abraham went down to City Point to meet them, and the result of the conference is that there is no peace as yet. They only demanded that all the property that has been confiscated shall be returned to them, that we give them their slaves back, pay all the debt that they have contracted, and give them th[e]ir Independence. and of course the thing was not to be talked of for a moment on our side, and so the conference closed, and the President has returned to the city.[32] so now I suppose that we shall have a vigorous prosecution of the war. I am sorry that the rebs was so blind that they will [not] see that their ruin is near at hand, and that it will soon become a nessity that they will have to lay down th[e]ir arms and submit to the terms that we may propose to them.

I do not think of any thing more that I need to write, only I do not want you to wait for me to write an answer to your lett[e]rs before

---

[32] This was the Hampton Roads Conference which took place February 3 on board the steamer *River Queen* at Hampton Roads off Fort Monroe, Virginia. Lincoln and Secretary of State William H. Seward met with Confederate Vice-President Alexander H. Stephens, former Confederate Secretary of State Robert M.T. Hunter, and Assistant Secretary of War and former U.S. Supreme Court Justice John A. Campbell. It was brought about by F.P. Blair who had previously met with Jefferson Davis. The conference failed because, as Griffith noted, the Confederates wished to remain independent and continue the practice of slavery, while Lincoln insisted on restoration of the Union. *Almanac*, 632-633; *Dictionary*, 371; *Encyclopedia*, Vol. 2, 919-920.

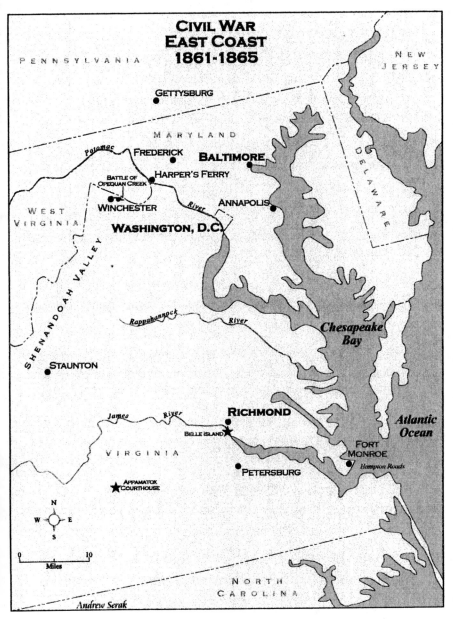

Map of Washington, D.C. and areas mentioned by Frank Griffith in his
Civil War letters. Produced for this volume by Andrew Serak.

you write to me, for you see that I do not have any time, only of an evening to write, and then I can not always write then. I have one to write to Carrie this week, and 25 to the different Div so you can see how much time I have. but I am going to write to you often if I do not do any thing more. now I do not want you to worry about me for it will not be long now before I shall be with you aga[i]n, not quite seven months, and I may come before that time even.

Kiss the little ones for me, and give my love to all the folks at home.

Yours,
Frank

Washington
Feb 10th/65

Dear Thank,

I recd your most wealcome letter last Wednesday but have not had time to write till tonight so you will see that I have something to do now. Wednesday night our Div met so I could not write that night, and last night I had company till ten Oclock, and to night I had an invitation to go down to Excelsior Div but I have stayed at home to write to you for I shall not have any more time till Sunday night, and then I have to write to Carrie for I have not answered her letter yet. and I owe Uncle Gifford one, too, and I have the minuites [minutes] of the last meeting to fix yet before next meeting night and they cover two pages of fools cap, and a lot of communications to write to the other Div, so you can see that I have plenty to do. and I hope that you will try and excuse me if I do not write you very long letters, or if I do not write more than once a week for some time to come.

I have not felt quite so well for the last two or thre[e] days, but feel <u>better</u> to night so that I think I shall be all right in a few days again. my side is some sore yet but does not pain me so much as it did. I wish that you was here so that you could join the Div with me and then you could help me do some of the writing. I tell you that we had a grand old time last Wednesday night. My <u>friend</u> that I told you about is the Presiding officer in the Div, and he wanted to resign and I did not want him to, and so after he had offered his resignation I got up and made a <u>speech</u> on the subject, and then a vote was taken, and

252

the Div voted Unanimous to not accept his resignation and so he has got to stay in his place. And now about that case. the lady has left the Div and her brother has been granted a withdrawal card so that we have got sh[e]d of them both. Our Paper made its first appearance that night and was a desided Success. your communication appeared in it and it was first rate. and I want you to write some more. the paper is called the strength of the Circle, and is Dedicated to Love, Purity and Fidelity. Our Div is Called Circle Div No. 17 and we have about 140 members, all soldiers, and 15 Lady vistors, so you can see that we are doing some good.

The weather has been verry cold for the last few days. there is about two inches of snow on the ground and there has been sleighing one or two days, but it is thawing some to day, but is freezing some now. I do not think that I owe Albert a lett[e]r for I have writt[e]n to him since I have been here and have not had a letter from him since I have been here. but I suppose that he did not get it, so I am going to write to him again soon.

There is a Drunkin man sitting by the table and talking to me so you can see what a good letter I can write to night. But he has solemly promised his word that he will go down to the Div next Wed[n]esday night and join the sons of Temperance. I have be[e]n talking to him to night about his wife and how glad she would be to hear that he had become a temperance man. I talked to him till he cried and he said that if we would take him in he would keep it. he is a well educated and smart, inteligent, and it seems such a pity that such men should die with the Delrum Tremers. there is a case up in the ward now and it is so, quite awful to hear him rave, and to hear tell of the awful sights that he says that he can see. God save me from such a fate as this.

We are going to have a Grand Initiation of the whole Order of the sons of temperance in the District of Columbia on next Wednesday night. the whole Div will meet on ninth street and march down to the Capital to the House of Representitives. and then we go to hear speeches made by sev[e]ral of the distinguished members of both houses. I suppose that we shall have a grand time, and I only wish that you could be here to see it, but I will tell you all about it in my next. Yes, I think that when my
[*next page missing*]

U. S. Christian Commission

sends this as the Soldier's messenger to his Home. Let it hasten to those who wait for tidings.

"Behold! now is the accepted time; behold, now is the day of salvation."

CENTRAL OFFICE:
11 Bank Street, Philadelphia.

BRANCH OFFICE:
No. 500 H Street, Washington.

Washington D C Feb 17th

Dear Thank.

I recd your most welcome letter to day of Feb 12 and 13 th and now to night I am going to try and write to you I have written only once a week since I have been here for I do not have only evenings to write now and I went to go to the Div one night and then I have an invitation to go to others almost any night and here I want to tell you something I am quite anxious to become a member of the Grand Div and as I can only become so by being elected Worthy Patriach of my own Div I am trying to do all that I can for the Div so that I may be elected so you will see that I have all that I can do at present and you will

Letter by Frank Griffith to his wife Thankful, from Washington D.C., February 17, 1865. Griffith Papers, Regional History Center, Northern Illinois University.

U.S. Christian Commission
sends this as the Soldier's messenger to his Home.
Let it hasten to those who wait for tidings.
"Behold! Now is the accepted time;
behold, now is the day of salvation."

Central Office: Branch Office:
11 Bank Street, Philadelphia.   *No. 500 H Street, Washington.*
[stationary letterhead]

Washington, D C
Feb 17th [1865]

Dear Thank,

I recd your most wealcome letter to day of Feb 12 and 13th, and now to night I am going to try and write to you. I have written only once a week since I have been here for I do not have only evenings to write now. and I want to go to the Div one night, and then I have an invitation to go to others almost ev[e]ry night. and here I want to tell you something. I am quite anxious to become a member of the Grand Div, and as I can only become so by being elected Worthy Patriarch of my own Div I am trying to do all that I can for the Div so that I may be so elected. so you will see that I have all that I can do at present, and you will please excuse me if I do not write more than once in a week. I shall always try and do that and more if I can, but as I said before I feel quite anxious about it.

I went to a new Div last night, it was the second since its Organization, and they called on me to make a talk. and I had to get up and do the best that I could under the circumstances which is not much at any time. I have not recd any communication from you for our paper that is to come off next week, but perhaps that I shall in your next letter. and now if you can find me a good Declamation in any thing that you can send to me so that I can be prepared to say something when they call on me, I shall be glad. any thing that will be either grand or firey. if you can find that old speech that I spoke once of, A Wards, send that or any thing else that you may think best.

I think that I am getting better all the time, at least I am more fleshy than I was. and I feel better than I did when I came here, but my side aches a good deal of the time, but I hope that I shall be better in the spring. No prospects of pay yet, and I do not think that we shall get any now till the first of March now. but the time when it will not

255

be necessary for me to write everything to you that I wish to say is fast approaching. only a little more than six months and I shall be free once more, and I begin to count the weeks and then the days. it looks long to look ahead, but short when it is past. it is almost six months since I left New Orleans and to look back it only seems so many weeks.

so you have got a <u>bile</u> [boil] on your arm. well, I think that I can sympathize with you. but still if I was there I would <u>pay</u> you off for laughing at me when I had them so that I could not sit down. I shall never forget how you and Sarah used to laugh with [when] I had to have a pillow in my chair to eat my meals.

Yes, I think that I should prefer that our meeting should be alone, but then I suppose that we shall be govern[e]d by circumstances. there is no news that I need to write that I can think of. Our Grand Demonstration Did not come off on account of Congress having night sessions, but is to come off some time in March. I have written to Albert last week. please to write often, and accept this from,

Frank

Washington, D.C.
Feb 19th 1865

Dear Thank,
you see that I have commenced you a lett[e]r on this large sheet, but I do not want you to think that it will be a verry long one for I do not know that I will have time to finish this to night. I have got to sit up and bake some <u>Beans</u> for breakfast, and I have been writing all the ev[en]ing, but I thought that I would leave off and commence a lett[e]r to you. if I did not have time to finish it and if you do find some mi[s]takes in <u>spelling</u> or writing you will please lay it to the <u>hand</u> and not the head for I have got in the habit of writing so fast lately that I do sometimes leave out a letter, and perhaps a word, now and then. but I shall always be glad to have you corect me at any time. and now that I am on this subject I noticed that in your last letter but one you left out three words, and spelled <u>with</u> "withe" and manner "maner," so I do not think that you have got much the start of me in that respect.

I am still getting better and I can see that I am getting fat again since I have been here. I tell you that I am getti[n]g to be a famous cook. I have made some biscuits and some pies, and tomorrow I am going to fry some <u>cakes</u>. I can make all kinds of soups and the like of that. and I am getting so that I like <u>cabbage</u> (is that spelled right?) and vinegar, but I cant go the Tomatoes yet, but am in hopes that I shall like them before I come <u>home</u>. I do not think that I shall be half so dainty as I was when I left, and I suppose that you will be glad of that.

I suppose that you [are] having one of the hardest winters that was ever known in that state. and the residents of this City say that this is the coldest winter that they have ev[e]r seen in this state. it has not snowed much here and we have had sleighing only two or three days. but it has been cold and freezing for the last month. the Ice in the river is about one foot thick and they are cutting it up to put in their Ice houses. To day has seemed like a day in April at home. it was verry pleasant, but is freezing some now. I have not had any more letters from Nettie yet and I think that I shall have to jog her memory a little on the place of her punctuality, dont you?

I think that you must have had a great time when the smoke house caught fire, and I suppose that you were half frightened to death. it is lucky that the house did not get on fire too. Now you ask me what I think of your going to live with Al this summer. now I do not like to dictate to you what you shall do, or what you shall not do. and if you think that you will be happier, or that the time will pass more pleasantly there than at home, or that <u>Mother</u> can get along well enough alone this summer, then I, perhaps it will be better for you to go. but Al will want a <u>team</u> if he goes to farming, and your folks have got none, and I could not give my consent to their having mine. and then as long as you are at home all the money that I can send you this spring will help you <u>all</u> for I cannot bear that my Mother shall suffer if I can help it. I know that it will [be] hard times this spring, and you will want all that we can sow. and then your folks have other children that can help them. and then I do not like to have the children come too much under your mothers influence. you will know the reason without my mentioning it to you. but there are somethings that I can not <u>forget</u>. I know that I am asking a great deal of you, and perhaps too much. and if I was only there I could tell you more than I can write. I know that you will think that I am selfish in this matter, but if you and Al were going to live alone I should think different about it.

but it is only six months now before I shall be home if nothing hap[p]ens to prevent. and perhaps I shall be home in the spring on a furlough. I hope so at least. and then perhaps I can make some arrangements that will [be] more satisfactory to you and all the rest. I know that it is asking a great deal of you to stay there and take care of my father and Mother, and that you will think that some of the rest of the children might do something too, and I think so too. but as the case now stands I do not see how I can do any better at pr[e]sent. but if I live till my time is out I will try and provide a home of our own somewhere, if it is ever so humble. and then I, and you my Darling, will be free to act for ourselves. but still I shall leave it to your judgement to do what to you seems best.

I think that we shall get our pay now the first of next month and then I can send you another hundred dollars, and I want you to keep this till a time of need for I fear that we have not seen the w[o]rst of the times yet. do not pay any debts that are not an absolute neces[s]ity for there is no telling when I shall get any more, and you may need it for something to eat yet. Now do not think hard of me for writing this plain to you, or think that I do not love you, for that is not the case at all. Oh, how many nights I have lain awake and thought of you and how lonesome you must feel. and then I know that you have trials and troubles that you will not write to me, and I have thought that if my life was only spared till I could see you again, Oh, how would I try to be more of a husband to you, that I might in the future make some amends for the past.

Now I want to ask you if you would like to belong to our Div of the Sons of Temperance. if so I am going to see if I cannot have you initated by Proxy so that I can write you more of the procedings. and then when I come home I can get you a card and we can join some Div there. so if you will just tell me what you think about it I shall be much obliged. we are having some fine times now. our paper comes off on the next wednesday night. we have had one and that was a decided success.

The Dr came in here to night and I had to stop and talk with him so I do not think that I shall be able to finish this to night. if there is any thing more that you want me to write please tell me and I will try and write it.

Write often and accept this from your,

Frank

258

Tell Mother that I will try and answ[e]r her lett[e]r this week

---

Washington
March 2[nd]/65

Dear Thank,
        Do you like that I should call you Thank, or had you rather that
I should call you Wife? you will excuse me if I do not write you a
long lett[e]r to night for I have got lots of writing to do. but I thought
that I would write to you first so that I should be sure to write to you
to night for I shall not have any more time to write this week as I have
to write the paper for our next meeting. I am getting along first rate
now and am getting fat again. my side is so much better that I think
that I shall get well now. and then I have a good living now so that
makes me feel a good deal bett[e]r.
        I recd your most wealcome letter yesterday, but could not write
last night for that was Div night. and here I want to tell you that I
want you to write to [me] twice a week if I do not write to you for I do
so like to get a lett[e]r from you often. but they help to pass off the
lonesome hours, and they are so lonesome lately that it seems as
though my time would now be out. and if I do not get yo[u]r letters
Wednesday and sund[a]y it seems so long. and after the first of April
I shall write to you often for I shall not have so much to do. now I
have to get up at half past four in the morning and work all day so that
I do not have any time till afternoon, and then only two hours from
two till four, and sometimes not that. but it is not very hard work and
it keeps me busy so that the time does not seem quite so long. I do
not know as you can read this. if not tell me and I will try and write
better.
        You say that you would like to come here to live if I would
only settle down to some honorable business. Now, I hope you do not
think that I would ask you to go any where with me into any
Dishonorable business for I hope that I shall always be able to get an
honest living, be it ev[e]r so humble. and that when my time is out
that I shall be able to find a home somewhere, though that [be] ever so
humble. I can not tell now what I shall do when I get home for I can
not tell what the circumstances will be then, but I hope that I shall be
able to do something. I am trying to get a furlough to come home and

259

see Father, but I do not think that I shall be able to do so before April. I know that you will do all in your power to make our home happy, and [I] too will do all that I can to make it comfortable and pleasant. so my Darling, be patient for it is only a little time now before I shall be there. My _friend_ _Arthur_,[33] that I have wrote to you about so often, and I have been building _air_ _castles_. and we have agreed to study _law_ when our time is out, and then go to _Kansas_ to _practice_. he has studied some, has a good education, and is on the whole a good fellow, though on some things we can not agree yet. we _agree_ _to_ _disagree_.

and now I am going to tell you something that will tickle you. we have made a _solemn_ compact that we will not make, buy, sell, nor _chew_ any more _Tobacco_ till our time is out. and it is two weeks to night since I threw away my tobacco and I have [not] taken any since. but I tell that it came hard at first. I had to chew sticks and such, and one day I took a rag to chew, but I do not hanker after it any more. and I think that if I can stand it till I come home [that] you will help me to keep the compact aft[e]r that, for when I want a chew you will give me a good _kiss_, wont you? and that will be bett[e]r than all the tobacco in the world.[34]

Yes, I got the stamps that you sent me and I will send you some money in this so that you can buy you some more. I have had my teeth filled this week and that cost me five dollars, and I want to keep a little by me but what I can send you I want you to ke[e]p for your self for you may need it. do not pay any debts more then you are obliged to. I am going to write to mother to night in this so I will close this. write often and [t]ell me if you got the _money_.

Frank

Washington
March 26[th]/65

----

[33] A. Lester Wilkinson, see letter of January 12, 1865.

[34] Civil War soldiers on both sides received tobacco rations. Some doctors recognized the health threat, and groups similar to the temperance movement distributed pamphlets to soldiers denouncing the use of tobacco. Varhola, _Everyday Life During the Civil War_, 107 & 109.

Dear Thank,

You do not know how glad I was to get your letter to day for it has been more than a week since I have heard from you and I had begun to think that you was sick, or that the high water had carried you off, or that you had forgot to write to me at all. I have writt[e]n one letter since I have heard from you, and to night I am going to try and write you another. I am <u>well</u> as I can reasonably expect to be at present. my side keeps getting better so that I hope that I shall get entirely well yet. I have got another letter from Nettie, but did not get any picture. I will send you the letter as soon as I can answer it and you can see for yourself the reason that she does not send it. The weather has been quite cool for a few days past, but is getting warmer now, and we may begin to look for some of those delightful days of spring now. there has not been any snow here this month and we have had some of the pleasantest days that I have se[e]n in a long time.

I went to <u>church</u> last Sunday night and I heard one of the best sermons that I have heard since I heard that one at our <u>church</u> at the time of the Quarterly meeting when that man from New York preached on the <u>Reserection</u>. his subject was on entire dependence on the mercy of <u>God</u> and <u>His</u> great goodness to us, and one thought that I had nev[e]r thought of before seemed to me something new. he was speaking of the great original Sin and said he was <u>glad</u> that our first parents had partook of the forbiden fruit. his reason was that by that act it had made us <u>all</u> sinners for said he if they had withstood the temptation and been saved it would not have removed the tree from the garden, but each one of us would have been exposed to the like temptation would have been placed before us all. and then whoever sined would have been totaly and irretrievably lost, for then the great Sin <u>offering</u> would not have been necessary and there would have been no escape. But now that we have all been made partakers of the sin so may we all be made partakers of that gr[e]at <u>salvation</u>. It was a new thought to me and it struck me as being a good one. I wish that you could have heard him speak for it was to me at least most interesting.

If I stay here in Washington till my time is out how would you like to come here so as to go home with me? you could leave the <u>children</u> there and come and stay three or four weeks and then we could go and see all of the sights, to the Capital, and the Navy Yard, and the Patent and Post offices, to Mount Vernon. and then it would be so pleas[a]nt to have you here to go home with me. I begin to count the days now till my time will be out, only 162 days, and they will soon pass away, wont they? ev[e]ry day counts one less but they look long to look ahead, yet the six month[s] that I have been here has passed off quickly. and the weeks come ar[o]und quickly, too.

I w[e]nt down to the Navy Yard yesterday for the first time since I have been in the city. the Monitor Montauc is there having some repairs. she was in the <u>blockade</u> off Charleston and bears the marks of Service. I counted fifteen places where the shots have struck her <u>Turet</u>, some of them only making a dent and some of them half the size of the ball. one shot went clear through her side just above the water making a hole that you could put yo[u]r head in, and several places on the deck where they had struck and then glanced off.[35] we had the liberty of going all over the back and I wished that you could have been there with me.

I am going to see what I can do towards getting a <u>furlough</u> next week and I will let you know the result.[36] but I must close this and go to bed. I will write to you again this week when I will have more time. accept this with the love of,

Frank

have you got the paper I sent you?
I have found an old letter of Netties that I had thought I had sent you before. I will send it now.

---

[35] *U.S.S. Montauk* was hit 47 times during the naval attack on Charleston, April 7, 1863. *Almanac*, 335-336.

[36] Griffith got his furlough in early April and spent at least a week, if not more, visiting his family.

Chapter 8

"There is no place like our home"
The War Ends, Washington, D.C., April - June 1865

Frank Griffith had often mentioned trying to obtain a furlough to go home and visit his wife, Thankful, and his father who was dying of lip cancer. However, the only leave he ever received occurred in April of 1865. He did not return to Washington, D.C. until April 23, thus he was not present when President Lincoln was assassinated on April 14, or for the turmoil the city experienced during the following days.

Griffith returns to duty as a cook for a hospital, as well as for several doctors. His former unit, the 116th New York Volunteer Infantry, had been on reconnaissance up and down the Shenandoah Valley. They received the news of Lincoln's assassination the following day, and left for Washington on April 20, arriving on the 21st in time to meet Lincoln's funeral train.

With the 116th now in Washington, Griffith once again has contact with a number of his friends from back home. The 116th is camped on Capitol Hill and spends the month of May guarding the "Old Capitol" and "Carroll Place" prisons. On May 23 and 24 Washington hosts a grand spectacle, a Grand Review of the Army of the Potomac, and the Armies of the West. A Day of Fasting and Prayer in honor of Lincoln was held in the city on June 1. Five days later, Frank Griffith is mustered out of the service. The 116th mustered out on June 8.

In the letters he writes home following his return to Washington, Griffith comments briefly on the death of John Wilkes Booth and the capture of Davy Herold. Rumors are rampant as to what will happen to those involved in the conspiracy to murder Lincoln. Rumors also abound as to when the men will be discharged from the army.

As the Confederacy falls apart, Jefferson Davis and members of his staff are captured. Griffith happened to be attending the play "Uncle Tom's Cabin" at Grover's Theatre on May 11 when the capture was announced. "And then there was a scene of the wildest excitement that I ever saw, such cheering. ev[e]ry one rose in his place and swung his hat and cheered... the band played the Star Spangled Banner and Yankee Doodle and then we cheered again."

On a more personal level Frank expresses the fear that he did not make a favorable impression when at home. He is as anxious as ever to hear from Thankful. As a member of the Sons of Temperance much of his free time has been taken up with attending meetings held by the various temperance divisions. Frank believes this group has saved him from drinking. He has been reading a book about the evils of drunkenness, and mentions a book that Thankful had given him to read on the subject, and how she must have seen his weakness early on. Thankful is sorry his Division will disband, and prays that God will keep him from becoming a drunkard.

John Griffith is now quite weak and near death, and Thankful and other family members are taking turns sitting with him every night. Hard as this may be, what really troubles Thankful are remarks that she has overheard which make her feel unwanted. Frank's father has finally made a will, but all that Frank and Thankful want are to be left alone in peace. Frank doesn't know what he will do to make a living after his return home. Thankful's brother Albert Myers has proposed purchasing a mill, but after his experience with Thankful's brother-in-law Horatio, Frank does not think much of joining in another partnership, unless Thankful approves. Frank has just about made up his mind to go west. Although Frank talks about the possibility of being discharged in his letter of June 3rd, he does not realize that in three days his dream of being mustered out will become a reality.

Washington
April 28th [1865]

Dear Thank,

I recd your letter yesterday, but have not had time to write till to night. and as I have got to sit up and bake <u>beans</u> I thought that I could not spend the time more pleasantly than to write to you for I know that you will be looking for a letter from me by the time that this gets there. I have got rested and I feel first rate now, much better than I have since I have been in the city. I have got your letter and am going to try and answer all of your questions if I can. I got along first rate with my journey.[1] I got here on Sunday morning. should have been here Saturday night but was hindered in New York for transportation. No, I did not come in a <u>Sleeping</u> car for they charged me $1.25 to stany [stand] and I thought that I could not come it any easier than to keep awake. no, I was not most sick but was some tired. I did want my coat one night a little while till they made a fire in the car, but on the whole was glad that I did not bring it. yes, I did find things in pretty good order when I came back. have had a <u>rain</u>. and one of the boys have gone to his company. The intense excitement has somewhat died away, but you can see in ev[e]ry face a <u>shade</u> of earnest thought, and it still continues to be the theme of conversation.[2] Boothe and his accomplisce Harold have been captured, both together. Boothe was <u>shot</u>, but Harold was taken alive and brought to Washington and is now safe in Prison.[3]
Sunday. [30[th]]

I hope that you will excuse me for not sending this letter

---

[1] Frank's return trip from visiting his family in East Concord, New York.

[2] President Abraham Lincoln was assassinated on Friday, April 14, 1865 by John Wilkes Booth at Ford's Theatre, and naturally everyone was shocked by this event and interested in who was involved.

[3] David "Davy" E. Herold and Booth were trapped in the barn of Richard H. Garrett, south of the Rappahannock near Port Royal, Virginia about 2 a.m. on April 26. Herold surrendered, but Booth was defiant and "ranted dramatically." The barn was set on fire, Booth was shot and then pulled from the burning building. He died about 7 a.m. His body was carried to Washington on the *Montauk*. *Almanac*, 681-682; Leech, *Reveille in Washington*, 408.

before but we have been cleaning house this week. and every night I have been too tired to write, but to night I thought that I would finish this and send it, and this week I shall have more time to write. I have been to church to night and have just got back, so you see that I do sometimes go to church here. I do not know what to write to you to night for my mind is full of the great events that are going on that I cant think of any thing else. the talk is now that we shall be discharged now before the first of June. I hope so, do you? and then I shall have time to talk to you enough to make up all that I do not write. how is father? I want to hear from him more often. the Body of Boothe was taken out into the river last night and Sunk.[4] and tomorrow there is to [be] some of his accomplises hung at the Arsenal in this city.[5]

Please to write often, and ac[c]ept this with the love of,

Frank

Washington
May 8[th]/65

Dear Thank,

I am still going to keep on writing to you if you do not to me. I have had only two letters from you since I came back and I am beginning to think that I did not make a verry favorable impression on you while I was at home. or perhaps that you are so busy that you

---

[4] After Booth's body reached Washington it was taken to the Navy Yard for identification, inquest and autopsy. Booth was buried at the Washington Arsenal, and in 1869 re-buried at Green Mount Cemetery in Baltimore. Secrecy concerning these events gave rise to many rumors. *Almanac*, 682; *Encyclopedia*, Vol. 1, 252.

[5] The hangings took place later. On May 1 President Andrew Johnson ordered nine army officers be named to make up a military commission to try the eight remaining conspirators, Herold, Samuel Arnold, George A. Atzerodt, Dr. Samuel A. Mudd, Michael O'Laughlin, Lewis Payne (Paine), Edward Spangler, and Mrs. Mary E. Surratt. After a lengthy trial in Washington the commission found all eight guilty on June 30, 1865. Arnold, Mudd, and O'Laughlin received life sentences, and Spangler was given six years. On Friday, July 7 Herold, Atzerodt, Payne, and Surratt, were hanged on the Arsenal grounds. *Almanac*, 684, 694.

Company I, 9th Veteran Reserve Corps, at Washington Circle in Washington, D.C., taken in April 1865. Frank Griffith was a member of this company. Courtesy of the Library of Congress, Prints & Photographs Division, Civil War Photographs [reproduction number LC-B8171-7804]

cant find time to write to me more than once a week, and then only a few hurri[e]d lines. but be that as it may I am going to inflict a letter on you twice a week till you order me to stop writing. you do not know how lonesome I have been since I came back and how anxiously I look for the mail, only to be disappointed ev[e]ry day. and then I wonder why you do not write often as you did before, and whether you, too, have been disappointed in me and do not care to write. but I am sure that if you only knew how I long for some kind token of remembrance from home you would not fail to send me a letter at least once a week.

We are having some of the pleasantest weather here that I ever saw. such beautiful sumers and ev[e]ry thing looks so fresh and nice that it makes me almost homesick to think of it. and last night I was setting here and looking out into the beautiful moonlight and I thought of the quiet and happy life that we used to live when I was at home, of all your past care and kindness to me unworthy as I have been. and I wondered if I should be as contented and happy again after I shall have passed from these scenes of strife and bustle, of noise and tumult. and then I wondered if your influence would be suffcient in the future as in the past to guard me from temptations that daily come in my way. and now that our Div is about to surrender it Charter, and we [are] about to withdraw from the Order, if I should be able to still say no to any of my friends when they ask me to drink with them. I believe that thus far my pledge has been my salvation since I have been here. but now that we are about to be released from its obligation, will I still have right principle enough to keep me from drinking and its twin vice.

You know that you once told me that I was of too yealding a nature, and I fear that your words wer[e] but too true. But if I have ever prayed, and I believe that I do sometimes pray though I am ashamed to say that I do not pray often, I have prayed that I might be saved from being a Drunkard. It has been the one fear of my life that in some weak moment when I was not on my guard that I might fall. Oh, you who can pray and know how to pray, pray that I may be saved from this. I do not know why this has come into my mind, or why I should write thus to you for I do not know that I shall have any more temptation than I have ever had, or that I shal[l] want to drink. but I have been reading a book lately called ten nights in a bar room, and the story has been running through my mind ever since.[6] did you ever read it? do you remember that before we were marri[e]d that you gave me the Inebriators hut to read, and that you recommended it to me as a good book.[7] I have often thought that your quick perception of character saw my weak points, and that you ment it as a hint to me, or rather as a warning. did you, dear? I at least took it so - and in my heart I [am] thankful [to] you for the interest that you manifested in me.

I have seen some of the boys of the 116th, but have not had time to go and see them yet, but am going there tommorrow night if I can get time[8]. Elijah Smith[9] and Charly Ballard[10] came down to see

---

[6] *Ten Nights in a Bar-Room, and What I Saw There*, by Timothy Shay Arthur, (Philadelphia: J.W. Bradley, 1859, c.1854). This book tells the story of the people in one small town after a bar-room opens. Respected members of the community, as well as young men with promising lives, are ruined and murder is committed. Even the buildings fall into disrepair. According to James D. Hart in *The Popular Book: a History of America's Literary Taste*, (New York: Oxford University Press, 1950), 109, T.S. Arthur was one of the most prolific temperance novelists, producing five per cent of all the volumes of fiction in the 1840's. By 1860 publishers estimated a million copies of his books had been printed. *Ten Nights in a Bar-Room*, first published in 1854 was his most popular title.

[7] I was unable to find the title "Inebriators Hut," but it could be *Confessions of a Reformed Inebriate*, by the American Temperance Union, NY, 1844.

[8] After reaching Washington on April 21 the 116th N.Y. was camped about five miles south of the city. It left that place on April 27 and marched ten miles around Washington and Georgetown to a site on the railroad, four miles north of the city. Letter of James F. Ryther of Co. H, dated 29 April 1865, held by Gordon G. Ryther.

[9] Elijah P. Smith was age 44 when he enlisted at Evans. He served as a private in Co. K until promoted to sergeant prior to May 1863. He mustered out with the company on June 8, 1865 at Washington, DC. *Registers*, 475. See also Appendix B.

[10] Charles H. Ballard was 18 when he enlisted at Brandt. A private in Co. K he was promoted to sergeant prior to May 1863, and to first sergeant prior to November 1864. He mustered out with the company June 8, 1865 at Washington.

me last sunday. the boys are all well, have lost only one man since I came from them.[11] they want that I should come back to the Co so as to come <u>home</u> with them, and I am going to try and get <u>transferred</u> if I can. they think that they will be mustered out by the first of June. I have not seen Birny yet, but shall when I go up th[e]re. There is to be a grand review of all the troops on the Old Bull run Battle field sometime this month, I do not know when. I should like to go and see it, but do not expect that I shall be able to get away from here.

The report here to night is that Kirby Smith has <u>surrendered</u> his forces to Gen Canby and with them all the troops west of the Mississippi river.[12] and if this is true all armed resistinc[e] to the Government will cease, only those Guerilla rebels are left. and soon the boys will come <u>marching home</u>, and how many <u>hearts</u> will be made glad. but how many, <u>alas</u>, will be made sad when they look in vain for some loved one that th[e]y have laid upon the altar of their country. and how shall we be greeted when we get there? will those who have stayed at home at their ease, and grown rich while we have stood between them and the foe, will they ever think of the <u>sacrifice</u> that we have made? will they remember that we have ever stood between them and their ruined homes and dissapated <u>hearths</u>, between them and the ruin that now covers the South, and honor [us] for this, for all that we have suffered, or will they only think of what they may make out of our necessities. But time will <u>tell</u>, and we can only leave it to time.

But I shall have to close this and go to <u>bed</u> for it is ten Oclock and I have to get [up] early now. I need not tell you to write to me often for I have said it to you so often, but try and not forget me quite, will you? Give my love to all who care enough to ask for me. kiss the Children for me, and acc[e]pt this from,

---

Registers, 372. See Appendix B.

[11] Andrew Wuest was 25 when he enlisted at East Hamburg. He served as a private in Co. K until he was killed in action on September 19, 1864 at Winchester, Virginia. *Registers*, 501. See also Appendix B.

[12] Griffith was speaking of Confederate General Edmond Kirby Smith and Major General Edward Richard Sprigg Canby of the Union, however this report was premature. Smith did not surrender to Canby until June 2, at Galveston, Texas. *Encyclopedia*, Vol. 4, 1811.

Frank

_____

Washington
May 11th/65

Dear Thank,

It rains so to night that I cant go out any where, so I am going to write to you although I sent you a letter to day or yesterday. I got two from you to day post marked the 8th and 9th of May and I noticed in one of them that you commenced it on the 3 of the month. I think that they were a long time in coming, or else the time seems long to me, but they were the last that I had and they were most wealcome. I do not know why you do not get more letters from me for I have sent you one twice a week since I have been here, so if you do not get more please don't blame me.

I am well now, better than I have been in a long time and have good hopes that I shall be well again. The talk is now when will we be mustered out. but I believe that it will be this month or the first of next, at least I hope so. I have been up to see the old Regt. Saw Lon and he looks as tough and fat as he can be. the boys all seemed glad to see me and want me to come back to the Co. I should like to verry much and perhaps shall [do] so as to come home with them. but I think that it will be better for me to stay here at present. and I do not think that the Dr will let me go now, for since I have come back I have had to take charge of the kitchen entirely and have all the cooking to see to, cook all the low diet, and have to cook for two Doctors besides, so you see that I have my hands full. I spoke to the Dr to day about my going back and he said that he could not spare me at all, said that he wanted me to stay and cook for him. and they say up in the ward that they have nev[e]r had their food cooked so well in a long time and do not want me to leave. I know that I rate a good deal better time here than I should in the Co for I have a good place to sleep and plenty to eat, do not have to be out any nights, can go any where that I please so that I am here to do my work. I have never had but two passes since I have been here and do not need any. I cooked the Dr a grand dinner yesterday. I will give you the bill of fare, there was three to eat: Roast beef, Mashed Potatoes, fried Eggs, fried Onions, Broiled fish, Asperegus, toast, Tea, coffee, apple sauce, and other things too numerous to mention. so you see that I am getting to be <u>Notorius</u>. perhaps it will be a good lessen to me for when we go to keeping house I shall know how to help you some, that is if you will let <u>me</u>.

You say that you are doubly lonely since I came back. and I suppose that you will that I had not come home at all till my time is out. and I am sometim[e]s sorry my self that I came, for the time seems so much longer since I came back. but then when I think how happy we were I can bear to be lonesome some for that. but then we had so little time to visit by ourselves. th[e]re was so many to see and talk to that my tongue ached for a week after I got back. but when I come again I hope that we shall have the satisfaction of knowing that I shall not have to go back again.

I saw <u>Birney</u> the other night, but he did not seem verry glad to see me. did not ask me any questions about home or any thing. I told him that I saw his wife and he said that she told him that I was there. I guess that she writes to him often. he was writing to her when I went there. Loren Johnson tents with him. he looks well and hearty. I have not had a letter from Dora in a long time, nor one from Nettie since I sent her that picture. I guess that she does not mean to write to me any more, but I think that
[*next page missing*]

Washington
May 14th 1865

Dear Thank,

I have sent you a letter since I had one from you, but I am going to <u>inflict</u> another on you to night for I have nothing else to do. and if you get tired of them you can lay them on the fire and give me credit for writing them. I am well as usual, only I have got a slight cold, nothing serious I hope. my side is much better that it was when I was at home, has pained me some to day, but it always does when I get cold. the weather is very fine now, not verry warm and such splendid nights, it makes [me] almost homesick to look out.

I suppose that you have heard that <u>old</u> Jeff Davis and his Staff have been <u>captured</u> and are on their way to this city.[13] I was down to Groves Theatre[14] last night to see Uncle Toms Cabin played. I would have given five dollars if you could have been there to have seen it. it was some of the most splendid acting that I ev[e]r saw, especialy the part of <u>Little Eva</u>, a little Girl as large as Nettie or not much larger, and the most beautiful one that I ev[e]r saw. she performed her part with[out] making a single mistake. it fairly made me <u>weep</u> to hear her talk to her <u>Pa</u>. and then the closing scene, I cant describe it to you, but if there is ev[e]r a chance I mean to have you see it. Once between the acts the Manager came on the stage and said that a dispatch had just been recd at the *Chronicle* Office Saying that Jeff Davis and his staff had been captured. and then there was a scene of the wildest excitement that I ever saw, such cheering. ev[e]ry one rose in his place and swung his hat and <u>cheered</u>. I do not cheer verry often but I could not help it then. there was a good many officers present and they shook hands and swung their hats and <u>cheered</u>. The band played the Star Spangled Banner and <u>Yankee Doodle</u> and then we cheered again. and amid the noise the curtain went up and the play went on again. I will send you a paper with this and another tomorrow if I can get one.

I do not know of any more news that I can write. I had a letter from your folks yesterday. Horati[o]s folks have gone somewhere, your mother did not say where. I have not seen any of the 116[th] since I wrote you last. I think that I shall go up there tomorrow night. but I think that I will close this and go to bed for I did not sle[e]p much last night. and then if I write two letters to your one I can not afford to write verry long ones. but if you can find time to write to [me] once in a while do so and they will be most <u>Thankfuly</u> received.

Frank

---

[13] President Jefferson Davis, his wife Varina, Postmaster General Reagan, presidential secretary Burton Harrison and several others were taken prisoner by Union troops during the early morning hours of May 10, 1865 near Irwinville, Georgia. Other members of the Confederate government were also taken into custody at other locations, thus the Confederate government was no more. Davis was taken first to Macon, Georgia and then to Fort Monroe, Virginia where he was imprisoned. He was released May 13, 1867 without standing trial. *Almanac*, 687.

[14] Grover's Theatre was located at Pennsylvania and E, not far from the President's mansion. Leech, *Reveille in Washington, 1860-1865*, map on end pages.

East Concord
May 14th 1865

My own dear Husband,
       your most kind letter of the eighth was received this afternoon
and I was so glad to hear from you. but I am very sorry that you do
not get my letters as I have not forgotten you or neglected to write to
you on account of cares, for this is the sixth time I have written and
you have been gone a little more than three weeks, when it seems that
it is as many months almost. You said you was so very lonely since
you went back. I believe I can sympathize with you only as you are
away from all kind home friends. but I feel that the time is not far
distant when you can come to us not to return to the noisy camp life.
And you wonder if you will be contented when you get home. oh, I
hope you will for it seems as though I never could bear to have you
away from me a month at a time again. for is it not sufficient to try
our constancy these three long long years that we have been apart.
have we not suffered thus enough? And if there is one cherished wish
in my heart it is that we may have a home all our own, and that I may
fill my place in such a way that home will be the dearest spot on earth
to you and our little ones. that it may take the place of clubs and
saloons and the like. not that I wish you never to enjoy your self with
your associates for I am not selfish, I hope. But that you may feel that
you are ever the most welcome there of any place in the world. oh
yes, I believe you will be content, wont you?
       I am sorry that your Div is going to disband. what is the
reason? for I believe it has been the means of saving the character of
many Soldiers who are only surrounded [by] those of their own sex,
and feeling so lonely and being tempted so strongly to drink, with out
the Pledge might have returned to their homes and dear friends
drunkards. I do believe you will have that strength given you that will
ever enable you to withstand temptations to drink. Do not be afraid to
say No for it will soon become a settled opinion among the boys that
you will not drink, and they will let you alone. oh, for your own and
your familys sake, do not drink. Yes, I will and do pray that you may
be kept from this. And may God in mercy answer, is and ever will be
my prayer. I do not know as I gave that book to you as a warning
more than I would to anyone, only as I thought if you had the result
pictured so plainly, so lifelike before you, that you never would so

want to taste the <u>wine when</u> it is red. But if it had, or if I have ever had any influence over you to keep you from yielding to temptation, I feel glad, nay <u>happy</u>, that through Gods help my life has not <u>all</u> been spent in vain. But you will weary of this uninteresting letter so I will leave the subject for the present.

Father is growing weak all the time. he cannot stand on his feet alone and only sits up a few minutes at a time. and it seems so bad that we can hardly stay in the room with him. we sit up with him every night.

[*next page missing*]

East Concord
May 20th 1865
Saturday evening

Dearest,

I have done work for to night and so to pass the hour before dark more pleasantly I am going to write to you. Your kind letters of the 14th & 15th were received last night and I was very glad to get them, more so for not looking for any before to night. and I thank you for writing so often. I am going to try and write oftener than I have for I have got done house cleaning, only white washing, and [I] think I shall do that Monday. and then I am not going to work so hard about the dradging work for it will be done for this spring. and I am going to quilt some, and cut some carpet rags so that when we go to living by ourselves we can have a carpet for our floor. if you can get the warp for me when you come home I can weave it and it will be nice. Lydia is here yet, Marth has been here to day. It is raining a little to night.

I never get tired of your dear letters, for now you are gone that is all the comfort I take, reading your letters and writing to you. <u>No</u>, not <u>all</u>, for I do enjoy the precious sessions of prayer. and were it not for the consoling soothing influence of the spirit of grace that I feel in my heart then I would often give away to the trials and darkness that sometimes surrounds me. and then the thought of your <u>dear</u> <u>Love</u> for me, unworthy as I ever have been, and of what you expect of me in your absence has ever been the guiding star of my life. for by it have I tried to shape the course of my doings. that at your return (if God spares you this long) you could say you were satisfied with what I had done. And when I read your letters so full of <u>Love</u> and tenderness I feel that I am fully repaid, and that you are satisfied.

I do not know what remark was that <u>you</u> heard when at home, but <u>I</u> have heard so many that I shall be glad to be away. not that your folks have not been <u>good</u> to me, for they have, and I shall ever <u>love</u> and respect them for it. But it has been said to me so m[any] times that they <u>promised</u> <u>you</u> we should have a <u>home</u> here while you was gone, that I have thought it was in regard of their promise alone that we staid, and not because of their <u>wanting</u> us. and it has made me so <u>very</u> lonesome that I have shed many tears on the account of it.

oh <u>Sha</u>, what is the reason I write so to you for you have trouble enough of your own. It is most dark and I shall have to close soon. How do you do now? and what do you think about coming home soon? Father is quite comfortable to day, but yesterday he had a real bad day. we have to draw him in a chair, back and forth, when he gets up. but he don't sit up, only a little while at a time. please write often as you do, and keep up good courage for the [en]d is at hand.

this from your Thank

To Frank

U. S. Sanitary Commission
[stationary letterhead, showing emblem]

Washington
May 26th [1865]

Dear Thank,

It is Nine Oclock but I am going to try and write you a few lines to night before I go to bed for I have had two letters from you since I last wrote, one yesterday and one to day. but I could not write last night, and to night I have had company till just now. but I mean to write as often as you do, and I think that I have since I have been back here. I was so glad to hear from you so often for I did not look for a letter till Monday. I always get yours on Mondays and Thursdays so that I have come to look for them on those days, and if I do not get them then I feel so disappointed and lonesome.

I am as well as usual, only I have got some cold and it makes my <u>side</u> pain me some. I have sent you some papers containing an account of the grand Review[15] so that you can read it better than I can write it to you. it was a grand sight and such a one I do not expect to see again in my life time if I should live to be an hundred years old. I wish that you could have been here to have seen it, but when I come home I will tell you all about it. I suppose that Lon will be home soon now for I hear that the Regt is to be sent home as soon as possible now to be mustered out. but I do not know when I shall come now, perhaps not till my time is out, so we had not better make any calculations on that.

I suppose that Mother feels better <u>satisfied</u> now that <u>Pa</u> has made his <u>will</u>. but they need not have been at all <u>uneasy</u> on our account for I have not asked any thing, and do not want any thing but to be let alone. do not say any thing to any of <u>them</u> about it, nor let them know that you know any thing about it. Do your <u>duty</u> in the future as I know that you have always <u>done</u> in the past, and when I get home, if that happy time ever comes, we will take care of <u>our</u> <u>selves</u> and the rest can do the same. but do not let them think that <u>you</u> <u>or</u> <u>I</u> are at all disappointed. I think that we can make a home of our own where we shall be at last free to think and act for our selves, and shall not be looked upon as though we were not <u>wealcome</u>. but for the present let us make the best of it that we can and look to the future for our reward.

I do not think that I shall try to get any business here for the city is full of men out of business so that it will be almost impossible to get any thing that will pay. I do not know what I shall do yet, but will find something when I get there. and I feel that with <u>you</u> and our dear little ones to help me that I can make at least as good a living as we have ev[e]r had there. and then when the time comes that I can

---

[15] The Grand Review was actually two parades held in Washington DC, where the Armies of the Republic passed in review before President Andrew Johnson, members of the cabinet, General Ulysses S. Grant, and other dignitaries. On May 23 at 9 a.m. General George Meade led 125,000 men of the Army of the Potomac up Pennsylvania Avenue where huge crowds of people watched for six hours. The following day Generals Sherman and Oliver O. Howard led nearly 100,000 men of the Western campaign in review. The crowds returned to cheer not only these more informal looking veterans, but also the assorted camp followers who marched along with them. *Almanac*, 689-690; *Encyclopedia*, Vol. 2, 860-861; Leech, *Reveille in Washington*, 414-417.

The "Red Star" Division of General Sherman's Army marching up
Pennsylvania Avenue, Washington, D.C. during the Grand Review on May
24, 1865. View taken from near the Treasury Building by Matthew Brady.
Courtesy of the Library of Congress, Prints & Photographs Division, Civil
War Photographs [reproduction number LC-DIG-cwpb-02822]

come home to you, to our home, wont it be so pleasant to be by our selves, to do, act and think for ourselves. Oh, let us try to make it to us the sweetest place on earth, so that we may say that be it ever so humble there is no place like our home. let us make it a place where love and harmony and the happiness of each other shall be our greatest pleasure.

Oh Darling, do you know that in all these three long weary years of war, when I have made myself a voluntary Exile from home and all that this world held dear to me, the thought of you, dear, has been the light of my life. and in the long dreary nights of dangers how I have passed the lon[e]ly hours in thinking of you and how happy we would be when I came back again. and I how I have prayed that I might be more worthy of your love that I might be more careful of your happiness
[next page missing]

———————

East Concord
[May] 28th [1865]
Sunday evening

Dear Frank,

to night I seat myself to write to you, but I do not know what to write for I have written two since your last was received, but that does not make any difference if I took a notion to write. Father is no better than he was the last time I wrote you, continues to grow weaker all the time, can hardly get off the bed alone. Mother is gone up to take Sarah home. Will has gone up to Johns to milk. Albert is here after Lydia, they are going home in the morning. I am so lonesome here lately that I can hardly stand it. seems as though Mother could not bear to have a laugh or joke at all, for every time we do so she says how can you bear to Will, and of course she means the rest of us as well. oh, I hope you will come home soon for if you was here it would be so much more pleasant, with your dear face and voice ever near me to comfort and cheer me. I do not know what makes me so down spirited lately, but I try to drive it from me all I can as I know it does no good and only frets those about me. and I know I have a cross to bear, and perhaps this is mine, and I ought to try to do it with patience and love. but at times the wickedness triumphs over the better principles of my heart and I murmur and complain. dear Frank, <u>pray</u> for me that I may be strengthened with grace from on high.

A[l]bert is here and he wants me to tell you that a mile from Pontiac there is a <u>mill</u> that he has been to work in this spring is for <u>sale</u> and he has a chance to buy[16]. Fay and Marth are going to stay here to night, and tomorrow night I am going to sit up with him [Father]. I have set with him two nights the past week and you don't know how lonesome I was all alone all night. He has had a very bad time for two or three days past with his stomach and bowels. He suffers so intensely that it does not seem as though he could stand it so long. and [*illegible word*] or could wish him to stay in this suffering long when <u>there</u> is no pain nor sorrow nor sighing. The girls are well. Nettie commences going to school tomorrow. Gertie says "<u>Ma</u> why don't <u>pa</u> come home I should like to know?' Old Mrs Calkins is to be buried tomorrow. I have got my straw all spun, and this week I am going to clean the house if I am well.

I wish you could go and see the grand reviews so that you could tell me all about it when you get home. I tell you, wont we enjoy ourselves if we are spared for you to come home and stay. Mell is not lame this spring or hardly since you went away. I have not been to church to day for it rained so hard and then I did not feel very well. Everything is very backward here about growing, and it is so wet that there is no chance to get in crops. please write often as you can and do not think that I have neglected to write or to think of you.

> your own dear
> > Thank
> To
> Frank

United States Sanitary Commission
[stationary letterhead]

---

[16] Both a grist mill and a saw mill were located in Pontiac which was located in Evans township, southeast of Angola, on a branch of Big Sister Creek. Truman C. White, ed., *Our County and Its People: A Descriptive Work on Erie County, New York*, Vol. 1 ([Boston]: Boston History Co., 1898), 553; French, *Gazetteer of the State of New York*, 290.

Washington
May 29th 1865

My Darling,

    I set down to night to write you a letter in reply to the one that I recd to day of the 26th, but I found a book on the table and I began to read, got interested, read till ten Oclock, and now I have just commenced your letter. so if I do not write you a very long one you must not think that it is because I do not like to write to you, but it will be for the want of time. I have to write to night for I do not expect to have another evening to myself till next Friday. now I suppose that you will want to know the reason and I can tell you. Tomorrow night I have to go down to Good Samaritan Div S[ons] of T[emperance] on some business. and the next night Our Div meets, I suppose for the last time as we propose to Surrender our Charter then. and the next night I have an invitation to go down on the Island to Excelsior Div as they are going to have a great time of it. you know that it is the Day of Fasting and Pray[e]r and I suppose that they will have some verry interesting exercises.¹⁷ so you see that if I do not write to you to night I shall have to wait till Friday, and I thought that would not do, <u>not</u> <u>hard[ly]</u> at all. so you see the consequence.

    I am well as usual and am enjoying my self as well as possible while I am away from <u>you</u>. I do not know of any news to tell you. there are so many stories about our coming home that I do not know what to tell you, but still I live in hopes that I shall get home in June, but may have to stay my time out yet. but then we need not make any calculations about it for there is no telling. I sent you two papers to day and will send you some more as fast as I can get them. we have not been paid off yet and I am out of <u>stuff</u>. [I] shall put the last stamp that I have got on this letter. but you know that it is always safe to trust in Providence, and that is what I propose to do for stamps in future.

    I am having a pretty good time now for I do not have as much

---

¹⁷ Thursday, June 1, 1865 was "a day of humiliation and prayer in honor of Abraham Lincoln." *Almanac*, 692. Both President Lincoln and Confederate President Jefferson Davis had proclaimed a number of days of "fasting, humiliation and prayer" as well as days of thanksgiving during the war. Woodworth, *While God is Marching On*, 100, 102 & 245.

Washington, D.C. April 1865.

While serving as a cook in the Veteran Reserve Corps, Frank Griffith often came down to this area to obtain beef. This view was taken in April 1865 and shows the cattle grazing on the "White Lot," located across from the Washington Monument. On the horizon at center is the White House, and at right the Treasury Building. Courtesy of the Library of Congress, Prints & Photographs Division, Civil War Photographs [reproduction number LC-B8184-10153]

work to do so that I think that I shall have some time to spare in the day. I have a nice ride in the Ambulance almost every day when we go after <u>beef</u>. we have to go about two miles down by the Washington Monument[18]. did I ever tell you any thing about it while I was at home? if not I will when I come again. it is not finished yet and I do not think that it ever will be, but it will be a grand thing when it is completed. I am going down to Mount Vernon before I come home if I can get a chance, and to the Patent Office, I have not been there yet, and to several other places that I want to see before I come home.

I went up to the old Regt the other day but did not see Birn[e]y. they expect to come home soon. I do not know when. but I shall have to close this and go to bed for it is nearly midnight. Please write often, and ac[c]ept this with all the love of,

Frank

U.S. Sanitary Commission
[stationary letterhead, showing emblem]

Washington
Jun 3rd/65

Dear Thank,

I have just got your letter of last Sunday and you can bet that I was glad for I had thought that you had forgotten me this week, or that there was something the matter, and I was anxious to hear from you. I am well as usual and that is all that I can hope for. ev[e]ry thing goes on just as usual. There was some excitement here this week about our being <u>mustered</u> out, but that is <u>played</u> out now. and the news is now that we shall have to stay [until] our time is out. but I still have some hopes that we shall have our <u>discharge</u> in the course of a few weeks, so let us <u>hope on</u>. There was an Order here that all men whose term of Service will expire before the first of Oct Should be mustered out

---

[18] Cattle grazed on land located at the southern end of the White House grounds, across from the Washington Monument grounds where the Army slaughtered them for beef. Stanley Kimmel, *Mr. Lincoln's Washington* (New York: Coward-McCann Inc., 1957), 47.

immediately, but the news is to day that this order does not have any refference to this <u>Corps</u>. but I think that there will soon be an order to discharge the whole of this corps.

I do not know what to tell Al about that mill <u>business</u> for I have never seen it and do not know any thing about it. what do you think of it? if I could go and see all about it I should know what to do. if I knew that I would be well enough to work in a mill I should think more about it. do you want to go there to live? you did not say any thing about what you thought about it. I do not want to pledge any thing till I have seen it. I have about made up my mind to go <u>west</u> when I get out of this so as to get out of the way of the most of my <u>Friends</u>. but if there is any chance to make any thing at that place I do not know, but it might be for the best. And then another thing, and the one that presents at present the strongest Objection, is that I have had about <u>enough</u> of this Partnership business, <u>don't</u> <u>you</u>? and I think that perhaps, on the whole, that what <u>we</u> do ever on after this had better be in a shape that we can <u>own</u> it <u>ourselves</u>. Please to write and tell me what you think of it for you know that your council is always <u>acceptable</u>.

Yes dear wife, I know that you do have a <u>cross</u> to <u>bear</u>, and for the three years that are now nearly passed it has been a <u>heavy</u> one. but do not <u>now</u>, I <u>pray</u> <u>you</u>, [now] that the time is so near at hand when I shall be with you again, to help you to bear the trials and burdens, do not <u>Faint</u> or lose your Patience. I know that the time seems long now to look ahead to, but then every day counts one less, and soon they will all be numbered. and <u>then</u> the <u>joy</u> of meeting again, to know that we shall not have so soon to part. Oh yes, we will try to live more for each other and to <u>promote</u> the comfort and happiness of each other. And till that happy time comes let us be <u>patient</u>, hoping for the best and believing that all things shall work together for good.

I do not know what to write more to you to night. I have been out ev[e]ry evening till 12 this week till to night, and I have staid at home to write to you. I have been to a Temperance meeting ev[e]ry night, and last night I went down on the Island to Excelsior Div as it was the day of Fasting and Prayer. we had some of the most interesting exercises that I have heard in a long time. but I think that I will close this and go to bed for I am sleepy. write often as you can and I will do the same.

Frank

The last surviving letter written by Frank Griffith to his wife Thankful from Washington, D.C., June 3, 1865, on U.S. Sanitary Commission letterhead. Griffith Papers, Regional History Center, Northern Illinois University.

P.S. why don't you write me a good (<u>Private</u>)

———————

This is the last surviving letter from Frank Griffith. He was mustered out just three days later on June 6, 1865 in Washington, DC.

SANDWICH G.A.R. POST No. 510 - 1915 -

Fifty years after the Civil War ended, Frank Griffith and members of the Sandwich, Illinois, Grand Army of the Republic Post Number 510 posed for this photograph taken on Memorial Day, 1915. Identified are:

1. F.S. Mosher (shoulder & arm)
2. Robert Buck
3. A. A. Hennis
4. Henry Hennis
5. Ed Coleman
6. C.C. Courtright
7. Robert Logan
8. O.M. Skeel
9. James Browning
10. Mr. Starkey
11. Jas. D. Brower
12. James Martin
13. F.A. Whitney
14. **Frank Griffith**
15. John Q. Adams
16. Robert Woodward
17. Eldridge Skinner
18. Henry Burchim
20. Henry Dannewitz
22. J.D. Kern
23. Silas Carner
24. A.M. Abbott

Credit: Original on loan from the Sandwich Historical Society.

Appendix A

The Family

Cornell, Cynthia Eudora Griffith - Born 1829, she was called "Dora" or "Dory" by the family. Dora taught school in Concord, New York ca. 1844-1855. In 1863 she and her husband Charles Cornell moved to the state of Maine.

Cornell, Charles - Frank's brother-in-law, apparently a farmer.

Griffith, Archibald - Frank calls him "Uncle Archie," perhaps a brother or cousin of John Griffith. He was an early settler of Concord, and benefactor of education. The Springville [NY] Academy was renamed the Griffith Institute in his honor.

Griffith, Carrie Annette - First child of Frank and Thankful Griffith, born June 5, 1860 in Concord, Erie County, New York. Called "Nettie" by her parents. Married Frank L. Voris, and had one son Harry Eugene Voris. Widowed in 1883, she married Eugene Stuart Williams on March 23, 1904. Carrie died February 16, 1942 in Sandwich, Illinois.

Griffith, Cora Elsie - Third child of Frank and Thankful Griffith, she was born October 21, 1868 in Springville, Erie County, New York. She married William C. Minard on October 14, 1886 in Kendall County, Illinois. They had two daughters Edna M. and Barbara Annette Minard. She died July 15, 1952 in DeKalb, Illinois.

Griffith, David E.- Frank's cousin, he was born in 1830. The son of John Griffith's brother Hezekiah and wife Sarah, they lived on a farm near John Griffith. He died in 1901.

Griffith, Edwin Clare - Only son of Frank and Thankful Griffith. He was born December 29, 1877 in Sandwich, Illinois, and died April 1, 1906 in Lincoln, Illinois.

Griffith, Frank Elnathan - Born April 26, 1835 in East Concord, Erie County, New York. Several sources list him as Elnathan, but he went by Frank after his marriage. He married Thankful Myers on April 6, 1859 in Ashford, Cattaraugus County, New York. He died November 17, 1921 in Sandwich, DeKalb County, Illinois. (see Introduction for additional information on Frank)

Griffith, Gertrude Mary - Second child of Frank and Thankful Griffith, she was born April 7, 1862 in Evans, Erie County, New York. Referred to as "Gertie" or "the Ba" by her parents, she was often sickly. She died in Angola, Evans township, New York in 1870.

Griffith, Harriet M. - Fourth child of Frank and Thankful Griffith, she was born June 26, 1871 in Erie County, New York. She married George John Bernard March 24, 1896 in Kendall County, Illinois. They had two children Gertrude Nell and David Griffith Bernard. She later divorced Mr. Bernard, and took care of her father from 1916 until his death. "Hattie" died in 1929.

Griffith, Harriet Sanford - Frank's mother, born ca.1803 in Columbia County, NY. She died ca. Spring 1866 in East Concord, N Y.

Griffith, John - Frank's father, born in New York State in 1796 to Samuel and Martha Griffith. He married Harriet Sanford in 1827. Moved to Concord, Erie County in 1833. A farmer most of his life, he also served as a Justice of the Peace. He died from cancer on his lip ca. June 1865 in East Concord, New York.

Griffith, Marcus Eugene - Frank's youngest brother was born in May 1850, and was known as "Gene" or "Eugene." He married Ruth, and died in 1925.

Griffith, Thankful Myers - Wife of Frank Griffith, she was born July 15,1840 in New York State to Mary Peirce and Jacob Myers. "Thank" died January 7,1900 in Sandwich, Illinois.

Griffith, William Henry - Frank's brother "Will" was born Jan. 20, 1844. He married Cora Tabor, and they had two sons, Glen and Dennis Griffith.

Hurd, Horatio S. - Thankful's brother-in-law, a farmer. Apparently Frank and Horatio had a partnership of some kind before Frank went to war. Frank's letters indicate he felt Horatio did not treat him fairly.

Hurd, Sarah P. Myers - Thankful's sister was born in 1836. She married Horatio Hurd and lived in Evans. They had at least five children: Anna A. died Sept. 11, 1863 (age 3), and Cora A. (1) five days later, both from typhoid, and they had three more daughters, Rose in 1864, Flora in 1868, and Susan in1870.

Kellog, Helen Amanda Peirce - Cousin of Thankful, she was born in 1835. Both Helen and her husband George P. Kellog were teachers.

Morse, John F. - Frank's brother-in-law, he had a farm near John Griffith. During the 1860's he also taught school.

Morse, Nancy Eveline Griffith - Born in 1831, Frank refers to his sister as "Eva." She married John F. Morse. They lived on a farm near the Griffiths during the 1860's, and had two sons, Frank M. and Carleton S. Morse.

Myers, Albert E. - Thankful's younger brother, he was born April 2, 1845 in New York State. He enlisted November 27, 1861 in the 78th New York State Volunteer Infantry serving as a private in Co. G. On July 12, 1864 the unit was disbanded and joined with the 102nd. He saw much fighting, and for a time was captured and held in Richmond. Albert mustered out December 24, 1864. He married Emma Amelia Ells on October 15, 1865 in Evans, New York, and ca. 1870 worked as a carpenter in the Evans/Angola area. Albert had three sons: Orson Gardner, born 1874, Floyd Edison, born 1881, and Gilbert Weldon born 1888. By July of 1881 he and his family were living in Missouri. Injuries suffered during the war caused him to be unable to work by 1890. In 1900 he was living in Butler County, Kansas. His wife died in 1909. In March 1915 Albert was living in Manatee County, Florida, and by March of 1925 he was a resident of the "Soldiers Home" in Los Angeles, California.

Myers, Elizabeth L. - Thankful's sister, was born May 1846, and was called "Lizzie" or "Libbie." She married Tertius L. Camp sometime after 1865. In 1900 Lizzie and her husband were living in Angola, New York.

Myers, George - Thankful's brother George, and wife Nell are mentioned having a baby girl, ca. summer 1863. He had died by 1900.

Myers, Jacob - Thankful's father, born 1810, married Mary Peirce, and did farm work, but did not own a farm. In 1850 the family lived in Concord, Erie County, in 1860 they lived in Yorkshire, Cattaragus County, and in 1870 they lived in Evans, Erie County. He died sometime after June 1885.

Myers, James W. - Thankful's brother was born in 1848. He may be the "Jay"who is mentioned in one of the Griffith letters. In 1900 he was living in Kansas City, Missouri.

Myers, Lydia E. - Thankful's sister was born in 1843, and had died by 1900.

Myers, Mary Peirce - Thankful's mother, born ca. July 18, 1808, she died sometime after June 1885.

Peirce, Ann H. - Thankful's cousin, daughter of Thomas Peirce. She was a teacher in Concord, and later became an artist in Springville, New York.

Peirce, Gifford - Born 1805, referred to as "Uncle Gifford." Gifford's wife was Mariette, and they had a daughter Helen Amanda. Gifford was a merchant in Concord.

Sanford, Nettie - A cousin of Frank Griffith, she lived in Brunswick, New York.

Spencer, Charles - Brother-in-law of Frank, he was the son of Asaph and Roxy Spencer.

Spencer, Sarah Ellen Griffith - Born in 1838, she was a teacher before her marriage to Charles Spencer. They had five children, Kinney C., Arthur C., Belle, Clark R. and Frank C. Spencer.

Stanbro, Catharine Griffith - Frank's oldest sister was born ca. mid-1820's. She married Henry C. Stanbro, ca. 1842, and had at least one son, Lanson Ashley Stanbro.

Stanbro, Lanson Ashley - Nephew of Frank, he was known as "Ashley." He was born in Concord in 1842, and married Thyrsa Bryant in April 1862. He also served in the 116th with Frank, but in Company C. Ashley was wounded in action at Port Hudson June 14, 1863 and lost his right arm. Following his discharge in November 1863 he returned to his wife and daughter, Catherine E., in Concord. They had four more children, Julius, Frank, Alice and Clark Stanbro. Ashley was a farmer in East Concord from at least 1873 to 1895.

Steele, Caroline E. Griffith - Frank's youngest sister was born in 1841. "Carrie" was a teacher before her marriage to John Corydon Steele, ca. late 1862. They had a baby girl ca. January 1864. Carrie died in 1925.

Steele, John Corydon - "Corydon," as he was known, was a Baptist Minister from Concord. Following his marriage to Frank's sister Carrie, they moved to Attica ca. 1863.

Treat, Fayette - Frank's brother-in-law, was known as "Fay." Born January 8, 1831, he was the son of John and Eunice Treat, neighbors of John Griffith.

Treat, Martha Esther Griffith - Frank's sister was born in 1832, she married Fayette Treat.

Appendix B

Muster Roll of Company K,
116th Regiment of New York State Volunteer Infantry
with additional Biographical Information

CAPTAINS

Ayer, James - Ayer was born Aug. 14, 1813 in Evans and spent entire life there prior to enlistment. In 1861 he became the town Supervisor. He enlisted at Buffalo, Sept 2, 1862, mustered in as captain Sept. 4, 1862. Ayer died of disease, May 22, 1863, at Camp Niagara, Baton Rouge, LA. He is buried in Forest Ave. Cemetery, Angola, NY.

Ferris, Warren T. - From East Hamburg, Ferris was 19 when he enlisted at Buffalo, Aug. 11, 1862. He mustered in as a 2nd Lieutenant in Company A, Aug. 12th. On Nov. 24, 1862 he was promoted to1[st] Lieutenant in Company K, and promoted to Captain, May 23, 1863. He mustered out with regiment June 8, 1865, Washington, D.C. In Nov. 1878 he was a clerk in Buffalo. Ferris served as President of the 116th Regt NY Veteran Association in 1881 and 1882, and as a member of its Finance Committee in 1887. He still resided in Buffalo in 1895.

FIRST LIEUTENANTS

Gould, Philip W. - Gould was 30 when he enlisted at Buffalo. He mustered in Sept. 4, 1862, and resigned his commission Nov. 23, 1862.

Ferris, Warren T. - (see above)

Dingman (Dingham), John H. - Born in 1840, he was 22 at enrollment at Evans, Aug. 8, 1862. He mustered in as a private in Co. A, Aug. 20, 1862; promoted corporal, Sept. 3, 1862; was wounded May 27, 1863 at Port Hudson, LA; promoted sergeant, Sept. 13, 1863; wounded April 8, 1864 at Sabine Cross Roads, LA; promoted 1st sergeant April 20, 1864. Dingman mustered in as 1st Lieutenant, in Co. K, on Jan. 13, 1865, and mustered out with regiment, June 8, 1865. From at least 1895 until 1911 he lived in Titusville, PA. He died in 1924 and is buried in McDowell Cemetery, Evans, NY.

SECOND LIEUTENANTS

Grannis, John W. - Born Jan.16, 1829, Grannis was a farmer when he enlisted at Buffalo on Aug. 26, 1862. He mustered in as a 2nd Lieutenant, Sept. 4, 1862, but resigned Sept. 30, (Oct. 15) 1862 due to poor health. In 1875 he was a farmer in Brandt, NY where he lived until at least 1895.

Cottier, Elisha B. - Born in New York City Nov. 23, 1831, moved to Buffalo in 1849. Age 31 at enrollment at Buffalo. Mustered in 2nd Lieutenant Oct. 1, 1862, commissioned 1st Lieutenant on June 23, 1863. Died of malaria, Aug. 21,1863 at Baton Rouge, LA.

Shepard (Sheppard), George H. - Born Sept. 5, 1830. Enlisted at Evans, Aug. 26, 1862. Mustered in private, Sept. 4; promoted 1st sergeant prior to May 1863; and mustered in 2nd Lieutenant, May 27, 1863; mustered in 1st Lieutenant Aug. 22, 1863, and mustered in as Captain, Co. A, Sept. 10, 1864. (Note that Clark, 346, says promoted to 2nd Lt. July 18, 1863, and to 1st Lt. April 12, 1864). Mustered out with regiment. In 1886 Shepard was President of the 116th Regt. NY Veteran Association. He was living in Clymer, NY in 1895, and he died Aug. 20, 1902.

FIRST SERGEANTS

Shepard (Sheppard), George H. - (see above)

Conger (Congar), Daniel C. - Age 43 at enlistment at Evans, Aug. 26, 1862. Mustered in private, Sept. 4, and promoted to sergeant prior to May 1863. Wounded May 27, 1863 at Port Hudson, LA. Promoted 1st sergeant Aug. 6, 1863. Discharged for disability May 2, 1864, at Rochester, NY. Buried in Jerusalem Corners Cemetery, East Evans.

Ballard, Charles, H. - Born March 18, 1842, Ballard was a mason at the time of his enlistment at Brandt, Aug. 27, 1862. He mustered in private, Sept. 4, promoted to sergeant prior to May 1863, and promoted to orderly sergeant, May 2, 1864. Received a slight wound in left hip Sept.19, 1864 at Winchester, VA. Promoted to 1st sergeant prior to Nov. 1864. Mustered out with regiment.

SERGEANTS

Gould, Joseph W. - Age 26 at enlistment at Evans, Aug. 30, 1862. Mustered in private, Sept. 4; promoted to sergeant, no date; deserted Nov. 8, 1862 at Baltimore, MD.

Ingersoll (Ingersol), Horace P. - Age 30 at enlistment at Evans, Aug. 26, 1862. Mustered in private, Sept. 4; promoted to sergeant, no date; promoted to 2nd Lieutenant in 75th Regiment, U.S. Colored Troops, March 3, 1863. From at least 1873 until at least 1895 he resided in North Evans. He died 1903, and is buried in North Evans Cemetery.

Smith, Elijah Porter - Born in 1817, Porter served in the "Patriot War" of 1837-1838. He was 44 when he left his wife and six children to enlist at Evans, Aug. 25, 1862. Mustered in private, Sept. 4; promoted to sergeant prior to May 1863. Mustered out with regiment. Operated Union Hotel in Angola in 1877, and still lived there as of 1895.

Doan (Doane), Valentine - Age 29 at enlistment at Eden, Aug. 26, 1862. Mustered in private, Sept. 4; promoted corporal prior to May 1863; returned to ranks, Aug. 6, 1863; promoted sergeant May 2, 1864. Mustered out with regiment. Lived in Angola in 1873, and died Nov. 4. 1894.

Sherman, Job B. - Age 22 at enlistment at North Collins, Sept. 2, 1862. Mustered in private, Sept. 4; promoted to corporal Dec. 12, 1862; wounded May 27, 1863, Port Hudson, LA; promoted sergeant, March 24, 1865. Mustered out with regiment. In 1895 he lived in Litchfield, MN.

Eno, Henry W. - Born in England, was 18 at enlistment at Brandt, Aug. 27, 1862. Mustered in private, Sept. 4; wounded May 27, 1863, Port Hudson, LA; promoted corporal Aug. 6, 1863; promoted sergeant May 8, 1864. Mustered out with regiment. Eno resided in Washington, DC in 1895, and in Anacostia, DC in1911.

Prescott, Albert D. (C) - Age 19 at enlistment at Hamburg, Sept. 2, 1862. Promoted corporal prior to May 1863; to sergeant, Aug. 6, 1863. Mustered out with regiment. He lived at Hamburg in 1873, in Lake City, MN in 1895, and at Sunnyside, WA by 1911.

Ewers, William C. - see listing under Privates

CORPORALS

Judson, Franklin M. - Born May 18, 1841, he was a farmer at enlistment at Brandt, Aug. 27, 1862. Mustered in private, Sept. 4, he was promoted to corporal, no date. Wounded May 21, 1863,at Plain Store, LA, Judson died of his wounds, May 23, 1863 and was buried near the battlefield.

Paxson (Paxon), Horace A. - Born in 1838, he enlisted at Eden, Aug. 27, 1862. Mustered in private, Sept. 4; promoted corporal, Sept. 4, 1862; wounded May 27, 1863, Port Hudson, LA. Transferred to Vet. Reserve Corps, Jan. 10, 1864. In 1873 Paxson lived in Springbook, and from at least 1895 until 1911 at Hamburg, NY. He died in 1925 and is buried in the Webster (Quaker) Cemetery, in Eden, NY.

Crawford, Harvey M. - Born Dec. 3, 1828, a farmer when he enlisted at Brandt, Aug. 27, 1862. Mustered in private, Sept. 4; promoted corporal, Oct. 21, 1862; wounded in ankle April 8, 1864 at Sabine Cross Roads, LA. Discharged for disability July 19, 1864, at New Orleans. Resided at Brandt Centre in 1873, and in 1895 at Farnham, NY, died 1903 and buried in Bradt Cemetery.

Dibble, John - Came to U.S. in 1859 from Germany. He was 23 at enlistment at Evans, Aug. 25, 1862. Mustered in private, Sept. 4; and promoted to corporal, April 1, 1865. Mustered out with regiment. From at least 1873 until at least 1895 he resided in Derby, but by 1911 he lived in Buffalo where he died in 1920.

Baldwin, Joseph Henry (Henry J.) - Age 19 at enlistment at Evans, Aug. 28, 1862. Mustered in private, Sept. 4, and promoted to corporal April 1, 1865. Mustered out with regiment. From 1895 until at least 1911 he lived in Fair Haven, Stearns County, MN.

Naigel (Naigle, Nagle, Nagel), William - Age 21 at enlistment at Eden, Aug. 27, 1862. Mustered in private, Sept. 4; promoted corporal, May 8, 1864; received slight breast wound Sept.19, 1864, at Winchester, VA. Mustered out with regiment. In 1890 he lived in Eden, and at Eagle Rock, PA. from at least 1895 to 1911.

Reifel (Riefel, Riefle, Reafer, Raefer), Austin - Born in Erie County (or Germany?) on Aug. 29, 1833, he was a farmer at enlistment at Brandt, Aug. 29, 1862. Mustered in private, Sept. 4, and promoted to corporal Aug.6, 1863. Mustered out with regiment. In 1873 he was living in Brandt, where he was farming in 1875. He died in 1878, and is buried in the North Collins Cemetery. [5'10", dark complexion, blue eyes and dark hair]

Wisinger (Weissinger, Wysinger), David - Age 19 at enlistment at North Collins, Sept. 2, 1862. Mustered in private, Sept. 4; wounded May 27, 1863, Port Hudson, LA; promoted corporal Aug. 6, 1863. Mustered out with regiment. In 1895 he lived in Prairie Center, KS.

Taylor, Douglass S. - Age 18 at enlistment at Evans, Aug. 26 (28), 1862. Mustered in private, Sept. 4; missing in action at Donaldsonville, LA, July 13, 1863; returned, no date; promoted to corporal May 2, 1864. Mustered out with regiment. He lived in Chicago, IL in 1895.

Avery, Richard H. - see listing under Privates

MUSICIANS

Carr, George W. - Born in 1837, by 1855 he was a farmer in Evans, where he enlisted at age 23, Aug. 27, 1862. Mustered in private, Sept. 4; appointed musician prior to May 1863. Discharged May 18, 1864. He was the first postmaster of the post office in Derby in 1874, and by 1878 he was employed there as a teacher. Carr served as Treasurer of the 116th Regt. N.Y. Veteran Association from at least 1887 to 1895. He still resided in Derby as of 1895. He died in 1908 and was buried in East Evans/Jerusalem Corners Cemetery.

Russell, Leroy J. - Leroy was 14 when he enlisted with his father, Warren K. Russell, at Evans, Aug. 30, 1862. Mustered in private, Sept. 4; appointed musician prior to May 1863. Mustered out with regiment. He resided in Angola from at least 1895 to 1911. He died in 1937 and is buried in the Forest Ave. Cemetery in Angola.

WAGONER

Crawford, Bela - Age 27 (37) at enlistment at Brandt, Aug. 27, 1862. Mustered in private, Sept. 4; appointed wagoner, no date. Died of disease, Oct. 27, 1863, New Orleans, LA.

PRIVATES

All mustered in Sept. 4, 1862, to serve 3 years and discharged June 8, 1865 at Washington DC, unless otherwise noted.

Ames, Acil (Ashael, Asahel, Ashel) Ebenezer - Born Aug. 14, 1835 in Poultney, VT, he moved with his family to Hamburg, NY in 1839. He married Harriet D. Brown Sept.17, 1860. He enlisted at Evans, Aug. 28, 1862, and was wounded in right side of neck May 21, 1863, at Plain Store, LA. Mustered out with regiment. The father of six children, he moved his family to Somonauk, IL in 1868, where he worked as a laborer and carpenter. A charter member of the Sandwich G.A.R. Ames died Nov. 21, 1916 at the home of his son Will, and was buried in Oak Ridge Cemetery, Somonauk.

Ames, Austin H. - Age 41 when he enlisted at Hamburg, Aug. 31, 1862. Transferred to Veteran Reserve Corps, Sept. 26, 1863, and discharged 1864. In 1895 he lived in North Evans, NY.

Avery, Edwin - Born April 9, 1838 at Collins. Enlisted at Evans, Aug. 27, 1862. Mustered out with regiment. He lived at Brandt, where he was farming from 1873 to at least 1895. In 1911 he resided in Silver Creek, NY.

Avery, Richard H. - Age 18 at enlistment at Evans, Aug. 29, 1862. Promoted to corporal Aug. 23 (26), 1863, returned to ranks, May 1, 1865. Mustered out with regiment.

Baker, John N. (M.) - Age 26 at enlistment at Evans, Aug. 26, 1862. In Feb. 1863 he was Post Baker at Camp Banks, Baton Rouge. Discharged for disability, April 10, 1864, at New Orleans, LA. In 1895 he lived in Eden, NY.

Barker, George W. - Born in 1832, he enlisted at Brandt, Sept. 3, 1862. Mustered out with regiment. He died in 1904 and is buried in the North Evans Cemetery.

Black, John - Age 22 at enlistment at Eden, Aug 31, 1862. Wounded June 14, 1863 at Port Hudson, LA, and transferred to Veteran Reserve Corps, Jan. 10, 1865. From at least 1895 to 1911 he resided in Greenfield, MI.

Bremiller (Bramiller, Braimmiler), Charles - Age 24 at enlistment at Hamburg, Sept. 2, 1862. Wounded May 27, 1863, Port Hudson, LA. Died of disease, Aug. 23, 1863, Baton Rouge, LA.

Brewer (Brower, Blower),William H. - Age 32 at enlistment at Evans, Aug. 27, 1862. Mustered out with regiment. In 1873 he lived in Evans, NY, but by 1895 he had moved to Demorest, GA.

Butler, John E. - Age 19 at enlistment at Eden. Mustered in Sept. 6, 1862. Mustered out with regiment. He resided in East Hamburg in 1873, and from 1895 to at least 1911 in North Collins. Butler died Dec. 22, 1924.

Cameron, William J. - Age 26 at enlistment at Evans, Aug. 25, 1862. Mustered out with regiment.

Craig, Charles E. - Age 22 at enlistment at Hamburg, Aug. 30, 1862. Taken prisoner Oct. 19, 1864, Cedar Creek, Va.; paroled, no date. Mustered out June 9, 1865 at Elmira, N.Y. In 1895 he resided in North Evans, and by 1911 he lived at Lake View, NY.

Crawford (Croford), Daniel - Born June 25, 1830. He enlisted at Brandt, Aug, 28, 1862. Wounded May 27, 1863 at Port Hudson, LA. Mustered out with regiment. In 1873 he resided at Brandt Centre, and in 1895 in South Dayton, NY.

Dash, Charles - Age 26 at enlistment at Brandt, Aug. 27, 1862. Mustered out with regiment.

Dean, Merritt (Merrit) - Age 19 at enlistment at Brandt, Aug. 30, 1862. Mustered out with regiment.

Dexter (Dieter), John M. - Age 21 at enlistment at Hamburg. Mustered in Sept. 6, 1862. Mustered out with regiment. He lived in Cherry Creek, NY in 1895.

Dibble, Cyrenus C. - Age 41 at enlistment at Evans, Aug. 31, 1862. Discharged for disability, April 19, 1864, at New Orleans, LA.

Drummler, William - Age 36 at enlistment at Evans, Aug. 25, 1862. Mustered in Sept. 4; no further record.

Eddy, Reuben - Age 18 at enlistment at Brandt, Aug. 27, 1862. Mustered out with regiment.

Evans, Ariel (Arial, Arilal) - Born Oct. 29, 1825 in Connecticut. He was a farmer when he enlisted at Brandt, Aug. 29, 1862. He died from inflamation of the bowels, Jan. 11, 1863, at Carrollton, (Greensville) LA. Buried at Brandt Cemetery.

Ewers, Joseph A. - Born March 1, 1821, he enlisted at Eden, Aug. 26, 1862. Received slight wound in right hip Sept. 19, 1864, at Winchester, VA. Mustered out with regiment. In 1873 he lived in North Evans. He died Feb. 17, 1892 and is buried in the North Evans Cemetery.

Ewers, William C. - Age 34 at enlistment at Eden, Aug. 26, 1862. Promoted to sergeant, March 4, 1863; returned to ranks, March 24, 1865. Mustered out with regiment.

Fairbanks, Marshall A. - Age 27 at enlistment at Evans, Aug. 25, 1862. Mustered out with regiment. In 1873 he resided at East Evans, and in 1895 at Evans, NY.

Fales (Fails), James H. - Age 25 at enlistment at Evans, Aug. 29, 1862. Died of disease, Nov. 11, 1863 at Evans, NY. Buried in North Evans Cemetery.

Fedick (Fedic, Frederick), George - Born in Erie County, he was a 29 year old farmer at time of enlistment at Brandt, Aug. 27, 1862. Wounded June 14, 1863, Port Hudson, LA. Mustered out with regiment. He lived in Springville, NY in 1895. [5'8", light complexion, blue eyes, brown hair]

Fedick (Fedic, Frederick), Nicholas - Age 26 at enlistment at Evans, Aug. 31, 1862. Mustered out with regiment. In 1895 he lived in West Valley, NY and in 1911 at Killbuck, NY.

Flint (Flink), John L. - Born in 1840, he enlisted at Brandt, Aug 30, 1862. Mustered out with regiment. He resided at Brandt from at least 1873 to 1895, but by 1911 was living in Los Angeles, CA. He died in 1914 and is buried at Brandt Cemetery.

Frary, Lyman M. - Age 26 at enlistment at Evans, Aug. 26, 1862. Died of typhoid fever, Nov. 21, 1862, at Fortress Monroe, VA, age 26 years and 8 months. He is buried in North Evans Cemetery.

Freeman, George A. - Born in 1838, he was 23 at enlistment at Evans, Aug. 26, 1862. Wounded May 27, 1863 at Port Hudson, LA. Mustered out with regiment. In 1873 he lived in North Evans, but by 1895 he lived in Buffalo, NY. He died in 1909 and is buried in the Forest Ave. Cemetery in Angola., NY.

Frost, James M. - Born in 1843, he was 19 at enlistment at Evans, Aug. 26, 1862. Taken prisoner April 9, 1864, at Pleasant Hill, LA, paroled, no date. Mustered out with regiment. He resided at North Evans from at least 1873 until his death in 1926, and is buried in the North Evans Cemetery.

Glosser, Conrad - Age 18 at enlistment at Eden, Aug. 28, 1862. Mustered out with regiment. He gave his address as Eden Centre in 1873, and as Eden in 1895.

Glosser, John - Age 23 at enlistment at Eden, Aug. 28, 1862. Mustered out with regiment. In 1873 he lived in Eden Centre, 1895 in Eden, and in Water Valley, NY by 1911.

Goff, Freeman C. - Age 32 at enlistment at Marilla, Sept. 3, 1862. Transferred to Co. C, no date; died Oct. 25, 1863 at Lancaster, NY.

Griffith, Frank Elnathan - Griffith was born in East Concord, April 26, 1835. He was employed as a mechanic when he enlisted at Evans, Sept. 2, 1862. Wounded April 9, 1864 at Pleasant Hill, LA. Transferred to Veteran Reserve Corps, June 20, 1864. Mustered out June 6, 1865 at Camp Fry, Washington, DC. [5'8", dark complexion, blue eyes, dark hair] (*see Introduction for additional information on Griffith before and after the war*)

Haggerty (Hagerty, Haggarty), John A. - Age 18 when enlisted at Hamburg, Sept. 2, 1862. Wounded May 27, 1863 at Port Hudson, LA. Mustered out with regiment. In 1911 he lived in Darlington, WI.

Hammond, Stephen (Steven) Vars - Age 40 at enlistment at Evans, Aug. 27, 1862. Mustered out with regiment. Buried in Evans Center Cemetery, Angola.

Hawks, George H. - Born at Evans Aug. 20, 1836. In 1855 he was a farmer in Brandt. He enlisted at Evans, Aug. 31. Died of disease July 10 (11), 1863, in the hospital at Baton Rouge, LA. Buried in Brandt Cemetery.

Hill, George M. - Age 26 at enlistment at Eden, Aug. 26, 1862. Mustered out with regiment. In 1873 he lived in Angola.

Hill, Milton H. - Age 19 when enlisted at Eden, Aug. 27, 1862. Wounded May 27, 1863 at Port Hudson, LA. Died of his wounds, June 1, 1863.

Ibach (Iback), Charles - Born in 1834, he was 27 when he enlisted at Evans, Aug. 29, 1862. Wounded in left wrist May 27, 1863, at Port Hudson, LA. Mustered out with regiment. Following the war he worked as a mule skinner and tanner, using his Civil War rifle to dispatch the mules. From at least 1873 until 1895 he lived in North Evans, where he operated a tannery for many years. By 1911 he lived in Derby. He died in 1921 and is buried in the North Evans Cemetery.

Ingersoll (Ingersol), Loyal C. - Age 28 at enlistment at Buffalo, Aug. 11, 1862. Mustered in Sept. 3, as private, Co. D. Transferred to Company K on Nov. 1, 1862. Deserted Dec. 31, 1862, at Carrollton, LA.

Killom (Kellom), Alonzo F. - Born in Erie County in 1836, he was a farmer in Concord from at least 1855 until he enlisted at Evans. Mustered in Sept. 6, 1862. Wounded in foot on June 14, 1863, Port Hudson, LA. Mustered out with regiment. In 1873 he was living in West Falls, NY. Killom died April 22, 1895, and is buried at Griffins Mills Cemetery, Aurora, NY. Griffith refers to him as "Lon." [5'8", light complexion, blue eyes, light hair]

Kinsley (Kingsley, Kinsly), Charles E. - Age 18 at enlistment at Evans, Aug. 25, 1862. He died of disease, at age 19, July 27, 1863, Baton Rouge, LA., and is buried in Evans Center Cemetery, Angola.

Ludlow, Lewis - Born in 1837, by 1855 he was a farmer in Hamburg. Ludlow was 25 at enlistment at Evans, Aug. 29, 1862. Wounded July 13, 1863 at Cox's Plantation, LA. Mustered out with regiment. In 1873 he lived in East Evans, 1895 in Evans, and by 1911 he was living in Derby. He died in 1912 and is buried in the East Evans/Jerusalem Corners Cemetery.

Lynn (Linn), Miner (Myner) D. - Age 20 at enlistment at Brandt, Aug. 27, 1862. He received a flesh wound in the back Sept. 19, 1864, at Winchester, VA. Mustered out May 29, 1865 at Mower Hospital, Philadelphia. In 1895 he lived in Charlotte Centre, NY.

Matteson (Mattison, Matthewson), William Harrison - Born Nov. 9, 1841, enlisted at Evans. Promoted to Reg'l Comm. Sergt., May 16, 1865. Mustered out with regiment. In 1873 he lived in Angola. Died Jan. 25, 1890. Buried in Brandt Cemetery.

Mills, Charles B.(M) - Age 18 at enlistment at Evans. Mustered in Sept. 6, 1862. Wounded June 14, 1863 at Port Hudson, LA. Discharged for disability, March 9, 1864, at New York City.

Naigel (Nagel, Nagle, Naigle), Charles - Age 25 at enlistment at Eden, Aug. 27, 1862. Promoted corporal, March 6, 1863; returned to ranks, prior to Nov. 1864. Mustered out with regiment. From at least 1895 to 1911 he resided at Eden Center. Died Sept. 21, 1914.

Ostrom (Ostrum), George V.(N, W) - Age 23 at enlistment at Evans, Aug. 26, 1862. Died of disease, Dec.16, 1863, New Iberia, LA.

Page (Paige), William B. - Age 26 (23) at enlistment at Evans, Aug. 26, 1862. Discharged for disability, Jan. 24 (28), 1864, at Buffalo, N.Y. He died August 23, 1893.

Patrick, Adrian - Born in Erie County, he was a farmer, age 25, when he enlisted at Hamburg, Aug. 30, 1862. Discharged for disability, Dec. 14, 1863, at St. Louis U.S. Army General Hospital, New Orleans, LA. From at least 1873 until 1895 he lived in Derby. [5'9", dark complexion, grey eyes, brown hair]

Pearson (Pierson), Luke - Age 32 at enlistment at Buffalo, Sept. 3, 1862. Transferred to Co. I, Sept. 1862. He was wounded in action, May 21, 1863 at Plain Store, LA, and died of his wounds, Sept. 8, 1863 at Baton Rouge, LA.

Phelps, Francis M. - Age 18 at enlistment at Evans, Aug. 26, 1862. Transferred to 163rd Company, 2nd Battalion, Veteran Reserve

Corps, April 28, 1865. Discharged for disability, July 8, 1865. He lived in North Evans in 1895.

Reifel (Riefel), Peter - Age 23 at enlistment at Evans. Mustered in Sept. 6, 1862. Wounded May 27, 1863, Port Hudson, LA. Discharged for disability, March 30, 1864, Rochester, NY. In 1873 he lived in Springville, 1895 in Buffalo, and by 1911 he resided in Angola.

Russell, Warren K. - Born in Vermont in 1819, he was employed as a butcher in Evans, NY in 1855. He was 42 when he enlisted with his son Leroy, at Evans, Aug 30, 1862. In Feb.1863 he was the Regimental Butcher at Camp Banks, Baton Rouge, LA. Promoted to Regt'l Commissary Sergeant on Oct. 1, (Sept. 26)1863. Dropped from Co. rolls Oct. 12, 1863. Discharged for disability March 1, 1865 (May 16, 1865), at Buffalo, NY. In 1873 he was living in Evans where he died in 1878. He is buried in the Forest Ave. Cemetery, Angola.

Slater (Staler), Theodore - Age 21 at enlistment at Evans. Mustered in Sept. 6, 1862. Wounded May 27, 1863, Port Hudson, LA. He died of disease at age 23, on Sept. 9, 1864, at Evans, NY, and is buried in the Evans Center Cemetery, Angola.

Smith, James H. - Age 21 at enlistment at Hamburg, Sept. 2, 1862. Discharged for disability, Jan. 25, 1864, at Buffalo, NY. By 1895 he was living in Bull City, KS and in 1911 he lived in Cottage Grove, OR.

Sooy, Franklin - Age 18 at enlistment at Hamburg, Sept. 2, 1862. Died of disease, Aug. 9, 1864, Philadelphia, PA.

Stone, James K. - Born Aug. 24, 1844, and was a farmer when he enlisted at Brandt, Aug. 30, 1862. Mustered out with regiment. In 1895 he lived in Granite Falls, MN and in 1911 he lived in Newark, NJ.

Taylor, Lafayette - Born Oct. 11, 1826, was a farmer when he enlisted at Brandt, Aug. 27, 1862. Mustered out June 29, 1865 at Mower Hospital, Philadelphia, PA. In 1873 he lived at Brandt, and by 1895 he was living in North Collins.

Taylor, Morris (Moris) - Born Nov. 11, 1835 in Cattaraugus County. He was a farmer when he enlisted at Brandt, Aug. 27, 1862. Mustered out with regiment. From at least 1873 to 1895 he lived at Brandt.

Thomason (Thonson), John A. - Age 26 at enlistment at Evans, Aug. 27, 1862. He died of disease, July 18,1863, at Baton Rouge, LA.

Tice (Tico),Wendell - Born in 1830, he was 31 when he enlisted at Evans. Mustered in Sept. 6, 1862. Wounded May 21, 1863 at Plain Store, LA, and transferred to Veteran Reserve Corps, Nov. 14, 1863. Died of disease Dec.1, 1863. He is buried in the Forest Ave. Cemetery, Angola.

Tromler (Tromber, Trommeler), William - Age 25 at enlistment at Evans, Aug. 25, 1862. Lost an arm from a cannonball, April 23, 1864, Cane River, LA. Discharged for disability, May 17, 1865, at Willet's Point, NY.

Vibbard, Wyman W.- Born Oct. 1, 1841 in Fulton County. He was a farmer when he enlisted at Brandt, Aug. 27, 1862. Mustered out with regiment. In 1911 he lived at Tama, IA.

Wait (Waite), Gurden (Giddon) F. - Age 18 at enlistment at Evans, Aug. 25, 1862. He was placed on sick since Sept. 2, 1864, and died of disease Sept. 4, 1864.

White, Ira - Age 26 at enlistment at Evans, Aug. 26 (25), 1862. Mustered out with regiment. In 1895 he lived in Norfolk, VA.

Whittemore (Whitmore, Whittmore), Horatio G. - In 1855 he was a farmer in North Collins, where he enlisted at age 33 on Sept. 6, 1862. Mustered in Sept. 9 as corporal; returned to ranks, Aug. 6, 1863. Transferred to Veteran Reserve Corps, Nov. 14, 1863, performing hospital duty. Died of dropsy Dec.17, 1863 at Baton Rouge, LA., age 35.

Wuest (Wurst, Wrust, West), Andrew - Age 25 at enlistment at East Hamburg, Sept. 1, 1862. Killed Sept. 19, 1864, Winchester, VA.

Zeigler (Zegler, Zigler), Philip - Age 18 at enlistment at Evans, Aug. 30, 1862. Transferred to Co. A, 19th Regiment, Veteran Reserve Corps, Oct. 3, 1863. Mustered out July 13, 1865 at Elmira, NY. In 1911 he lived in Franklin, PA.

Information taken from: *The One Hundred and Sixteenth of New York State Volunteers*, by Clark; *A Record of the Commissioned Officers, and Privates, of the Regiments Which Were Organized in the State of New York...*, Vol. IV, by New York Adjutant General's Office; *Register of Officers Commissioned in the Volunteer Regiments from the State of New York, 1861-1865*, New York Adjutant General's Office; *Civil War Military*

Discharges & Pensions, by Jewitt; *Some Deaths in Erie County, N.Y. 1863*, by Jewitt; *New York Soldiers in the Civil War*, Vols. 1 & 2, by Wilt; *Roster of All Known Remaining Members of the 116th Regiment N.Y. Vol. Infantry*, by Carr and Stambach; Memorial *Services in Memory of Ira Ayer, Capt. Co. A, 116th N.Y. Vols.*; *First Re-Union of the One Hundred and Sixteenth New York Volunteers*; *Roster of all Known Surviving Members of the 116th Regiment New York Volunteer Infantry Prepared for the 32nd Reunion of the Regiment Held at G.A.R. Hall, Buffalo, N.Y. Aug. 26, 1911*; Military Register, Company K, 116th Regiment, New York Volunteer Infantry (original poster).

Appendix C

116th New York State Volunteer Infantry Field and Staff Officers, and men from other Companies in 116th mentioned in Griffith letters

<u>FIELD AND STAFF</u>

COLONELS

Chapin, Edward Payson - Born August 16, 1831 in Waterloo, NY, Chapin had been practicing law in Buffalo for about nine years. Soon after the war started he raised a company for the 44th Infantry, of which he became Lieutenant-Colonel. Wounded at Hanover Court House in May 1862 he was in Buffalo recuperating when the 116th was being formed. Chapin was commissioned Colonel of the 116th Aug. 11, 1862 and mustered in Sept. 5, 1862. He was commanding a brigade, leading troops across a field when a Confederate bullet pierced his head and he died May 27, 1863, at Port Hudson, LA. Promoted to Brigadier General, posthumously on May 27, 1863. Chapin is buried in Waterloo, NY.

Love, George Maltby - Born in Buffalo on January 1, 1831, Love served previously as Sergeant-Major of 21st Infantry, and Captain of Co. A, 44th Infantry. He mustered in as Major of the 116th on September 4, 1862. He was wounded in action at Port Hudson on May 27, 1863, commissioned a Colonel June 23, 1863 and was in command of a Brigade for a portion of the time. Love was breveted a Brigadier General, and awarded the Medal of Honor for capture of the battle flag of the 2nd South Carolina at Cedar Creek, VA on October 19, 1864. He mustered out with regiment in June 1865. He remained in the Regular Army after the war, and on March 7, 1867 he was appointed a 2nd Lieut. and was awarded four brevets for service. On March 1, 1875 Love was promoted to 1st Lieut., and engaged in garrison and frontier service until he retired March 15, 1883 for disability incurred in the line of duty. Love died March 15 1887, and is buried in Forest Lawn Cemetery in Buffalo.

LIEUTENANT COLONELS

Cottier, Robert - Age 46 at enrollment at Buffalo, Aug. 19, 1862. He mustered in Sept. 5, 1862. Cottier resigned May 27, 1863.

Higgins, John - Age 29 when enrolled at Buffalo, Aug. 21, 1862. He mustered in as Captain of Co. D on Sept. 3, 1862. On July 18, 1863 he mustered in as Major, and on Sept. 14, 1863 as Lieutenant Colonel. Higgins resigned Sept. 19(17), 1864.

Sizer, John Mappa - Sizer was 22 when he enrolled at Buffalo, Aug. 24, 1862. He mustered in as Captain of Co. G on Sept 3, 1862, and was promoted to Major on Sept. 14, 1863. He served on the staff of Gen. Emory as Acting Assistant Inspector General, ca. Feb.-April 1864, and was mustered in as Lieutenant Colonel on Oct. 30, 1864. Sizer mustered out with regiment. In 1879 Sizer was President of the 116th Regt. N.Y. Veteran Association.

MAJORS

Love, George M. - Promoted to Colonel, May 28, 1863. (see listing above)

Higgins, John - Promoted to Lieut. Colonel, Sept. 14, 1863. (see listing above)

Sizer, John Mappa - Promoted to Lieut. Colonel, Oct. 30, 1864. (see listing above)

Carpenter, George W. - Age 28 at enrollment at Buffalo, Carpenter mustered in as a 1st Lieutenant in Co. I on Aug. 31, 1862, and was Commissioned a Captain Jan. 14, 1863. He was wounded in action, Oct. 19, 1864 at Cedar Creek, VA. On Feb 3, 1865 he was commissioned Major, and mustered out with regiment. In 1895 he served as President of the 116th Regt. N.Y. Veteran Association, and lived in Watertown, Coddington County, SD.

ADJUTANTS

Weber, John Baptiste - Weber was born in Buffalo in 1842. A 2nd Lieut. of Co. F, 44th Infantry, he was appointed 1st Lieutenant and Adjutant of 116th on August 8, 1862. He was detached on brigade staff for a time. On Nov. 7, 1863 he was discharged for promotion to Colonel 89th Regiment U.S. Colored Troops. Following the war he served as Assistant Postmaster of Buffalo. In 1870 Weber ran against Grover Cleveland for Sheriff of Erie County. He lost that election, but won the position in 1872.

From at least 1881 to 1884 he was associated with the wholesale grocery firm of Smith & Weber. In 1884 Weber ran for U.S. Congress and was elected, serving two terms. President Benjamin Harrison appointed him Commissioner of the Port of New York. Weber was living in Buffalo in 1895, and in 1901 he was Commissioner General of the Pan American Exposition company. He died in 1926 at age 84.

Nial, John C. - Age 18 when enrolled at Buffalo, Aug. 22, 1862, Nial mustered in a private in Co. G, on Sept. 3, and was soon promoted to 1st Sergeant. He was promoted to Sergeant-Major, on Nov. 23, 1862; mustered in as 2nd Lieutenant of Co. E, July 18, 1863; as 1st Lieutenant on Sept. 14, 1863, and mustered in as Adjutant Nov. 8, 1863. Nial mustered out with regiment. In 1895 he lived in St. Louis, MO.

QUARTERMASTERS

Adams, James - Age 38 when enrolled at New York City, July 14, 1862. Mustered in as 1st Lieutenant and Quartermaster Sept. 5, 1862; resigned, Sept. 14, 1862; official date of discharge listed as Dec. 16, 1864, no service rendered. In 1895 he resided in Buffalo.

Fargo, Willitt (Willet) H. - Age 25 when enrolled at Baltimore, MD, Sept. 15, 1862. Mustered in as 1st Lieutenant and Quartermaster on Sept. 30, 1862, and resigned Nov. 25, 1862.

Goslin, Alexander M. - Age 23 when enrolled at Buffalo, July 29, 1862. Mustered in Sergeant, Co. C on Sept. 3; promoted to Quartermaster-Sergeant, Sept. 5, 1862; mustered in as 1st Lieutenant and Quartermaster, Nov. 26, 1862; detached on brigade staff March 1864. He was discharged May 14, 1865 to accept promotion to Captain and Asst. Quartermaster U.S.A. Volunteers. He resided in Akron, NY in 1895.

Miller, George W. - Age 30 when enrolled at Buffalo, Aug. 15, 1862. Mustered in a Sergeant of Co. D on Sept. 3, 1862; mustered in as 2nd Lieutenant of Co. I on Sept. 14, 1863; promoted to 1st Lieutenant, Co. D on Jan. 1, 1864; wounded in action, Oct. 19, 1864 at Cedar Creek, VA; commissioned Quartermaster June 17, 1865, but not mustered in; mustered out with regiment.

SURGEON

Hutchins, Chauncey B. - Age 35 when enrolled at Buffalo. Mustered in as surgeon Aug. 1, 1862; was detached on staff of Gen. Emory as Medical Director, ca. Feb.-April 1864; and mustered out with regiment. In 1895 he lived in San Francisco, CA.

ASSISTANT SURGEONS

Lynde, Uriah "Uri" C. - Born March 26, 1834 in Concord township, Lynde became a school-teacher. In 1856 he began to study medicine, graduating from Buffalo University in 1859. From 1859 to 1862 he practiced medicine in Springville. He was 28 when he enrolled at Buffalo to serve in the 116th and raised Company F. Mustered in as First Assistant Surgeon on Aug. 29, 1862. He was placed in charge of the hospitals at Springfield Landing near Fort Hudson, LA. Following his resignation on Oct. 18, 1863 he returned to the study of medicine and in the spring of 1865 graduated from Jefferson Medical College in Philadelphia. Lynde continued practicing medicine in Springville until 1872 when he moved to Buffalo, specializing in surgery. In 1895 he still resided in Buffalo.

Howe, Carey W. - Age 25 when enrolled at Buffalo, Sept. 1, 1862. Mustered in as Second Assistant Surgeon Sept. 5, 1862, and resigned, Jan 6. 1863. He lived in Buffalo in 1895.

Coventry, John M. - Age 26 when enrolled at New Orleans, LA. Mustered in as Assistant Surgeon April 22, 1863, and resigned, Sept. 14, 1864. He lived in Windsor, Ontario, Canada in 1895.

Shaw, M. Eugene - Formerly Assistant Surgeon with 89th Infantry, Shaw was 22 when enrolled in 116th at Morganza, LA, March 8, 1864. He mustered in as Assistant Surgeon, May 12, 1864, and mustered out with regiment.

CHAPLAINS

Modisett (Moddesit, Modesitte), Welton M. - Age 47 when enrolled at Buffalo. He mustered in as chaplain, Sept. 5, 1862, and resigned, June (July) 23, 1863. In 1895 he lived in Buffalo.

Gordon, Hiram J. - Gordon was 34 when he enrolled at Stevenson, VA. Mustered in as chaplain March 25, 1865, and mustered out with regiment.

NON-COMMISSIONED STAFF

SERGEANT MAJORS

Clark, Orton S. - The son of Zenas Clark, he was 23 when he enrolled at Buffalo, Aug. 18, 1862. Mustered in Sergeant Co. C, Sept. 3, 1862; promoted Sergeant-Major, Sept. 5, 1862; promoted to 2nd Lieutenant, Co. A, Nov. 8, 1862; mustered in 2nd Lieutenant, Co. A, Nov. 22, 1862; promoted to 1st Lieutenant, Co. A, May 21, 1863; mustered in and commissioned May 21, 1863; wounded July 13, 1863 Cox's Plantation, LA; detached on Brigade Staff for a time; mustered in Captain Co. H, July 25, 1863; mustered out with regiment. Clark wrote the official history of the 116th, *The One Hundred and Sixteenth Regiment of the New York State Volunteers*, published in 1868. He was Secretary of the 116th Regt. N.Y. Veteran Association in 1873. In 1895 he resided in Minneapolis, MN.

Nial, John C. - Promoted to 2nd Lieutenant, July 23, 1863. (see listing under Adjutant)

Hair, Richard M. - Age 21 when enlisted at Buffalo, Aug. 22, 1862. Mustered in private, Co. I, Sept. 3, 1862; promoted Corporal, Nov. 8, 1862; promoted 1st Sergeant, April 11, 1863; wounded in action at Port Hudson, LA, May 27, 1863; promoted Sergeant-Major, July 18, 1863; and discharged Sept. 26, 1863 to take promotion of Sept. 19, 1863 to 1st Lieutenant and Adjutant of 89th U.S. Colored Troops. In 1895 he lived in Brookfield, MO.

McGowan, Raymond - Age 22 at enrollment at Buffalo, Aug. 15, 1862. Mustered in as private in Co. D, Sept, 3, 1862; promoted Corporal prior to May 1863; wounded May 27, 1863, at Port Hudson, LA; promoted Sergeant-Major, Sept. 23, 1863; promoted to 2nd Lieutenant; mustered in as 1st Lieutenant of Co. C, March 10, 1865; mustered out with company. In 1895 he lived in Grand Rapids, MI.

Stadin (Statten), Oloff (Orlof) W. - Age 28 when enlisted at Buffalo, Aug. 1, 1862. Mustered in as private in Co. G, Sept. 3, 1862; promoted Corporal, Jan. 23, 1863; wounded May 27, 1863, at Port Hudson, LA; promoted Sergeant, Oct. 18, 1863; promoted Sergeant-Major, April 1, 1864; mustered out with regiment. Saw prior service as Sergeant, Co. C, 1st Sharpshooters.

QUARTERMASTER SERGEANTS

Goslin, Alexander - Promoted to Quartermaster, Nov. 23, 1862.(See listing under Quartermaster)

Danner, Michael, Jr. - Age 24 when enlisted at Buffalo, Aug. 28, 1862. Mustered in as Sergeant in Co. C, Sept. 3, 1862; promoted to Quartermaster-Sergeant, Nov. 23, 1862; mustered out with regiment. He resided in Joliet, IL in 1895.

COMMISSARY SERGEANTS

Claghorn, Josiah L. - Age 29 when enlisted at Buffalo, Aug. 12, 1862. Mustered in private in Co. A, Aug. 20, 1862; promoted to Commissary Sergeant, Sept. 3, 1862; discharged Oct. 4, 1863 for promotion to 1st Lieutenant and Quartermaster 89th U.S. Colored Troops. In 1895 he lived in Wauseca, MN.

Russell, Warren K. - enlisted at Evans, Aug. 30, 1862. Mustered in as private, Co. K, Sept. 4; promoted Commissary Sergeant, Sept. 26, 1863. (see listing in Appendix B)

Matthewson, William Harrison - Age 24 at enlistment at Evans. Mustered in as private, Co. K, Sept. 4, 1862; promoted Commissary Sergeant, May 16, 1865. (see listing under Matteson in Appendix B)

HOSPITAL STEWARD

Nichell, Charles F. A. - Son of Dr. Henry Nichell of Buffalo, he had nearly completed his medical education before enlisting at age 18 at Buffalo, Aug. 12, 1862. Mustered in as private in Co. H, Sept. 3, 1862; promoted to Hospital Steward, Sept. 12, 1862; mustered out with regiment. After finishing his medical training Nichell practiced in Buffalo in 1867.

PRINCIPAL MUSICIANS

Martin, John - Age 24 at enlistment at Evans, Aug. 2, 1862. Mustered in as private, Co. A, Aug. 20, 1862; appointed musician, no date; "Leader of Band," promoted principal musician, March 1, 1865; mustered out with regiment.

Knapp, Julius L. - Age 18 at enlistment at Marilla, July 19, 1862. Mustered in as private in Co. I, Sept. 3, 1862; appointed musician prior to May 1863; promoted principal musician, March 1, 1865; mustered out with regiment.

COMPANY A

Ayer, Ira - Captain - Ayer was born Dec. 26, 1802. He had been a supervisor of the town of Evans in 1857, 1858 and 1860. He enrolled in 116th at Buffalo, Aug. 12, 1862. Mustered in as Captain Co. A, Sept. 3, 1862; resigned due to illness, March 1, 1863. Ayer died July 28, 1889.

Wadsworth, Charles F. - Captain - Age 26 when enrolled at Buffalo, Aug. 21, 1862. Mustered in as 1st Lieutenant, Co. D, Sept. 3, 1862 and mustered in as Captain of Co. A, May 19, 1863. On June 16, 1863 Wadsworth left the 116th under orders to report to Washington, DC, and resigned Aug. 18, 1863. In 1895 he lived in Geneseo, NY.

Newton, Jacob C. - Captain - Age 22 when enrolled at East Hamburg, Aug. 9, 1862. Mustered in private in Co. A, Aug. 20, 1862; promoted 1st Sergeant, Sept. 3, 1862; mustered in 2nd Lieutenant, Nov. 24, 1862; mustered in Captain, Oct. 12, 1863; discharged due to disability, Sept. 9, 1864. He resided in Los Angeles, CA in 1895.

Clark, Orton S. - First Lieutenant - (see listing under Sergeant Major)

White, Horace Wayne - First Sergeant - Age 23 at enlistment at Hamburg, Aug. 6, 1862. Mustered in private in Co. A, Aug. 20, 1862; promoted Corporal, Sept. 2, 1862; promoted Sergeant, Nov. 9, 1862; promoted to 1st Sergeant, Jan. 1, 1865; mustered out with regiment. In 1895 he lived in Hamburg, NY.

Woods, Robert H. - Corporal - Age 18 at enlistment at Buffalo, Aug. 4, 1862. Mustered in private Co. A, Aug. 20, 1862; promoted to Corporal, Jan. 1, 1865; mustered out with regiment. From at least 1895 to 1911 he lived in Farmington, NM.

Cook, Andrew - Private - Age 18 at enlistment at Evans, Aug. 2, 1862. Mustered in private, Co. A, Aug. 20, 1862; mustered out with regiment. In 1895 he lived in Caro, MI, and by 1911 he resided in Grand Rapids, MI. Cook died in 1916.

Oatman, Leroy S. - Private - Born July 6, 1844 at Hartford, Washington Co., NY, the son of Lyman and Desire Oatman. The family came to Erie County in 1848. He enlisted at Evans, Aug. 4, 1862. Mustered in private, Co. A, Aug. 20, 1862; promoted Sergeant prior to May 1863; wounded in action May 21, 1863, Plain Store, LA; returned to ranks, Dec. 15, 1863; Regt'l Ordnance Sergeant, Dec. 26, 1863; mustered out with regiment.

On July 31, 1867 he married Lucinda E. "Lucy" Stray, and they had two children, Helen and Edna. In 1868 he established a drugstore in Angola which he ran for 16 years. In addition he served as a special deputy clerk of Erie County, was a Justice of the Peace, was an active member of the Angola Board of Education, and in 1876 was Master of Evans Lodge No. 261 of the Masons. In 1887 Oatman was President of the 116th Regt. N.Y. Veteran Association, and in 1895 served as 1st Vice President of the group. Oatman died in 1904 in Buffalo and was buried in Forest Ave. Cemetery, Angola.

Sawdy, William H. - Private - Age 44 at enlistment at Evans, Aug. 8, 1862. Mustered in private, Co. A, Aug. 20, 1862; wounded in action May 27, 1863 at Port Hudson, LA; furloughed and never reported back to company, listed as deserted April 13, 1864 at New Orleans, LA.

COMPANY B

Gray, Wilson H. - Captain - Age 19 at enrollment at Buffalo, Aug. 23, 1862. Mustered in 1st Lieutenant, Co. F, Sept. 3, 1862; wounded in action May 27, 1863, at Port Hudson, LA; mustered in Captain, Co. B, Aug. 1, 1863; discharged for disability, Aug. 15, 1864. Following the war he lived in Toledo, OH, and in 1895 in Detroit, MI.

Weeks, Henry W. (W. Henry) - Private - Age 21 at enrollment at Lancaster, Aug. 6, 1862. Mustered in private, Co. B, Sept. 3, 1862; discharged for disability, June 4, 1863. In 1895 he resided in Buffalo.

COMPANY C

Brown, George N. - First Lieutenant - Age 27 at enrollment at Buffalo, Aug. 26, 1862. Mustered in Sergeant, Co. C, Sept. 3, 1862; promoted 1st Sergeant prior to May 1863; mustered in 1st Lieutenant, Sept. 14, 1863; commissioned Aug. 17 (18), 1863, date of rank June 8, 1863; discharged for disability, July 27, 1864. He lived in Buffalo in 1895..

Stanbro, Lanson Ashley - Private - Age 20 at enlistment at Sardinia, Aug. 11, 1862. Mustered in private, Co. C, Sept. 3, 1862; wounded in action and lost his right arm June 14, 1863, at Port Hudson, LA; discharged due to his wounds, Nov. 9, 1863, at

Rochester, NY. In 1873 he was farming in East Concord where he still resided in 1895. Nephew of Frank Griffith. (see also listing in Appendix A)

COMPANY D

Rohan (Rowan), John H. - First Lieutenant - Age 21 at enrollment at Buffalo, Aug. 18, 1862. Mustered in Sergeant, Co. D, Sept. 3, 1862; promoted to 1st Sergeant no date; mustered in 2nd Lieutenant, Co. E, Jan. 5, 1863; transferred back to Co. D, March 8, 1863; mustered in 1st Lieutenant, Co. G, June 15, 1863; mustered in Captain, Co. G, March 9, 1864; wounded in action, Oct. 19, 1864, Cedar Creek, VA; mustered out with regiment. In 1895 he lived in Fort Wayne, IN.

Miller, George W. - First Lieutenant - Age 30 at enrollment at Buffalo, Aug. 15, 1862. Mustered in Sergeant, Co. D, Sept. 3, 1862; mustered in 2nd Lieutenant, Co. I, Sept. 14, 1863; promoted 1st Lieutenant, Co. D, Jan. 1, 1864, mustered in April 12, 1864; acting Regimental Quartermaster, March 1864; wounded in action Oct. 19, 1864, at Cedar Creek, VA; promoted to Quartermaster, June 5, 1865, but not mustered; mustered out with regiment.

McCumber (McComber), John Milton - Private - Born in Delaware. In 1855 he was employed as a mason in Colden, NY where he enlisted at age 32, Aug. 27, 1862. Mustered in private, Co. D, Sept. 3, 1862; died of typhoid fever, Aug.4, 1863, in hospital at Baton Rouge, LA. Left a wife Hannah and a son Eugene.

COMPANY E

Swartz (Swarz, Schwartz), Henry A. C. - First Lieutenant - Age 21 at enrollment at Buffalo. Mustered in Sergeant, Co. G, Sept. 3, 1862; promoted 1st Sergeant no date; mustered in 2nd Lieutenant, Co. D, Sept. 14, 1863; transferred to Co. E, Dec. 27, 1863; mustered in 1st Lieutenant, Co. F, Sept. 18, 1864; transferred to Co. E, Feb. 12, 1865; mustered out with regiment. In 1895 he lived in Buffalo.

COMPANY F

Crary, Charles S. - Captain - From Springville, he was 20 when he enrolled at Concord, Aug. 12, 1862. Mustered in 1st Sergeant,

Co. F, Sept. 3, 1862; mustered in 2nd Lieutenant, Dec. 3,1862; mustered in 1st Lieutenant, Co. H, June 5, 1863; transferred to Co. F, Sept. 14, 1863; mustered in Captain, Co. I, Feb. 12, 1865; wounded in left shoulder Oct. 19, 1864, at Cedar Creek, VA; mustered out with regiment.

Mayo, Samuel A. - Corporal - Age 26 at enlistment at Concord, Aug. 13, 1862. Mustered in Corporal, Co. F, Sept. 3, 1862; wounded in action at Donaldsonville, LA on July 13, 1863, and died of his wounds at Baton Rouge, LA, August 8, 1863.

Shoemaker (Schumacher), Henry - Corporal - Age 18 at enlistment at Concord, Aug. 13, 1862. Mustered in private, Co. F, Sept. 3, 1862; promoted corporal, March 1, 1865; mustered out with regiment. From at least 1895 until 1911 he resided in East Dubuque, IL.

Ferrin, William Augustine - Musician - Age 19 at enlistment at Concord, Aug. 8, 1862. Mustered in musician, Co. F, Sept. 3, 1862; discharged by order of Secretary of War, Oct. 29, 1863, at New Orleans, LA. In January 1864 he started the *Chronicle*, in Concord. In 1865 be became City Editor of the *Buffalo Express*, and later Editor of the *Cattaraugus Republican*. From 1876 to 1880, Ferrin was Secretary of the 116th N.Y. Veteran Association. In 1895 he lived in Salamanaca, NY.

Hoverland, Frederick E. - Private - Age 18 at enlistment at Concord, Aug. 13, 1862. Mustered in private, Co. F, Sept. 3, 1862; wounded in shoulder May 21, 1863 at Plain Store, LA; mustered out with regiment. From at least 1895 until 1911 he lived in Leaf River, IL.

Johnston, Lorenzo - Private - Age 25 at enlistment at Concord, Aug. 13, 1862. Mustered in private, Co. F, Sept. 3, 1862; mustered out with regiment. In 1895 he lived in College View, NE.

Johnston, Marion F. - Private - From Ashford, he was 18 at enlistment at Concord, Aug. 9, 1862. Mustered in private, Co. F, Sept. 3, 1862; received a severe wound to right temple, Sept. 19, 1864, at Winchester, VA; discharged for disability, April 3, 1865. He resided in Fairhaven, MN in 1895.

McClure, Julius A. - Private - Age 42 at enlistment at Concord, Aug. 8, 1862. Mustered in private, Co. F, Sept. 3, 1862; discharged for disability, May 10, 1864, at New Orleans, LA. In 1883 he was employed as a shoemaker in Concord, and by 1895 he lived in Fitch, NY.

Shultes (Shulters, Shultus), Franklin C. - Private - Born in Concord Jan. 8, 1844, he was 18 at enlistment at Concord, Aug. 11, 1862. Mustered in private, Co. F, Sept. 3, 1862; discharged for disability, May 1, 1864 at Alexandria, LA. In 1895 he resided in Springfield, NY.

Tyrer, Hiram A. - Private - Age 18 at enlistment at Collins, Aug. 14, 1862. Mustered in private, Co. F, Sept. 3, 1862; died of chronic diarrhea, May 7, 1864, at Marine Hospital, New Orleans, LA.

Weber, James B. - Private - Age 19 at enlistment at Concord, Aug. 9, 1862. Mustered in Sergeant, Co. F, Sept. 3, 1862; returned to ranks, March 18, 1865; mustered out with regiment. In 1873 he was President of the 116th Regt. N.Y. Veteran Association. From at least 1895 to 1911 he resided in Springville, NY. (Griffith refers to him as "Birney")

COMPANY G

McGowan, James S. - Captain - Born in Buffalo in 1836, the son of Andrew and Mary S. McGowan. On 1861 he was employed as a "weighman" in the Buffalo grain trade. He enrolled at Buffalo, Aug. 23, 1862. Mustered in as 1st Lieutenant, Co. E, Sept. 2, 1862; mustered in Captain, Co. G, Sept. 14, 1863; resigned, March 8, 1864, at Franklin, LA, probably due to ill health. He married Elizabeth Blaney on July 21, 1864, and they had two children, Richard B. and Blanche Marie. The couple separated ca. 1888. In 1895 McGowan lived in Buffalo. He died of apoplexy/alcoholism in the Police Station on July 17, 1902. He was buried at Holy Cross Cemetery.

COMPANY H

Woehnert, John G. - First Lieutenant - Age 27 at enrollment at Buffalo, Aug. 25, 1862. Mustered in private, Co. H, Aug. 26, 1862; promoted Sergeant, Aug. 28, 1862; wounded in action, May 27, 1873 at Port Hudson, LA; promoted to 1st Sergeant prior to Aug. 1863; mustered in 1st Lieutenant, Sept. 14, 1863; mustered in as Captain, Co. B., Jan. 7 (8), 1865 at Washington, D.C.; mustered out with regiment.

Ryther, James F. - Corporal - Age 18 at enlistment at Evans, August 14, 1862. Mustered in private, Co. H, Sept. 3, 1862; promoted corporal, Jan. 12, 1865; mustered out with regiment. In 1895 he lived in West Seneca, NY. Buried in North Evans Cemetery.

COMPANY I

Irwin (Erwin), Edward - First Lieutenant - Age 24 at enrollment at Buffalo. Mustered in as 2nd Lieutenant, Co. I, Aug. 31, 1862; mustered in 1st Lieutenant, Nov. 8, 1862; resigned, Oct. 14, 1863. In 1895 he lived in Buffalo.

Morgan, William J. - First Lieutenant - Age 21 at enrollment at Buffalo, Aug. 18, 1862. Mustered in private, Co. I, Sept. 3, 1862; promoted Sergeant Sept. 4, 1862; promoted 1st Sergeant no date; mustered in 2nd Lieutenant, Nov. 8, 1862; wounded in action May 27, 1863 at Port Hudson, LA; mustered in as 1st Lieutenant, Co. B, Aug. 10, 1863; transferred back to Co. I., Sept. 14, 1863; mustered in as Captain, Co. B, Oct. 24, 1863; and transferred to Co. C., April 12, 1864. Mustered out with regiment.

Information taken from: *The One Hundred and Sixteenth of New York State Volunteers*, Clark; Buffalo Evening News, 9 November 1963; *A Record of the Commissioned Officers, and Privates, of the Regiments Which Were Organized in the State of New York....*, Vol. IV, New York Adjutant General's Office; *A Compendium of the War of the Rebellion*, Dyer; *Our County and Its People: a Descriptive Work on Erie County, New York*, White; *Centennial History of Erie County, New York*, Johnson; *New York in the War of the Rebellion 1861-1865*, Phisterer; *The Honors of the Empire State in the War of the Rebellion*, Townsend; *Annual Report of the Adjutant-General of the State of New York for the Year 1903, Registers of New York Regiments in the War of the Rebellion*; Courier & Republic, 28 October 1864; *History of the City of Buffalo and Erie County*, Smith; *First Re-Union of the One Hundred and Sixteenth New York Volunteers*; Courier, 28 September 1864; *Roster of all Known Surviving Members of the 116th Regiment New York Volunteer Infantry Prepared for the 32nd Reunion of the Regiment Held at G.A.R. Hall, Buffalo, N.Y. Aug. 26, 1911*; 1855 Census, Erie County, New York; *History of the Original Town of Concord, Being the Present Towns of Concord, Collins, N. Collins and Sardinia, Erie County, New York*, Briggs; *New York Soldiers in* *the Civil War*, Vols. 1 & 2, Wilt; *Roster of All Known Remaining Members of the 116th Regiment N.Y. Vol. Infantry*, Carr and Stambach; www.bufnet on 10/30/2000.

Appendix D

Chronology of the 116th New York State Volunteer Infantry*

1862

July   7   Gov. Morgan issues order to raise new regiments in
                each of New York's 32 senatorial districts

Aug. 11- Sept. 3   116th N.Y.S.V. Infantry organized at Fort Porter/
                Camp Morgan, Buffalo

Sept.   2   <u>Frank Griffith enlists at Evans, Erie County, New York</u>
        3   116th mustered at Fort Porter, Co. K received short
                furlough to enable members to settle affairs at home
        5   116th minus Co. K, leaves Buffalo via the Erie Road
        7   Arrived at Baltimore, Maryland; attached to Emory's
                Brigade, 8th Army Corps
        8   Encamped near Druid Hill Park, Baltimore at "Camp
                Belger" until Nov. 5; Col. Chapin and experienced
                officers drill and instruct men
        10   <u>Co. K leaves Buffalo</u>
        11   <u>Co. K arrives at "Camp Belger" near Baltimore</u>

Oct.   9   Brigade organized to which 116th assigned
        12   Started on expedition to Gettysburg, Pennsylvania
                against Stuart
        13   Arrived at Gettysburg
        14   Marched through village, bivouacked near Cashtown.
        15   Left Gettysburg
        16   Arrived back at "Camp Belger,"Baltimore
        18   Raised flag pole, camp renamed "Camp Chapin"
        28   Ordered down town to quell expected riot

Nov.   2   Orders to prepare for distant service, to join Gen
                Bank's Louisiana Expedition, Dept. of the Gulf, 19th
                Army Corps

---

* **<u>Underlining</u> shows where Griffith spends time apart from 116th.**

321

Nov.	5	Left Baltimore, embarked on the "Robert Morris" and "Baltimore" passing down the harbor; transferred to steamship "Atlantic"
	13	Arrived at Fortress Monroe, Virginia
	18	Marched to Hampton village. Received first pay
Dec.	2	Fortress Monroe
	4	Bank's expedition sailed from Fortress Monroe, on steamship Atlantic
	5	Encountered a heavy storm lasting two days
	13	Reached Ship Island, Mississippi in the Gulf of Mexico
	14-28	Drilling and other preparations at "Camp Canaan"
	29	Embarked on steamer "North Star"
	30	Entered the Mississippi River and at 8 p.m. anchored off New Orleans, Louisiana
	31	Landed at Carrollton, "Camp Love"

1863

Jan.	1	"Camp Love," Carrollton, spent month here drilling
	12	Received first mail since leaving Fortress Monroe
	22	March of the Brigade on the "Shell Road"
Feb.	2	Embarked on the river steamer "Che-Ki-Ang"
	4	Arrived at Baton Rouge, Louisiana
	5	Pitched tents at "Camp Banks," Baton Rouge
March	9	Received shelter tents to replace "A" tents
	14	Started for Port Hudson
	15	Steamer Mississippi exploded at 2 a.m., retraced route and bivouacked at Morticeno Bayou
	16	Marched to Baton Rouge and embarked on boat
	17	Landed at Winter's Plantation and marched through the swamp on a reconnaissance, remaining at the Plantation until 21st
	22	Returned to Camp Banks, Baton Rouge
April	3	Detachment left at Fortress Monroe arrived

April	4	Moved to "Camp Niagara," Baton Rouge
May	19-20	Started again toward Port Hudson
	20	<u>Griffith absent sick at Baton Rouge, at least into June</u>
	21	*Battle of Plain Store.* Loss in regiment, 13 killed and 44 wounded
	24	Port Hudson surrounded
	27	Assault on Port Hudson. Loss in regiment, 22 killed and 85 wounded, including Col. Chapin
June	6	On skirmish line at Port Hudson
	14	Second assault on Port Hudson. Loss in regiment, 5 killed and 23 wounded
	19	<u>Griffith at Camp Gatt, Baton Rouge convalescing, through Aug. 13</u>
July	2	Marched nearly to Plain's Store, where a wagon train had been attacked, to reinforce the escort and returned in evening to Port Hudson
	6	Rumors that Vicksburg had surrendered to Grant
	7	Rumors confirmed. Flag of truce received from Port Hudson
	8	Port Hudson surrendered
	9	116th NYSV & 2nd Louisiana march inside Port Hudson to receive surrender, in evening embarked on steamer and moved down the river toward Donaldsonville
	10	Landed at Donaldsonville, Louisiana
	13	*Battle of Cox's Plantation*, at Bayou LaFourche. Loss in Regiment, 5 killed, 23 wounded, and 21 prisoners, Confederate victory.
Aug.	1	Embarked on steamer "Excelsior" and landed at Baton Rouge, at Camp Niagra for a week
	9	To Fort Williams, Baton Rouge for garrison duty
	27	Ordered to New Orleans
Sept.	2	Embarked on steamer "Iberville" and proceeded down the river

Sept.	3	Reached New Orleans. Transferred to the "Alexandria" and started on the Sabine Pass Expedition
	7	Sighted the coast of Texas at Sabine Pass
	8	Confederates disable gunboats at Sabine Pass and we started our return
	9	On half rations and becalmed in the gulf for two days
	11	Gunboat towed us toward the mouth of the river
	12	Entered the mouth of the Mississippi
	13	Landed at Algiers, opposite New Orleans
	16	Ride on railroad cars to Brashear City
	17	Crossed Berwick Bay to Berwick City
	18-25	At Berwick City
	26	Marched though Pattersonville, Louisiana, camped after 9 miles, and remained there till Oct. 3
	28	Reconnaissance to Centerville, Louisiana
Oct.	2	Camp Misery, Bayou Teche, on the road to Texas
	3	Marched through Franklin, Louisiana and camped
	4	Marched 12 miles
	5	Marched 12 more miles
	8	Marched through New Iberia, 16 miles
	9	Marched 10 miles to Vernillion Bayou, skirmish
	11	Marched through Vermillionville 14 miles to Carrion Crow Bayou, remained there 9 days
	15	Skirmish at Carrion Crow Bayou
	21	Marched through Opelousas to Bayou Barri Croquet 17 miles, and remained there 10 days
Nov.	1	Turned back, camped at Carrion Crow 17 miles
	2	Marched to Vermillionville 14 miles
	3	Awakened after midnight, forced march of 15 miles in five hours to Bayou Grand Coteau to reinforce Burbridge's Division of the Thirteenth Corps
	4	Returned to Vermillionville
	16	Left Vermillionville, began march back to Camp Pratt
	17	Marched to New Iberia, remained there through until Jan. 7

1864

Jan. 6   Awoke to find about two inches of snow on the ground

7   Marched from New Iberia towards Franklin 10 miles

8   Marched 10 miles, camping at Harding's Plantation

9   Arrived at Franklin

15   Moved for winter quarters to better ground at "Camp Emory," Franklin, remained there through March 4

Feb. 3-4   <u>Griffith at work at Brigade Headquarters for Col. Love</u>

5   Pole and flag raising at Franklin

9   All companies working on some ornament for the camp

March 10 - May 22   RED RIVER CAMPAIGN

15   8 a.m. began marching from Franklin on Opelousas Road, 16 miles

16   Marched to Camp Pratt, 18 miles

17   Marched to Vermillion Bayou, 16 miles

18   Crossed Carrion Crow Bayou and camped 1 mile beyond, 16 miles

19   Marched through Opelousas and Little Washington, 16 miles

20   Day of Rest

21   Marched 17 miles to Bayou Bouef

22   Crossed Contableau Bayou and through Holmesville, 14 miles

23   Passed through Cheyneyville, 13 miles

24   Marched to Gov. Wells plantation, 17 miles

25   Reached Alexandria on the Red River, 13 miles

26-27 Rested at Alexandria

28   Started up the Natchitoches Road, along Bayou Rapides, 18 miles

29   Entered the pine woods of Louisiana, 9 miles

30   Marched to Cane River, 21 miles

31   Crossed the Cane River and camped in woods, 7 miles

April 1   Marched 16 miles

2   Reached Natchitoches, Louisiana, 5 miles

April	3-5	Rest
	6	Left Natchitoches following the advance troops, marched 14 miles
	7	Marched to Pleasant Hill, 22 miles
	8	Marched 8 miles by noon. *Battle of Sabine Cross Roads*. Regiment lost, 2 killed, 19 wounded and one missing
	9	Marched back to Pleasant Hill, 10 miles. *Battle of Pleasant Hill*. Regiment lost 2 killed and 10 wounded, <u>including Frank E. Griffith</u>
	10	Left Pleasant Hill at 2 a.m., marched 21 miles to Yellow Bayou
	11	Marched 14 miles to Grand Ecore, remained there 10 days
	13	<u>Griffith sick at Grand Ecore</u>
	22	116th left Grand Ecore at 4 a.m.
	23	Halted at Cane River at 1 a.m., having marched 45 miles in 21 hours. *Battle of Cane River* (Monet's Ferry). Regiment lost one man wounded.
	24	Entered Pine woods on return march
	25	Reached Alexandria
	28	Moved camp closer to the city, remaining there until May 13
May	1	<u>Griffith convalescing in Marine Hospital, New Orleans thru at least June 14</u>
	5	116th began work on the "Red River Dam" on north side of river, rations reduced to one third
	9	Dam broke early in the morning, four of the gunboats passed over the rapids
	12	Balance of fleet passed the rapids. 116th crossed the river to Alexandria
	13	Started back toward the Mississippi River
	16	*Battle of Mansura Plains*, Louisiana. No losses
	17	Crossed the Atchafalya River at Simmsport
	20-21	Marched 34 miles to the Mississippi River at Morganza, camped there till July
June	14	Review by General Sickles, Inspector General, U.S.A.

June	20	<u>Griffith, still in New Orleans, transferred to Veteran Reserve Corps</u>
	27	Moved camp a little down the river
July	2	116th embarked on river steamer "Colonel Cowles" at Morganza
	3	Arrived at New Orleans
	4	Transferred to ocean vessel "Mississippi"
	5	Left New Orleans and proceeded down the river
	12	Reached Fortress Monroe, Virginia, and ordered on to Washington, D.C. 116th now in 1st Brigade, 1st Division, 19th Army Corps, Army of the Shenandoah
	13	Landed at Washington, D.C. at 7 p.m. President Lincoln and Secretary Stanton drove down to the landing
	14-23	Snicker's Gap Expedition
	14	Marched to Tennallytown in the night
	16	Forded the Potomac River at Edward's Ferry
	18	Over the mountains at Snicker's Gap
	20	Forded the Shenandoah River and at night back again and over the mountains at Snicker's Gap
	23	Crossed the Chain Bridge and bivouacked within the defenses of Washington
	24	<u>Griffith on guard at barracks hospital in New Orleans, thru August 29</u>
	26	Marched by way of Rockville, Turnpike
	26-31	Harper's Ferry, Va, "roustabout"
	28	Crossed the Monocracy River and to Frederick, Maryland
	29	Passed through Harper's Ferry and to Bolivar Heights, Virginia
	30	Marched back through Harper's Ferry
	31	Arrived at Frederick, Maryland
Aug.	5	On the cars at Monocracy and off for Harper's Ferry
	6	Climbed Maryland Heights, then marched through Harper's Ferry, and up to Bolivar Heights
	7	General Philip Sheridan arrives and assumes command

Aug.	10-Sept. 10	Reconnaissances up the Shenandoah Valley and Harper's Ferry vicinity
	10	Passed through Charlestown, Virginia
	11	Marched to White Post, Virginia
	12	Marched to Newtown, Virginia
	13	Marched to Cedar Creek, Virginia
	15	Marched back to Winchester, Virginia
	18	Marched back to Charlestown, Virginia
	22	Marched back to Bolivar Heights, Virginia
Sept.	4	Shirmish near Berryville
	14	<u>Griffith at Battery Barracks, New York City, until at least Sept. 22</u>
	19	*Battle of Opequan Creek,* near Winchester, Virginia. Regiment lost 9 killed and 38 wounded
	20	Crossed Cedar Creek and nearly to Strasburg, Virginia
	22	*Battle of Fisher's Hill*, Virginia. Regiment lost 1 killed and 9 wounded
	23	Advanced up the valley
	24	<u>Griffith to Cliffburne Barracks, Washington, D.C.</u>; 116th advanced as far as New Market, Virginia
	29	<u>Griffith to Fry Barracks, Washington, D.C., through May 1865</u>
	29	Marched to Mount Crawford, Virginia
	30	Marched to Harrisonburg, Virginia
Oct.	6	116th left Harrisonburg, returned to New Market, Virginia
	7	Regiment on duty as rear guard of the army
	10	Reached Cedar Creek and bivouacked
	15	Reconnaissance to Strasburg, VA
	19	*Battle of Cedar Creek*, Virginia. Regiment lost 7 killed, 44 wounded and 10 prisoners
	20	Skirmish at Fisher's Hill, Virginia
Nov.	9	Moved back to Middletown, Virginia
	12	Skirmish at Newtown, Virginia, 1 man wounded
	30	Moved to camp near Stevenson's Depot, near Winchester, Virginia until March

March	6	Moved closer to Stevenson's Depot until April 4
April		<u>Griffith on leave to East Concord, New York, ca. early April</u>
	4	Advanced up the Shenandoah Valley toward Washington, D.C.
	7	Bivouacked one mile from Winchester, Virginia
	9	Received news of the Lee's surrender to Grant at Appomattox Courthouse
	10	Moved back to Summit Point, Virginia
	15	Received news of the assassination of President Lincoln
	20	Started on cars for Washington, D.C.
	21	Met funeral train at 8:40 a.m.; at 9:45 arrived in Washington, D.C.
	23	<u>Griffith returns to Washington, D.C. from leave</u>
	30	Ordered to report to General Auger and went into camp on Capitol Hill; 116th now with 1st Brigade, Dwight's Division, Dept. of Washington
May	1-June 5	Assigned to duty as guard of "Old Capitol" and "Carroll Place" prisons in Washington. D.C.
	23	Grand Review of the "Army of the Potomac" at Washington, D.C.
	24	Grand Review of the Armies of the West, at Washington, D.C.
June	1	<u>Day of Fasting and Prayer, in honor of Lincoln, Washington, D.C.</u>
	5	Order received directing our muster out
	6	<u>Griffith musters out, Washington, D.C.</u>
	8	116th mustered out of service at Washington, D.C.
	11	116th leaves (on train) from Washington at 1:25, reaching Baltimore, Maryland at 7 and leaving there at 11:30 p.m.
	13	Arrived in Elmira, N.Y. at 5 a.m. and at Buffalo, N.Y. at 3 p.m. Marched through Buffalo to Fort Porter.

June	13	Allowed go home until the 19th since paymaster had not arrived
	19	Returned to Camp Morgan (Fort Porter), Buffalo (no paymaster)
	24	Reported to Camp Morgan (no paymaster)
	26	Reported to Camp Morgan, and by 10 p.m. all in 116th fully paid. Regiment disbanded

116th New York Volunteer Infantry Statistics

Mustered into Service Sept. 3, 1862	929
Recruits including colored cooks mustered later	44
Total membership of Regiment	973

Killed	67
Wounded	291
Twice wounded	10
Died from wounds	43
Discharged for wounds	37
Died from sickness	89
Discharged for sickness	87
Transferred to Veteran Reserve Corps	38
Transferred to other Regiments or Branches of the Service	79
Mustered out with Regiment	408
Unaccounted for	125

[*note that some men are listed in more than one category*]

Information taken from: Frank Griffith's letters; *The One Hundred and Sixteenth Regiment of New York State Volunteers*, Clark; *A Compendium of the War of the Rebellion*, Vol. 3, Dyer; *Centennial History of Erie County*, Johnson; *New York in the War of the Rebellion 1861 to 1865*, Phisterer; *History of the City of Buffalo and Erie County*, Smith; *Memorial Services in*

Memory of Ira Ayer, Capt. Co. A, 116th Vols.; Ryther chronology; *Souvenir 116th Reg't New York Vol. Infantry Twenty-fifth Anniversary of Muster into the U.S. Service*; *Roster of All Known Remaining Members of the 116th Regiment N.Y. Vol. Infantry*, Carr and Stambach; Military Register, Company K, 116th Regiment, New York Volunteer Infantry [original framed poster]

Bibliography

116th New York Volunteers, *First Re-union of the One Hundred and Sixteenth New York Volunteers*. [Buffalo]: n.p., 1873

Adams, George Worthington, *Doctors in Blue: The Medical History of the Union Army in the Civil War*. New York: Henry Schuman, 1952

Ames, William S., "acil ebenezer ames," E-mail to author, 25 October 1999

"An Illustrated Historical Review of Western New York's Role in the Civil War," (supplement), *Buffalo Evening News*, 9 November 1963

Ancestory.com - Individual Database Search Results on Civil War soldier Arthur L. Wilkinson, 20 March 2000

Anders, Curt, *Disaster in Damp Sand: The Red River Expedition*. Indianapolis: Guild Press of Indiana, 1997

Arthur, T.S., *Ten Nights in a Bar-Room, and What I Saw There*. Philadelphia: J.W. Bradley, 1859

Attie, Jeanie, *Patriotic Toil: Northern Women and the American Civil War*. Ithaca, NY: Cornell University Press, 1998

Beecher, Harris H., *Record of the 114th Regiment, N.Y.S.V.: Where it Went, What it Saw, and What it Did*. Norwich, NY: J.F. Hubbard, Jr., 1866

Benjamin, Marcus, ed, *Washington During War Time: A Series of Papers Showing the Military, Political, and Social Phases During 1861 to 1865*. Washington, DC: National Tribune Co., 1902

Boatner, Mark Mayo III, *The Civil War Dictionary*. New York: David McKay Company, 1973

Briggs, Elizabeth and Colin J. Briggs, *Before Modern Medicine: Diseases & Yesterday's Remedies*. Winnipeg, Man.,Canada: Westgarth, 1998

Briggs, Erasmus, *History of the Original Town of Concord, Being the Present Towns of Concord, Collins, N. Collins and Sardinia, Erie County, New York*. Rochester: Union and Advertiser Company's Print, 1883

Brooks, Stewart, *Civil War Medicine*. Springfield, IL: Charles C. Thomas, 1966

Brooksher, William Riley, *War Along the Bayous: The 1864 Red River Campaign in Louisiana*. Washington, [DC]: Brassey's, 1998

Brown, Richard C., *Erie County and the Civil War*. Adventures in Western New York History, Vol. 18. [Buffalo, N.Y.]:Buffalo and Erie County Historical Society, [1973]

The Buffalo City and Erie County Register and Business Directory: Including a Directory of Farmers for 1870. Rochester: C.C. Drew, 1870

Buffalo Express, 30 November 1863; 1 December, 1863

"Buffalo in the Civil War" [newspaper clipping scrapbook] Buffalo and Erie County Public Library, Buffalo, NY

Capers, Gerald M., *Occupied City: New Orleans under the Federals 1862-1865*. [Lexington]: University of Kentucky Press, 1965

Carr, George W. and H.E. Stambach, *Roster of All Known Remaining Members of the 116th Regiment N.Y. Vol. Infantry*, Buffalo: Hauser & Plogsted, 1895.

Clark, Orton S., *The One Hundred and Sixteenth Regiment of New York State Volunteers: Being a Complete History of its Organization and of its Nearly Three Years of Active Service in the Great Rebellion*. Buffalo: Matthews & Warren, 1868.

The Commercial Advertizer Directory for the City of Buffalo, Buffalo: R. Wheeler & Co., 1861

Cosgrove, Charles H., *A History of the 134th New York Volunteer Infantry Regiment in the American Civil War 1862-1865: Long Night's Journey into Day*. Studies in American History, Vol. 16. Lewiston, NY: Edwin Mellen Press, 1997

Dallas, Mary Kyle, "The Neglected Warning or The Trials of a Public School Teacher," Street and Smith's *New York Weekly*, January 21, 1864, Vol. XIX, No. 9. Albert Johannsen Collection, New York Weekly, AP2. S8734 1864a Ovsze, Rare Books and Special Collections, Founders Memorial Library, Northern Illinois University, DeKalb, IL.

DeForest, John William, *A Volunteer's Adventures: A Union Captain's Record of the Civil War*. New Haven: Yale University Press, 1946

Department of Commerce and Labor. *Head of Families at the First Census of the U.S. Taken in the Year 1790 - New York*. Washington: Government Printing Office, 1908

Drake, Paul, *What Did They Mean By That?: A Dictionary of Historical Terms for Genealogists.*[Vol. 1.] Bowie, MD: Heritage Books, 1994

_____, *What Did they Mean By That?: A Dictionary of Historical Terms for Genealogists, Some More Words, Volume 2.* Bowie, MD: Heritage Books, 1998

Dyer, Frederick H. Dyer, *A Compendium of the War of the Rebellion,* Vols. 1 and 3. New York: Thomas Yoseloff, 1959

Encyclopedia Americana, International Edition, Vol.11. Danbury, CT: Grolier Incorporated, 1998

Ferris, Zebulon Papers, A68-144, Buffalo and Erie County Historical Society, Papers I, Family Correspondence 1856-1882; Papers IV, 116th Regiment N.Y.S.V.

Fox, William F., *Regimental Losses in the American Civil War, 1861-1865.* Albany, NY: Albany Publishing Company, 1889

French, J.H., *Gazetteer of the State of New York: Embracing a Comprehensive View of the Geography, Geology, and General History of the State, and a Complete History and Description of Every County, City, Town, Village, and Locality.* 10th Edition, [Syracuse: R.P. Smith] 1861

Geary, James W., *We Need Men: The Union Draft in the Civil War.* DeKalb, IL: Northern Illinois University Press, 1991

Geiger, Lillian, *A History of the Town of Concord.* [Buffalo]: Buffalo and Erie County Historical Society, 1971

Goins, Charles Robert and John Michael Caldwell, *Historical Atlas of Louisiana,* Norman: University of Oklahoma Press, 1995

Greene, David L., "What is Genealogical Scholarship?" *New England Ancestors*, Holiday 2000 issue

Hart, James D., *The Popular Book: A History of America's Literary Taste.* New York: Oxford University Press, 1950

Heidler, David S. and Jeanne T. Heidler, eds, *Encyclopedia of the American Civil War: A Political, Social, and Military History.* 5 vols. Santa Barbara, CA: ABC-CLIO Press, 2000

Heinl, Robert Debs, Jr., *Dictionary of Military Quotations*, Annapolis, MD: United States Naval Institute, 1966.

Historical Data Systems, Inc., http://civilwardata.com. Information on Arthur L. Wilkinson, 5 December 2000

Holcomb, Julie, ed, *Southern Sons, Northern Soldiers: The Civil War Letters of the Remley Brothers, 22nd Iowa Infantry.* DeKalb:

Northern Illinois University Press, 2004

Hollandsworth, James G. Jr., *Pretense of Glory: The Life of General Nathaniel P. Banks*. Baton Rouge: Louisiana State University Press, 1998

Illinois. DeKalb County. 1870 U.S. Census, population schedule, microfilm M539, Roll 215. Founders Memorial Library, NIU
_____ 1880 U.S. Census, population schedule, microfilm T9, Roll 202. Founders Memorial Library, NIU
_____ 1900 U.S. Census, population schedule, microfilm Roll 297. Founders Memorial Library, NIU

Jackson, Ronald Vern, *New York 1860 Buffalo (Census Index)*, Salt Lake City: Accelerated Indexing Systems International, 1987

Jerger, Jeanette L., *A Medical Miscellany for Genealogists*. Bowie, MD: Heritage Books, 1995

Jewitt, Allen E. Sr. and Joyce S. Jewitt, *Civil War Military Discharges & Pensions*. Hamburg, NY: Allen E. Jewitt, Sr., 1984

Jewitt, Joyce S., comp., *Some Deaths in Erie County, N.Y. 1863*. Hamburg, NY: Joyce S. Jewitt, 1984

Johnson, Crisfield, *Centennial History of History of Erie County, New York: Being its Annals from the Earliest Recorded Events to the Hundredth Year of American Independence*. Buffalo: Matthews & Warren, 1876

Johnson, Ludwell H., *Red River Campaign: Politics and Cotton in the Civil War*. Kent, OH: Kent State University Press, 1993

Josephy, Alvin M., *War on the Frontier: The Trans-Mississippi West*. Alexandria, VA: Time-Life Books, 1986

Kenamore, Bruce, Letter to author, 6 March 2000

Kett, Henry F., *The Voters and Tax-Payers of DeKalb County, Illinois*. Chicago: H.K. Kett & Co., 1876. Reprint with index by DeKalb County Historical Society. Evansville, IN: Unigraphic, Inc., 1977

Kimmel, Stanley, *Mr. Lincoln's Washington*. New York: Coward-McCann Inc., 1957

Leech, Margaret, *Reveille in Washington 1860-1865*. New York: Harper & Brothers, 1941

Long, E.B. with Barbara Long, *The Civil War Day by Day: An Almanac 1861-1865*. Garden City, NY: Doubleday & Company, 1971

Lowry, Thomas P., *The Story the Soldiers Wouldn't Tell: Sex in the Civil War*. Mechanicsburg, PA: Stackpole Books, 1994

Marshall, Florence Houghton, *1870 Census, Somonauk Township, DeKalb County, IL*. [DeKalb: F.H. Marshall], 1994.

_____, *1880 Census, Somonauk Township, DeKalb County, IL*. [DeKalb: F.H. Marshall], 1985

McArthur, Sullivan F., letter 30 September 1862. Buffalo and Erie County Historical Society, A64-38 McArthur Family Collection, Folder 2

Memorial Services in Memory of Ira Ayer, Capt. Co. A, 116th N.Y. Vols. Buffalo: Webster Brothers, 1890

Michigan Cavalry, 7th Regiment, 1862-1865. *Roster of Survivors of the Seventh Michigan Cavalry and Muster Out Rolls of the Regiment*. [Ann Arbor, MI]: Register Pub., 1895

Military Register, Company K, 116th Regiment, New York Volunteer Infantry. *"116th NY Vol Inf. Co. K"* [original poster like item] from Esther Williams via e-mail to author, 15 September 1999

Moneyhon, Carl and Bobby Roberts, *Portraits of Conflict: A Photographic History of Louisiana in the Civil War*. Fayetteville: University of Arkansas Press, 1990

National Geographic Society, *Battlefields of the Civil War* (map printed for the special publication *The Civil War*). Washington, DC: National Geographic Society, 1974

New Topographical Atlas of Erie Co., New York: from actual surveys especially for this atlas. Philadelphia: Stone & Stewart, 1866.

New York, Erie County. 1850 U.S. Census, population schedule. Micro-publication. Buffalo and Erie County Library, Special Collections

_____ 1860 U.S. Census, population schedule. Microfilm 0803751, [on loan from] LDS Library, Salt Lake City

_____ 1870 U.S. Census, population schedule. Microfilm 0552429, [on loan from] LDS Library, Salt Lake City

New York (State) Adjutant General's Office, *A Record of the Commissioned Officers, Non-Commissioned Officers, and Privates, of the Regiments which were organized in the State of New York and called into the Service of the United States to assist in suppressing the Rebellion, caused by the Secession of* some of the Southern States from the Union, A.D. 1861, as taken from the Muster-in Rolls on file in the Adjutant-General's Office, S.N.Y. Vol. 4, Albany: Weed, Parsons & Co., 1865

_____, Annual Report of the Adjutant-General of the State of New York for the year 1903, Registers of New York Regiments in the War of the Rebellion, Vol. 35. Albany: Oliver A. Quayle Co., 1904

_____, Register of Officers Commissioned in the Volunteer Regiments from the State of New York, 1861-1865. Albany: Charles van Benthuysen & Sons, 1868

Northup, Solomon, Twelve Years a Slave. Edited by Sue Eakin and Joseph Logdon. Baton Rouge: Louisiana State University Press, 1968

Oehser, Paul H., The Smithsonian Institution. Boulder, CO: Westview Press, 1983

Phisterer, Frederick, New York in the War of the Rebellion 1861 to 1865, 3d ed. 5 Vols. Albany: J.B. Lyon, 1912

Portrait and Biographical Album of DeKalb County, Illinois. Chicago: Chapman Brothers, 1885

Roberts, Robert B., Encyclopedia of Historic Forts: The Military, Pioneer, and Trading Posts of the United States. New York: Macmillian, 1988

Robinson, E. and R.H. Pidgeon, comp., Atlas of the City of New Orleans, Louisiana. New York: E. Robinson, 1883

Roster of All Known Surviving Members of the 116th Regiment New York Volunteer Infantry Prepared for the 32nd Reunion of the Regiment Held at G.A.R. Hall, Buffalo, N.Y. Aug. 26, 1911. Buffalo and Erie County Historical Society Collection

Rumbarger, John J., Profits, Power, and Prohibition: Alcohol Reform and the Industrializing of America, 1800-1930. Albany: State University of New York Press, 1989

Ryther, James F., letters of 1862 and 1863, held by Gordon G. Ryther, West Oneonta, NY

Sandwich Free Press, 25 November 1915, 30 November 1916

Sifakis, Stewart, Who Was Who in the Union. New York: Facts on File, 1988

Smith, H. Perry, ed. History of the City of Buffalo and Erie County. 2 vols. Syracuse, NY: D. Mason & Co., 1884

Souvenir 116th Reg't New York Vol. Infantry Twenty-fifth Anniversary of Muster into the U.S. Service. Buffalo: Haas & Klein, 1887

Townsend, Thomas S., *The Honors of the Empire State in the War of the Rebellion.* New York: A. Lovell & Co., 1889

United States. National Archives, Washington. Military Records, Griffith, Frank E., Co. K. 116 NY Inf.
_____, Washington. Pension Records, Ames, Acil E., File SC-181,242
_____, Washington. Pension Records, Griffith, Frank E., C-2509-042

United States. War Dept. *The War of the Rebellion: A Compilation of the Official Records of the Union and Confederate Armies.* Series I, Vol.34, Part 1. Washington: Government Printing Office, 1891

Varhola, Michael J., *Everyday Life During the Civil War.* Cincinnati, OH: Writer's Digest Books, 1999

Vogel, Michael N., Edward J. Patton, and Paul F. Redding, *America's Crossroads: Buffalo's Canal Street/Dante Place.* Buffalo, NY: The Heritage Press, 1993

Webster's Ninth New Collegiate Dictionary. Springfield, MA: Merriam-Webster, Inc., 1991

White, Truman C., ed., *Our County and Its People: A Descriptive Work on Erie County, New York.* Vol 1. [Boston]: Boston History Co., 1898

Wiley, Bell Irvin, *The Life of Billy Yank: The Common Soldier of the Union.* Baton Rouge: Louisiana State University Press, 1998

Wilt, Richard A., *New York Soldiers in the Civil War.* Bowie, MD: Heritage Books, 1999

Winters, John D., *The Civil War in Louisiana.* Baton Rouge: Louisiana State University Press, 1991

Woodward, Jane S., *Men of Medicine in Erie County 1821-1971.* Buffalo: County of Erie Medical Society, 1971

Woodworth, Steven E., *While God is Marching On: The Religious World of the Civil War Soldiers.* Lawrence: University Press of Kansas, 2001

Works Progress Administration, comp., *Index of 1855 Census, Erie County, New York, Exclusive of Buffalo, Part 1 and 2.* Buffalo: n.p., 1941

INDEX

349

ABOUT THE AUTHOR

Born and raised in St. Charles, Illinois, Joan Metzger received a degree in American History from Mundelein College in Chicago in 1972. She performed photograph preservation and research duties at the Arizona Historical Society in Tucson, Arizona for nine years before returning to Illinois in 1987. In 1991 she received her Library Science degree from Northern Illinois University in DeKalb, Illinois. Currently she is employed as the Assistant University Archivist in the Regional History Center at NIU.

Joan has been interested in history since grade school. She has written several articles for historical journals, and served as photo editor for *Celebrating History: A Pictorial Essay of St. Charles, Illinois* (1990). She has been a member of a number of historical organizations including the Adobe Corral of the Westerners, and formerly acted as an interpreter and served on the board of the Garfield Farm & Tavern Museum.

The author lives in DeKalb with her husband Allan, where they enjoy the nature in their back yard, as well as that viewed from their bicycles and kayak.

Frontispiece is an original pen and ink sketch
by David F. Driesbach, DeKalb, Illinois.